PRE-ADAMITE MAN

DEMONSTRATING THE EXISTENCE OF THE HUMAN RACE UPON THIS EARTH 100,000 YEARS AGO!

(1888)

Contents: Adam, Menes, Egypt; Cain; On the Banks on the Nile; Spiritism; The Ark and the Deluge; Ebb and Flow of Empires; Structures of Etruria; Ten Thousand Years of Italic Tradition; The Genesis of Nations; Human Skeletons in the West Indies; and more.

Paschal Beverley Randolph

ISBN 1-56459-825-X

Kessinger Publishing's Rare Reprints
Thousands of Scarce and Hard-to-Find Books!

- -

We kindly invite you to view our extensive catalog list at:
http://www.kessinger.net

PREFACE TO THE FOURTH EDITION.

SINCE I printed the first copies of this work, the opinions of mankind regarding the origin of the race and its varied divisions, have essentially changed, and to-day the Spirit of Research is active as ever. Up to the present, the book has had mountains almost insurmountable in its path, but hath overcome all obstacles, until now, through the energy of Publishers who appreciate the labors of the humble but fearless student of Truth, WM. WHITE & Co., Boston, Mass., it takes its place among the few books destined to do good and outlive the error it was created to combat. It hath outlived adversity; hath become a standard authority in the world of letters on the subject whereof it treats, and in the future, as in the past, will do much toward disabusing the Public Mind on the subject of the ANTIQUITY AND ORIGIN OF MAN.

P. B. RANDOLPH.

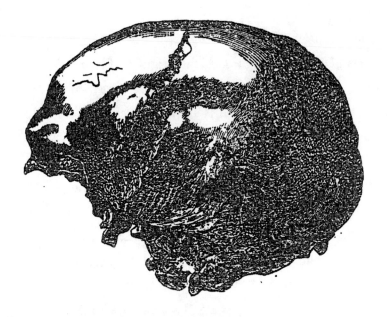

Sketch of an undoubted Pre-Adamite Skull, now in possession of the London Geological Society (supposed to be 100,000 years old.)

CONTENTS:

PART II. ANCIENT EUROPE.

CONTENTS.   vii

and Adjustments of the Roman Year and Calendar, from Romulus to
Pope Gregory..Page 199

CHAP. VI.—Silence and Ignorance of the Clerical Writers relative
to the most important and curious facts of so-called Contemporaneous
History.............. ....Page 225

CHAP. VII.—Ethnological ; The Genesis of Nations....Page 238

CHAP VIII.—The Gorilla vs Man ; Is the latter but a developed
form of the Mammalia ? or is he the INITIAL TYPE of a new range of
terrestrial existence—of a new class and kingdom of Nature ? If the
latter, what a future lies before him !......................Page 251

PART III. FOSSIL MAN.

CHAP. I.—Discovery of Human Skeletons in the West Indies, the
Kirkdale Cavern, Quebec, Caverne de Engboule, Florida, and else-
where, from 50,000 to 150,000 years old ; Human Remains from Gravel
Hills ; "Flint Weapons.".............................Page 277

CHAP. II.—The skeleton of a Whale found with a human weapon,
in a Scotch hill ; The fossil Elks and human bones of Ireland ; Human
remains and Elephants' teeth found in non-tropical climates, indicating an age of 38,000 years at least ; Mr. Koch and his flint arrow-heads
from the "Drift ;" Human remains found in a Rocky Mountain gold
hill... Page 295

CHAP. III.—John Elliott in the "Geologist" on Fossil Man, and re-
mains found in Durham ; The Heathery-Burn Discoveries ; Professor
Huxley, F. R. S., on the celebrated "Muskham Skull ;" The Trent
Skull and its dimensions ; Human remains from Neanderthal ; The
Belgian Skull, found with the bones of Bears, Hyenas and Elephants :
The Massat and Mecklenburg Skeletons ; Dr. Schauffhausen on the
"Plau Skeleton ;" The Mewslade Skull ; The Seonen Cranium ; The
Montrose and boat-shaped human skulls ; The Eastham Skull and its
measurement ; Skull of a Gorilla compared with that of Man ; Skulls
from Etruria, and their dimensions ; Human Bones from Switzerland ;
Copenhagen fossil skulls compared with that of an Ashantee Negro ;
Professor Owen on Ancient Crania ; The Engis Skull, "the oldest
record of man on earth ;" The Dolichocephalic crania ; Apes, Man,
Chimpanzes, Negroes ; Table of the oldest human relics found with
fossil mammalia ; Tables of the Earliest Evidences of the Human
Race..Page 303

CHAP. IV.—Proceedings of various Geological Societies, and discoveries of fossil man by their members ; "Flints in the Drift ;"

PREFACE.

Adam was not the first man! The writer and compiler of this book believes this affirmation. The reader of this book will also believe it after its perusal. The work is written, not for fame or emolument, for the writer has no need of either, but because there was and is a need for just such a book as this. Of course much more can be said to the purpose on the subject of Human Antiquity than this volume contains. It will be said in future editions. Those who adhere to Adam, as the ancient lady did to her Total Depravity, will be troubled by this book, and will denounce all Adamicides in general. This cannot be helped. The truth *must* come up sooner or later, and the quicker the better for the world. Here it is! at least a portion of it. At first my search for materials was unrewarded ; but patient industry, long-continued research, an indomitable resolution not to be foiled, a lively consciousness that I was doing mankind and the world a service, and one that would be acknowledged by *unbiased* minds, at length resulted in placing so much material at my command, that it became difficult to decide what to admit and what to reject. So much for devoutly believing in the magic word—TRY! The exigencies of the war at the magic word—TRY! No subject with which the human mind can grapple—save only one—that of immortality—the triumphant Fact of our continued existence after life's fitful fever shall have been ended—is fraught with more intense interest than that upon which this work treats.

Bulwer says, in the preface to Zanoni, that now-a-days one can hazard nothing in print without authority, or scarcely quote Shakespeare without citing chapter and verse. This is the age of facts—the age of facts, sir; to which truth we most heartily assent. Facts are stubborn things. In this book I have demonstrated two propositions : 1st, That a certain portion of Ancient, as well as Modern. History is a " gigantic swindle ;" and, 2d, That Adam was not the first man ;—in short, that Pre-adamite men existed on all the continents of the globe certainly 35,000, and probably 100,000, years prior to the date usually assigned to that rather mythical personage ; and this Fact is one that—it not being possible to be set aside—will have to be taken, no matter how bitter the pill, and digested accordingly.

The following are a few of the authorities consulted in the preparation of this volume :

Lord Lindsay on the " Anakim ;" " Angels, Cherubim and Gods"—London, 1861 ; Abydenus—" Fragment of Berosus ;" Apollodorus, with Heyne's notes ; Arrian ; Avienus—Festus ; Birch and Derougé on the " Egyptians ;" Benjamin of Tudela ; Wm. Brade's " Sphinx of History ;" Beyers' Notes to Selden—*De dis Syrius ;* Bampton Lectures—Mansell's ; Luke Burke's " Future ;" Botta's " Nineveh ;" Baron Bunsen's " Egypt's Place in Universal History ;" The Bible—nine different versions ; Cory's " Fragments of Ancient History"—Berosus, Syncellus, &c., &c. ; Bishop Colenso's " Pentateuch Critically Examined ;" Basil Cooper's (B. A.) " Hieroglyphical Date of the Exodus ;" Candlish's " Contributions to an Exposition of Genesis ;" Miss Fanny Corbeaux on " Egypt ;" Champol-

lion's " Egyptian Researches ;" Ctesias ; Cratylus ;
Donaldson's Works ; " Flint's in the Drift ;" " Genesis
of the Earth and Man." edited by Reginald Stuart
Poole, Esq., British Museum : Diæarchus' History of
the " Reign of Alexander the Great ," Dr. Edersheim's
" History of the Jews," edition of 1856 ; Eusebius'
Chron. ; Hardy's " Eastern Monachism," and " Manual
of Budhism," London, 1861 ; Eustathius ; Eratosthenes ;
Encyclopædia Britannica ; Encylopædia Americana ; Ra-
pin's English History ; The " Veil of Isis ;" " Mysteries
and History of the Druids ;" Francis Newman's " He-
brew Monarcl.y :" " Fossil Man"—London Register ;
Editor of, and contributors to, " The London Geolog-
ist ;" Foster's " Arabia ;" Cyril Graham— Quarterly
Review, July—Oct.. 1859 : " Hieronymian Hebrew—
a Grammar of the Sacred Language"—Wm. Beeston,
London, 1843 ; *The Samaritan Pentateuch*, of Nablous,
Syria, examined by the writer hereof in Jerusalem ;
Horace Welby's " Life, Death and Futurity"—*the Eng-
lish Edition ;* Herodotus ; Lucian ; Lepsius ; Homer ;
" Kings of the East ;" Miss Angharad Lloyd ; Lowth
on the Scriptures ; Manetho ; Mantell's " Fossils of the
British Museum ;" Vaux " Nineveh and Persepolis ;"
" Pre-adamite Man ;" Pliny ; Ptolemy ; Pompeius ; Pe-
cocke's " History of the Arabs ;" Prof. Wilson's " Pre-
historic Man ;" Strabo ; The " Timæus and Scholium ;"
Travels of Sir John Chardin ; American Journal of
Science and Arts ; Trogus ; " Unpointed Text of the
Book of Genesis ;" Xenophon, and many others, need-
less to here enumerate at greater length.

INTRODUCTORY.

Who ever heard of th' Indian Peru?
Or who in venturous vessel measured
The Amazon huge river. now found true?
Or fruitfullest Virginia who did ever view?

Yet all these were, when no man did them know,
Yet have from wisest ages hidden been;
And later times things more unknown shall show;
Why then should witless man so much misween
That nothing is but that which he hath seen?
What if within the moon's fair shining sphere,
What if in every other star unseen.
Of other worlds he happily should hear?
He wonder would much more; yet such to some appear!
                                    SPENSER—*Faerie Queen.*

Adam was not the first man! Men—whole nations of men—civilized men, not only lived before the period usually ascribed to Adam, and to Eve, his wife, but lived at least *thirty-five thousand,* and with even greater probability, *one hundred thousand years ago.* This fact, startling as it may appear to the mass of superficial readers, is one so clear and plain as to be demonstrated with as much ease as a good geometrician could solve the thirty-fifth problem of Euclid.

Thousands of years before the 4004th year of the world before Christ—the date of its creation, according to the Christian and Hebrew systems of chronology, the Plains of Asia, over which I have recently traveled (while collecting materials for the series of books, of which this is the first,) abounded and teemed, not only with populous centers of civilized life, but with the ruins of scores of cities, the very memories of whose names, and of those who once lived in them, were forgotten by, or had possibly never been known to, the dwellers in the towns, the ruins of which we now exhume from beneath the sterile sands and burning deserts—the mute but eloquent record that

" Once upon a time a strange, and mighty people were."

I believe with Luke Burke, from whose works I have largely availed myself in the second part of this volume, (and to whom I tender my sincere thanks for the excellent privilege,) that " History," especially Ancient History, in some portions thereof, at least, approaches very nearly to being totally unreliable, and to discover, correct, and prove which, such glorious intellects as those of Neibuhr, Baron Bunsen, and Luke Burke were devoted through long and laborious years.

For our dearly loved, but by the masses, our unappreciated America, I have engaged in a task similar in kind and intent, though perhaps not in quality, exhaustiveness, or scope, to that so triumphant one performed by the first two above-named heroes of a battle-field greater than marshalled armies ever trod upon, and who are now, let us hope and believe, gathering a new and better sort of laurels in the

Lands beyond the swelling flood, the kingdom o'er the sea

of Death; and the third of whom, to the eternal disgrace of Literary England, is now laboring for the World and fighting for the truth, against obstacles, and an antagonism so great and bitter, that every true and honest heart shudders at the sad spectacle of the terrible and unequal contest.

Invent a murderous shell, and England will make you a gartered knight ! Devote a life to letters or to science, and she sneeringly bids you starve ! Be a William Armstrong, and she will pour millions in your lap! Be a Luke Burke, and you cannot raise money enough to print a pamphlet once a month, although that pamphlet contains truths a million times more valuable to the human race than fifty myriads of Armstrong guns! But this is the fate of genius; this is the way of the world. Let us hope that it will not always be so!

Burke made an independent discovery of the vast antiquity of man, in a field that no mere geologist, ethnographer, or antiquarian had dreamed of exploring; for he demonstrated the age of the Cyclopæan structures of Greece and Etruria, (the substance of which is herein embodied) and discovered many a new law of matter, mind, and the universe. His reward for these *original* demonstrations was in effect "a crust and a garret!" William Armstrong finds an old gun in Warwick Castle, and its original in the Hall of Arms in Malta, where myself saw it in 1862. He seizes on the idea they embody; makes a gun after the pattern of these old fusils—a gun by the way that is far more dangerous to its *friends behind*, than to its *foes before it*, at any range or rate : he christens it after himself, and rolls in knighted wealth as a consequence. The sun that rose on Calvary, and nooned on Galileo, now shods its rays on Burke, and withers, but, thank heaven! cannot utterly destroy. The reader will please pardon this tribute of gratitude to a great man.

I purpose to write concerning the Pre-Adamite men. In the columns of the New York *Tribune*, in the summer of 1855, I think it was, there appeared an article which perhaps millions of people read and passed over without a thought, but which in its final effect upon my mind, entirely changed the current of my life—especially my intellectual life. The article is here partly quoted from memory, but is quite correct so far as it goes : " In sinking one of 95 artesian wells across the Egyptian Delta, by French engineers, under the orders of a Turkish Viceroy, the borer came in contact with what afterward proved to be an immense statue of Rameses, or Rhampses II., the great Sesostris, who lived, according to one Egyptological authority, some 1350 years before Christ ; and 1400, 1800, and 2185 B. C., according to others. Probably all are wrong. The base of this statue was 12 feet, or thereabouts, beneath the surface ; and its discovery throws much light on a question purposely veiled in darkness by the Rabbins of the Jewish faith. After reaching the base of the statue they continued to bore, and from an additional depth of 32 feet, the borer brought to the surface many fragments of pottery, some of which evidenced considerable taste and art in its structure. Now, according to Lepsius, and other Egyptologers, the vertical rising of the floor of the Delta, from the overflowing of the river, is at the mean rate of $3\frac{1}{2}$ inches per century. Accordingly, these bits of pottery must have been manufactured by the hands of civilized men 13,500 *years ago !*"

A clearer statement, from the pages of a recent volume, by the late Baron Bunsen, will throw additional light on the subject : " Mr. Leonard Horner (Transacactions of the Royal Society,) has established the fact from researches made near Cairo, pertaining to the geological history of the alluvial land of Egypt, that Egypt was peopled by those who made pottery 11,000 years before Christ. Mr. Horner was in Egypt during the process of boring for water by the French engineers (in the area of Memphis, and but a short journey from any one of a dozen pyramids or more.) It had previously been settled, upon strictly scientific grounds, by Lepsius and other distinguished *savants*, that the vertical rise of the floor of the Delta from sedimentary deposits, caused by the annual Nilotic overflow, was at the rate of 3½ inches per century. Mr. Horner found the.deposit at the colossal statue of Rhampses II., to be 9 feet 4 inches in depth, which gives, at the above rate of increase, the item of 3,215 years for *that* particular accumulation of-mud. But, let it be remembered, he found the mud to be 32 feet deep *beneath* the base of the statue, giving a total of 41 feet 4 inches. The last or lowest two feet were found to consist of sand, below which it is possible there may be no true Nile sediment in this locality, and we thus have but a total of 39 feet 4 inches, from which it follows that the lowest deposit of mud was made there 10,285 years before the middle of Rhampses' reign, 11,646 years before Christ, or exactly 13,508 years ago (1862). The deeper parts of this accumulation, says Leonard Horner, are probably more compact in structure, from the long applied superincumbent pressure, and therefore their age may be, and probably is, far greater on that account, than that arrived at by the application of the chronometric scale of 3½ inches per century, obtained by measuring the superficial and specifically lighter part of the accumulated mass."

The unscientific reader may possibly cavil at such astonishing results, until he comprehends *how* the conclusions were arrived at. A few words will thoroughly ventilate the subject: 1. The river Nile annually overflows the greater part, if not the whole, of the Egyptian Delta—a tract of alluvial land numbering millions of acres; and upon which the proud river leaves a thin scale of mud every year, which mud it brings from the wash of the mountain streams of southern and central Africa—Dongola and Nigritia generally. II. The statue alluded to was, of course, built,

not in a pit, but upon the surface of the ground, yet it
was found 9 feet 4 inches below it. How came it
there? "It might have sunk!" True, it *might*, but
then, again, it might *not!* for at its base was found, at
various distances, such lighter things as bits of broken
clay-pots, charcoal, burnt stones and bricks, on the
same level, which could not possibly have been the
case if the statue had been gradually sinking; for its
immense weight would have provided for the statue a
far quicker and deeper grave than the other things
possibly could have found, by reason of their vastly inferior specific gravity. The statue, then, was found exactly on the surface upon which it was originally
erected, but that surface was exactly 9 feet 4 inches
beneath the present one. III. Sinking being thus out
of the question, the accumulation of nine feet and over
of Nile mud, must be attributed to the waters of the
annually overflowing river. IV. The age in which
Rhampses II. reigned is known approximately. A mean
being taken, we judge that the middle of his reign
must have fallen, probably more, but certainly not less,
than 1,350 years before Christ. It is absolutely certain
that it could not have been one hundred years either
before or after that date. V. The result is a mere arithmetical one, for we accept the 1350 years, and allow
one hundred years for every 3½ inches of mud from the
foot of the statue to the present surface of the ground.
VI. The deposit may have, during some of the centuries, been more or less than 3½ inches, but the average
gives that rate and no more. Remote as is the date
of 13,500 years from the present time, which these
probings have disclosed, they have not enabled us to
attain the hoped-for object of discovering an approxi-
mative link between historical and geological time. No
trace of an extinct organism has been turned up to

take the formation of the alluvial land of Egypt beyond that modern epoch from which, in our artificial systems, we are used to carry back our geological reckonings. In the lowest part of the borings of the sediment at the colossal statue of Rhampses in 1854, at a depth of thirty-nine feet from the surface of the ground, consisting of true Nile sediment, the instrument brought up a fragment of pottery, now in my possession, which *fragment must be the record of man's existence* 13,375 years before A. D., 1854.

In another pit, 354 yards north of the statue, and 300 from the river, similar fragments were brought up from a depth of thirty-eight feet. Fragments of burnt brick and pottery have been found at even greater depths, in localities near the river, ten and sixteen miles below Cairo.

At Sigiul fragments of both were found in the sediment from between forty-five and fifty feet from the surface; and in boring at Bessousse they were brought up from a depth of fifty-nine feet below the surface! Now, by a rule applied elsewhere, the Sigiul pottery tells of man, at the lowest, having lived there 20,000 *years ago!* Baron Bunsen concluded from the above, and other data, that "man lived on this earth not less than 20,000 years before Christ, and that there is no valid reason for assigning a more remote beginning for our race." Heartily accepting the Baron's first conclusion, I feel compelled to reject his last, for reasons presently to be developed.

Some few months after the *Tribune* article had set me thinking on the subject, the following fragment from Syncellus attracted my attention, and provoked to further inquiry and investigation. I strove to accept nothing that was not well authenticated, and to reject everything that would not bear the closest normal criticism.

The fragment alluded to gives a portion of the Chaldean (Babylonian) chronology, as subjoined :

9 Sari of 3,600 years, consequently 32,400 years
2 Neri " 600 " " 1,200 "
8 Sossi " 60 " " 480 "

Total years,   34,080

Again, we have the following rather startling items of chronology, all of which concern *post*-diluvian dynasties, and if they are true we must carry back our chronological reckonings many thousand years more than we usually do.   Here are the extraordinary lists :

1st Dynasty, 86 Chaldean Kings reigned, years, 34,080
2d " 8 Median " . " 224
3d " 11 Chaldeans " " " 258
4th " 49 " " " " 458
5th " 9 Arabians " " " 245
6th " 45 Assyrians " " " 526
7th " 8 " " " " 122
8th " 6 " " " " 82

Total, Kings, 222   Years, 35,995, but say 36,000

A tolerably long stretch of either the truth or time. My opinion is that the truth is *not* stretched half so much as at first sight might appear.   Probably good reason exists for assigning a hoary antiquity to everything that pertains to ancient Chaldea ; but when we are shown, in addition to the above, a list of the reigns of ten *ante*-diluvian kings or dynasties, who reigned for 432,000 years, we feel that we are either walking on ground not the most solid ; in fact, that we are reading something very much akin to the mystical writings of Plautinus, Budha or Jacob Boehm, or the dreamy platitudes of Swedenborg, or, not rising so high as

these, that we are having a pre-edition of the senseless
and ridiculous nonsense whereof so much has been
foisted upon a too credulous world within the present
century, by such men as Joseph Smith. When we read
in the Talmud, Rabbi Dimis' account of having sailed
three days between two fins of one fish, and that the
ship flew through the water faster than an arrow from
the bow; or when we read in Budhistic books that the
inhabitants of the sixth heaven, or Bramah-loka, live
sixteen thousand years, every day of which is equal to
sixteen hundred of our years, their entire age being
nine thousand two hundred and sixteen millions of
earthly years, we reject the whole as either utterly absurd, or conclude that a mystical meaning is couched
beneath the statements, which meaning lies so deep that
we forbear to trouble ourselves with the business of
exhumation.   Like the nonsense just alluded to is, at
first sight, this Chaldean story of nearly half a million
years ; and yet there must be no inconsiderable amount
of truth buried under the vast pile of rubbish.   Our
reason may reject the conclusions of Leonard Horner ;
we may smile at old Syncellus, and laugh outright at
Herodotus, Manetho, Plato and Bunsen ; and yet, just
as soon as we hear the little word "geology," we find
it almost impossible, without grains of allowance
amounting to thousands of years, to accept the chronologies of the Jewish Rabbins, which assign but six thousand years as the epoch of the Genesis both of the earth
and man.   I do not deny, as many others, that six
thousand years ago there lived a man in the East, the
father of a tribe, nor that his name was Adam ; but I
do maintain that he was neither the first man, the only
man, or the only man of that name, for it can be clearly
and distinctly proved not only that there were other
men, but others bearing that identical name, and myth-

ical Adams, *quantum sufficit* beside, as well as others
whose names in other tongues are the exact equivalents
of the Hebraic Adam, or Adamah. There are hundreds
of legends extant concerning the original protoplast
afloat in the world, and especially in Oriental lands.
The Chinese records tell us that Pu-An-ku, the primeval man, came out of the mundane egg ; that he lived
eighteen thousand years ; and they speak of events that
transpired among their ancestors one hundred and
twenty-nine thousand six hundred years ago ! The
simple and effective answer to such assertions is, that
neither the work of human hands, nor the records of
human thought, could by any possibility survive such
an enormous lapse of ages ; nor, if immortality be
a fact, which I certainly affirm, does it seem to me possible that anything short of the intelligence and memory of the infinite God, could retain and grasp, over the
yawning gulph of dead years, the remembrance of what
took place at the further end of the tremendous hiatus !

Palœontology, ethnology, archæology, geology and
chronology, are intimately correlated arcs or segments
of the great circle of the Sciences, and they grow into
each other as naturally as sunshine does into smiles and
beauty ; and the study of one inevitably leads to that
of another, so that a question asked of one science very
often evokes and provokes a dozen answers from as
many more. Thus we ask concerning the antiquity of
man : "Did all men originate from a single pair of protoplasts, and were these latter the Adam and Eve that
we read about ?" No sooner do we ask these general
questions, than a dozen sciences present us with their
several and diverse replies. Comparative anatomy
and physiology, comparative philology, geology, geo-
graphy, craniology, theology, and, strongest of all, ethnology ; all these and more are ready with responses,

and these responses give one vote in the affirmative, to at least two in the negative.

The article in the *Tribune* prompted the writer not only to ask these questions, but to engage in studies and travels, extended to Europe, Asia, Africa, Central and South-western America, at a cost of much time and some thousands of dollars, in order to investigate the subject in all its bearings, a digest only of the results of which, this volume contains. I have freely availed myself of Bunsen's researches, and of Luke Burke's writings. To Prof. Levisohn, of the Russian Bishopric in Jerusalem ; Prof. Wilson ; R. S. Poole, Esq., whose works I profited by ; to the authorities of the British Museum Library in London ; to similar authorities in Paris and Munich ; to Prof. Krause, Mr. Ducat, our Consul, and other gentlemen in Jerusalem and other parts of Syria ; to Mr. Goddard, our Consul-General at the Court of His Polygamous Majesty, Abdul Aziz, Constantinople ; to Captain Giacomo, Consular Interpreter thereat ; and to Mr. Charles Trinius and other gentlemen, for the kindness shown, facilities for investigation afforded, and information tendered, I am duly grateful ; as well as to many others in various parts of the world, for assistance rendered me while searching for evidences of the existence of PRE-ADAMITE MAN.

Part First.

CHAPTER I. MENES—ADAM.

WHOEVER has wandered amid the stately ruins of Karnac, and El Uqusor, the palaces, tombs and dungeons, the massive statuary, pylons and hypæthral temples of the hoary old Land of the Pharoahs, of Moses and Thothmes, Joseph and Potiphar, must have felt, as I did, that the civilized world as we now know it, is very young indeed.; and that its proudest structures are infantile compared with the massive and aged grandeur of other civilizations, upon the ashes and ruins of whjch the Present may be said to have been builded.

Reader, let us imagine ourselves to be on the banks of the Nile. We are there. Tread lightly, my fellow-traveler ; we are on holy ground, here in Egypt, holy by reason of the awful shadows that enshroud its Past. Look ! yonder is the grand Memnon—him whose voice trilled in the morning, and melodiously called the Thebans to their matutinal devotions—to holy prayer to the Lord of Life and Light·;—the same God whom you and I worship—but under anothei name—called them to prayer through stony lips, just as the morning sun tipped them with his rosy light. Tread lightly ! for we are walking over the graves of kings and nobles,

high-born dames and stately lords!—aye! we are treading on the tombs of Dead Nations; we are walking on
the graves of Music, and of Art, Governments. laws
and languages, and of high and wondrous learning!
Tread lightly! for we are now in the land that Menes
ruled; and Menes is he whom we know in Genesis
under the name of Mizraim, and he passes there as the
grandson of Noah; but the era of Noah is four thousand,
that of Menes six thousand years ago! Menes was
but an innovator—a conqueror, in all probability. At
all events, he was a great king and mighty, and it is
mainly through the telescope he and his times afford us,
that we are enabled to see through the gloom into the
light beyond. and we are astonished at the spectacle
disclosed; for instead of finding a new state of things,
we only discern a new beginning—a new order. In
other words, Menes and his throne at Memphis—a city
near Cairo, and a long way below Thebes—were but
the last mile-stones on a road so long, that the farther
end is hidden in the night-time of the world. He and
it are but one link in a chain of kings, thrones and ages
—and that link the one nearest our own times, yet six
thousand long years off! We arrive at this result by
counting, first, the periods of the Dynasties, the dates,
and order, and duration of which are proximately
known. There were thirty dynasties, the names of
which are here withheld, simply for the reason that no
one would take any interest in reading them. Suffice
it that the names of the kings of all these dynasties,
from Menes to Alexander, from Alexander to Said
Pacha, the present ruler, are known. as well as the
number of years each monarch governed the land.
These figures give about six thousand years in the aggregate, on the authority of the best students of Egyptian History in England. France and Germany. Now

it is plain that if Adam lived in Syria, Assyria, Mesopotamia, Armenia, or thereabouts, six thousand years ago, as the Bible tells us—and it is not my purpose at this point to dispute its truth—and Menes also lived at that date, the latter could *not* have descended from the former, for the reason that Adam had not lived long enough to have a family of sons sufficiently numerous to build one of the largest and finest cities in the Ancient World, nor to turn the course of one of the mightiest rivers on earth; for, be it known, King Menes caused a new channel to be dug for the river, in order that he might have a convenient place to build his Memphis on; and the space thus reclaimed was scores of thousands of acres in extent. Again: it is doubtful if any of Adam's children, supposing there *was* an Adam, six thousand years ago, while their father was yet a young man, had developed the art of sculpture and architecture to the extent of being capable of carving from a single stone such splendid statuary, and of erecting such buildings as Menes' city was graced with. The Adamites and Memphians were not even cousins german, for reasons already stated; and, consequently, the king and his people were undoubted Pre-Adamites. Again: Menes and his race were not autocthonic where we find them; but had moved away from a place called This, located far above where Karnac now stands. When they came down the Nile to build a new city, and to found a new Empire, they had left an old one—had exhausted the resources of a worn-out nation, and immigrated *en masse* to localities where they speedily developed new ones.

Within the last twenty years there has quietly grown up a scientifically-founded scepticism, which has spread so widely and gone so deeply down, that every class of society is more or less affected by it, and that to an extent almost too great to be readily believed. The scepticism I allude to is that regarding the literal correctness of scriptural statements in reference to God, Nature, human origin and our final destiny. It does not follow that this has in any degree retarded the growth of vital piety, for many an intellectual doubter is in heart and in practice a religious man ; on the contrary, the religion of these days is one of the understanding, not of blind credulity as formerly ; and I believe that—if the entire Bible, from Genesis to Revelation, should prove to be other than what is claimed for it, notwithstanding all that, Christianity, in its essence and benignant spirit and sway, would thrive quite as well, and perhaps more rapidly thereafter.

The first quarrel between Science and the Bible was that of Astronomy, in the person of Galileo, against the religious but ignorant zeal of the past, and Astronomy carried the day, after a rather bad rolling in the dust. Then came the case of Geology against Moses, and Moses gracefully retired. Then comes " Adam vs. many another First Man," and we are fighting that battle to-day. Science is about to settle for ever one of the most vexed question that ever came up for human discussion. Arrayed in martial panoply on the one hand stands a vast army of men who will not see ; and on the other a smaller army of men, each armed with a couching-needle, wherewith they propose to remove the cataracts from the eyes of those, who, on being told that Man can rightly claim an antiquity vastly more remote than has been assigned him, have persisted in declaring that they " can't see it."

The learning of the world, its talent and its genius, is now gathering, preparatory to grappling with the great problem of Man's genesis and his destiny. Nor can the discussion and the combat be much longer delayed. The issue is not at all doubtful.

The question would long since have been settled, had we any faith in ancient chroniclers; but there is so much of apparent fable in their account of ancient times, that if we do not reject them altogether, we at least require a great deal of concurrent testimony before we accept their statements. Herodotus seems to have been an honest man, but a rather credulous one, else he would not have sent down to us along with his undoubted truths, so much of nonsense as he has, and which was palmed upon him by the priests of Memphis. Manetho is no better. Indeed it is doubtful if we have much that he wrote, *as* he wrote it; for many of the fragments that have reached us bear the imprint of other hands than his, affixed too, long after he left the earth. These alterations of his text doubtless took place in the Helleno-Egyptian age, and suspicion points her finger at Ptolemy Mendesius as one, if not the principal, interpolator.

With the remark, that the Priests of Memphis told Herodotus that Menes, the founder of the New Egyptian Empire, began his reign 11,340 years before the rule of the last king of the 23d Memphite dynasty, and that he gives us this as veritable history, I proceed to quote, first a fragment of Manetho, and second, the conclusions of Baron Bunsen, based upon it, and other authorities concerning the early days. Manetho says:

"The first [man], in the opinion of the Egyptians, was Hephæstus, (afterwards the god Phtha,) who is also celebrated among them as the inventor of fire. From him proceeded Helius (Ra, another god); afterwards Agathodæmon; then, Kronos, (Seb, another god); then Osiris; then came Typhon, the brother of Osiris;

then came Horus, the son of Osiris by Isis, his wife.
These were the first who reigned amongst the Egyptians. Down to Bydis the royal authority was transmitted successively in uninterrupted series during
13,900 years. After the gods, heroes reigned for 1,255
years; then, again, other kings reigned 1,817 years;
then thirty other Memphite kings for 1,790 years; then
ten other Thinite kings 350 years. A dynasty of ghosts
and heroes then followed, during 5,813 years," making
a grand total of twenty-four thousand, nine hundred
and twenty-five years—of Egyptian history; and yet
Egypt was but a baby nation compared to others, and
its civilization quite imperfect contrasted with civilizations that were cotangent and contemporaneous with it.

Bunsen's deductions, in brief, are as follows:—

"FIRST AGE OF THE WORLD. THE HISTORICAL PRIMEVAL WORLD.
CREATION TO FLOOD. B. C. 20.000—10.000.

"FIRST PERIOD. *Formation and Deposit of Sinism.* B. C. 20,000—
15,000.

"Primitive language, spoken with rising or falling cadence; eluci-
dated by gesture; accompanied by pure pictorial writing; every
syllable a word, every word a full substantive one, representable by a
picture.

"Deposit of this language in Northern China (Shensi), in the country of the source of the Hoango (Sinism).

"The *earliest* polarization of religious consciousness; Kosmos or
Universe, and the Soul or Personality. Objective worship, the firmament; subjective worship, the Souls of parents, or the Manifestation
of the Divine in the Family.

"SECOND PERIOD. *Formation and Deposit of Primitive Turanism;
the Eastern Polarization of Sinism.* B. C. 15.000—14,000.

"Pure agglutinative language; formation of polysyllabic words
by means of the unity of accent.

"Origin of particles, words no longer substantive and full, but denoting the mutual relation of persons and things; finally, of complete
parts of speech.

"Deposit of this stage of formation in Thibet (Botiya language).
Germ of mythology in the substantiation of inanimate things and
properties.

"THIRD PERIOD. *Formation and Deposit of Khamism and the Flood;
Western Polarization of Sinism.* B. C. 14,000—11,000.

"Formation of stems into roots, producing derivative words: complete parts of speech, beyond the distinction between full words
(nouns, verbs, and adjectives) and formative words, B. C. 14,000. De-

clension and conjugation with affixes, suffixes, and endings ; stage of the Egyptian. B. c. 13.000. Commencement of symbolical Hieroglyphics. i. e., picture-writing : but without the introduction of the phonetic element, or designation of sound. B. c. 12.000. Deposit of this stage of language in Egypt owing to the earliest immigration of West Asiatic Primitive Semites. Invention of, or advancement in, hieroglyphic signs : the phonetic element introduced, by means of the establishment of ideographs to express a syllable, without reference to the original meaning ; primitive syllabarium. B. c. 11.000. THE FLOOD. CONVULSION IN NORTHERN ASIA. EMIGRATION of the Arians out of the country of the sources of the Oxus (Gihon) and Jaxartes, and of the Semites out of the country of the sources of the Euphrates and Tigris; B. c. 11,000—10,000.

" SECOND AGE OF THE WORLD. FORMATION OF HISTORICAL TRIBES AND EMPIRES OF ASIA. FLOOD TO ABRAHAM, B. c. 10,000—2678.

" FIRST PERIOD. *History of Egyptian Deposit.*

" The period of the Nomes, and the formation of Osirism or the psychical element of religion, and basis of the union : provincial solar worship : beginning of Egyptian nationality........ B c. 10.000.

" Beginning of the formation of castes ; priests and warriors.

" Close of the Republican period in the Nomes......B. c. 9086.

" Bytis, the Theban Priest of Ammon, the first Sacerdotal King. B. C. 9085

" Duration of the Sacerdotal Kings, according to Manetho [?]. 1855 years ; end of Sacerdotal Kings................B. C. 7231.

" SECOND PERIOD. B.c. 7250—4000. *History of Egyptian Deposit.*

" Beginning of Elective Kings B. c. 7230.

" Duration of these, according to Manetho, 1817 years ; end B. c. 5414.

" Beginning of Hereditary Kings in Lower Egypt, B. c. 5413.

" Duration of them, according to Manetho, 1790 years ; end B c. 3624.

" The Contemporaneous Thinite Princes before Menes, during the

" *General Epochs of Asiatic History. Establishment of Semism in Armenia, Assyria, and Mesopotamia, and the Kossite Turanian Empire.*

" Complete severance of Western and Eastern polarization by the separation of the Semites and Arians.

" Establishment of Semism in the formation of affixes.

" The Triliteral system, as exclusive formative principle.

" The Turanian Invasion and Empire : Nimrod, the Kossian.

" Assembly of peoples at Babylon (watch-tower), and Semitic Polarization and Emigration.

" Journey of the Arians from Upa-Meru to Sogd and Bactria.

" *General Epochs of Asiatic History. Establishment of Iranism and the Egyptian Hieroglyphics.*

" Perfect formative language ; the united races of the Aryans and their gradual separation as Kelts, Armenians, Iranians, Greeks, Slaves, Germans, &c. B. c. 7250—5000.

" In this period the individual formation of the separate races of northern and southern Semites.

" Formation of the Aryan kingdoms in Central Asia as far as

last 350 years of the pre-Menite period, according to Manetho, collaterally with the Memphites.
B. C. 3974—B. C. 3624.

" Consequently a double government: the Upper Country (Abydos)—the Lower Country (On, Heliopolis).

" Development of the three forms of worship in their separate characters: Set (Delta)—Ra (Heliopolis, Heptanomis)—Ammon (Thebes = City of Ammon : Osiris gradually becomes the object of worship of the whole confederation.

" THIRD PERIOD. *History of Egyptian Deposit.*

" Menes, King of all Egypt ; Osiris-Union and the consciousness of Egypt being a kingdom.
B. C. 3623.

" Pyramids built in the First Dynasty..............B. C. 3460.

" Animal worship introduced, improvement and establishment of writing, beginnings of Literature ; Second and Third Dynasty (contemporaneous : Beginnings of the Ritual)................B. C. 3400.

" Building of the largest pyramid (second of Herodotus)
B. C. 3280.

" Nitokris and the tomb in the pyramid of Menkeres (the third)
B. C. 2957.

Northern Media, and to Kabul and Kandahar. B. C. 5000—4000.

" *General Epochs of Asiatic History. Power of Chaldeeism and Khamism. Beginnings of writing with Letters by the Semites.*
B. C 4000—2878.

" The Aryans migrate into the Indus country.........B. C. 4000.

" Formation of a powerful Chaldean Empire in S. Babylonia.

" Beginning of Chaldean series of Kings in Babylon...B. C. 3784.

" Zoroaster, the Seer and Lawgiver of Bactria..B. C. 3500—3000.

" Building of the city of Babylon 2000 years before Semiramis (Temple of Belus).....B. C. 3250,

" Abraham (Abram) born in Ur of the Chaldees........B. C 2927.

" Abraham withdraws to the south-western part of Mesopotamia with his father..B. C. 2900."

What an amazing stretch of semi-historical time! And yet modern research, while it rejects every thing that bears the faintest resemblance to myth, establishes the fact that even the enormous lapse of time above recorded is based more on the truth than upon fable.

The Persians, in their Dabistan, and other books, tell us such strange stories of past time, and so earnestly, that despite ourselves we are inclined to listen to, if not believe them ; and after we deduct nine-tenths of the years in their chronologies, we still have left a period of time compared to which Menes and Memphis are but of last year.

According to the authority just named, Time, from all past eternity, has been divided into a succession of cycles. During each of these there exists a class of beings, intelligent, progressive, immortal, who all die when the cycle ends, except a single pair, who become mysteriously changed, and give birth to the progenitors of the beings of a new cycle.

At the end of the great cycle that preceded the present one, the last survivor was a being named Mahabad; and he was the first lawgiver, priest and king. He had thirteen descendants, to whom he taught all the primitive arts, by whom he was succeeded, and who were the first teachers of the human world. All this happened a great many thousand years ago. During the reign of the last of those kings—Azorabad, a good and pious man, the world became crrupted by fraud, violence, chicanery, and loose passions, from which it was at length saved by Jy Affram, a devout man, who, at the instigation of a messenger direct from heaven, assumed the cares of State, and restored order and happiness by very summary dealings with the vicious and unwise.

The new dynasty, thus founded, came to an end by the miraculous disappearance of its last king, Jy Abad, and the world again relapsed into an awful state of violence, crime and confusion. It was again redeemed as it had been; but once more fell; but this time lower than before. A merciful God again smiled upon, and saved the race from complete wreck and ruin. All was of no avail. The drama was again enacted, and with the same results. A vast number of ages had now elapsed, and God determined to make use of their evil habits in order to put an end to the whole population of the cities of the world ; and accordingly he let loose all the restraining cords, and murder, war, lust and rape very speedily accomplished His will, and hurried them over the ramparts of eternal gloom and death. When all this was done, God called into existence a being named Kyomurz, or Gil-Shah ; and he was the father of all the present human race—that is to say, of the Persians. " Gil" means " clay," " Shah" means " king," " Kyomurz" means " First Man." Thus we have the first king ; earth-king ; king of the earth, and Adam. The time that has elapsed since Gil-Shah lived must be computed at not less than one hundred thousand years.

In this identical book, whose antiquity is very great indeed, we learn that a certain king of their country was in the habit of fighting pitched battles with the Deeves—an order of disembodied gentry, who took to building cities in the province of Mazunduran ;* he defeated them, but the remains of their cities still remain. This is a very pretty conceit, but have we not something very like it concerning battles with spiritual beings, led on by Michael and Satan ? Is there the remotest connection between the two—accounts ?

How strange it is that, try as we may, we cannot reach an absolute historical commencement of any an-

---

* Recently, while travelling in Oriental lands in company with a " Heathen" friend, who was well read in Oriental lore, beside being an excellent English and German scholar, our conversation turned on " Who built Persepolis, Baalbec, and the Pyramids ?'' Said he, seriously, " They are too collossal to have ever been erected by human hands of the present race or orders. My opinion is that they are the remnants of a gigantic race of intelligent beings, compared to whom we are the veriest pigmies. Such people did once live, and they, and not the present race of mortals, built those vast monuments !" " When ?" " Allah knows ! There is but one God ! Perhaps one hundred thousand years ago."

cient nation? Let us fly as high and as far as we may, and alight upon the hoariest spot on earth. and yet we are only at the hither end of long dynastic lines! In the very oldest mythologies now extant, we perceive evidences of second-handedness; no matter whether we seize upon the Chinese annals, extending back, with probable truth, from eight to twelve thousand years, or take those that Manetho and Herodotus have handed down the ages; or those which were extant hundreds of years before either of them walked the earth, all alike yield the same results. The Greek historian and the Egyptian scholar alike, are but latter-age men! We find no new thing, either in what they have given, or in what we reach from beyond them; but we always find derived knowledge, theory, myth —selected from the "has been," or the "once upon a time"—something that *was*, but which had ceased to be —the mournful remnants of the foretime, the ruins and *debris* of what once was comparatively perfect; vast systems that had grown up, matured, fallen into dissuetude and decay, and finally gone out like an oil-less lamp! The oldest mythologies, Greek, Roman, Egyptian, Indian, Bactrian and Assyrian, are but new pictures of old facts long antecedent to *their* time.

Said my rather free-thinking, Moslem friend, to me one day as we were taking our coffee and smoking our chibouques under the shade of the sycamores in the Ezbekiah, Cairo: " I have lived seven years in Europe; have mastered four languages; have fitted myself for my Shah's service (military engineering,) under the tuition of English, French and German masters, and of course have had abundant opportunity to observe. The result of these observances are that all you, people of the West, are *one-sided* and *fanatical!* You are the best mechanics in the world; are rich and powerful,

but—excuse me!—are not very wise with all your
knowledge.   You laugh at our Koords, who, disdain-
ing all your prosaic theories of Creation, boldly assert
that *they* did not spring from your Adam, but were
begotten of women created especially for that purpose
by Allah, through the instrumentality of the Ginns
(spiritual beings) ; and yet, while you thus laugh, you
at the same moment tell us impossible tales of five
hundred distinct nations of men all springing from one
common pair !   This is more absurd than the Koordish
legend.   You know that the 112th chapter of the
Koran tells us—and perhaps you would do well to
consider its teachings—that " God never begat, nor
was begotten ; neither had He any equal ;" He was
never incarnate in any body, nor took a female companion or a child.   I do not know, but I *feel*, that God is
a being too vast for human comprehension ; and I
believe that this God is He who created man, solely
and alone ; but you believe that another God, in association, made man.   I am believing the truth ; you are
accepting a Shemitic myth !   I believe that this earth
has, for millions of ages, been the scene of human acti-
vities ; you, that it is but a few thousand years old !
Your God is human ; mine is celestial.   I am a be-
liever in one God ; you have a score or two—French,
American, English, African, Jewish, Russian, Scotch —
in fact all sorts of gods ; and you degrade the noblest
faculties of your souls, and bow down, not to the
august Creator, the great Mind of minds, but to a
series of conventional gods.   I suppose that Time moves
in cycles, and that each has its peculiar order of intelligent beings, both like and unlike the present race of
men.   By and bye these last will disappear, as others
have before them, and be superseded by a loftier race
of immortal beings.   We are but the initial types of

glorious races to come after we are gone to act our
parts in another drama, in another stage of being!
You, as well as myself, have been amongst the Ansai-
reeh of Syria, and have gratefully listened while I
translated for you their sublime cosmogonical theories.
You know how eloquently they spoke of the five ages
before the present race of men inhabited the earth,
and of the Djân, the Ramm, the Tamm, the Bann, and
the Djam, all of which lived long ages before your
Adam.   You perhaps understood that those five orders
of intelligent beings were men as you and I are. They
were ; and believe me, the legend is more than a mere
figment of imagination ; for behind there lies a vast
deal of sober truth ; and in these orders you can easily
see the faint but certain record of long lines of kings,
nations, religions and political systems—forms of faith
and records of past human action.   And these five orders of fanciful-looking beings mean nothing more nor
less than so many recollections of the human foretime,
stretching away into the dim distance, beyond the epoch
of some of your geological ages, whose days are centuries long.

Allah slowly plants a garden, but he plants it very well!

Do you remember the day that your friend, Mr. Ducat, and Professor Krause, yourself and I, strolled
out to see the 'wailing place' of the Jews, near the
mosque El Aksur, in Jerusalem ? And do you remember the historical fact that Jerusalem was known four
thousand four hundred and seventy-nine years ago, and
that the story that Melchizadek founded it, is not
true ? Well, on that very day an Arab, in digging a
a well, found a jug-handle of a form and material
so entirely different from any other discovered in modern times, that it attracted the attention of learned
men. Well, again, did you observe that on the handle

was a peculiar figure? That was the figure of the
sun ; precisely such as had before been found amidst
the ruins of Nineveh and Memphis, Tanta and Heliopolis ; and consequently it spoke, not merely of four
thousand five hundred, or five thousand years ago, but
it speaks of the early days of the Chaldean empire ;
of commerce and art ; and hints, not merely at the
Jebusite reign, but of Ninus and of Nimrod. When *they*
lived, you must ask your Western scholars, but probably in the days of the nations called the Djân.
Chaldea was an early nation, and yet, in my opinion, science will yet prove her, old as she is, to have
been of Indo-Germanic origin ; and so with many
other of the nations of Asia, particularly those upon
the Western portions thereof. No, no, my friend, do
not put yourself to the trouble of believing that the
present is the first, or only, family of men that have existed on this globe. Men, nations, civilizations, all,
like the seasons, move in cycles, and each round of ages
is but a varied repetition, on a larger or smaller scale,
upon the same general theatre, of events that have,
time and again, been enacted and observed. Just
look at yonder moon : it rises, falls, comes up and goes
down again ; the same unvarying round forever and
forever. So the earth, and man, and nations, and civilizations, and historical and unhistorical epochs and
eras. They all rise, grow, flow, reach a perihelion
splendor, and then a night, and then again a new moon,
a new day. But come, let us fill our pipes. Philosophy
is tiresome!" And he became silent. I could not
help marveling at such things falling from an Oriental's lips, nor wondering at the dogged persistency
with which he clung to the notion that all we of the
Western world, were at this very moment, not only
idolators, but actual Polytheists ; but aside from that,

and one or two other matters, I could not but admit
that his remarks were, to say the least, very suggestive. In another work I shall detail many strange
things derived from my intercourse with this man.

It is held by a great number of scholars that the
words in Genesis, "Let us make man in our own
image," does not warrant the assumption that the person there spoken of was the *first* man on the earth, but
implies that man, as he then existed, did not so exist as
the intellectual and moral image of God ; consequently
Deity determined to make man *in* that image, though
to whom God alluded when he said, "Let *us* make
man," is not yet apparent, but will be before we conclude this book. Another reading of the 26th verse of
Genesis, 1st chapter, might be : "Let us create other
men in another and better moral mould than those who
now exist." But as this exegesis might be set down as
a mere quibble, I trust no weight will be attached to
it, for it is not safe to even attempt to build up a theory,
or to establish any hypothesis, the grounds of which
are not solid and based on the very truth-itself ; for
though a false doctrine or system may pass current, and
be successful for a while, yet in the end, both the system
and its authors are sure to sink into a night that knows
no ending ; hence, if my theory cannot stand on better
authority than perverted texts of either Scripture or
Science, nothing is more absolutely certain than that it
is destined to a very limited career in the worlds of
Letters and of Thought. It has already been admitted
herein that the name Adam is one used to signify a particular individual ; but it has also other meanings, as.
for instance, Genesis vi. 1—7 : "And it came to pass,
when ha-adam (the Adam—the Adamites) [1] began to
multiply on the face of the earth, and daughters were
born unto them, that the sons of God ("sons of the

gods" is the true rendering) saw the daughters of the
ha-adam that they were fair (literally *goodly*); and
they took them wives of all which they chose.[2]   There
were giants (Nephilim) in the earth in those days;[3] and
also after that, when the sons of God (of the gods) came
in unto the daughters of ha-adam, and they bare *children*
to them; the same became mighty men, which were of
old, men of renown.   Literally these *were* the mighty
ones which *were* of old-time men of renown.[4]   And the
Lord said: I will destroy the ha-adam whom 1 have
created ... for it repenteth me that I have made
them."[4]   Now the events here related refer, not to the
days of Adam, for, according to Scriptural chronology,
no less than 1556 years had elapsed since creation,
and 626 since Adam's death.   In Hebrew the prefix
" ha " is equivalent to our " the," and is, of course, an
" article," while " Adam " was both a proper individual
name, and also a collective patronymic, like " Anakim,"
" Israel," " Jacob," " Gideon," " Dan," and " Reuben ;"
though in some sense the term " Adam " differs from the
others, inasmuch as it was a "generic epithet." " Adam,"
without the article, was the name of the Hebrew protoplast; it then became the name of himself and wife;
then it became that of any one of their descendants, and
then to any multitude thereof; and, by a synedoche, or
extension of meaning, is applied to the whole human
race.   Says a recent British author, on this very point :
" When ' Adam' does not signify the man whose proper
name it was, nor relate to his time, it is *properly* a
generic epithet, but used as a collective noun, and signifying ' The Adamites,' including none *beside* them,
and excluding none *of* them."   " Ha-adam" is a vague
singular, but virtually a plural.   The Septuagint has
" ha-adamah," which, in my opinion, is the better rendering of the two.   Adam also signifies " redness,"

"red-earth," "red-men;" so does "Edom;" so does
"Hamor," which latter is also a generic epithet; a
male patronymic; a female name; a collective noun,
and a special hero of the Bible. In quoting the passages from vi. Genesis, we encounter something more
than has yet appeared, for instance: ¹"When 'ha-adam'
(the Adamites) began to multiply." Can this passage
mean "When *that* particular branch of the human
species began to increase?" Such is, at least, the implication; as also that other branches *had already*
stocked the land. Indeed, the fact that there *were*
other tribes of men, not of Adam's race, is clearly and
emphatically stated in the same quotation; and they
are called the sons of God, as Adam's offspring are
called after *their* great progenitor. Some writers have
claimed that these sons of God were spiritual beings;²
but this cannot be possible, seeing that such are neither
in the habit of marrying flesh-and-blood women, nor
capable of becoming the fathers of such a goodly race
of mortals as became the mighty men of old. These
sons of God were therefore of another race than the
Adamites, as were also the people mentioned in the
next verse totally distinct from either of the human
races just mentioned.³ "There were Nephilim (giants)
in those days." Now this passage neither states nor
implies that the giants were overgrown specimens of
humanity, such as we see in these days in museums, but
they were a race of men of exceeding stature. "Men
of old, men of renown."⁴ It appears that there was a
hoary antiquity ascribed to those who lived in the
Noachian Age, even according to Genesis; and this
passage plainly indicates a Pre-Adamite race, or races
of men. "It repenteth me that I have made the
ha-adam."⁵ And God promised to destroy them—and
did, all save Noah and the people in the Ark—all of

the Adamites except eight persons, but not all of *mankind*, by as many millions, as will be hereinafter seen.

Let us push our inquiries one step further in the same direction.

___

CHAPTER II.

CAIN—HIS WIFE—JOB.

GEN. iv. 13–26 : " And Cain said unto the Lord, My punishment is greater than I can bear. Behold thou hast driven me out this day from the face of the earth ; and from thy face shall I be hid ; and I shall be a fugitive and a vagabond in the earth ; and it shall come to pass, that every one that findeth me shall slay me. And the Lord said unto him, Therefore, whosoever slayeth Cain, vengeance shall be taken on him sevenfold. And the Lord set a mark upon Cain, lest any finding him should kill kim. And Cain went out from the presence of the Lord, and dwelt in the land of Nod, on the east of Eden. . . . And Cain knew his wife, and she conceived, and bare Enoch ; and he built a city, and called the name of the city after the name of his son Enoch. And unto Enoch was born Irad : and Irad begat Mehujael, and Mehujael begat Methusael : and Methusael begat Lamech. And Lamech took unto him two wives : the name of one was Adah, and the name of the other was Zillah. And Adah bear Jabal ; he was the father of such as dwell in tents, and of such as have cattle. And his brother's name was Jubal : he was the father of such as handle the harp and organ. And Zillah, she also bare Tubal Cain, an instructor of every artificer in brass and iron : and the sister of Tubal Cain was Naamah. . . . And Lamech said unto his wives, Adah and Zillah, Hear my voice. ye wives of Lamech, hearken unto my speech : for I have slain a man to my wounding, and a young man to my hurt. If

Cain shall be avenged seven-fold, truly Lamech seventy and seven-fold. .... And Adam knew his wife again, and she bare a son. and called his name Seth : For God, said she, hath appointed me another seed instead of Abel, whom Cain slew. And to Seth, to him also there was born a son ; and he called his name Enos : then began men to call upon the name of the Lord."

Now several noteworthy things here present themselves, which we will glance at, *seriatim :* 1st. Adam and Cain and Eve were all of that particular branch of the human family then existing—three persons. Cain having killed Abel at home, surely did not allude to his parents when complaining that whoever found him would slay him! Although he was a murderer himself, it is not likely that he deemed his father and mother capable of the same dreadful crime. It is far more reasonable to conclude that he feared the punishment due to murder. If he so feared, then three parts of one grand conclusion instantly present themselves : 2d. There must have been some other human beings beside his family, in existence, and these others were not a few, but many, as is implied by his " Whosoever shall find me." These others were of a different race than Adam, and by reason of their numbers, must have been of a race who had existed in that region long antecedent to Adam and Eve. Nothing is mentioned about other brothers of Cain, for further along we are told that Eve's third son was expressly given to fill up Abel's—the dead man's—place. Of sisters of Cain nothing is said, and on this point we have no right to go behind the record, and suppose that Adam had a number of female children. But, supposing that Adam *had* daughters, it is not likely, in the first place, that Cain would have been afraid of a few women ; nor that, if such existed, that they would have sought the

life of one brother, by way of revenge for the slaying
of another one, in the second place; and in the third,
it is not likely that, supposing such sisters to have been
in existence, (first), that Cain and Abel had been guilty
of incest with them, and raised up sons; and (second)
it is not likely, supposing such to have been the case,
that they would have slain Cain in revenge of Abel's
death at his hands, for the sons of Abel would have
feared the *lex talionis* at the hands of the sons of Cain.
It was not his sons, nor Abel's, for there were none
such, nor of his sisters, that Cain was afraid.   Again,
it is not likely that Adam was guilty of the dreadful
crime of which reason demands that we exculpate
both of his sons.   Who then was Cain in fear of?   What
grounds had he?   The text obliquely answers these
questions : He was fearful of the penalties exacted for
murder.   These penalties imply human society, and
human codes of Law, hence a state of advanced civilization ; and the people who had, at that early period of
time, advanced far enough to frame and execute such
laws, were of course of an entirely distinct branch of
the *genus homo ;* for it cannot be supposed for an in-
stant that Cain would have feared the vengeance of
savages or barbarians, supposing that such existed ;
for men, savage or civilized, act from settled motives ;
and if savages existed in those days, they could not
have any motive in avenging Abel's murder.   But,
admit that such savage men did exist, it is clear that
they were not related to Cain, and were, consequently,
Pre-Adamite men.

   In the next place, it is clear that there were other
people than the Adam family in existence, else why
was a mark put upon Cain to protect him from human
vengeance ?   As to the nature of this mark, or why
God connived at Cain's escape, no remarks need here

be offered, although if this whole account should turn out to be either a myth, tradition, or allegory, we may be able to answer both of these queries. Nothing can ever induce a rational man to the belief that the Infinite One either sanctioned murder or incest among men at any period of human history. I feel that such a defense of God is gratuitous, yet it seems *apropos* at this early period of our investigations, for the question is but opened; we are only at the beginning, and a splendid vista lies before us. . . . . " And went out from the Presence—and dwelt in the land of Nod, eastward of Eden." Here two new questions come up: 1st. Why did Cain go there? The reply is, " To get where his crime was unknown, and where he would be safe from the 'clutches of the law.' " And 2d. Did he go to the wilderness—to live and labor alone? The first answer replies to the second question. He did *not* go to the wilderness, but to an inhabited land, where he " knew his wife." Who was she? Not his sister, for reasons already given. She must therefore have been either a daughter of the land he fled to, or a woman of the people of whom he was afraid before he emigrated. In either case she was not a relation of his, and was, consequently, a Pre-Adamite. Again: a single person could not build a house alone, much less a large number of houses; and even if he could do so, he *would* not, unless there were people to occupy the aforesaid houses. Well, in this land of Nod, whither Cain fled, he builded a city, and called it Enoch, after his son. Who were the helpers of Cain in this work of building? Why build a city for a single family—Cain's? Who were Zillah and Adah, Lamech's wives? Not of Adam's race, assuredly. Well, Cain went to Nod, married, had children, and grandchildren, and built a city; his descendants began to raise cattle, and had invented the

Harp and the Organ ; had learned how to make brass,
and fashion it and iron into useful implements, and all
within a period of one hundred and thirty years, for it
was all accomplished before the birth of Seth, who was
born when Adam was one hundred and thirty years
old, and it was not till *after* Seth's birth that Adam
begat sons and daughters ; and before Adam had
daughters at all there were Adah. Zillah, Seth's wife,
Cain's, and the wives, mothers, daughters and sisters
of all the people who helped Cain to build his city !
In the second verse of Genesis iv., it is said that Cain
was a tiller of the land, and in the same verse that
Abel was a keeper of sheep.   In the last verse of
same chapter, "Men began to call upon the name of the
Lord," *i. e.*—worship God. Now, observe : 1st. Men
cultivate land for either a livelihood, or for profit.
They keep sheep for the same purpose ; yet why, in
that climate—and it matters little whether Adam and
his family dwelt in the region where Damascus now
stands, as one tradition claims, and where his head lies
buried to this day, according to a second legend ; or in
Mesopotamia ; or in Southern Armenia ; or near the
Ural mountains ; or near Jerusalem, or on the plains
now submerged beneath the Caspian Sea ; or in Central Persia, according to as many other traditions ; it
matters not, I repeat, which of these may be the true
locality. No adequate motive or necessity could possibly exist, either for keeping sheep or cultivating the
soil as a profession, if there were but four human beings
on the earth.   The very fact that such professions were
pursued, implies the existence of other human consu-
mers of the commodities—wool, meat, milk, cheese,
butter, fruits and vegetables, thus produced. 2d. Adam
and his family knew but one God, the Creator, and yet
we are told that in the 105th year of Enos' life, and

the 235th of Adam's, and while only Adam, Eve, Seth, Cain, and thirteen others, including five women, were yet alive. that " The people began to call on the name of the Lord." This implies two things: First, that there were others beside these seventeen people in existence, for *they* already "called on the name of the Lord;" and secondly, that the hearts of those others were then, for the first time, withdrawn from the worship of their old gods, and directed to the worship of the God of Adam and his family ; for it cannot be supposed that Cain, who had too good reason to remember, had forgotten God in the land to which he fled. But it *is* likely that he worshiped in repentance in his new home, and won the nations over, so that they began to forsake their old, and conform to a new and loftier system of worship. It strikes me that this last passage presents a formidable obstacle in the path of those who insist, on Scriptural grounds, that all mankind originated with the Edenic protoplasts.

While on the Scriptural part of this investigation, I call attention to a few more passages, after which there are some things to be said on the Bible generally, of great interest to all who admire that most wonderful of all books that was ever written.

Turn to Job. chapter i. 6, and chapter ii. 1 : "There was a day when the sons of God came to present themselves before the Lord, and Satan came also among them. And the Lord said to Satan : Whence comest thou ? And Satan said : From going to and fro in the earth, and from walking up and down in it." In noticing these passages it must not be forgotten that the entire sublime Book of Job is, beyond all doubt the oldest in the Bible—not excepting Genesis. This latter Book is a collection of separate narratives, usually attributed to the pen of Moses—as is also the Book of Job—but probably without good reason. The Pentateuch, or a part of it, at least, may have been, and probably was, compiled by the great Legislator ; but Job is the work of a single pen ; is a connected story throughout; and the grand, magnificent, and lofty style in which it is written, differs so greatly from that of Moses, as to leave no doubt that it was the work of another, and widely different order of genius. The date usually ascribed as that of Job, is 1520 before Christ, but this assignment is made not on the very best authority, viz., that of the Jewish Rabbins. The entire Talmud, as was demonstrated to me while in Jerusalem, to my entire satisfaction, abounds, not merely with numberless chronological, geneological, and historical falsifications, and perversions, but with the most puerile and absurd statements ; as, for instance, that one of their Rabbins once went hunting ; started a hare ; the animal, to save itself, plunged into a dark lane—a sort of tunnel ; the Rabbi pursued it incessantly for three whole days and nights, and then discovered that during all that time he and the hare had been running through the marrowless shin-bone of the defunct Ogg, King of Bashan !--and there are actually hundreds of volumes of just such ridiculous nonsense ; and these self-same worthies have tampered with every page of the Old Testament that they chose to, thus compelling the scholars of Christendom to find the world's history, bit by bit, and scrap by scrap, from ten thousand graves, where they have lain entombed for ages. But they will do it, and in accomplishing the mighty task, will do the worlds of Letters and Religion a service and a benefit, incalculable by the human mind, as at present constituted. To resume : Job, or the " Poem," as not a few regard it, was of Chaldean origin ; and if the splendid tale is a record of a human experience, then that experience was undergone by a man who, in all probability, was not related to the "Rabbins" even in the ten-thousandth generation or degree. The reasons for this opinion will be manifest in chapters further on.

Many readers regard the "Satan" mentioned in Job, as the very Devil incarnate in the human form. The notion is childish—the idea an unworthy one. That term is one signifying falsity in the abstract, *i. e.*, an oppugnment, a negation, the spirit that opposed the Good. The sons of God referred to, are, doubtless, the same race of Pre-Adamite men, already treated of, while the "Satan" here can mean no other than the doctrine-mongers of the land —a class of idolators—a people distinct from either the Adamites, or the righteous people above noticed.

Science, especially Astronomy, requires a long time for development, and yet in this exceedingly old book we read passages that indicate a close acquaintance with it. We read of Arcturus, Orion—" the sweet belts of Orion," of Pleiades, and " the sweet chambers of the South," and even with eclipses of sun and moon ;*

---

* In all ages and among all nations the eclipses of the Sun and Moon have excited an unusual degree of interest in the minds of the masses. For many centuries they were looked upon with that awe and reverence which the human mind in its uncultivated state is apt to bestow upon all phenomena which appear strange and unintelligible. And even at the present day there are many who ascribe peculiar power to the Sun and Moon. The Egyptians, Chaldeans, Indians and Chinese, each began to observe these phenomena at a very remote period. We have satisfactory evidence that the Egyptians recorded observations more than 1600 years before Christ. and the Indians at a yet earlier day. In fact, it has recently been proved beyond a doubt, that we have the record of a remarkable phenomenon which was observed in the year 2460 B. C., or some centuries before the " universal flood"—according to the Hebrew chronology, or the systems of reckoning usually accepted. At a very early day, the Chaldeans knew a

while other passages show that even Physiology was
tolerably well understood.   Job speaks of kings and
thrones and diadems ; so that monarchies already existed in his days.   Even the arts of criticism and
authorship were common in his time, for he expressly
wishes that his adversary had written a book—that he
might "Review" it?   The 35th verse of the 38th chapter looks very like an allusion to the modern electric
telegraph.   And in passing, I will mention that while
in Egypt I became satisfied from evidence there presented—from Macrinius, I think—that something very
similar must have been known to one of the Cleopatras,
else how did she "send news by a wire to all the cities,
from Heliopolis to Elephantina, on the upper Nile?"
The word "Jordan" in the 41st chapter is believed to
be an interpolation, or to refer to another than the
Syrian river, for Job lived in Idumea, and far away
from the Jordan.

CHAPTER III.

THE NILE.

Aimard, in a recent work on South America, says a
thing so happily, that I cannot forbear quoting it here :
" Learned men have endeavored to prove that America
was quite new, comparatively with the ancient known
world.   This hypothesis is absurd, quite as absurd as

period of 223 lunations (or eighteen years) when the same eclipses
were reproduced. This leads us to suppose that they were careful
observers, and had made considerable progress in the science of Astronomy. One of the early Chinese Emperors founded a school of Astronomers, whose duty it was to predict all remarkable eclipses, and
on failing to do so, paid the forfeit with their lives. In a subsequent reign, YHANG, the Astronomer Royal, announced two eclipses
which did not take place, and in order to save his head, he said it was
not because his calculations were erroneous, but that the Heavenly
bodies deviated from their regular course out of respect to the virtues
of the Emperor.

that which asserts that this land was peopled from Asia, by means of Behring's Straits. The imposing ruins of Palenque, the city recently discovered in Yucatan, prove not only a more remote antiquity than the Egyptians have preserved for us, but still further, a civilization that the ancients (Oriental) never possessed. The Red race, whatever may be said, has no relation whatever with the White, Black or Yellow races, and is, like them, primordial and autochthone. On this subject we remember a repartee made one day by a Comanche Chief to a missionary, who—we don't recollect exactly to what purpose—was endeavoring to prove that there had not been an aboriginal race in America, grounding his argument rather clumsily, we think, upon that passage of the Bible, which says that Noah had *three* sons, one of whom peopled Asia, the second Europe, and the third Africa, and that thence it followed that the inhabitants of the New World must be descended from one of these three children of Noah. " Brother," said the Indian, " The Father has forgotten this—they who preserved the tradition of this Noah have only given him three sons, because at that period our land was not known ; if it had been, there would certainly have been a fourth, you may depend upon it !" The reply is worth being written in letters of gold. As with the Indian, so with many another race of men.

To aid us in our researches the Genius of History bears us back and down, through the long lane of the centuries. until we stand face to face with Hipparchus, Euctemon, Meton, Ptolemy, Eratosthenes and Autolycus; where we rest a while, and resting, sigh " There's no beginning here!" Once more we take wing, and after a vast flight through the Glimmer, we halt to talk with Herodotus, Manetho, Berosus and the Babylonian illuminati, every one of whom repeats the same mono-

tonous song of, " No beginning here !" Especially is
this true of those whom in this chapter we are treating
of—the Nilotic branch of the human tree. Having
parenthetically glanced at other races, let us now return to our starting-point—Egypt, and to Menes—that
wonderful man, who left his father's house, and kingdom, and the lovely city of his birth—the ancient This,
in Upper Egypt, probably in the latitude where afterwards stood the famous Abydos, to found a new kingdom—to erect a new empire.

Menes had two sons, one of whom, Athothis, succeeded him on the throne, but whether of Upper or
Lower Egypt, is not exactly known ; if it was, it would
matter little. But what is of vast importance in this
connection, is that this king Athothis, five thousand
nine hundred and forty years ago, was a very liberally
educated man—indeed a man of profound learning and
scientific attainments ; for we are assured on the very
best, and unmistakable authority, that he was not only
a munificent patron of literature, but was himself an
author of excellent works upon Physiology and Anatomy.* Now if literature and art had reached thus
far at that early date, it follows that they must have
been developed by some other race of men than those
claiming the Adam of the Hebrews, as the primeval
originator. The simple fact is, that in this first beginning of what is fairly proved to be comparatively
modern Egyptian History, we are simply becoming
acquainted with a people who had already worn out
one phase of civilization. and were then beginning to
found a new order of things, just as had been probably
done before—just as will be done again and again,
until Time himself shall have grown hoary with age!

* See " Early Egyptian History." London : 1861. Macmillan & Co.

We must go away from Egypt—old as she is, and at least in *four* different directions, before we arrive at any thing like a true beginning of the great civilized drama ; for we can *never* reach that of Man himself ; true, we can guess—and that is all. In Memphis—on the pyramid-plateau—on the site of Cairo, and westward of the present Egyptian capital, the sacred Bulls, Apis and Mnevis, were worshiped in the days of Menes—a fact so pregnant with meaning, and one that so clearly points backward to a human antiquity, compared to which the era of Menes is but of yesterday, that the wonder and astonishment is indeed great, that European Egyptologers have not perceived it long ago. That fact is this : These sacred Bulls were supposed to symbolize Life—the Principle of Animation. In these Bulls the god Pthah, Sokar-Osiris, (Life,) was resident. This Bull-worship was not indigenous to Nilotic lands. It was an importation from Western Asia, was borrowed from the banks of the Euphrates, and the Bull-worship of Memphis was but a locally modified service of what had been a nation's faith in Babylon, thousands of years before the Meneites' progenitors had dispossessed the Nigritian kings and founded This. The proof of this is clear, and has been demonstrated by recent discoveries in Egypt, and in Birs Nimroud. We know when Bull-headed gods, and living Bulls were introduced into Egypt ; we know that the early nations copied the examples of each other ; we know that this mode and form of worship was in vogue in Babylon, Nineveh, and Nimroud, in their palmy days ; and we know that these palmy days stretch away vastly beyond the horizon of Time, bounded by Menes, Apis, Osiris and Memphis. The golden calf made by Aaron for the Children of Israel, was but this identical Bull-worship, modified and adapted to the demands of a somewhat

differently organized people. The same people worship
the gold in another shape ever since that day. Does
any other people? This relapse of the Hebrew wanderers into Memphite idolatry, disgusted, discouraged,
and so enraged their great leader, that he threw down
and broke the two tables of the law, which had cost
him the labor of forty long days to engrave, while
alone upon the Asiatic mountain; and no wonder! It
was enough to provoke Moses—or any other man.

In a large tomb near the Pyramids, is the picture of
the preparation of a feast. A man has just killed a
cow, is sharpening a *bronze* knife on a *steel* rod, while
an *iron* pot of three legs is boiling over a fire! The
colors explain the metals. . Bronze, iron, steel, five
thousand eight hundred years ago! Surely Adam's
children had not yet experienced that stern necessity,
which is the mother of invention, to such a degree, in
less than two centuries from Adam's creation, as to
lead to these important results! Were not these results the product of centuries of human experience,
then already long since passed away? Is not this the
most reasonable view?

The first Pyramid was built, according to the best
authorities, about two hundred years after Menes came
to lower Egypt; and one of the tombs near it is
ascribed to the butler of a king then upon the throne;
and on the walls of this tomb are pictures of *cabinet-
makers, boat-builders, sail-makers,* and *glass-blowers.*
Each one of these trades, of course, imply at least a
score of others; else whence their highly-tempered
steel tools, planes, saws, needles, looms, and so forth?
There are no iron mines on the banks of the Nile : there ·
are no copper mines there either; but the first must
have been obtained in South-western Africa ; the latter
from the Asiatic deserts—perhaps from Wadi—Maghra,

in the Sinain wilderness; for the mines there give abundant evidence of having been worked a long, long time ago, probably in the days of the Pyramid-building—perhaps anterior thereto. A people must have been far advanced to have been able to make as excellent edge tools, as were in use when those vast buildings were reared. Another picture represents the Egyptian king in the act of slaying his captives, who are evidently Asiatics, but as far unlike any known nation, as the Negroes are unlike the modern Greek. Who, and what were, this captive people? Sons of Adam? Mercantile arts were pursued, as well as war; for we find pictures of bartering; exchanging leopard-skins and other peltry, for coin and other commodities; and those skins were foreign produce; Egypt having neither leopards nor pearls of her own—and strings of pearls are represented. The ancient people tanned leather, blew glass-bottles, made wine, hunted, fished, farmed; were floriculturists, tamed beasts, dyed cloth, imitated precious stones; played on flutes, harps, lyres, a sort of guitar; and, in brief, possessed an hundred arts, which arts are proved to have existed, by sculptures on the monuments, and in papyri manuscripts, taken from tombs, where they had lain five thousand long years and more; and it is difficult to understand how such an amazing advancement could have taken place in so short a time, supposing that the Adam of Genesis was the first and only created man, as it would be for a Mohawk Indian, fresh from the woods, to give a learned lecture on analytical geometry, or the calculus of variations.

Little by little we are unraveling the tangled skein of Time and human history. I have already had occasion to connect Egypt with Assyria, in the matter of the Bulls. Long before the Bull worship became part

of the national practice on the Nilotic shores, Babylon
was a city of a million inhabitants ; one Nineveh had
already fallen and crumbled into dust, and a new Nineveh had, like the fabled Phœnix, arisen from its ashes.
Babylon was built before the Deluge, and, old legends
tell us, survived it. True, 2,233, B. C., is the date
of the building of that remarkable city on the Plains
of Shinar, assigned by James, the British king's trans-
lators of the Bible ; but it is one purely arbitrary, and
wholly unwarranted, as our researches will presently
demonstrate ; for if we add a term equally long, we yet
fail to reach Babylon's era. She was a mighty centre
of a mighty belt of nations, and the sculptors of her
sister city, Nineveh the second—built, as I have said,
thousands of years before—were carving out of solid
stone the monstrons winged Bulls—the identical Bulls
that now grace the Halls of European Museums. The
great city of the Jebusites (Jerusalem) had waxed old ;
Joppa (Jaffa) was an old sea-port ; Damascus, the
queen of cities, was a very ancient town, and one whose
origin man cannot fix ; and a hundred other human
hives were thronged with busy life many a long century prior to four thousand and four years before
Christ ; and if we take our stand upon the towers of
any one of those places—and from them interrogate
China as to *her* age, she replies, " O, sons of Belus, and
Nineveh, thousands of summers had passed over my
head ere thou wert born among the nations !" And
probably China would speak the truth, for her chronology extends many thousands of years beyond the
Mosaic ; while that of the Hindoos is older still, and
has *astronomical records* to prove its truth, such as the
occultation of some stars, the conjunction of some
others, and the heliacal rising of others still. Nor will
it do to attempt to account for the correctness of these

recorded events, on the hypothesis of "back reckonings," because, although possible, it is improbable.
Men never act but from motives of some sort of interest : and no nation, especially the Hindoos, had or has
any *inttrest* in telling falsehoods to posterity—always
excepting the Jews—and *they* had a powerful motive,
namely, the desire to prove themselves God's chosen
people ; and their desire to appear as the "First
Family." But—Science is telling *her* story now ! Scripture is common human property, and no more belongs
exclusively to Eber's children, than sunshine does to
Africa alone ; and as Scripture itself does not claim
to give chronological accounts of creation and human
events, it is but right that its friends clear it of the
rubbish attached to it by interested parties, and let the
sublime Book stand for what it really is—a dateless
narrative of certain past occurrences. I have seen it
suggested by a British writer, quite recently, that in the
legacy left by Joseph to his children, called the Book
of Genesis, or the Beginning, that we have an *ancient
oratorio*, transcribed from an Oriental tragedy. Another writer expresses his profound conviction, that in
Genesis we have but the lucubrations of some of the
visionary Rabbins of the olden time. I reject both notions, because we know it relates historical facts. The
sublime thoughts in Genesis were never achieved by a
playright, nor were they the invention of any mere
literateur. The world's best thoughts were then, as
now, the world's own property, and by that world were
treasured and housed in books—printed or written,
both on parchment and the tablets of human memory.
To this common *cache* the writers of old were indebted
for the priceless fragments they have bequeathed us.

    There is a chronology of Soul as well as of material
history ; and not by the study of material things alone

shall we arrive at the age of man or of the world ; but
by the study of the human mind itself, and it alone, shall
we solve the great problem ; for the birth and death
of Ideas are the true mile-stones on the great path that
man has traveled. There are no abortions by Thought's
great mother—Nature. Her children take a long time
to gestate, and a still longer one to be born and reared ;
and thousands of years are often consumed in the processes. For instance, let us take two ideas : 1st. That
wars are not necessary ; 2d. that all men are naturally
brethren. Both of these ideas were, thousands of years
ago, born into the world ; the first is part of every
man's internal, but not of his practical consciousness ;
and the second — embodied in the Golden Rules of
Brahma, Confucius, Budha and Jesus, has not yet reached
the outer, from man's inner world. A great idea requires not less than five thousand years for an orbit.
Give us the known succession of ideas, and we can
come far nearer to deciding how old the human world
is, than by the study of all the monumental records in
existence, save when those monuments are themselves
the idea expressed in stone—as, for instance, the obelisque or the scarabeus. As a whole, the world develops, and ideas are climacteric—crude, less crude, fine,
polished — and then they beget new ideas, thought-
babes, which, though different from the parents
themselves, are, nevertheless, a decided improvement.
Illustration : The idea of a God, beginning with ele-
mental worship, idolatry, polytheism, and so on, from
the crude concept of the savage, to the sublime idea
attempted to be grasped by modern genius. Probably
the space of time between the two poles of this central
Thought of thoughts must be measured by thousands of
—centuries, shall I say ? Take another instance : the
birth of the Promethean instinct—Fire, and its uses.

What a wide gulph of years separates us from that early time when man discovered the art of making and using fire! How long it took him to learn to melt the ores; how long from the first rude casting to the last cylinder, for some grand "Naugatuck" or "Vanderbilt," "Persia" or "Adriatic," "Great Eastern," or "Roanoke?" Nay. How long did it take to develope the mageric art—to pass by slow degrees from the simple broiled or roasted lump of meat, to the *patés* and *entreés* of a Parisian *chef de cuisine?* Bring two men together : one shall be one of Livingston's Makalolos, the other the chief cook of Napoleon, the Unsatisfied ; contrast them—and the difference is as that of one to one-hundred ; and yet the art of the last is unquestionably but the out-growth of the first. Put the question : How long would it take Zambuzi to equal Alexis Soyer—how many generations would it require ?

The people who dwelt in This, and who afterwards founded Memphis and erected Thebes, were, beyond all reasonable doubt, a branch of that singular tribe of people now called the Basinjes, remnants of whom are still to be found in Central Africa, occupying that splendid series of basins—the great lake-region— through which the Zambezi and the Leeambye roll their magnificent tides, which now embraces lakes Ngami in the south, Tsadi in the north, Dilolo in the west, and Taganyika and Nyanja in the east. This whole region was once only a single lake, but one nearly three thousand miles long, by one thousand in width ; and there cannot be a doubt that recent geological changes—though an event geologically recent, may mean twice ten thousand years ago !—drained all but the above five portions through the fissure of Mosi-oatunye. These Basinje people are, in form, stature and feature, far more like the ancient Egyptian type, than

are the Copts, who claim to be the descendants of Menes
and the Pharoahs.   New conditions, localities, and
climates develop new habits, customs, languages, forms
of thought and worship ; and if, as is probable, on the
occurrence of that terrific earth-quake which opened
the fissure of Mosioatunye, and emptied the lake of its
waters, the remnant of survivors emigrated in search
of a new home, which they at length found on the
banks of the Nile, how long must it have taken them
to rise above and out of their barbarism, to develop
a new form of thought, a new language, and to found
a new empire?   How long must it have taken this
primitive people to subdue the possessors of the coveted
soil ; to engraft on their own sacerdotal systems the
to them—new order of things which they found?
How long before their simple language became so
altered and enriched by contact with, and absorption of,
that of the conquered race, and the nations with whom
they were commercially related, west, east, and north
of them, as to become an entirely distinct tongue?
Bunsen tells us that ten thousand years are not sufficient! but Bunsen is not an absolute standard—at least
with us Americans, whatever he may be to Europeans.
The Baron peoples Egypt from Asia ; I prefer to people it from Africa—and. I think, with far more reason ;
contending that a tribe or tribes of Central Africa,
driven out by some cataclysmal event, migrated to the
banks of the Nile, and there founded a new nation, just
as was done on our shores, and is being done on the
Pacific at this very time.

Wherever a new race of men settle with, or in proximity to, an old one, the habits of both become measur-
ably at first, and finally, inextricably blended.   While
by association and intermarriage, the language of each
becomes so mingled with the others' vernacular, and

with other tongues, that, in the course of time, an entirely new language is produced. On the Western coast of America the English is rapidly changing both its structure and its volume, owing to foreign admixtures, and to the physical and organic changes in the people, from climate and custom. The "Pigeon English" of Chinese ports, illustrates this point admirably. It is already a common dialect, and will one day boast an extensive literature. "Pigeon" means "Business." I take you to a friend of mine in Canton, and—"*Mi Chin-chin you, this wun velly good flin belong mi; mi wantchie you do plopel pigeon along he all same fashion along mi; spose no do plopel pigeon, mi flin cum down side mi housie, talkey mi so fashion, mi kick up bobbery along you.*" Such is the way in which I introduce you to another trader with whom you desire to deal, and: "*Me savey no casion makery flaid; can secure do plopel pigeon long you flin all same fashion along you.*" And the business is done perfectly satisfactorily to the three parties.

Let us sail right across the sea to the Northwest coast of America, and land at Fort Vancouver. Here we shall find a new language even more remarkable than Pigeon English, because it has a dozen or a score of elements, while that has but two—English and Chinese. At the Fort we find twenty different Indian languages; the Chinese, the Sandwich Island dialects, English, French, Spanish, Portuguese, and a dozen others besides, all contributing to one common end— the formation of a new tongue, that in time will surpass all the rest; for though the Onomatopœic process is a slow, it is, nevertheless, a sure and perfect one. Mr. Clark's friends used to salute him with, "Clark, how are you?" and now the common salutation of everybody, instead of "How de do," is "Clak-ho-ah-yah?"

"He-he" means laughter ; " Tala" (dollar) means
money ; " Ting-ling" is a bell ; " Tum-tum," a waterfall ; " lip-lip," to boil ; Rum is " lum ;" fire is " Paia ;"
to-morrow is " tumola ;" " lamestin" and " lakles" are
la medicin and *la grasse ;* and yet there are thousands
born every year to whom this apparent jargon will be
vernacular ; and, with the amplitude of soul which ex
perience and age will give this new people, their lan
guage will expand and refine just as the Anglo-Saxon
and the Gaulic has, and as the Nilotic speech did a
hundred ages ago ; for the same great natural and intellectual forces are in operation now as then : and
only the element of Time is required to produce results
quite as profound and startling in the world's Future,
as the Past has witnessed.

<hr>

CHAPTER IV.

ASIA—AFRICA—PEOPLES.

In speaking of China, with reference to human antiquity, I am tempted strongly to present philological
reasons why the claims of the inhabitants of that singular country *to* a vast antiquity, are entitled to far
greater respect than has generally been accorded them ;
but as such a disquisition would be unsuited to the majority of readers, by reason of its dryness and techni-
calities, I shall postpone its consideration in the present
volume, merely remarking as I pass, that, according to
certain distinguished philologists, there are but *two*
roots from which all languages sprung.   There are two
general and grand systems – two poles, so to speak—a
positive and a negative, and between these two, and
springing from them as an arch from its pillars, all languages had their development.   These two, the Aryan,
from which came, in addition to hundreds that are

dead, and other hundreds that are living, the tongues, dialects, and languages now spoken by the British, Celtic, Gallic, Sclavonian, Persian, Hindoo, Greek and Italian peoples ; and the Semitic, or Turanian, the root of as many more, such as the Turkish, Hungarian, Tartar, Thibetan, and similar tongues. Now this pleasant theory is all very good, and, but for one little hindrance, would be quite acceptable, and that is : It is not true ! for there is no more relationship between the thirteen hundred tongues of the North American Indians and the Semitic and Aryan root languages, than there is between a potato and a melon. There are not less than forty-five hundred languages now spoken on the earth ; and assuming that an equal number have become obsolete and dead, we have nine thousand distinct forms of human speech. Now if the whole human family sprung from the Adam of Eden six thousand years ago, the linguistic faculty must indeed have developed at a prodigious rate. But the formation of language is *not* a rapid process, even under the most favorable circumstances. Philologers tell us that thousands of years are requisite to the formation of a perfectly new tongue, from elements furnished by an old one. Bunsen says ten thousand years ! Taking the best possible view of the case, it is not to be conceded that these nine thousand, or even two thousand, forms of speech, could have developed out of the one tongue spoken by the Adam of Genesis. [It will be observed that I have conceded that there *was* such a personage, and that he was the Hebraic, and, possibly, the Caucasian protoplast, but not at all that he was the *originator* of either the Negro, Egyptian, Assyrian, Chinese or American Indian races of men.]

China has a bewildering antiquity, even if we only allow her the usually accorded forty-one centuries.

But what are we to say to the records now in France, captured by the French Commission, which speak of events of eight thousand years ago ? What are we to think of Mariette's mummy, believed to be ten thousand years old ? Is it all myth, all fable ? By no means ! Every nation under heaven, our own beloved America especially, has a buried history, as well as the living one, recorded on paper and in human memories. There are missing chronicles of all the peoples, but pre-eminently so is this true of China ; for even the vastly ancient records that have been found, undeviatingly point backwards to ages, so remote that the epochs of Adam and Eve, and Menes and Cain, and the building of the antediluvian city of Enoch (Babylon,) are but comparatively recent. China, according to Huc, the French traveler, and others, and her own records, was, once upon a time, in that long, dark night, or early twilight of human story, the theater of a most wonder- ful and mysterious event—a national cataclysm, change, upheaval—not produced by human means, nor yet by that strange flood of Noah or Deucalion, recorded of Anno Mundi, 2,348, because the legend is known to be older—we having quite as much right to believe the records of one nation as we have to credit those of another ; nor is there any just reason for accepting a rabbinical legend or account, and rejecting a Chinese one ; especially in view of the fact that the former stands already convicted of historical dishonesty, while no such charge can be laid at the doors of the Chinese annalists. They give us allegory and tradition, but no deliberate falsehoods.

Kong-foo-tse (Confucius,) who lived in the sixth de- cade of the Sixth Century before Christ, speaks of, and names, both men and books, who, and which, in his day, were of a hoary antiquity ; as also does the great Chi-

nese Philosopher, Laou-tze, who was born B C. 604 ;
and the " Book of Reason and Virtue " claims to contain the sum total of the wisdom of the " Ancients of
years," and to be " full of profound knowledge, whose
very obscurity was a recommendation."   When Confucius first arose, he did so as an innovator on a system
of religion that had become corrupt and effete, merely
by reason of its extreme age.   Of course, at that time,
the worship of Foh, or Budha, was then unknown, for that
celebrated Mendicant had not then arisen in India ; or
if he had, his system was confined to his local and personal adherents.   In the days of Confucius, a new order
of things was established on the ruins and *debris* of
the old ; and there can be no doubt but that there was
some truth in the traditions of his day, which affirmed
that " there once existed on the soil of China, a mighty
nation at the very head of civilization, in ages so remote that their historical monuments have been lost or
submerged in the deluge of the waters of oblivion."*
The spirit-rapping, and magical religions of China,
which Confucius superseded by a better, or eclectic
system of his own, was itself, like Mahometanism, Brahminism, Budhism, and some later forms of religion, but a
remodeling of other precedent systems, that had, probably, existed during long previous ages ; and the proof of
this is, that all the most ancient records point to some
dead parent of the religions which themselves commemorated. A singular confirmation of the truth of Solomon's
apothegm, " There is nothing new under the sun !" is the
fact that the great, valuable, and strange philosophical
system of Rosicrucianism, probably the most perfect
system of human thought the world has ever seen, or
will ever see, inasmuch as it alone, of all others, has re-

_____

*Brade's "Sphinx of History"—article—" Asiatic Mysteries ;"
page 253.

solved the mysteries of human origin, nature, and destiny; and which, though long considered to be dead and buried, has within twelve years been revived in Germany, France, England—under a Grandmastership; and in America, (New York,) and also in California, in all of which places it bids fair to do a vast amount of good in the direction of dispelling many of the clouds that obscure the mental vision of the race. This great system, once supposed to have originated in Germany in the 16th century; afterwards fathered on the ancient Greeks; then attributed to India; finally reaching a home in early Egypt, is now found to have been an old story with the Chinese who lived scores of ages before it became a wandering star in other lands. Astrology, medical and judicial, the search for the Philosophers' Stone, the Elixir of Life and Immortality; and, in short, all the Hermetic and Spiritualistic mysteries, table-turning, *et hoc genus omne*, all and each of them were as familiar to and with the inhabitants of Ancient China, as they were to the Confucianists twenty-five hundred years ago, and to the mystical philosophers of the present day, in America and Europe. What, then, must be the age of those peculiar ideas? What ages must have rolled away since the absolutely original man lived on earth!

Many modern scholars believe that the Adam of Genesis was not the first or only created man, and I perfectly coincide with them. Indeed it is demonstrable, even from Genesis itself, that he was not; and this is quite as certain as that creation did not take place in the period of one hundred and forty-four hours, although there is no question that the authors of the original legend, afterwards copied in the Book of Genesis, believed that such was the fact, not on the authority of their own positive knowledge, or divine revelation, or of dreams or visions, but on the authority of traditionary legends that were current when they wrote. It is but of little use for us to speculate at this point concerning the origination of the human race, whether by the "Development theory," or by a sudden Deific ictus, so long as we are ignorant of even who our well-attested human grand-sires were; for we have a long list of human relatives before we get to the Gorilla-cousins of Monsieur Geoffroy St. Hillaire. When the stupendous Mammoth, the Iguanodon, and the ponderous Dinotherium, tramped over the earth, like walking thunders, and woke the deep solitudes of primeval forests with their terrific roars. Man was a listener and spectator, and he beheld the wanton sports and gambols, and the fearful battles of the monstrous Saurians, and the huge Palæotheria, and the Mylodonic beasts, unmoved perhaps, perhaps in mortal fear and terror; but that he *did* witness these things I shall prove before this book is ended.

Could we, in these days, summon the shades of Plato and Eudoxus, and demand of them an answer to such questions as our subject suggests, with what rapture would we listen to the storied legends and strange traditions regarding primeval and autochthonic man! How eagerly, and how gratefully we would drink in Egypt's ancient story, as understood, and current, when they were studying Philosophy under priestly masters on the banks of the Nile, and in the marble halls of Heliopolis, or, perhaps, beneath the massive pylons of the very Temple of the Sun, where now stands that single lonely obelisque, mournfully telling the wondering on-looker, the pilgrim from far-off lands, that "Once upon a time a mighty city had there stood, and marvelous things been taught." Strange things they must have learned during their long initiation of thirteen years! But

Plato and Eudoxus are both asleep, or else refuse to come. They have no affinity with jumping-tables, like so many of their disbodied brethren are said to. What a pity! Could we only snatch an hour's chat with the ghosts of the architects of Baalbec, how pleasant it would be? Or if they would deign to tell us *when* that wondrous town and temple were built? and why? and by whom? Or who laid the foundations of Jaffa? or of Beyrout? or of lovely Damascus? Aye! or if they would point out when and by whom the city of the Jebusite, old Jerusalem, was reared on Zion, Moriah, and the twin hills, it would be a great satisfaction. Or if some obliging ghost would but whisper in our ear who was really the original Chinaman, we would cheerfully forgive him any little fright he might occasion us. But, seeing that not one of these answers have been printed in the papers of the day, the ghosts are exceedingly reticent upon the subject. Let us hope they will finally relent.

It is held by several talented writers that once upon a time Egypt was ruled by a race of Negro Kings, and that that people dictated laws to the nations from the columned halls of Karnac. Of course I do not dispute these writers ; for not being familiar with their authorities, it would not be either courteous or safe to do so ; but *if* a dynasty of Negro monarchs reigned over Egypt since the days of the Adam of Genesis—I say that *if* such a fact is really true, then I cannot see it. Such may have been the case, antecedent to the first Memphite dynasty, but not since. On the walls of the tombs of Beni-Hassan, between Memphis and Thebes, are numerous representations of Egyptian Kings and captives, the latter in chains and undergoing the punishment of the bastinado, applied to the feet. If these tombs, as some think, represent events of Egypt's early days, it follows that the Negro Kings must have reigned, not at Karnac, but further up the river towards Dongola, and long prior to the founding of either Memphis, Thebes or This: and not only so, but at a period so remote, that we are startled at the figures. The Pyramids of Ghizeh had begun to wax old when Abraham, the Chaldean father of Israel, was yet unborn ; and in a long line of centuries—6,000 years— from the present to King Menes, there was no Negro King over Egypt—neither before or after Thebes was built. Before Menes we are told of the reigns of eight gods, succeeded by a short line of three hundred and forty-five High Priests. These last were extinct five thousand years before Horus (son of Osiris). Then came a reign of twelve lineal gods ; and then twelve more; and it was fifteen thousand years from Osiris to King Amasis : the whole embracing a period of 35,000 years, without one single Negro King. It may be that the writers alluded to, imagine that because there were Ethiopian monarchs over Egypt, that therefore they were Negroes. A mistake, but a natural one. Negroes are Africans, but all Africans are not Negroes. It is doubtful if the Negro, since the world began, ever even approximated to such a high state of civilization as he has attained on Northern American soil ; but that he will achieve great things in the future, is, of course, but a mere question of time. What I wish to deduce from all this is, that over five thousand years ago the Negro was just as we find him to-day, so far as color and feature are concerned. In these respects he has been without variableness, neither shadow of turning —any other color. Climate, therefore, had nothing to do in making him the hue he is ; for in Africa, beneath the torrid sun, and in cold Icelandic regions, he and his children retain the same complexion, save where amalgamation bleaches it. The notion that the "curse of Cain" is the cause of his sable hue, has long since been discarded by all people of common sense. He must, therefore, be a distinct species of the *genus homo*; for, differing so totally from the sons of Adam, he could not have descended from the same source, and is, consequently, and beyond all doubt, a Pre-Adamite Man! because, *à fortiori*, the sun had not shone hot or long enough to tan him black, on the hypothesis that he originated from the Adam and Eve of Genesis. The differences between the Negro and all other Oriental races, is too apparent, and pronounced, to leave room to doubt that he is a distinct species of the human family—but a species destined to power and greatness.

CHAPTER V.

THE BIBLE—THE APOGRAPH.

THE Hebrew chronology is said, by what is considered as being competent authority, to be at fault in many respects, and, indeed, to be totally unreliable, anterior to the epoch of Solomon, that is, 1,015 years B. C. In reference to all dates back of that, we are said, on Bunsen's authority, to have but the records of the wild dreams and vagaries, and sometimes criminal statements of the Rabbins of Alexandria and Jerusalem. We are able to fix the date of Solomon by means of other than Scriptural testimony, with which, however, it accords. Those means consist of monuments, historical dates and narratives of contemporaneous events, derived from a hundred different sources. We are certain of what took place in some parts of the world 2,877 or 2,900 years ago. And at that point we are adrift, so far as Rabbinical chronology is concerned.

By means of the same process, we reach Menes from Solomon, and still on, into the deeps of Time.

The quaint old Sir Thomas Browne truly said that "The number of the dead long exceedeth the number of the living—or that shall live; and the Night of Time far surpasseth the Day." It seems strange, however, that men should willingly and zealously attempt to falsify the story of that "Night," merely for the sake of making facts conform to their ill-digested hypotheses. Yet so it is; and of all things else the Bible has been tortured and twisted to effect this end more than any other book ever written by mortal hands, or conceived in the human brain. The text of the Bible has been so willfully tampered with and perverted from its true meaning, that I venture to affirm that it has been, and still is, the cause of more unbelief, disbelief, and atheism, than any other one thing in Christian lands. The Book is plainly one whose sphere lies in the Moral world, and not in that of Science at all; and whoever seeks to interpret it so as to make it sanction his own vagaries, had better be about something else, for which he is better adapted. Conscientious men sometimes attempt the impossible task of reconciling Genesis and Geology, Creation and Astronomy—and make lamentable failures, as a matter of course. Had Hugh Miller been less honest, he had not slain himself. He tried to harmonize Science and Genesis, and failing—died. The Bible, as it stands before us to-day, is to be received for what it claims to be, not for what its unwise friends claim for it. Genesis gives what looks like either *two* distinct accounts of the creation of *one* man; or an account of the distinct creation of *two* men! Before proceeding to the consideration of this part of our subject, it is meet first to make a few preliminary remarks. It is quite evident that Moses, or whoever else wrote

the Book of the Beginnings, or Genesis, must have so
written on the authority of legend, tradition or hearsay; else by direct inspiration, revelation, or vision;
for of course, supposing that Moses was the author,
and the Hebrew chronology is correct, it was impossible for him to write, of his *own knowledge*, concerning
events which took place over fifteen hundred and
seventy-one years before he was born. In these days
we reject the Persian and Budhistic systems of metem-
psychosis, and refuse to believe that either Moses or any
other man, while in one body, saw and carefully noted
events which he remembered when, ages subsequently,
he occupied another. We cannot believe that he
beheld things, and wrote accounts thereof, on the banks
of the Nile, or in the Syrian Deserts, which had occurred nearly sixteen hundred years before.

Science knows nothing about inspiration. That pertains to the domain of the psychologist and theolo-
gian. A man's visions may be all very satisfactory
and consoling to himself, and to whoever else chooses
to believe them; but they are not considered sound
evidence in modern courts—and, because they *are*
visionary, are rejected by all sensible juries—either in
the box, or in the world. Legends of all sorts, and
traditions of all kinds are, and from immemorial time
have been, accepted for what they intrinsically may be
worth, in the latter case frequently for a great deal
more, and as they are usually based upon the truth,
they generally bring a fair price in the world's great
literary marts. The original writers of the Pentateuch must have given us apographs, more or less correct, of what, to them, seemed original truth. That they
did so, is proved by the fact that we now have possession of very many of the identical legends whence
those of Genesis were undoubtedly taken. They must

have jotted down the traditions current in their day and age, concerning the great human origines. I say " they," for the reason that Genesis is. in these days, almost universally conceded to be, not a continuous narrative from a single pen, but a series of fragments by different authors, cemented into one semi-consistent whole. The book tells us, in plain language, that this world of ours, all the beautiful things in and on it ; the sun, moon and stars ; the great fish, and the seas in which they swim ; the crawling worm and noble man ; lovely Eve, and all other things above, below, around and within this globe of ours, was created out of Nothing, by the gods (Elohim,) in six days, or one hundred and forty-four hours. Thus stands the account.

Now, it so happens, that by virtue of a singular disturbing cause, inherent in most men—the meddling propensity—that these six days of creation, these one hundred and forty-four hours. have been so stretched that now they mean any period of time, from a century to six geological ages—from thirty-six thousand five hundred days, to two hundred and fifty millions of years; and yet they cry " give ! give !" and all this in direct face of the fact that the Bible speaks of the evening and the morning as one day ! The grand and simple story is perverted, defaced and stultified by interpretations and exegeses, as violent as they can be, and such as would drive the writers of Genesis to distraction, could they witness the very pleasant way in which their works are dealt with. If the writers of Genesis had meant to say that the process of creation occupied a million of years or of ages, surely they would have so placed it on the Record ! The book says, and means, that the gods, (Elohim, for not till long afterwards was the term Iveh, or Jehovah used,) did, out of Nothing, create this world and man in six literal days. We have two accounts, but the same space of time is assigned in both. The Bible says, and means, that a man was made out of the dust of the ground, and that after he was duly finished, life and a soul was imparted to the clay by the process of breathing into his nostrils on the part of the Elohim. After this, the man was put into a garden. After a while, Elo a saw that the man needed what as yet he had not, and yet could not very well do without —a wife; and so, the man having been put to sleep, Elohim cut his side open and removed a bone, whereof he fashioned another human being, pleasantly varying somewhat from the first one. This couple got along very comfortably until a serpent tempted and seduced Eve, who did the like by her husband. And one time, as Elohim was taking a "walk in the garden, in the cool of the day"—for the weather was sultry—the transgression was discovered, and Eden was forthwith vacated.

The same people who contend for geological ages, also maintain that the serpent of Genesis means the Devil, or a snake acting as his proxy. But the Bible says a "serpent," a "beast of the ground," and it means a snake, and not a devil; if it did, it would have so been written. Nowhere in the Sacred Book is it stated, or the implication warranted in the slightest degree, that Satan was a fallen angel of God. John Milton had not written "Paradise Lost" in those days. Nowhere is it stated that fallen angels became evil spirits, tempting man to ruin and destruction. Those who think that the " Lucifer, son of the morning," mentioned in Job, means the devil. are not familiar with ancient astronomy, the convertibility of astronomical terms, the ancient names of Saturn, ancient races, forms of religious faith, nor with Semitic forms of

speech. Such forced interpretations of Scripture have
been the cause of much discord in the human family,
and have divided mankind into thousands of sects, each
one thirsting for the other's blood and ruin. They have
begotten carnage, blasphemy, bigotry, and hatred; sown
more discord, falsified more truth, promoted more irre
ligion, created more party-feeling, repressed more
learning, stultified more common sense, and been a more
terrible bane of civilization and true religion, than any
other thing under the sun. Why do they not let the
Bible alone, and by teaching its morals, and spreading
its ethical light, seek to illumine the profound heathen-
ism of the world? not all of which, exists either in
Africa or Boroboola Gha!

Beyond all reasonable doubt, Moses, "who was
learned in all the learning of the Egyptians," also
knew their theories of the human origines, as well as
their current legends and traditions, most of which had
been grafted from an Asiatic stock upon African stems,
long before his cradle was found in the bushes of
Rhoda by the King's daughter, of Royal Memphis.
Long, long before the Hebrew Law-giver had listened
to the promptings of ambition, old Chaldea's poets had
sung of a "time in which nothing rested but black
darkness, and an abyss deep of waters," which fragment differs but little from the second verse of Genesis:
" And the earth was without form, and void, and darkness was upon the face of the deep; and the spirit of
God moved upon the face of the waters,"—a passage
whose awful sublimity is not always seen and appreciated by those who read it. There is every reason to
believe that the latter description was not written till
thousands of years after the former had been crysta-
lized in the legendary consciousness, the faith and belief of an entire family of nations—great and civilized

peoples, dwelling in cities scattered thickly over the
plateaus of Eastern Asia, and along the banks of the
Euphrates ; and of whom Herodotus and Manetho
were as ignorant as they were of Canada and New
Orleans :—quite as ignorant as we are of who built
the WALLED LAKE,* a work not done by the present
race of Indians, from whose labors it differs as widely
as does the Cyclopean structures of Etruria, or a Ro-
maic hut from a Greek Temple.

Long before Menes founded Memphis, the Phenician
sages had taught of a "turbid Chaos and black as starless
night, over which swept breezes of thickened air ;" and
the hosts that peopled India were probably quite as

---

* The wonderful walled Lake is situated in the central part of
Wright county, Iowa. The shape of the lake is oval. It is about
two miles in length, and one mile wide in the widest part, comprising
an area of some two thousand acres. The wall enclosing this lake is
over six miles in length, and is built or composed of stones varying
in size from boulders of two tons weight down to small pebbles, and
is intermixed with earth. The top of the wall is uniform in height
above the water in all parts, which makes its height to vary on the
land side, according to the unevenness of the country, from two to
twelve feet in height. In the highest part the wall measures from
ten to twelve feet thick at the base, and from four to six at the top,
inclining each way—outward and inward. There is an outlet, but
the lake frequently rises and flows over the wall. The lake at the
deepest part is about ten feet in depth, and abounds with large and
fine fish, such as pike, pickerel, bass, perch, etc. The water is as
clear as a crystal, and there is no bubbling nor agitation to indicate
that there are any large springs or feeders. Wild fowl of all kinds
are plenty upon its bosom. At the north end are two small groves
of ten acres each, no timber being near. It has the appearance of
having been walled up by human hands, and looks like a huge fort-
ress, yet there are no rocks in that vicinity for miles around. There
are no visible signs of the lake being the result of volcanic action, it
being smooth, and the border of regular form. The lake is seventeen
miles from Boon river on the west, and eight miles from Iowa on the
east, and about one hundred miles from Cedar Rapids. It is one of
the greatest wonders of the West.

familiar with the same idea. Indeed the same sublime
notion that has been handed down to us in Genesis,
constituted the starting point of a number of Oriental
cosmogonies. Let us, then, accept the first verses of
Genesis at their proper value. It is unfair to distort
the Scriptures till they accord with either science, or
the peculiar notions of theologians. The language in
which they were written is susceptible of correct translation into all the European tongues ; and when the
writers say " two" we have no right to aver that they
mean "ten." The Book of Genesis is a compilation
of many fragments, probably not collected, but adopted,
and adapted by Moses ; and it is criminal to attempt
to make them conform to modern science. To do so
is to rob them of their sublimity, weaken their power,
ruin their meaning, destroy their moral force and sense,
beget a thoughtless, heedless scepticism, and to arouse
a bigoted antagonism, and provoke the sneers of the
unthinking multitude. Our simple duty is to free them
of the vicious interpolations of the Hebraists. It is
generally admitted by Biblical scholars, that the first
verse of Genesis is to be regarded as a preface to what
follows, and that the second one belongs to an account
which ends at the fourth verse of the second chapter,
and which embraces one narrative of man's creation ;
while the second chapter, from the fourth verse, gives
a totally distinct account of the same, or another creation ; and many persons believe that an enormous interval of time elapsed between the separate events
recorded there.

In this work, up to the present, the existence of the
Mosaic Adam is not contested, but conceded ; my design not having heretofore been to prove him a myth,
but to show that, admitting him to have existed, he was
neither the first or only created man. The Adam of

Genesis may be a myth ; he may have been a miraculously created man ; he may have been an immigrant from other parts of Asia, or may be the Ideal Hero of the poets who sung of Auld Lang Syne when this world was six thousand years younger than it is to-day. In either case it matters little, so long as we can prove man's antiquity to be immeasurably greater than is usually believed.

No one, let it here be distinctly understood, once for all, can entertain a profounder respect for the truths contained in the Bible than the writer of these pages. Its moral teachings, its inculcations of the Golden Rule, its sublime prophecies of good to come, and its lofty eloquence, all challenge his deepest regards. But it does not follow thence that he is bound to accept either the absurdities, interpolations, puerilities, or falsehoods of the Rabbins, and others, merely because they happen to be bound up within its lids, along with much that is unquestionably sublime and true. There are things in the Bible concerning Deity, that, it seems to me, very narrowly approach downright blasphemy ; while other things so derogate from the Infinite Dignity and overwhelming Majesty of the Eternal God, that it is *impossible* for a normal healthy mind to regard them with any thing but absolute horror.

Concerning miracles : 1st. Man's origin may have been, literally, as stated in Genesis, but if so, the process was discontinued after the first experiment, for natural processes have long since superseded miracles. 2d. We are told that the first woman was taken out of man. This I do not believe, seeing that it is impossible, has been all along the ages, and will be so through the limitless eternities. Neither can I believe that the Infinite, Awful, Eternal One, ever had a child by any woman in the physical sense, virgin or matron ; and I

say it with all respect, for I believe in Jesus Christ—
but in a moral—not in a miraculous sense. It is
equally impossible for me to believe certain other
things, deemed by some people essential to a blessed
immortality. No man was ever yet a Deicide!—God
has never yet been slain—for no human being was, or
ever will be, capable of killing God! No spear wielded
by human hands has ever yet penetrated the sides of
the Awful Lord of Glory—the Infinite, Supreme, Ever-
living God! True, all these things *may* once have
been; but as I am unable to grasp the miraculous prin-
cipia of their evolution, they must, by me, be set aside
till they can be comprehended, it being my opinion at
present that we owe all these accounts of miracles to
the idealizations of the custodians of the Bible long
ages ago. Again, it is not at all plain to me, first, how,
and for what reason, God was in the habit of walking
in the garden in the cool of the day, seeing that he is
a spirit. Second, how and by what means Adam knew
about Eve's building up, or manufacture, from a rib?
third, how he knew that the rib was taken from his
side by God, (from whose sublime dignity and majesty
the whole thing derogates,) when and while the man—
this identical Adam himself, was in a deep sleep?

In the first chapter of Genesis it is said that the
birds were created before the beasts, and the beasts
before Adam; but in the next chapter the birds and
beasts are said to have been made out of the dust of
the ground, and to have been brought to Adam to see
what names he would call them; and, consequently,
Adam was made *before* the beasts. Let us compare a
few of these pasages:

Gen. I. First Account.	Gen. II. Second Account.
1st. Preliminary preparations.	1st. Preliminary preparations.
Gen. 1st to 11th verse.	Gen. ii., 4-7.

2d. Creation of the Vegetable kingdom. Verse 11-14.

3d Arrangement of heavens and creation of animals. 14-26.

4th. Creation of Man (MALE and FEMALE!) *at the same time!* Verse 26 to end.

5th. [It is conceded that the verses 1 to 4 of the second chapter belong to the first one.] Sabbath instituted. Gen. ii, 1-4.

2d. Formation of Man—a single male *only*—out of dust. Gen. ii., 4-7.

3d. The planting of the Garden of Eden, and commands to the man concerning it. 8-18.

4th. Formation of beasts and fowls out the ground for man The result. 19-21.

5th. Formation of Eve from a rib taken by Elohim from Adam's side, while that individual was asleep. Adam sees her, likes and names her :— The institution of Monogamic marriage and the Edenic state of life. 21-25.

GENESIS 1ST CHAPTER.

In the beginning God created the heavens and the earth. 1-11.

And God said, Let the earth bring forth grass, the herb yielding seed, and the fruit-tree yielding fruit after its kind whose seed is in itself, upon the earth, &c.; (to verse 14.)

14th. And God said Let there be lights in the firmament of the heaven to divide the day from the night, and let them be for signs, &c.; (to v. 20, and Gen. ii. 1-4.*

And God said, Let the Waters bring forth abundantly, &c., to verse 24.

V. 24. And God said, Let the Earth bring forth the living creature after his kind, cattle, and creeping thing, and beast of the Earth after his kind. And it was so.

V. 25. And God made the

GENESIS 2D CHAPTER.

These are (the following are) the generations of the heavens and the earth when they were created, in the day that the Lord God made the earth and the heavens, and every plant before it was in the earth, and every herb of the field before it grew : for the Lord God had not caused in to rain upon the earth, and there was not a man to till the ground.† But there went up a mist from the earth and watered the whole face of the ground. 4-6.

And the Lord God formed man of the dust of the ground, and breathed into his nostrils the breath of life ; and man became a living soul. . . . And the Lord God planted a garden eastward in Eden : and there he put the man whom he had formed . . . And out of the ground made the Lord God to grow every tree that is pleasant to the sight, and good for food ; the tree of life also in the midst of the garden. and the tree of knowledge of good and evil, (to v. 10.)

V. 15. And the Lord God took the man and put him into the

---

* Was this a second creation? Verses 3. 4 5, tell us that day and night and light already existed.

† This implies that agriculture was not the result of the curse as the earth needed tilling before either the man or his criminal son was in existence.

beast of the earth after his kind, and everything that creepeth upon the earth after his kind. And God saw that it was good.

V. 26. And God said, Let us make man in our image, after our likeness ;—[Can it be possible that the gods here alluded to were deified heroes, such as both before and after the supposed date of the transactions, here recorded, were worshiped in Babylon, Egypt, Nineveh, and Phenicia?] and let th m have dominion over the fish of the seas, and over the fowl of the air, and over the cattle, and over all the earth, and over every creeping thing that creepeth upon the earth . . . So God created man in his own image, in the image of God created he him, male and female created he them . . . And God blessed them, and God said unto them, Be fruitful, and multiply, and replenish the earth, and subdue it : [Then it appears that the earth, even before the " Fall," was in a condition that needed subduing? Alas! alas! one after another, our long cherished notions are being melted away.] and have dominion over the fish of the sea, and over the fowl of the air, and over every living thing that moveth upon the earth . . . And God said, Behold

Garden of Eden, to dress it and to keep it. . . . And the Lord God commanded the man, saying, " Of every tree of the garden thou mayest freely eat ; but of the tree of the knowledge of good and evil, thou shalt not eat of it : for in the day that thou eatest thereof, thou shalt surely die. . . . And the Lord God said, It is not good that the man should be alone ; I will will make him an help meet for him. . . . And out of the ground the Lord God formed every beast of the field. and every fowl of the air ; and brought them unto Adam, (ha-Adam - the man,) to see what he would call them. [Does not this remarkable sentence, as well as the 8th. 9th. 10th, 11th. 12th. and 13th verses of Gen. iii. and the 9th and 10th verses of chapter iv. *directly challenge, or deny* God's omnipotence and omniscience? To me it certainly seems so. Can this be due to the Rabbinical tamperings heretofore alluded to? Or is this, as well as other parts of the Pentateuch, a legendary fragment? Is the whole a myth? Is the whole book a material symbol, in the depths of which great spiritual truths reside, as is claimed by the Swedish Seer, Swedenborg? Or, intermingled with the original text of the Books, do we find the crude speculations of undisciplined minds? These are all serious questions, and are not to be passed over lightly. For if this Book of Genesis be proved not what it claims to be, then nothing on earth can prevent an overwhelming revolution throughout the whole of Christendom. If Adam's story be proved a myth. and the fall, and the Scriptural account of the peopling of the world, then the whole Messianic doctrine must fall, never to rise again ; and *practical* Christianity supersede the *mystical* — a change that some people will not regret. Indeed. I have heard several good men already praying devoutly that the Christian reli-

I have given you every herb bearing seed, which is upon the face of the earth, and every tree, in which is the fruit of a tree yielding seed; to you it shall be for meat . . . And to every beast of the earth, and to every fowl of the air, and to everything that creepeth upon the earth, wherein there is life, I have given every green herb for meat. And it was so . . . And God saw everything that he had made, and, behold, it was very good.

And the evening and the morning were the sixth day.

Thus the heavens and the earth were finished, and all the host of them.

And on the seventh day God ended his work which he had made; and he rested on the seventh day from all his work which he had made . . . And God blessed the seventh day, and sanctified it: because that in it he had rested from all his work which God created and made.

gion might speedily be superseded by the religion of Jesus Christ—and, somehow, at the conclusion of these prayers, I could not help responding "AMEN!"] . . . And whatsoever Adam called every living creature, that was the name thereof. . . . And Adam gave names to all cattle, and to the fowl of the air, and to every beast of the field :.But for Adam there was not found an help meet for him. [Here are two extraordinary circumstances related : 1st. The number of living species now amounts to so many millions that it would require ten lifetimes to name them. 2d. Language is known to be a thing of growth—progression to be a law of life; how, then, did this protoplast acquire language and names to give the beasts? Let it be remembered that God is a spirit—the God of Heaven—not using vocal speech—and that Eve was not yet created, and therefore could not converse with Adam. Was the God of Genesis a material being? This is implied both in his speech with Adam, and his "walking in the garden in the cool of the day." All this is very curious—but quite explicable—further on.]

And the Lord God caused a deep sleep to fall upon Adam, and he slept; and he took one of his ribs, and closed up the flesh instead thereof; and of the rib, which the Lord God had taken from man, made he a woman, and brought her unto the man. And Adam said, This is now bone of my bone, and flesh of my flesh : she shall be called Woman, because she was taken out of man."

It is clear to every attentive reader that these two chapters cannot possibly relate to the same event; for the whole procedure essentially differs from beginning to end. The first chapter relates to a creation of the human species, totally distinct from another one occurring, perhaps, millions of years afterwards—when

the earth had performed one great cycle, and the former race of men had worn out both the world and
themselves.   Not to enlarge on this subject, it yet becomes my duty to point to a few other things which in
dicate at least two distinct orders of men—merely remarking, as we pass, that the God of this part of
Genesis is the Elohim.   Jehovah—correctly Iaveh—
literally, the Eternal —the God that was, and is, and is
to be—was not known till long subsequent to the
events above recorded.   And the Elohim, so far from
being the Infinite One, are properly classible among
the Spiritual intelligences—deified men, living or dead.
There are numberless gods, of whom are predicated
speech, power, life and action, mentioned in the Bible ;
for instance, those who fought against Sisera, Lucifer,
Baal, Baal-zebub, Astarte (Ashtoreth), and others, particularly the gods of the nations circumscribing Israel,
who were all intelligent beings—that is to say, spirits
or men.   In the present instance, we are forced to reject the spiritual hypothesis, and conclude that the
heathen gods—before the advent of a mere mechanical
and material iconolatry—were human beings.   The
God who walked in the garden, and the gods of whom
Melchizadek was *not* high priest,* the wrestling gods ;
the gods of the giant sons of Anak (which giant race,

---

* This Melchizadek king of Salem was not Shem, the Holy Ghost,
nor an Adamite ; for the Order of which he was a priest, existed, according to Parkhurst, prior to the events of the Creation recorded in
the first chapter of Genesis—and perhaps the second.   Christ was a
priest after Melchizadek's Order.   The priesthood was hereditary,
and this mysterious priest of a Pre-Adamite Order, and king of a Pre-
Adamite city, had, of course, a Pre-Adamite Pedigree.   Many proofs
exist that his history has been tampered with ; as that he neither had
beginning nor end, but a charmed life like Valmondi, *le juif errant*, or
Croly's "Salathiel."   Perhaps he was a Rosicrucian of the Ravalette
stamp, and possessed the elixir and the " wondrous stone !"

be it known, existed before the flood, and existed *after* the flood; which, therefore, on a Biblical guarantee, did *not* destroy all human beings, save those who were in Noah's ark.) We are told, and I most certainly believe, "that no man hath seen the Infinite God at any time," consequently the God of Adam was not the Eternal One; but either a local Deity or a Representative of THE ONE. The last supposition seems unreasonable. The three Gods that appeared to Abraham, as well as all other gods who "did *eat*" as they did, are not of heavenly Genesis. The God of Abraham Isaac and Jacob, was not the God of other nations, nor could he—on other, and quite apparent grounds—have been the Eternal. The witch of Endor saw gods ascending out of the earth; and we have so many repetitions of the title, that it is difficult to determine the real from the genuine.

The Adamic Pedigrees do not accord better than the two cosmogonies:

GEN. IV.	GEN. V.
Adam —Eve—Abel—Cain.	Adam, Eve, Cain, Abel—Seth.
Cain—Wife—Land of Nod—Enoch.	Seth—Enos—Cainan—Mahalaleel.
Enoch—Irad, Mehujael, Methusael —Lamech.	Mahalaleel—Jared—Enoch—Methuselah.
{ Lamech--Adah, Zillah, two wives.	Methuselah—Lamech--Noah.
{ Lamech—Adah, Jabal—Jubal.	Noah—Shem, Ham, Japhet, from
{ Lamech—Zillah—Tubal-Cain.	whom the world was peopled.
Adam, Eve—Seth.	

This speaks for itself, nor is it possible to reconcile such discrepancies, for not only do the names differ, but in one case the world is peopled through Cain, and in the other through his brother Seth!

In this connection another singular thing presents itself. We are told in Genesis vii. 21, that "All flesh died that moved upon the earth, both of fowl, and of cattle, and of beast, and of every creeping thing that

creepeth upon the earth, and every man : All in whose
nostrils was the breath of life, of all that was in the
dry land, died." And yet in the 10th chapter, after
the subsidence of the Flood, the sons of Shem, Ham,
and Japhet are enumerated by name, and " By these
were the isles of the Gentiles divided in their lands ;
every one after *his tongue*, after their families, in their
nations ;" and " These are the families of the sons of
Noah, after their generations, in their nations : and by
these were the nations divided in the earth after the
flood." Two most extraordinary things appear here :
1st, If all flesh died in the flood, who were the " Gentiles" whose lands were divided (among themselves) by
the sons of Shem, Ham, and Japhet ? That is what I
am anxious to discover ! Have we not more " Rabbinical" work here ? and, secondly, these Gentiles, these
gentile nations, spoke *various tongues ;* and that, too, a
long time before the building of the city of Enoch (On,
Babylon,) or its immense Observatory : and the word
" Isles" certainly implies Navigation, for Isles cannot
be on the main-land, unless, indeed, the Oases of Sin,
of Shur, and Zahara are to be accounted such. These
things seem strange, and unaccountable, save on certain
hypotheses already indicated, if not expressed, in these
pages. I have no apology to make, in thus handling
the Scriptures ; for no improper spirit prompts me, but
only the love of truth itself. The moral teachings of
that book, and all its sublime, ethical, and religious
truths, will stand. To me they are sacred, and I disturb them not at all ; but its historical parts have
been aforetime so tampered with that it is now difficult
to separate the text from the alterations and interpolations. No mere Rationalism lies at the fountain head,
nor am I alone in questioning the historical accuracy of
the Pentateuch. Long before I had been tempted to visit

the Orient, men from the very bosom of the conservative Church of England had led the way that I
am following, viz: Benjamin Jowett, M. A., Regius
Professor of Greek in the University of Oxford; Mark
Pattison, B.D. ; C. W. Goodwin. M.A.; Baden Powell, M.A.F.R.S., Savilian Professor of Geometry in
the University of Oxford ; Henry Bristow Wilson, B.
D. ; Vicar of Great Staughton, Hunts ; Rowland Wil-
liams, D.D., Chaplain in Ordinary to the Queen, Head
Master of Rugby School, Chaplain to the Earl of Den-
bigh ; in " Essays and Reviews ;" besides a number of
equally intelligent scholars of our own dear America.
And now, even as I write, there comes to us from over
the broad Atlantic another eloquent protest against
the historical inaccuracies of the Book of Genesis, and
of the entire Pentateuch, from a Bishop of the Church
of England—the Right Reverend John William Colenso, D.D., Bishop of Natal (Africa).   This prelate,
after years of patient study, has arrived at the conclusion that he must reject the entire Pentateuch, both as
a historical narrative, and as a Divine revelation.   I
refer my readers to his work—" The Pentateuch and
Book of Joshua Critically Examined," and content myself with quoting a few of the objections raised, remarking, as I do so, that the discoveries now being made
concerning those books, and the antiquity of man, are
rapidly but surely demolishing the whole system of
Christianity, and just as rapidly paving the way for the
advent of the *Religion of Jesus Christ :* destroying the
letter and the form, but preserving the *Spirit* and the
Soul ; dispersing the clouds that envelope Jesus and
the Past, and fixing Him and His Imperial Truths in
frames of shining light, so that all can see their glowing
beauties, and every thirsty soul drink at the fountains of
living water.   Says the Bishop : My knowledge of

Geology satisfied me that a universal deluge, such as
the Bible manifestly speaks of. could not possibly have
taken place in the manner described in Genesis, not to
mention other difficulties which the story contains. . . .
The result of my inquiry is the conviction that the Pentateuch, as a whole, cannot possibly have been written
by Moses, or by any one acquainted personally with
the facts which it professes to describe; and further,
that the so-called Mosaic narrative, by whomsoever
written, and though imparting to us, as, I believe it
does, revelations of the Divine will and character, cannot be regarded as historically true.

The Bishop then proceeds to say that, for the best of
reasons, he must reject many things, as I have myself,
and on the same ground, viz. : that the original Book
has unmistakably been tampered with, by additions,
interpolations, glosses, and subtractions. He cannot
believe, nor could I, when overlooking the river, that
the waters of the Jordan ever stood in heaps, like solid
walls, yet kept running all the while ; nor that the sun
and moon stood still in the heavens at the command of
Joshua, or any other man ; nor that Egyptian magi-
cians. or any one else, ever transformed rods into living
serpents. He cannot believe that the God of Heaven
ever sanctioned rape. murder, slavery or incest. He
cannot probably believe that Cain's descendant went
bodily to Heaven ; nor that in the second year of the
Hebrews' flight from Egypt, that they numbered six
hundred and three thousand five hundred and fifty men,
—fighting men, over twenty years of age. All who
have ever been in the Deserts of Sin and Shur, as I
have. and where this vast host is said to have been,
will know at once that by no possibility could every
available spot of cultivable land in that whole region
from Sinai to the Middle Sea, from the River of Egypt to

the gates of Ramleh, afford food enough in one year to
support that number for a single week ; while *water*
enough for such a host could not have been had any-
where—and yet this host of over six hundred thousand
could have been but about half of the entire number
of people in that hegira, for there were the women,
children, and the aged men.   He cannot believe that
the Gileadites slew of the Ephraimites, their brethren,
forty-two thousand men ;   that the Benjamites killed
forty thou..and men of Israel ; nor that the latter re-
taliated, and killed forty-three thousand Benjamites,
" all mighty men of valor ;" nor that the Philistines
slew of Israel thirty thousand men ; or that the former
had thirty thousand chariots ; or that David slew forty
thousand Syrian horsemen ; or that Pekah, King of Israel, slew of Judah, in *one day*, one hundred and twenty
thousand men, all valiant and brave ; or that he carried
away captive sons and daughters, women and fair mai-
dens, to the number of two hundred thousand ; nor that
Abijah, with four hundred thousand men, went out to
fight Jeroboam, with eight hundred thousand, and beat
him, leaving half a million of Israelites dead on the
field, to say nothing of his own probable losses—a
carnage simply impossible.   Waterloo's bloody field
counted less than five thousand dead ; and *Antietam*,
Fredericksburg, and *Baton Rouge*, with their mighty
hosts, backed by Parott guns, shell, shrapnel, grape
and Minnie-bullets, rifled cannon and revolving pistols,
swords, carbines, thirst and heat, and all other dreadful enginery, did not send half that number of souls
to pardon and to God ! How, then, is it possible to
believe these Rabbinical statements? But we have
not yet done with the Book.   How can we believe
that twelve thousand Israelites slew all the males of
an entire nation--the Midianites—and took captive

all théir little ones and women, without the loss of a single man! Surely this beats the "nobody hurt" of Sumpter and Moultrie! Is it possible to believe that by command of Moses all these prisoners,.except the virgin girls, were butchered in cold blood—all, all killed, except these thirty-two thousand little maids? Is it possible to credit the tale that Moses—that great man, could order the wholesale slaughter of not less than sixty-eight thousand children and women? This is not all: These (forty-eight thousand) women represented an equal number of men, for they were the mothers and wives of Midian, and consequently the number of victims is swelled to the enormous amount of one hundred and sixteen thousand! This valiant deed was achieved by twelve thousand Israelites, who. besides this slaughter, must have each man taken eight captives, and sixty-seven head of cattle; making a total of eight hundred and eight thousand head—and "nobody hurt" on their side! Now, when such absurd things are palmed off on us by whoever interpolated them in the Scriptures, we may well pause before we accept as literally, absolutely, technically true, the previous account of the Creation and of man.

A very few more observations on Scripture, and I have done. The first relates to the "giants." It is said that Ogg, king of Bashan, could only sleep in comfort on a bed twenty-seven feet long and twelve broad, because he was so large. Now I have no manner of doubt but that races of gigantic men did live in the early days, but if Ogg had been a little smaller he would have suited me better. Baron Bunsén, speaking of the wanderings of the early Chinese and Turanian races, says that: Wherever they went they found the land occupied by Barbarians, represented as being of prodigious stature; and in the records of old Se-

mitic and Turanian empires, we find traces of the existence of gigantic races of men.

Genesis tells us that man was made of the dust of
the ground, but also that other human beings—in Job.
xxvi. 5—probably a Chaldaic fragment—were made
from *under the water*. The passage says in English
"Dead things." But the Hebrew says "Rephaim"—
"dead men—giants; "things" not belonging to the
text. These Rephaim, dead men, giants, were not
Adamites. The "Rephaim," "giants," "Anakim"—
"dead great-ones,"*—are convertible synonymes, and
their origin was not the same as that of other men. I
conclude this chapter by quoting one of England's
noblest scholars: "Mankind sprang not from one, but
from many centers over the globe!" and "Turn whith-
ersoever we may, on every hand, we behold the giant
shapes of ancient empires, which flit like dim shadows
evoked by a master hand!"

CHAPTER VI.

VARIOUS HUMAN BEGINNINGS.

We have long since left, but will now return, to the
columned grove of the Memnonium, and Osiride avenues; at least we have lost sight of the hoary old land
which boasts them. In thus returning, we feel as if we
were coasting the head-lands of eternity on a dark and
stormy night. We know who built Thebes, Memphis,
Heliopolis, and we think we know who founded mighty
Babylon; but we do not know who built Gilgal of the
nations—the modern Jiljulio, nor Jerusalem, nor Jaffa,

---

* Cyril Graham - Quarterly Review—July–October, 1859, has given
us an extraordinary account of certain deserted Oriental cities, with
houses as perfect as those of Pompeii, but in their stone doors and
large dimensions, showing all the impress of a gigantic race of men.

nor Damascus, nor Bagdad, nor Baalbec. In fact, we do not *know* even who built Naples, in Italy. We do not rightly understand the Genesis of modern, much less of ancient nations, or who the Mound builders of America were. Indeed the British pedigree itself is in considerable confusion even now; for it is held by clever people on England's shores that "The English are of Israelitish origin—descended from Joseph, through the Angles and Saxons, who came originally from the country near Caucasus, to which some of the ten tribes were carried away, and whence the inhabitants were removed to occupy Samaria, where they were obliged to dispossess a people whose legends claimed an antiquity considerably older than the Israelitish one," which, as it extended to Adam, would give them the precedence, so far as age is concerned. We have already seen that, cotangent with Egyptian civilization under Menes, were other civilizations vastly older, and, as we shall see, quite as perfect, and having cosmogonical theories equally worthy of attention. I proceed to present a few out of hundreds that might be produced. Let these suffice; *non cuivis homini contingit adire Corinthum,* says Horace, to which we reply: True, we may not reach our Corinth—the First absolute man, but at least we are on the fair road to the coveted goal.

Two worthy sons of Scotia were once disputing each other's pedigree and their respective lengths. Donald had "bagged" fourteen hundred years in triumph, but was routed, horse, foot, and artillery, by Grant, who said: "Tut, mon! when the gude Laird was making Adam, the clan Grant was even then as thick and numerous as the heather on yon hills!" I do not wish to copy Grant, but it certainly seems to me that at the date, six thousand years ago, of Adam's asserted creation great and civilized nations were strewn about·

Asian, African, European, and even American soil, a great deal thicker than heather on some Scotch hillsides. My reasons for this belief will be given first, after which we will try to find still stronger testimonies to the existence of Pre-Adamite Man.

My theory is that there may have once existed an approximately true account of the Origines, but that the magnates of Israel, who had exclusive possession of it, had not virtue enough to restrain them from meddling with it in a variety of ways since the earliest epoch of their People's history. Science will yet restore the lost links of human story, and we shall know it as it really was, and that, too, without a Gorilla at the farther end. The true Scriptures relate to man's comparatively early days, if not to his absolute origin—this latter being a question that must be eventually decided upon on an entirely different sort of evidence from that which we are now discussing—and from any hitherto resorted to, or depended on. Here, in my opinion, are some of the methods by means of which the Origines have been enveloped in almost impenetrable clouds—my authority being " Edersheim's History of the Jews, 1856," and contemporaneous literature on the same, and cognate subjects. These authorities inform us that, as the result of long continued and earnest investigation, they find that when the spirit of the reality, indicated by the type (in ancient sacred Scripture), was lost sight of, and the type alone remained, the latter was either mistaken, or *purposely* accepted, for the reality itself, in consequence of which a direction altogether new and erroneous was given to religious thinking, which being pursued, led at length to complete apostacy. The Rabbins frequently, in order to substantiate some new conceit, or fanciful hypothesis, violated the very rules of grammar and the construc-

tion of sentences, and they not only determined the
meaning of words by tradition, but they devised and
applied new meanings for old words. Words were
split in two or three, and meanings given the component parts merely on euphonic grounds, because their
sounds were like other words whose meanings they
wanted the new word to imitate or conform to. Sometimes they traced words to cognate languages, or their
meanings were elicited from parallel passages. The
Hebrew is written wholly with consonants, and the
vowel-points, a comparatively modern innovation, are
added afterwards. But a sentence, written *without*
these points, has a totally different meaning from the
very same letters, in the very same sentence, written
with them. In a word, the Hebrew is a double language ; 1st, the Ancient tongue ; and, 2nd, the same
with the Masoretic, or traditional vowel-points. The
first connected, or compiled and collated, form of the
Old Testament was unpointed, though even then its
texts had already been tampered with ; and out of that
form was begun to be translated into Greek, in Egypt,
under Ptolemy Philadelphus. It was completed by
different scholars, and their translation is called the
Septuagint, because seventy men of seventy minds, seventy notions of their own, and seventy conceptions they
each wanted to send down the stream of time, performed
the work. In the next place let me observe that there
is a direct relationship, in sound at least, between the
Ancient Hebrew, Sanscrit, Arabic, Syriac, and Æthi-
opic languages, of which the Rabbins took good care
to avail themselves when they came across a word of
similar euphony, but different meaning, that suited their
purposes. The Masoretic, or pointed, Hebrew did not
come into use till one thousand years after the Septuagint—sufficient time for both to be corrupted in.

I give a few instances in proof of what vast changes in
meaning are given to ancient Hebrew records by the simple process of pointing, or attaching vowel signs thereto.
The same passages are given, from the accepted versions of the Bible, and from the unpointed Hebrew text.
I quote from the celebrated work of Henry F. A.
Pratt, one of the best Hebrew scholars of the present
century : Gen. x. 11, 12, referring to Nimrod—"And
the beginning of his kingdom was Babel, and Erech,
and Accad, and Calneh, in the land of Shinar. Out of
that land went forth Asshur, and builded Nineveh, and
the city Rehoboth, and Calah, and Resen, between
Nineveh and Calah : the same is a great city." This
identical passage, as it existed in unpointed Hebrew,
thousands of years before the Masoretic vowels were
invented, reads, word for word, as follows, still referring to Nimrod : " Now the beginning of his kingdom
was Babylon, and he extended, and fortified, and established it, in the land of Shinar. From this land he
went out into Assyria, and built Nineveh, and the public places of the city, and (its) wealth : this was a
great city." The difference here is startling—no less
than the removal of the names of six apocryphal cities
from the text, besides the exchange of the name of a
person (Asshur, Assyria) for that of a country.

Joshua xxiv. 19: "Ye cannot serve the Lord ; for
He is an holy God, He is a jealous God ; He will not
forgive your transgressions, nor your sins."—Bible,
Masoretic pointing. Unpointed text : " Then Joshua
said unto the people, Cease not to serve the Creator ;
for an holy God is He ; a jealous God is He (He would
be) that will not (would not) forgive your transgressions and your sins." What a difference ! What a
defence of God ! Job ii. 9 : " Curse God, and die"—
his loving wife's advice to her lord, according to the

pointed text. But the real sentence is, "Humble thyself before God, for thou art dying." It needs but a very little common sense to make this matter plain, even to unlearned readers. In the common version, Jacob wrestles with an angel, and gets his hip sprained ; but according to the unpointed Hebrew, he was caught in a storm in a torrent-bed, and hurt himself in trying to save his property, in his flight making all sorts of promises of living a better life, if God would spare him and his. He was so spared, and hence he was converted, got religion, and a new name. Once more : The Bible tells us that "The serpent was more subtle," etc., to the end of the account. The word translated "serpent" is "The Nachash," and it has at least *forty* meanings *besides* that of "serpent," and does not then mean a literal, spiteful, fanged, crawling snake, but a *snakish*, cunning thing. No snake ever yet talked either English or Hebrew, and never will. Eve's tempter was just such an one as in these days tempt other Eves, viz.: a snake on two legs, college-bred, and broad-clothed. It was a man ! The word is a proper name, chosen for its fitness of application to Eve's human tempter, just as we do in these days. It means a "seducer," a "corruptor," and, on the supposition that the whole cosmological account is a record of real events, and not a mere tradition, legend or myth, it is clear that the Nachash was nothing more than a man of a different race from Adam, who succeeded in making Eve his victim, in some way that disagreed with her and her husband. This something given or administered to her, could not have been a material thing, or a fruit of any kind, but was some sort of knowledge the couple had not previously possessed. The whole account is significant as it stands, but it must have been more so, before the Jews altered it to suit themselves. The curious on this head are referred to the Jewish Talmud and the Kabbalah, the writings of the Jewish Hagadists, the system of Philo Judæus, the Halacha, and especially to the two cabalistic works, Sepher Jezirah, and the Sohar, and the works of Drs. Shammai, Hillel, and Eidersheim; and, rising from the perusal of any of these works, the reader, in my' opinion, will not want further evidence that we have ·for ages been accepting Rabbinical nonsense and blasphemy, for sacred wisdom and divine truth. One of these Rabbinical books, the Hagada, makes God Himself second to Moses, God having to obtain Moses' permission to enlighten the world! And another cabalistic work rejects the whole story of Adam and Eve, and insists that the origin of the human race was in this wise: The whole atmosphere is peopled with aerial intelligences, having sense, shape, and ambition. These beings came, and still come, to earth, and at first met with certain refined material essences and elements, thus originating the human race. When the first autochthones existed, and their number is not hinted at, these aerial beings entered—the female into the male autochthone, and the male spirit into the female autochthone, either of which spirits found, and find, or achieve, incarnation in human form through the natural processes. The Kabbalah gives another theory, not worth being reproduced. It differs from both the others, however. This same Talmud declares God to be only Chief Rabbi in Heaven; his assessors are the angels; when God and they disagree, they choose an earthly arbitrator to decide between them! God cannot, and will not, devote all his time to business, but spends, daily, three hours in study; three in the commissariat department, providing provisions for the world; three in playing with Leviathan, and three in governing the universe; the remaining twelve hours being spent in *curtained apartments!* After Abel's death, Adam deserted Eve, and cohabited with two she-devils, Naama, and Selith, the concubines of Samael, the angel of poison. This worthy took up with Eve, and they twain begat Asmodi, who became chief of the devils. Indeed Adam had, and kept, a whole harem of very beautiful and quite bewitching lady-devils; while Eve became a perfect Messalina along with devils of the opposite gender, albeit she carried the business too far, too grossly, and too openly. It was held that not only devils, but ghosts, of both sexes, could, and did, hold intimate relations with both men and women, and that offspring resulted from these unions!

It is somewhat remarkable that those who so delighted in perverting Scripture, and assigning but a single origin to man, should not have taken pains to exclude all those passages which relate to independent and different origines, as, for instance, those already quoted, and such passages as this, from the 33d chapter of Deuteronomy: "Give ear all inhabitants of the world: both sons of Adam, and sons of Ish;" and Isaiah 31st, "Then shall the Assyrian fall . . . And the sword, not of an Adamite, shall devour him." These two races, of Adam and Ish, are mentioned more than *seventy times* in the same sentences.

Before proceeding further, I desire to call attention to the following passages, which are held by some Biblical scholars to imply, if not directly indicate, the existence of non-Adamic man: Romans v. 14; Job xxxviii. 7. "Lucifer" is, by the commentators alluded to, supposed to mean a Pre-Adamite King who sustained defeat. Satan the same :—Proverbs viii. 31; Isaiah xiv. I am indebted to a friend at my elbow, as I write these pages, for the last few items, and must admit that I cannot see the indications as plain as he does, not having a copy of the unpointed text of the Bible at hand for verification.

Let us now glance at a fragment of the Chaldean Cosmogony, according to Berosus.* There was a time when nought but darkness and an abyss of waters existed. In this abyss resided most hideous things, the product of a two-fold principle. There appeared men, some with two wings, others with fins and two faces. They had one body, but two heads; one male, the other female. Genitally, they were likewise double. Other human beings there were, some with legs and horns of goats; some with horses' feet; others with equine hind-quarters and human bodies, like hippocentaurs. Bulls were there also bred, with human heads; dogs with fourfold bodies and fishes' tails; horses with men's heads; horses dog-headed; men with horse-heads or horse-bodies; all of which monstrosities were sculptured in the temple of Belus at Babylon. These living things were as they were, because Order had not yet conquered Chaos. They were governed by a woman— Omoroco,—i. e. Thalath—Thalassa—the Sea. Presently Belus—i. e. Baal—Lord—God, came and cut the woman asunder, and of one half of her he formed the earth, and of the other half the heavens; and at the same time destroyed all the animals within her. All this (he says) was an allegorical description of nature, for, the whole universe consisting of moisture, and animals being continually generated therein, the God Belus took off his own head, upon which the other gods mixed the blood, as it gushed out, with the earth; and

---

* Cory's Fragments - Berosus, quoted by the Greek writer, Alexander Polyhistor, preserved by Eusebius.

from thence was formed true men. A sort of "Development theory" in disguise.

This is the reason, says the record, that men are rational beings, and endowed with Divine instincts and knowledge. Belus divided the darkness, separated heaven from earth, subdued Chaos, and reduced the universe to order. The afore-mentioned animals were not able to stand the light, and therefore perished; whereupon Belus, desirous to improve the scene they had occupied, compelled one of the subordinate gods to decapitate himself, and mix the blood with the earth. He did so. and there sprung into existence other men and animals of a higher order. Belus also made the sun, moon, stars and planets. Such, according to Polyhistor Alexander, is Berosus' cosmogony. Luke Burke, commenting on this extract. observes. that the account is not over consistent, and thinks that it evidently reflects the conjectural interpretations of historians and commentators, rather than the actual creed of ancient Chaldea. The monstrous animals are symbolical of natural forces, and are such as are common to all nations of antiquity, as is proved by the slabs of Nimroud and Nineveh, exhumed by Layard and others—both the legends and the slabs being vastly older than the modified Hebraic cosmogony, or its original man.

Here is a Scandinavian cosmogonical fragment: in the prose Edda is a conference between Gangler, the Question-asker, and Har, Jafnhar, and Thridi, the answerers. This is the substance of the Legend: Niflheim was formed long ages before the earth was made In the middle of Niflheim was the spring Hvergelmir—the source of twelve great rivers, that of Gjöl being the nearest to the abode of Death. In the southern sphere. or region, was the world called Muspell. It is too glowing and light for any but those belonging there. He who sits at its borders, or on its lands-end to guard it, is called Surtur. In his hand he bears a falchion, with which, at the end of the world, he will vanquish all the gods, and then consume the universe with flaming fire:

> "Surtur, from the South, wends
>   With seething fire;
> The falchion of the Mighty One
>   A sun-light flameth.

> "Mountains together dash,
>   Giants headlong rush,
> Men tread the paths to Hel,
> And Heaven in twain is rent"

Völuspá.

To Gangler's inquiry, as to the state of things ere the races mingled and distinct nations came into being, the following reply is given:

When the rivers that are called Elivagar had flowed far from their sources, the venom which they rolled along hardened, as does dross that runs from a furnace, and became ice. When the rivers flowed no longer, and the ice stood still, the vapor arising from the venom gathered over it and froze to rime, and in this manner were formed, in Ginnungagap, many layers of congealed vapor, piled one over the other.

That part of Ginnungagap that lies towards the north was thus filled with heavy masses of gelid vapor and ice, whilst everywhere within were whirlwinds and fleeting mists. But the southern part of Ginnungagap was lighted by the sparks and flakes that flew into it from Muspelheim.

Thus, whilst freezing, cold, and gathering gloom proceeded from Niflheim, that part of Ginnungagap looking towards Muspelheim was filled with glowing radiancy, the intervening space remaining calm and light as wind-still air. And when the heated blast met the gelid vapor it melted into drops, and, by the might of him who sent the heat, these drops quickened into life, and took a human semblance. The being thus formed was named Ymir, but the Frost-giants call him Orgelmir. From him descend the race of the Frost-giants (Hrimthursar.)

To the inquiry, "where dwelt Ymir, and on what did he live?" Har replies: "Immediately after the gelid vapors had been resolved into drops, there was formed out of them the cow Audhumla. Four streams of milk ran from her teats, and thus fed she Ymir."

"But on what did the cow feed?" asks Gangler.

"The cow," answered Har, "supported herself by licking the stones that were covered with salt and hoar frost. The first day that she licked these stones there sprang from them towards evening the hairs of a man, the second day a head, and on the third an entire man, who was endowed with beauty, agility and power. He was called Bur, and was the father of Bör, who took for wife Besla, the daughter of the giant Bölthorn. And they had three sons, Odin, Vili, and Ve; and it is our belief that this Odin, with his brothers, ruleth both heaven and earth, and that Odin is his true name, and that he is the most mighty of all the gods."

After this the sons of Bör slew the giant Ymir, and when he fell there ran so much blood from his wounds that the whole race of the Frost-giants was drowned in it, except a single giant, who saved himself with his household. He is called by the giants Bergelmir. He escaped by going on board his bark, and with him went his wife, and from them are descended the Frost-giants.

Then the sons of Bör dragged the body of Ymir into the middle of Ginnungagap, and of it formed the earth. From Ymir's blood they made the seas and waters ; from his flesh, the land ; from his bones, the mountains ; and his teeth and jaws, together with some bits of broken bones, served them to make the stones and pebbles.

With the blood that ran from his wounds, (added Jafnhar,) they made the vast ocean, in the midst of which they fixed the earth, the ocean encircling it as a ring, and hardy will he be who attempts to pass those waters.

From his skull, (continued Thridi,) they formed the heavens, which they placed over the earth. and set a dwarf at the corner of each of the four quarters. These dwarfs are called East, West, North, and South. They afterwards took the wandering sparks and red hot flakes that had been cast out of Muspelheim, and placed them in the heavens both above and below, to give light unto the world, and assigned to every other errant corruscation a prescribed locality and motion.

To the giants were assigned as a dwelling-place the outward shores of the great encircling ocean. Within, round the earth, the gods raised a bulwark against their turbulence. This bulwark, to which they gave the name of Midgard, they formed from Ymir's eyebrows ; and, finally, they tossed Ymir's brains into the air, and they became the clouds. As it is said in Grimnis-mál :—

Of Ymir's flesh was formed the earth ; of his sweat (blood), the seas ; of his bones, the mountains ; of his hair, the trees ; of his skull, the heavens ; but with his eyebrows the blithe gods built Midgard for the sons of men, whilst from his brains the lowering clouds were formed.*

---

* *Prose Edda*, sec. 4—8, in Mallett's *Northern Antiquities*, Bohn's Edition, pp. 401—405.

The next step in this collation of cosmogonies takes us to the wilds of North America. The traveler Hearne has, fortunately, saved from oblivion a curious fragment of tradition current among the "Northern Indians," the name by which the tribes around Hudson's Bay are designated by the servants of the Hudson's Bay Company. This story is told as follows:—

"They have a tradition among them, that the first person upon earth was a woman, who, after having been sometime alone in her researches for berries, which were then her only food, found an animal like a dog, which followed her to the cave where she lived, and soon grew fond and domestic. This dog, they say, had the art of transforming itself into the shape of a handsome young man, which it frequently did at night, but as the day approached, always resumed its former shape, so that the woman looked on all that passed on those occasions as dreams and delusions. These transformations were soon productive of the consequences which at present generally follow such intimate connections between the sexes, and the mother of the world began to advance in her pregnancy.

" Not long after this happened, a man of such a surprising height, that his head reached up to the clouds, came to level the land. which at that time was a very rude mass; and after he had done this, by the help of his walking stick, he marked out all the lakes, ponds, and rivers, and immediately caused them to be filled with water. He then took the dog and tore it to pieces; the entrails he threw into the lakes and rivers, commanding them to become the different kinds of fish; the flesh he dispersed over the land, commanding it to become different kinds of beasts and land animals; the skin he also tore in small pieces, and threw it into the air, commanding it to become all kinds of birds;

after which he gave the woman and her offspring full
power to kill, eat, and never spare, for that he had
commanded them to multiply for her use in abundance.
After this injunction. he returned to the place whence
he came, and has not been heard of since."*

The simple juxta-position of these three fables presents us with a curious illustration of the mythic affinities which connect together different, and often widely
separated regions of the earth That we have here to
deal with affinities of genuine connection, with evidences of a *bona fide* transmission of thought, and not
with mere chance coincidences, is obvious at a glance.
The subject, in each case, is nothing less than the creation of a universe, the grandest theme that could be
offered to human contemplation. In each case. the
work is accomplished by means which never could
spontaneously or directly suggest themselves to any
one, for there is nothing in the nature of things to
countenance any such working. In each case the formative material is the body of a slaughtered animal; an
old woman in the first instance, a giant in the second,
and a dog in the third, and in two of the cases the distribution and transmutations of the several parts of
these beings are strikingly analogous. In the third,
the mechanism is more simple, and, though differing in
detail, bears out in the main the fundamental idea of
the others. Nor do the affinities stop here. The agent
in two cases is the supreme divinity of each region, in
the other he is obviously an equivalent being, though
merely described as a man of prodigious stature. In
the Babylonian fable we have but two personages mentioned, in the two others we have, so to speak, three—

---

* Journey to the Northern Ocean in the years 1769—72. Lond.
1795, p. 342.

a dog being added in the one, and a cow in the other. In two cases we have a woman as part of the machinery, in two we have also a giant. The idea of eating is similarly duplicated. The old woman feeds upon berries, the giant lives upon the milk of the cow, who in turn is supported by licking the stones covered with hoar frost. And even the idea of the young man is common to both the northern fables, for while the cow is licking the stones Bör gradually emerges; he comes after the cow as his equivalent does after the woman, and then appears in each case the creative agent.

And now, after these coincidences, comes a set of contrasts which are not the least interesting part of the story, since they prove that none of these versions is a direct copy of either of the others, but rather an analogous, though independent, working up of some common material—of some fundamental fable now, to all appearance, perished. In the Scandinavian legend it is the first personage who is destroyed, in the Chaldean it is the second, and in the American it is the third. This looks something like a sequence of eras in the three versions. It is, at all events, in the analogy of transitions, very frequent in mythic fable.

It is obvious that it would never occur to any human being, as a preliminary idea, to suppose that this universe was formed out of the body of a slaughtered woman, giant, or dog. Such conjunctions could only arise in the course of association. The mind must be prepared for them by a special train of thought, and this fact dispels all idea of independent origins, and makes it plain, even in the absence of special evidence, that all three legends have had but one fundamental source. What that source may be, it is impossible to conjecture, from the materials supplied by the legends themselves; but the difficulty is not so formidable when

we take into consideration the analogies afforded by
the numerous parallel conjunctions which the study of
general mythology presents.   One point will easily be
admitted, even at this early stage of our inquiry —viz..
that it is only in symbolic language, and in metaphoric
picture writing, that we can expect to find the source
of such extraordinary' associations.   In this view it
may be that the giant, the woman, and the dog, are but
different symbolic expressions of some one idea, or set
of ideas, or that they imply the transfer of sympathies
and prerogatives from one personage of a legend to
another, just as the most sacred symbol in one creed
may be an abomination in another.

These legends also present a very interesting geographical relation.   The mythology of the North is connected by many links with the religious traditions of
the Persic or Iranian family, 'and the migrations or conquests of the Scythic tribes offer a ready means of ac-
counting for the affinity; nor could we at first sight turn
to a more probable source of connection with the regions of North Eastern America, than the explorations
and colonizations of the bold ocean wanderers of Scandinavia.   Yet there is nothing in the fables that speak
of relatively recent connections.   They rather point to
times when some common tradition was delivered to all
three, and in the course of ages modified to the existing
forms.   The tradition of Babylonia is plainly very ancient ; the creed of the North reaches back to unknown
times ; while the American fable, though handed over
to literature but yesterday, as it were, carries with it
no more appearance of juvenility than either of the
others.

The curious legend of which we have here presented
three versions, in as many different regions, has evidently traveled much farther than this.   An allusion

is made in the Dabistan to a local Hindu tradition, which reported that the world was formed of the skin of a Rakshasa or Demon, but we can only speak from memory, as we have not, at the moment, an opportunity of verifying the passage. There is, however, in one of the hymns of the Vedas, a description of the mystic sacrifice of a primeval being named *Purusha*, which has evident bearing on the present range of thought. The following is the substance of the legend, which our space compels us to condense :—

" This victim, Purusha, born primevally, they immolated on the sacrificial grass." They divided him into parts. The Brahmin was his mouth, the Rajanya his arms, the Vaisya his thighs, the Sudra sprang from his feet. The moon was produced from his mind *(manas);* the sun from his eye ; Indra and Agni from his mouth ; and Vaya from his breath. From his naval came the atmosphere ; from his head the sky ; from his feet the earth ; from his ear the four quarters ; and " *so they formed the worlds.*"*

A very distinct version of the original story has also existed, or still exists, in the cosmogonical traditions of the inhabitants of the Marian islands, as the following passage will show :

Pontan (they say) who was a very ingenious man, lived for a long time in the imaginary regions of space which existed before the creation. At his death, he commanded his sisters to form, of his breast and shoulders, the heavens and the earth ; of his eyes, the sun and moon ; and of his eyebrows, the rainbow.†

The tradition seems even to have traveled farther than this, for the Tangaloa of Tahiti " formed the ocean

* Prichard (*Physical History of Mankind*, vol. v., p. 176) quoting Freycinet, &c.

† Muir. Original Sanscrit Texts, p. 7.

from the sweat of his brow— so hard did he work in
making the land."* And there are, we believe, some
other fragmentary vestiges or allusions, to which at the
moment we cannot distinctly refer. But even those
that are unequivocal form a curious series of facts, and
evidently point to wide-spread and remote relations
among the families of man ; but such relations have
nothing to do with the speculative dreams so fashiona-
ble in the last generation, and not yet wholly forgotten
by the present, relative to the primeval peopling of the
earth, and the branching out of a primeval faith into
an infinitude of local superstitions.

Mr. Kohl, in his KITCHI-GAMI, or Wanderings round
Lake Superior, gives a variety of Indian traditions,
which he collected with care and judgment. The Ojib-
beways (he remarks) and, indeed, nearly all the Northern American Indians, situate their paradise to the
West.

" The Sacred Land of the West," beyond the Western Ocean, on the borders of the earth, and " The Sacred isles of the West," were familiar ideas to the
ancient Greeks. The paradise of the ancient Irish,
Hy Brasail, was an island in the Western Ocean ; that
of the Tonga islanders—the island *Bolotoo*—was situated in the *North*-west of the world. The *Amenti*, or
Hades of the Egyptians, like the Elysium of the Greeks,
was also in the West, and so of several other traditions.

When we come to stratify and analyze these and
their correlative legends, it becomes apparent that the
West was the original place of the paradise of departed
heroes, and that it was only in long subsequent ages
that this paradise was transferred, first to the North-
west, and finally to the North and East, when it

---

* Latham. *Varieties of Man*, p. 193.

became connected with *Initial* as well as *Terminal* myths.

In answer to Mr. Kohl's inquiries relative to the ideas entertained by the natives, on the subject of their paradise, he observes :—

Here my friend began telling me of a great, straight path, and its branch and side roads ; of a great strawberry that lay in the path of souls ; of a river, and a serpent before the entrance to paradise. And as the description was not very intelligible, one of the Indians called for a pencil, traced a rude diagram, and after some preliminary explanations, continued as follows :

" When men die they all go, after death, along the path of souls. On the centre of this path thou seest the strawberry lying on one side. It is extraordinarily large, and is said to taste very sweet. A man stands by it, who invites all passers by to taste it. But they must not accept it, for whatever soul does so is lost at once. Those that resist continue their journey prosperously till they come to paradise. It is, altogether, a journey from three to four days. Then a large broad river bars the way. Over it there is no regular bridge. Something that looks like a great tree-stump lies across it. Its roots are firmly fastened on the opposite shore. On this side, it raises its head, but it does not reach quite to the land. There is a small gap over which the souls must hop. The log, too, is constantly shaking. Most of the souls spring across, balance themselves properly, and save themselves. Those, however, that jump short, or slip off the bridge, fall into the water, and are converted into toads and fishes."

This paradise is very beautiful ; it was formed by *Menaboju* (the Hiawatha of Longfellow) at the command of the Great Spirit, and the souls there " are always merry, happy, and contented, play the drum all day and night and dance. They live on a variety of mushroom, and a species of wood that resembles the phosphorescent wood that is seen shining in our forests."

From another source the author learns that, " After the strawberry, a huge dog lies in the path. This dog, when sitting, is as big as a house. He watches the path, allows every one to pass unhindered Westward, but does not suffer any one to return from the world of souls to the East."

His informant also added that what seemed to be a log stretched across the river, was, in reality, a serpent, whose windings produced the trembling of the apparent log.

Many of the circumstances of this journey of the dead have direct affinities with the Mexican notions on the same subject, and no slight analogy also to the Hadaic journey of Classical fable. The bridge and its casualties is an important idea in Mahommetan legends. only that the log and serpent are there replaced by a razor. These connections between the Old world and the New, are extremely interesting, since they speak of inter-communications of which history has preserved no trace.

CHAPTER VII.

COSMOGONICO-CHRONOLOGICAL.—CATACLYSMS.

There is nothing more uncertain than chronology, as may easily be seen by the following :—Creation took place according to :

Septuagint, date of the Flood, (Before Christ, 3,246), years ago,		5,108
Septuagint, Creation's date......................	"	7,371
Ussher, Creation to present time.................	"	5,867
Hebrew Talmud....................	"	5,673
Byzantine Chronicles............	"	7,371

Julian Period	"	6,576
Desvignolles	"	8.788
Fourier	"	17.090
Chinese	"	498.600
Chaldean	"	473,000
Samaritan Pentateuch (Nablous, Syria)	"	6.167

And Plato tells us that the Atlantis (Isle of Delights) sunk in the ocean 9,000 years before the age in which he lived. One account tells us that Noah's Flood took place, B. C. 2,348 ; and another fixes that of Deucalion at 1,503 B. C. ; while the Deluge of Xisuthrus, dates at least 10,000 years before the Christian era.

The Thibetan Chronology—semi-Budhistic	before Christ,	11 869
It is known that Budha died	years ago,	3.384
The progenitors of the present race of Turks had great kingdoms in Asia	"	4.211
Chinese records (probable?) extend	"	63,000
And they ousted nations who had occupied the soil for 7,000 years.		
But totally divested of traditional elements, it is certain that the Chinese empire was an old one	"	5.164

A Chinese work, dating six hundred years before Christ, speaks of the " advantages of *ancient* systems of Education !"

Turning from China to Japan, we hear things quite as astonishing as any yet listened to, for their annals declare that they were ruled for fifteeen millions of years by celestial spirits, and then by human emperors for fifteen thousand years ; to which must be added six hundred, and one thousand eight hundred and sixty-two years, a total of seventeen thousand four hundred and sixty-two years. Their history is satisfactorily traced to 700, B. C.

The next step we take shall be to Hindostan. One of their periods, the Satya Yug, is now elapsing ; at its commencement the Seventh Menu, one of their ancestors, lived three million eight hundred and forty-two

thousand nine hundred and sixty-two years ago. But
their claims are well founded as far back as five thousand years ago. The Budhistic cycles of chronology are
something startling, if for no other reason than their exceeding *modesty.* Here they are, according to the sacred
books of the great Mendicant Order. There is a number known to the Budhists called an Asankya ; it is expressed by a unit and one hundred and forty cyphers.
The square of that constitutes an Anta-Kalpa ; and the
square of that in turn constitutes the number of years
since the first Budha ceased to preach, and attained
Narwana, or celestial beatitude. To-day there are hundreds of millions on this earth, who believe the whole
of this monstrous system, so far as figures go. Just
imagine a human intellect capable of grasping a number
only to be expressed by the figure 9 at the left hand of
one hundred and eighty-two million places of figures !
To give the reader something of an idea of only an
Anta-Kalpa, we will quote from a Cingalese author.
" Were it to rain as violently as rain ever fell, for the
period of eleven years, all over the earth, the number
of drops would not extend to an Anta-Kalpa. Were
an angel to fly from heaven once in ten thousand years,
and touch with a silk handkerchief, as lightly as possible, a rock five million acres in extent, and twelve
thousand miles high, it being as hard as diamond, the
handkerchief would have worn the rock entirely way ;
and a bird carrying away the dust of it, one speck at a
time, and being twelve thousand years on his outward,
and twelve thousand more on his inward flight, would
have taken the rock entirely away, and the angel and
the bird would have abundant time to repeat the experiment twelve thousand times between the commencement and ending of the period of a great Kalpa, or
Maha-Kalpa.

If we turn to the Babylonian chronologies, we are forced to reject their enormous statements and claims; but, while doing so, are compelled to admit that thousands of years before the date of the Man of Eden, the Babylonians had attained a high state of civilization, it being perfectly clear that nations capable of having such sublime conceptions of creation, of time, or duration, and the world of thought generally, as they unquestionably had, must have, long previous to the beginning of the six thousand years of Genesis, passed through that primitive barbarism which we erroneously attach to all ancient peoples. My own opinion is, that this world has witnessed more than one civilization, quite equal in degree, if not in kind, to that now existing.

Babylonian, Egyptian, Ninevite and Egyptological researches, have, through Bunsen, Layard, Muller, Schelling, Von Humboldt, Wilson, and others of the great galaxy of Scientific Stars, demonstrated the total unreliability of Theological chronologies; and the barriers which Jewish superstition and Christian sloth have erected upon God's free field of human history are, thank Heaven, being rapidly and forever broken down.

On the banks of the Nile we find that lofty arts, sciences, letters, and a high degree not only of civilization, but of learning, and luxury, existed in great perfection six thousand years ago.

All things advance from imperfection towards the perfect; but the rate of progress is necessarily slow. Nations, languages, science, art and intellectual systems do not, like the fungus, spring up in a night, nor wither in a day; but, like the cedar and the oak, are of slow but solid growth, and when they die, die hard. They do not perish swiftly, but become gradually extinct. Nations are like men; they are born, reach the virile age, reach maturity, and grow old. The process, where a nation springs out of barbaric or savage conditions, requires immense periods ; and in reference to Egypt, it must have required thousands of years to develop the state of things found there when Menes turned the channel of the Nile.   Bunsen gives 20,000 years B. C. as the date of the Beginning of what we find in Egypt 4000 years B. C. ; because it would require not less, but probably more, than that length of time, to develop one or both of the two vast families of languages in the East, namely, the Semitic and its antipodal speech, from which he thinks all modern tongues have sprung ; though how he connects either the languages of North and South America, and the monosyllabic tongues of China, with one or the other of these primitives, is hard to be seen.*   The Sanscrit is one branch of the early tongue, and is known to have been a dead language 4500 years ago, or long before Moses, and even then it was the offspring of other dead tongues.

The writer of this work cannot believe that all languages sprung from one or two sources, or that the human race had its origin with the Adam of Scripture, for the reason, among others :—First, that it is IMPOSSIBLE that any of the Nigritian races, the American Indian—many distinct varieties both in North and South America—and the Chinese, could have sprung from one common stock.   Intermarriage could never change people as we see them, had all originally been alike.   True, the darker races bleach whiter by amalgamation with lighter races ; but no possible amount of admixture will ever make people change from white to jet black, the originals being white in the first place. Take it as you will, here is a fact that cannot be gotten

* That eminent scholar's researches convinced him that Abraham was the first really historical personage of Genesis, for reasons already developed herein.

PRE-ADAMITE MAN.   113

over. Undoubtedly, all men are entitled to rights alike,
and are equally to be regarded as heirs of immortality :
but they are not all descended from one original pair.
In the great battle of the Polygenesists against the
Monogenesists, the former carry the heaviest artillery.
During the entire historical human period, the same
identical radical differences that exist between men of
different continents to-day, have existed ; and this is
proved by monuments, statuary and sculpture of all
kinds, and wherever discovered.   The Negro, the
Mongolian, and the man of Caucasian lineage, present
the same respective features—the first, in hue, shape and
outline ; the second presents the same sallow, flat face,
oblique eyes, high cheeks ; and the third, the same lofty-
browed bearing now, that they each did fifty centuries
ago : nor is it likely that the respective branches of the
human family would, or will change, save only by amalgamation, in the next 500 generations.   It follows, then,
that the idea of a single origin for all men *must* be
abandoned ; and only two other hypothesis are possible : first, that man sprung, through the Development
process, *via* Baboons, Gorillas, etc., or that he came
into being at a score of points of locality and time.
As yet, I see no reason to accept the former repugnant
notion, and cannot understand the *modus* of the latter.
We cannot believe ourselves developed Monkeys, even
with an interval of a million ages separating us from
them.   We reject the thing in scorn, and will continue
to do so until reason and science demonstrate our
error ; and with this peculiar phase of the Development and Monogenetic theories goes that of the Deluge, and some other notions based on the accounts in
Genesis.   With the " Garden" goes the " Ark" and the
" Flood"—as being universal ; and yet there was a

flood or floods, that probably swept millions of human beings out of existence. But of this more anon.

It is maintained by learned men that, geographically, man began his career, not in Syria, but in what is now a barren wilderness, on the northern slope of the Hindu Kush. The "Garden," therefore, stretched to the Taurus and the Polar Sea; eastward to the Altai, or Celestial Mountains of the Chinese; and its western boundaries were Ararat and Caucasus. This land was watered by the Oxus, Euphrates, Jaxartes and Tigris.* It has also grown to be a cardinal doctrine with the same scholars that, by a dreadful catastrophe, brought about by earthquakes, fire, water and wind, volcanoes and noxious gasses, not only were vast numbers of human beings swept away, but the very face of the region was changed; and the Caspian Sea and Lake Ural were formed, and a temperate climate was changed into one of frost and snow. The Hebraic legend in Genesis, the Bactrian one in the Véndidâd, and at least half a score of others, so strongly confirm the same story, that it is reasonable to suppose that it has a foundation in truth; albeit it is certain that more than one boat-load of men and animals survived the occurrence, whether there was only one or several deluges. Wherever these traditions of a flood have been found, they are connected with legends older still.

---

* Geological research has proved that a vast inland sea existed aforetime, which filled the whole space between the site of Constantinople on the west, and Turkistan on the east—a length of 2,000 miles, by about 1,000 broad. The Caspian, the Seas of Azoff and the Aral are but small ponds left when this great sea was drained. How and when this latter event took place is, of course, not precisely known; but that it was the result of causes, presently to be noticed, there can be no reasonable doubt. My theory, though novel, is worthy of scientific examination.

On the Couteau des Prairies, situated between the Missouri and Minnesota rivers, in the Western part of the American Union, is the identical spot where Creation first begun, many centuries before the great freshet, or flood ; at least such is the tradition and belief of many independent Indian tribes—and it is quite as reliable as any other. When the flood took place, many centuries ago, and destroyed all the nations of the earth, all the Indian tribes assembled in the Couteau des Prairies, to escape from the impending watery ruin. After they had all gathered there from every part, the waters still kept rising, till they finally entirely covered them, and changed their bodies into red pipe-stone, which pipe-stone abounds there till this day. While all the rest were drowning, one young virgin girl—Kwaptahw—caught hold of the foot of a very great bird that was flying over, and by it was carried to a safe place on the top of a high cliff, not far off. This bird was the War Eagle ; and by him she became pregnant of twins—a boy and a girl, and from these two the whole red-skinned world was peopled. This legend resembles, in some features, others that are a great deal more popular, especially in the miraculous and conceptional elements. Equally singular with the above are some of the Eastern legends not yet mentioned; for instance, that of the Arabs, to the effect that Creation began in the center of what now is Mecca ; that Adam was over one hundred feet high, and Eve nearly the same ; that Paradise was situated in the heavens ; and that the Fall was not only a moral, but also a physical one ; that Adam fell on a mountain in Ceylon, and Eve on Arafat, a hill near Mecca ; that being separated, they began to search for each other ; Adam beginning to travel on foot, in hopes of finding her, each footstep being one hundred miles in length, and a city arising wherever his foot rested ; he finally rejoined his wife on Arafat, where they lived till death ; Eve being then buried at Jeddah, a port on the Red Sea, where her tomb—two hundred feet long—is still to be seen. Arabian legends tell us that the tombs of Noah, Abel, Joshua and Moses, are each one hundred feet long. Also that, on ordinary occasions, God speaks in pure Arabic, save when mercifully inclined, when he adopts a Persian dialect.

Miracles, such as these and others, may have once occurred, but they have long since ceased. Science can take no notice of a miracle ; the two names are antipodal. Science and miracle are deadly foes, and whenever they meet in the shock of warfare, one party invariably suffers defeat, and that party is not Science. Galileo's world moved, then it did not ; but then again it did.

Science is called upon to account for the Deluge, or tell us how the universal testimonies all to the same general purport originated. She does so ; and not only tells us why and how the catastrophe —this Flood—happened, but she also tells us, very nearly, *when* it occurred. Of course the Deluge must have been a human reminiscence, else we should not hear of it. The catastrophe was the result of natural law, totally independent of any miraculous element whatever ; and we now know that the Deluge could not have happened much, if any, less than twenty-two thousand years ago, but with greater probability, not less than forty-two thousand years have elapsed since the greatest of these events—for there has been more than one—recorded itself, and engraved its history on the tablets of tradition. It may not be known to the general reader, but it is a well-attested fact, nevertheless, that, in addition to the diurnal and orbital motions of the earth, there is a third, an oscillating motion, requiring vast periods of time for

the accomplishment of one movement. This motion is
that of the deviation of the earth's axis, and by means
of it the poles, and therefore the equator also, are
shifted, and a great change takes place in the temperature, not only in polar, but in all other regions of the
globe ; and the cold is greater or less, for a period, at
the middle of one of these oscillations, than at the end.
It is believed that when this movement of the earth
reaches one extreme, there is a terrible degree of cold
at the poles, and consequently vast accumulations of ice
are gathered there ; and it is certain that the poles
have been permanently shifted more than once. The
coldest recent period occurred at the poles ten thousand one hundred and fourteen years ago, and of course
the earth there is now gradually verging toward the opposite extreme, and the climates of America and Europe
are undergoing rapid changes on that account. The
greatest recent degree of heat occurred at the poles not
less than twenty-two thousand years ago, in consequence
of the deviation of the earth's axis ; and the melting
of the ice on that occasion may have been the cause of
Noah's Flood—for it is certain that it has not a date
within the truly historical and monumental periods ;
and these carry us—the first to Menes, and the second
to nearly, or quite, double that length of time.
But we have distinct accounts of *two* Oriental floods ;
the first of which could not have taken place less than
forty-two thousand two hundred years ago ! Subsequent
to the assigned period of the last flood, we have great
nations in the East:—

We know that Menes lived, years ago,.................. 6000
And kings reigning in This, Upper Egypt, for years..... 350
And kings reigning in Lower Egypt, for years.......... 1790
Secular princes, } of all Egypt (Bunsen's authority).. { 1817
Sacerdotal princes, } { 1855

Since the Flood, years must have elapsed to the number of, at the very lowest, Bunsenian calculation 11,812

The Baron's conclusions are arrived at mainly on philological grounds. They may be unsatisfactory to some readers, and are not at all relied on here to prove the existence of Pre-Adamite man, as we are enabled to do *that* on totally independent grounds.

To trace the growth and culmination of languages, and seek to establish man's antiquity by that course, is a task which, although it might be done, is not my province in this book, though there are many solid arguments to be adduced from that direction, such, for instance, as the following : The Sanscrit is but an off-shoot of another language, yet in the days of Moses, itself was a *dead* language. The Rig-Veda is written in that "sacred tongue," yet the Rig-Veda is at least eighteen hundred years younger than another sacred volume, written in a language quite as ornate, full and complete as that of the Vedas—the Egyptian "Book of the Dead!" The Iranian languages were an improvement on Turanian stocks; and the number of these off-shoots are to be counted by the hundred; and yet there is another, and totally distinct, class of languages —the Semitic, quite equal to the others, and which was developed in as early ages of the world.

The Arabs, and the Aryas of India, have an old legend, that a tribe of what they call Geni—but which were probably as solid men as themselves—inhabited the earth before Adam, and who spoke a polished language; which race of beings all died out many ages before their successor, Adam, was created. Another tradition is to the effect that in the primeval ages two separate races of men inhabited India, who spoke languages so pure and perfect that nothing equal thereto has ever been heard since, and will not be until a perfectly true man, in all respects, shall arise to redeem and save all the nations. I now leave the philological argument for others to adduce, merely remarking that Abraham, went to Egypt nearly thirty centuries before Christ was born; and he found there a vast and populous kingdom, and a language exhibiting abundant proofs of long cultivation. It is not possible to tell now what language was spoken first; we can no more answer that question than we can tell who named the lands spoken of in Gen. ii., supposing that Book to be what is claimed for it; or how and where King David got his knowledge that the world was round! The fact is, that there must have been civilizations on this earth an enormous number of ages ago, and languages that have all passed away, leaving not a wreck behind to tell that such things were. It is highly probable that Plato's Atlantis was not a figment of poetic brains; and that "ocean beds may now be stretching beneath the weltering seas, which, over wide-extended regions, have been once the busy continents and islands of an inhabited and civilized world;" and so far from man having had an origin even forty thousand years ago, recent discoveries lead us to the belief that that enormous period may be at least doubled, and yet be within moderate bounds!

It has been proved, by Bunsen and others, that Egypt was an organized State 5,863 years before Menes, or nearly 12,000 years ago; and taking the first year of that date as a point of departure, we demonstrate a human antiquity which was ancient even then! The grounds upon which this conclusion is based are the following:—

First. The six days of creation, 6,000 years ago, are not geologically satisfactory; nor is the matter any clearer when these six days are stretched into six or

sixty millenia ; for so far from there having been but
six great Geological Periods, the number usually allot-
ted and insisted on, that number does not express the
half. Mon. D'Orbigny, in his *Podrome de Palœon-
tologie*, has demonstrated twenty-nine of these periods,
in every one of which both plants and animals existed ;
and as since he wrote, the remains of man have been
found, coupled with those of animals long since extinct,
and which animals lived in a period so remote, and
under such climatic conditions, that it was deemed by
the Geological schools utterly impossible that human
beings could have existed contemporaneously, it follows
that man *may* have existed during any one, or the
whole of these twenty-nine, or rather thirty Geological
periods. The six usually accepted are the Azoic ; Si-
lurian—Old Red Sandstone ; the Carboniferous ; Per-
mian and Triassic ; Oolitic and Cretaceous ; and the
Tertiary day, or periods.

Second. The Babylonian kingdoms long ante-dated
the earliest Egyptian governments.* In Egypt, several
distinct forms of Religion had grown up, decayed, died
out, and been superseded by others, before the era of
Menes. This King established in his realm an old
Asiatic Mythical Religion—Osiris worship—which
worship was preceded by that of Num, 1 ; Amun, 2 ;
Ra, On, 3 ; Set—Seth—Seti—Suth—Saturn—Phœnician worship. 4 : Ptah, 5 ; and with that of Isis and
Osiris, six forms of Religion—State Religion, up to the
days of the Thinite conqueror.

Eusebius tells us that between these reigns of gods
and the commencement of human kings, a vast period
of time elapsed ; the Theocratic form of government being exchanged for that of the Nekyes (Souls of Dead

---

* Egypt's Place in Universal History, Vol. IV., page 635.

men—priestly administration) : which in turn was superseded by a long reign of demi-gods. Bytis was the first of the sacerdotal kings. His place is at the head of the Nekyes Priests, and it was 13,900 years from the beginning of the reign of the first-named god to the beginning of the reign of Bytis. The reign of the Manes, or Spirits, lasted 5,813 years. making a total of 19,713 years from the reign of the first-named god to the end of that of the last ghost—Manes—Nekyes.

But these enormous lapses of time may be objected to. Well, we will leave out the reigns of both Gods and Ghosts, yet still there remain the 6000 years to Menes, and the reigns of four Dynasties of Human Kings *prior* to him, extending over a space of 5812 years, and giving us a sum total from the storming of Fort Sumpter to the first King, of the first of the above four dynasties. of nearly 12,000 years.

Third. The Chaldees had a story about the Flood and Ark, ages before one of their race (Abraham), carried the tale to Egypt and Syria, and that the story in Genesis is but a copy of the older one, as is also that of Creation, Adam, the " Fall," the " Ark" and " Deluge," there can be no more doubt than that light opposes darkness. It is not hard to demonstrate the mythical, allegorical, and typical character of much that we have been accepting as true, in both profane and sacred history.

The Babylonians and Chaldees had an Adam-Kadmon, or first man—and had also ten epochs from their head mortal to the Flood, just as the Hebrew story has ten generations from Adam to Noah. The first epoch, according to the Chaldaic Historian, was that of ALORUS, and extended to the beginning of the Second Epoch—

Lunar years ago*.......	86,000
The Second. Epoch of Aloparus, lunar years ago...........	10,800
The Third, Epoch of Almélon, lunar years ago............	46,800
The Fourth, Epoch of Ammenon, during whose reign Oannes, a fish-man, came out of the Red Sea, to teach mankind, lunar years ago....................................	43,200
The Fifth, Epoch of Melagarus (a second Merman Teacher, came out of the sea), lunar years ago................	64,800
The Sixth. Epoch of Daonus, lunar years ago..............	36,000
The Seventh, Epoch of Edoranchus (another Merman who came to teach the human race), lunar years ago........	64,800
The Eighth, Epoch of Sancharis, lunar years ago...........	36,000
The Ninth, Epoch of Otiartes, lunar years ago.............	28,800
The Tenth, Epoch of Xisuthrus, the Man of the Flood, lunar years ago....................	64,000
Total, from Alorus to the Deluge, lunar years ago, say......	432,000

Now let us see if the story of the Flood in Genesis is original or not. The reader will please read Genesis. 6th chapter, 13th verse, *et seq.*, at the same time that he peruses the following account given by the native historian, Berosus :[†] "Kronos (God, Set, Seth, Saturn), revealed to Xisuthrus, in a dream, that on a (certain) day the Flood would commence, in which all mankind would perish. That he must bury all the books in the city of Helios, Sippara, and forthwith build a ship five stadia long (3,125 feet), and two stadia broad (1,250 feet), for himself and wife, children and next of kin. He must load it with food for his family, and also for the animals of all sorts, fowls and quadrupeds, which he was to embark with himself in this *great* (Eastern) ship. Xisuthrus asked Set where he was to sail to ? who replied, " to the gods, with a

---

* That is to say, lunar years ago, when the account was written, which, of course, necessitates an addition of some thousands of years at the present date.

† See Eusebius III.; Syncellus, page 30 ; Bunsen's Egypt, Vol. IV., page 369.

prayer that it may fare well with mankind." All of
which was done according to the command of the god.
"After this the Flood came. As soon as it ceased,
Xisuthrus sent out birds ; but they, finding neither
food nor resting-place, soon came back to Xisuthrus in
the ship. . . . A few days after, he again sent out
birds, for the second time, but they also returned, and
with mud upon their feet. . . . A few days after, he
again sent out birds, *for the third time, who did not
return.* Then Xisuthrus knew that there was land
again. . . . Now, he took out some of the planks,
and saw that the ship was landed on a mountain. . .
He went out with his wife and daughter, and the
builder, and threw himself upon the ground, and prayed,
and built an altar, and offered sacrifices upon it. . . .
After the sacrifice, those who had come out disappeared. . . . Those who had remained behind looked
for them, and called to them by their names. in vain ;
but a voice answered them out of the air : ' Fear God ;
for he has (they have) been taken up to the Gods, because he (they) feared God :¹ his wife, and his daughter, and the builder, have shared the same honor : Go
back to Babylon [Bab El—Gate of God], and com-
municate *to mankind the books that are concealed at
Sippara :*² the place where they were was in Armenia. . . . Upon this they offered sacrifice, and
went their way to *Babylon.* . . . On the Gordiæan
Mountains, pieces of the ship which stranded in Armenia, are still to be seen. . . . They built a temple
and *restored* Babylon." . . . Notice, first—That here
we have the probable original of the " Translation of
Enoch ;" and, second—Even according to the old
legend. all mankind were not destroyed. God had
taken the patriarch, his wife, daughter and the builder,
to heaven, bodily ; yet those left in the ark were to

repair to Babylon and reveal the contents of the Books that had been hidden—(from whom? to whom?) It is plain that Babylon was not destroyed, neither was Sippara.

Note here, First : (still remembering that the above is a Chaldean legend,) That Abraham was a Chaldean, and therefore perfectly familiar with it, and that he undoubtedly transmitted it to his descendants, some of whom wrote it out as we find it in Genesis, barring the rabbinical additions to it, and others of whom have so garbled it as to necessitate long and laborious researches, in order to get at the original truth. Second : The whole Pentateuch was not written in Moses' day, for proof of which, see the very suggestive assertion in Gen. xxxvi. 31, where kings of Israel are alluded to (some hundreds of years before Saul was elected first to that office,) in such a way as to imply that that Book was written *after* there were kings over Israel. Third : It is also worthy of note, that Jehovah was *not* the God worshiped by the Israelites during the " Forty Years in the Wilderness." Let whosoever disputes this, refer to Amos v. 21 to the end, and be convinced.

There are proofs extant that the Bible has been tampered with, no matter whether it be regarded as the work of the copyist or of inspired penmen. I have an opinion that there is a great deal of Man, and but a very little of God about the Pentateuch portion of it, as the Book now stands, however much of the latter there may have been originally. If the Hebrew Bible was an original revelation from God, then it is certain that those to whom it was given altered it in such a manner as to make it appear to be a very imperfect apograph of that original revelation ; or else they changed it so as to make it conform generally with legends and traditions vastly older than itself. Be this as it may, the following facts have a very important bearing and significance: The great question of the Bible's authenticity has to be met in this age. The thing cannot longer be avoided. If it is an original inspiration, it will stand; it but a copy of older cosmogonical theories, that fact will stand also; and in either case the event will be the firmer establishment of God's Truth, whether that truth be written on the rocks alone, or partly on parchment, paper, or man's conscience. We know, according to Egyptian monuments, records and traditions, that civilized people dwelt on the banks of the Nile not less than nine thousand five hundred years before Menes, at the lowest calculation;* we know that Genesis resembles older cosmological accounts; we know that the story of the "Fall" was not original with the Hebrew nation, but that in various shapes the legend existed before Menes;† and knowing all this, many an honest man in

---

* Egypt's Place in Universal History, Vol. IV , pp. 57, et seq.

† Of the connection of the serpent with the temptation of Eve, we have heard a strange story related by an American traveler in Egypt, who was noted among his companions for his willingness to intrude upon out-of-the-way and admitted-to-be dangerous places. An Arab guide, perceiving this peculiarity, offered, for a consideration, to conduct him into the interior of one of the large pyramids, and show him a room, upon the walls of which was a picture no Frank had ever seen. The bargain was at once consummated, and the parties entered the structure, and after sliding down an inclined plane of some hundred feet, they came upon a large room, out of which led a narrow and half choked-up communication with an adjoining apartment. This apartment reached, the Arab lit his torches, and exposed to the astonished gaze of the traveler, a painting fresh as if the work of yesterday, representing a serpent with human arms and legs, handing an apple to an Egyptian woman; both figures relieved by the conventional trees peculiar to such early art. If this story be true—and we have no reason to doubt its authenticity—we have a pictorial representation of the Fall of Man, possibly more ancient than even the Mosaic account. —*Harper's Magazine.*

these days feels it a duty to probe the matter, even at the risk of being regarded " Infidel." But such a stigma can only be applied by the ignorant and bigot. Men who love truth and serve God are above that weakness, and will not quarrel with Science, even if she proves all the Adams to have been not human beings, but Ideal Men. Let us now present a few curious things that throw much light on the borrowed and mythical elements in the Book of Genesis :

I In the comparatively modern Pentateuch we read of Seth as being the son of the first man ; but in far older accounts (Assyrian Monuments,) the same character is God, from whose son, Enosh, the world was peopled. (See Gen. v.)   Now Set was at one time Sothis' (Suthi, Sirius, the Dog Star,) and afterward Saturn ; there are, consequently, unmistakable mythological elements in Genesis.

II. The Phœnicians were neighbors of the Egyptians. The Hebrew Jacob, wrestled with God, (Elohim,) and was hurt in the thigh ; in consequence of this he was called Israel, which means " Wrestler with God."   But long previous to Jacob the Phœnician Hercules had wrestled with Typhon, (the Sun-god at the meridian ;) he was wounded in the thigh, and he was thence named Palaimon Yisrael, " the wrestler with the god."   But,

III. Jacob wrestled with his twin-brother, Esau, in his mother's womb ; so had Acrisius with *his* twin-brother, Prœtus, in the womb of their mother.

IV. Esau, Jacob's brother, was a hairy, rugged man. But so. also, long before him, was the Phœnician Usov—Isauv, Esau, Isa—Jesus !

V.—A. The Phœnicians had a Qayan (Kain—Cain) before the Hebraic one.

· B. And they had also a first man—earth-born—(Adam—Kadmon).

c. Also a Tubal-Qayan—(Tubal-Cain—Worker in Brick—Craftsman).

D. They had also an El-Saddai, as the Hebraic Al-Shaddai—(God Almighty).

E. They had also a Sydyk—(Zadeq—Malki-Zadeq—Melchizadek)—the Redeemer, Redeemed, the Just, the Eternal ; Priest of the High.

F. Jacob saw Heaven open, and angels ascending and descending on a ladder, and he named the place Beth El (House of God). But before that the Phœnicians had a similar Beth-El (God's House), and so had the Egyptians their Hath-hor, which means precisely the same thing.

G. Circumcision was an old Aramæan custom, and commemorated the cutting off of his own head by Kronos-El, the Phœnician god. It was not, therefore, original with Abraham, but was adopted by him.

H. The account of the proposed sacrifice of Isaac by Abraham was but a revival and adaptation of an ancient Phœnician Myth. The Arabic legend says Abraham was about to offer up Ishmael, not Isaac ; and at Muna, near Mecca, not in Jerusalem ; in other respects the three versions are alike, but the Hebrew one is the youngest.

VI. Genesis, certainly written not earlier than Moses' time. and probably not till centuries had elapsed after his death, speaks of the building of the Tower of Babel. But Babylonian traditions, handed down to us, demonstrate that that event, as described in Genesis. was but a copy of a legend very old, at least three thousand years before the foundation of Memphis by the Thinite monarchs. (See Syncellus.) Hippolytus, (Hæres, v. 7, p. 97), tells us that the Chaldeans called the man who was born of the earth, but who afterwards became a living soul, Adam.   The Gnostics, also, speak of a god Adamus.

VII. No living man can reconcile the discrepancies and flat contradictions of the 4th and 5th chapters of Genesis.   But when we call to mind the fact that Seth was God's primitive name in Asia, (as was Shem that of the sun), long before the founding of the first Egyptian empire; and that "Enos" is the Aramaic word for " MAN ;" that "Adam," "Adamah," or "Ha-Adam" is in Hebrew; and that "Enos," therefore, means "The Man," the whole thing becomes as clear as daylight; and it is equally discernible how the Myth came where we find it.

VIII.—A. It is repugnant to reason—in fact, utterly so—to imagine it true that the Men of Genesis ever lived to the ages there stated.   No two versions of the Bible agree as to these apocryhal years.

B. Philology and tradition alike demonstrate that many of the names of those supposed long-lived Patriarchs, are not those of Men, but of Epochs, periods or reigns.   On these grounds they are understandable, and on no other   But—

c. I reject even this interpretation, philologically demonstrated though it be ; and unhesitatingly set these patriarchs, and their ages, down to the credit of the Rabbins, who, in my opinion, invented them ; or if they did not invent them, they gave new readings to very old accounts.   But again :

D. Supposing the numbers usually accepted as meaning the ages of the Patriarchs to really mean the period of the duration of the reign of certain ideas, or forms of religious worship, or even of political dynasties, the account would then stand thus :—

Giving us a period of over eight thousand years between the end of Shem's rule and the " Beginning." This view I present for what it may be worth. The suggestive idea here presented appears to have escaped the vigilance of Biblicists, so far as I am aware.

F. If we apply the same touch-stone from Shem downwards to Abraham, we have a grand total of eleven thousand two hundred and ninety-one years. And all this from the Bible ; singularly substantiating Egyptian chronology.

IX. Turn we now to Babylon once more. Nimrod is not named at all among the monarchs of the first Chaldean dynasty. He preceded them. He was not a Chaldean, but an Ethiopian, or Kossic-Turanian King. Now, Berosus gives us the names of eighty-seven Kings of that first dynasty ; and we have, from the reign of the first King of that dynasty, to the sack of Babylon by Zoroaster, which took place before Christ two thousand two hundred and thirty-four years, a semi-historical period of over thirty-five thousand years! But, suppose we omit the whole of the eighty-seven Kings, and fall back on certain history : in this case we have a period of ascertained dates, ending at the three thousand seven hundred and eighty-fourth year before Christ, or, years ago, five thousand six hundred and forty-six, (1862.) It is certain that Nimrod lived, flourished and triumphed, built cities and carved winged-bulls, a very long time before the beginning of the fifty-six centuries just mentioned. But:

X. This Nimrod was a Kushite, (Kossian) and spoke a Turanian language, and therefore *preceded* those Kings, and nations who spoke the Semitic tongues, which were a development of a much earlier age. Heber lived two thousand years before Abraham ; the latter lived not less than twenty-eight hundred years before Christ, at the lowest calculation ; and between Heber and the first Chaldean King of the last dynasty, at least five thousand years intervene ; and Nimrod existed before the first dynasty. It is worthy of note that the first account we have of him in the Bible is in a fragment interpolated in the geneology of Kham, Genesis viii—12, where it had no right to be placed, save by Hebraists, who despised all rights whatever, except their right to falsify. Nimrod's period is one of vast and hoary antiquity ; and yet when he went to fight and build on the plains of Babylonia, he found there a settled state of things, and a civilization of a high order ; just as the early Egyptians did when they conquered and supplanted the Kings of This, in Upper Egypt.

Turn where we may, toward any point of the compass, it is utterly impossible to find anything that even distantly approximates a real beginning—an original people—save only one, and that one the Negro. A few zealous Scientists, more zealous than wise, endeavor to make us believe that the first couple begat children, which children afterwards scattered about the earth, and that the physical conditions of climate, water, soil, valley-life, mountain existence, and so-forth, gradually tanned some, and blanched others, to such an extent that, in process of time, the world became peopled with nations as we know them now—from the splendid jet black men of Africa, to the pearly beauties of the State of Maine—where dwell the handsomest white women on the habitable globe—in Portland especially. The Monogenesists alluded to, are in fault. All men—Negroes excepted—now living, are hybrids, or rather concrete men, formed by intermixtures, carried on through countless ages.

Which ever way we look we find no true beginning, but only irruptions, immigrations, revolutions, and dynastic changes. Many a long century before either Nimrod or Babel, the Table-lands of Asia, were thickly strewn with mighty cities. When Solon, the learned Greek, was at Sais, in the Egyptian Delta, he asked the scholars of that country certain questions about the Origines of themselves and other nations, and the priests answered that they could show him Athenian names of his countrymen, who lived nine thousand years before the date of the conversation (which occurred in the reign of King Amasis, B. C. 619.) They not only told him about *one* disastrous Flood in his own land—for the Egyptians knew nothing about a deluge in theirs—but of *many* that had aforetime swept the lands of Greece and other nations, as with a destructive broom. They imputed his ignorance of these several cataclysms to the fact that, in those days, letters were not well cultivated in Greece; and therefore but few or no records were made—which few, if there were any, probably were lost in the general ruin. Solon was astonished at all this; but still more so when they told him that their sacred books contained a record of their institutions for eight thousand years: but of Solon's, for one thousand more: "These records state that your country (Greece,) once checked the advance of a mighty power, which threatened all Europe and Asia, bursting in upon them from the Atlantic Ocean.

For at that time the Atlantic was navigable, and beyond the Straits which you call the Pillars of Hercules, there was an island larger than Lybia and Asia put together. . . . Now on this great island, in the Atlantic, there was a vast and powerful kingdom. . . . This united Empire attempted to subjugate your country, O Solon, and ours. . . . Then your country arose and . . . drove back the aggressors, and erected columns to commemorate the victory. . . But at a later period extraordinary earthquakes and floods took place, and in one fatal night and day the whole of your fighting men there collected together, were swept off from the face of the earth, and at the same moment the Atlantic Island sunk into the ocean." [*Extract from the Timœus.*]

Bunsen says, in his last work (1862,) that, " There is nothing improbable in itself in reminiscences and records of great events in Egypt nine thousand years before Christ ; for, as we have seen, the Origines of Egypt go back to the ninth Millenium before Christ," (nine thousand years, or nearly eleven thousand, dating from the present time). There never was but one such conqueror as the Atlantean hero, and that hero was Nimrod, the Kossian, the "mighty warrior before the Lord ;" and his date cannot be lower than seven thousand, but probably was not less than twenty thousand years before Christ.* According to the same high authority, the Egyptians made the Origines of Asia, that is, the Asiatic peoples, antecedent to theirs, and, as they displaced an already settled people, and their own records reach back nine thousand years before Christ, the very latest date of their immigration to the Nilotic banks, cannot be lower than the

* Egypt's Place in Universal History, Vol. IV., pp. 462, *et seq.*

11000th year B. C.; and is probably twice as great, even on the testimony of Horner and Marriette. The history of the world is post-diluvian and ante-diluvian, and the barrier that divides them is the last of the so-called Floods, and there were civilized States in Asia as far antecedent to that event as we are subsequent thereto. This gives not less than twenty-six thousand years, at the farther end of which, civilized nations unquestionably existed on the Nile; for it is *impossible* that the Deluge can have happened later than from twelve to fourteen thousand years ago, and probably long before that; and it seems to me that this tradition was a hoary one, even in the earliest days of the first Chaldean monarchies—those that preceded Nimrod—on the assumption of only one deluge; but there were more floods than one—if not, whence the American legends?

A summary of results deduced from Bunsen's and other Biblico-Egyptological research, will present the following approximations toward, if not, the very truth itself, independent of my own reasonings and researches, or any other authority adduced herein : —

Creation of Man in the dim background of Time......		UNKNOWN.
Civilized Nations on the Plateaus of Eastern Asia.....	B.C.	35,000
Earliest Date of the Founders of the Thinite Nation...	"	28.000
The Flood in Asia and part of Europe...............	"	21.000
Date of Nimrod, Atlantis and Babylon................	"	16.000
Date of Ghost-worship in Egypt....................	"	12,000
Date of Menes....................................	"	4.200
Date of Abraham, probably not less than............	"	2,900
Date of Moses....................................	"	1,900
Date of Solomon.......	"	1,015
From First Civilization known, to Christ	"	35,000

These figures appear alarming, but we have it in our power to *prove*, equally high, if not higher human dates than these as will be seen in both the second and

third parts of this work. The " Flood," itself, may be
dismissed in a few words. I consider the testimony to
that event as being unimpeachable. There must have
been, at least, two great cataclysms in Asia and Africa,
besides others of equal magnitude in America—the
last of the former of which was caused by the shifting
of the axis of the earth, from causes already stated
herein. The melting of the ice at the Poles, the bursting of volcanoes and other frightful convulsions of this
last event, caused the molten bowels of the earth to
move, and in their movements, mountains, islands, continents were upheaved in some portions of the globe,
and other mountains, islands and continents sunk to
rise no more. Vast floods of water rushed down
from either pole ; myriads of peoples, scores of nations, attained immortality in the twinkling of God's
eye ; and their souls, in millions, rose to heaven and
entered the portals of disbodied glory, while their
fleshly forms sunk, food for fishes and for worms, leaving only here and there a fragmentary bone or skeleton, to become in future ages, after other upheavals,
mute but eloquent witnesses to the fact that there did
exist, once upon a time, Pre-Adamite races of men.

The particular event here alluded to, is the Oriental
" Flood" of Noah, Deucalion and others. But there
was one before that. I allude to the " Mysterious
Event" so dimly alluded to in early Chinese annals ;
and, perhaps, may be the same terrible catastrophe
alluded to by the Priests of Sais, in their conversa-
tions with Solon, something like six centuries before
the Christian Era.

Upon geological, astronomical and other grounds,
I have reached the conclusion that, at a period not less
than 42,000, nor more than 58,600 years ago, there
occurred the most tremendous event this earth ever

witnessed, or ever will witness, until a final convulsion shall hurl it out of being—as a habitable globe. It is known that the Planets of the Solar System are interdependent, and mutually connected ; and from researches conducted for long years, I conclude that about 58,600 years ago, the planet of this system then revolving on its axis in an orbit between those of Mars and Jupiter, BURST asunder—scattered into a million fragments, the larger ones now constituting the Asteroids, and named Juno, Vesta, Pallas, Ceres, and so on, to the number of a hundred or more, and the smaller bits of which are now revolving at greater or less distances apart, in a track or belt, so situated as to be crossed by the earth from the 10th to the 24th of every November, at which time we are visited by showers of meteoric stones, attracted then by the globe, and which fragments once formed part of the now shattered world. Millions of such fragments are yet flying through space in elliptical orbits ; but their number will continually lessen as Novembers pass, for then

"We gather them in! we gather them in!"

As the result of this bursting, I conceive that this earth suddenly changed its axis and its angle toward the ecliptic pole ; the sun melted the ice at the earth's poles ; the melted mass in the earth's bowels became disturbed, and it vomited forth fire and flame from a hundred volcanic mouths ; and Strombolic craters rained down fire enough to bury a thousand Sodoms and Gomorrahs.* Earthquakes rent the globe almost asunder ; scores of Asiatic, European, African and American cities—peoples, nations, were hurled into fiery and watery graves ; the Atlantis island sunk to

* The reminiscences of these scoriac rivers—these floods of sulphurous fire, in my opinion, furnished the basis of the Sodom and Gomorrah stories.

rise no more; the great lake of Central Africa was drained; the British Islands were riven from Continental Europe; the vast region of Africa between the sixteenth and thirty-fourth parallels of latitude, and now known as Zahara, was upheaved from the bottom of the Salt Sea; the Hesperidean lake of Diodorus Siculus, situate in Afric's heart, ceased to be; the regions of the Atlas and the Soudan were tossed up from briny depths; the Arabian Peninsula, the Deserts of Shur, Sin and Lybia, the Salt-Kuvcers of Persia, the prairies and deserts of America, and the sterile steppes of Russia, Tartary and Siberia, appeared with all their dreary majesty and horror on the world's surface. By this great convulsion, Japan was torn from China, the Caribbean Islands wrenched from Columbia's main, and the Greek Archipelago was brought into being. The climates of whole continents and zones were changed; men and animals, in countless millions, perished on this earth, and the entire face of nature assumed an altered aspect. I have myself picked up many a sea-shell and fossil tooth on Zahara's burning sands, miles and miles from the sea coast. I believe that I have handled things fashioned by the hands of men who lived before that awful ruin fell upon them. I believe that the Cyclopean structures of Etruria pertain to men who were on earth at that period; and that Palenque, Labhak, Copan, Uxmal, Kobah, Chichen. and Cuzco, are American remnants of that terrible devastation! If I am alone in this belief—so be it; I believe it. . . . Death rode in many chariots on that awful day; and men and animals perished by sulphuric, nitrogenic, and carboniferous blasts; and that they alone escaped who occupied peculiar localities, is quite plain. That climates changed at that time, is proved by the bones of tropical animals, and remains of tropical plants now found

in frozen regions ; and the plants and remains of northern fauna now exhumed from tropical graves. I do
not say that all these things were so ; I merely affirm
that, to me, they seem to appeal and cling to reasoning
and reasonable minds, with all the force of Revelation.

Such, then, are my reasons for rejecting the historical and some other pretensions of the Pentateuch.
Accepting the Bible as a moral guide, so far as it leads
to virtue and to God, yet boldly casting away its crudities and imperfections, whether of Rabbinical origin or
not, but in so doing I ape neither the flippant raillery
of Voltaire, the dreamery of Dupuis, nor the bitterness
of a Fuerbach, or a Compte. I simply follow Truth.

Part Second.

THE SPHINX OF HISTORY: HER TRIAL.

TOPIC FIRST.

CHAPTER I.

THE RIDDLE OF THE SPHINX: ITS SOLUTION.

Asia, with all her weight of years, is younger than
Europe! And here are my reasons for thinking and
saying so, albeit many of them are borrowed from the
great man spoken of in the introductory chapter of this
work. Others of the views are mine own ; while from
a broad field I have taken special pains to garner such
treasures as I found, and which I thus use, not for selfish
purposes, but for the healing of the people of the nations
of that mental strabismus which, whenever they look
for their great fore-parents, either light on Adam, on
one side, or a ringtailed monkey or chimpanzee on the

other, instead of glancing down the vast avenue of the
Ages, and resting upon the manly forms of civilized
progenitors, whose origin is not to be found either in
Eden or Chaillu-ville, in Adam-Kadmon or *Adam
Gorilla.*

The Editor of "THE FUTURE," in the pages of his
matchless journal, writing on the general subject of this
volume, says, most eloquently, that :—

The time has gone by when any serious opposition
can be expected, on the part of intellectual men, to the
presentation of mere facts. The age. indeed, has become, in a paramount degree, an age of facts, and abundant facilities exist for laying before the public all novelties in this line. Science has fully emancipated its
eyes and ears and hands, but the case is very different
when we come to its brain. The man of detail is free
and honored, but the reasoner is ever an object of suspicion, or even of aversion, unless he can manage to
reason in accordance with established opinion. After
all, man is yet but a child ; in favored spots, his senses
are relatively matured, but his brain is everywhere in
an undeveloped condition. The age of Philosophy has
yet to come : there is no adequate provision for the
thinker.

Existing science is rich in materials, but it is relatively poor in philosophy, deficient in organization and
low in the general character of its reasoning ; hence
the scope for discovery in every direction, for all who
can aim at it through the higher methods of organization, analysis, and synthetic evolution. But if this may
be affirmed with any justice of physical science, historical science may, as regards genuine argument, almost
be called a virgin subject, for, with special exceptions
here and there, we have gone on supinely leaning on
tradition, bowing to authority, arguing in vicious cir-

cles, and weighing one unproved assertion against another unproved assertion.

It will be firmly insisted on and practically proved herein, that the historical sciences can only be rationally studied by a rigid and exclusive adherence to those methods of inductive research which have made the physical sciences what they are. There is but one rational method of reasoning, and that is by rejecting all conjecture and credulity, and advancing methodically from certainty to certainty. The moment this method is applied to ancient history its entire structure totters and becomes disintegrated, and facts begin to assume new and wholly unlooked-for combinations and meanings. Hence the startling positions announced, and to be announced, in these pages.*

There is a Europe of which history knows nothing; there is an antiquity which had grown gray and venerable ages before her birth; there are monuments on which she pours darkness instead of light—fossils of a perished world, mementoes of a story longer and stranger than her own.

One power alone can give us back this Europe, this antiquity, this lost story, even in part. That power is *Science*—to her, then, shall we look for light and guidance in this journey into the long forgotten past. History would here be but an *ignis fatuus*, cheating us with phantasms and false hopes, plunging us, ultimately, into inextricable difficulties. Why should we listen to her in cases about which she knows nothing.

History is the daughter of Tradition and Credulity, the foster-child of Hypothetical Criticism. What could reasonably be expected from such a parentage, and such an education, but that which we have got—illusion?

---

* Of " The Future," whence this and many following analagous extracts are taken.

Were an inhabitant of some other sphere to alight
suddenly upon this earth, ignorant of its history, its
literature, and its languages, but with senses capable of
taking cognizance of the facts around him, and a mind
adequate to the due intelligence of the information thus
communicated, what would be his conclusions relative
to the past history and present condition of the races
with whom he was thus brought suddenly into contact?

We will suppose him landed upon the continent of
America, amid the bustle and din of one of the great
cities of the Union. We will suppose that having duly
scrutinized the novelties before him, he advances into
the country, penetrates the forest, traverses the prairie,
goes everywhere, sees everything. What are the historic inferences which these observations must naturally
suggest to him? They will necessarily be to the following effect :—

Here is a region, (he will say,) where dwell two
widely separated races, types of two epochs and two
social conditions, equally far apart. On the one hand
is the dusky Indian with the forest and the prairie for
his scene of action, the bow and the tomahawk, the
bark canoe and the snow-shoe, the wigwam and the
painted skin, the pipe and the string of wampum for
his sole wealth, protection, shelter and ornament; on
the other, an entirely different race, with all the appliances of an advanced civilization. Between these great
extremes there is nothing intermediate. The palace
displaces the wigwam, the steamer the canoe, the rail-
road the narrow trail. Antiquity and To-day sit side
by side.

For the savage, there is no history; what he is
now, he was of old. But there must be a history for
civilization; for civilization is a growth, the expression

and result of a long and eventful struggle. Yet here
are no traces of this struggle or of this growth, no
youth or infancy in any of its stages. No ruins, no
dismantled fortresses or crumbling palaces, or antique
walls, or half-buried cities, meet the eye ; all is new,
from the mansion to the hut. But civilization must
have had stages and fluctuations, and these must have
left vouchers of one kind or other. Everything ancient
could not have been thus completely swept away without humanity itself being swept away with it. No ;
this region never could have been the parent of its present civilization, nor is it possible that races incapable
of accepting this civilization, when offered to them,
could have been its actual creators. It must be exotic,
like the race which holds it ; it must have entered this
region fully formed ; and I must search elsewhere for
its early annals.

For America, read Africa ; for the United States,
Egypt : change a few phrases into their required equivalents, and in this account of a modern colony, you
have the story of the old Nilotic civilizations.

We search Egypt in vain for any trace of the antecedents of its great monuments ; yet the oldest of these
monuments are the mighty pyramids, the wonders of
the world—wonders even in Egpyt, the land of wonders.
Equally vain would be our search through Africa for a
race or nation capable of originating and developing
such a civilization as these monuments imply. The
races of Ethiopia and the North have been unable to
preserve even what they received, and all else in Africa
is barbarian. These mountains of burnt and unburnt
brick, of cut stone and polished granite, speak unequivocally of high natural talent, much acquired knowledge, ages of labor and training. If races possessing
these requisites were ever indigenous in Egypt, they

have left no successors behind them. Individually and
collectively, the pyramids imply a vast aggregate of
labor, wealth, time and ingenuity. Viewed as temples
and public monuments, they are works which only great
empires could erect; viewed as *bonâ fide* tombs, they
speak of wholly fabulous resources ; yet these empires
and their resources repose immediately upon primal
barbarism, as the monuments themselves do upon the
rock and sand of the desert. We no more find beginnings in ancient Egypt, than we find them in modern America.

What is true of the pyramids is equally true of the
other great classes of Egyptian monuments. From the
pyramids to the cavern temples and tombs on the one
hand, and to the exposed temples and palaces on the
other, the transition is sharp and abrupt ; without any
intervening links. The pyramids are monuments of
extreme simplicity ; the temples generally display the
prodigality of ornamentation and detail. The pyramids are without hieroglyphics ; everything else in
Egypt is literally covered with writing. Such transitions as these form no part of the spontaneous life of
a nation. They are invariably the result of compul-
sion and external force. In the most restless and progressive races, conservatism and the tendency to innovation are balanced forces, and change is ever a compromise. In the nations of the East conservatism rules
supreme, and, to all appearance, has ever done so. It
would be vain to seek there for any important spontaneous innovation in the usual habits of thought or action. All human experience, indeed, is decisive against
the possibility of such clear, sharp transitions in the
nature and style of great public works, as we have
here, by any other force than external conquest ; for
we have not now to deal with one of those cases in

which a later age seeks to imitate or reproduce the styles of antiquity, but with one of those in which ancient custom is rudely superseded by entirely new ideas.

Whether we view the pyramids as modified temples, or as *bonâ fide* tombs from the beginning, they must equally have been, in their day, part and parcel of the national thought and feeling, religious as well as civil, and nothing but an imperious necessity could have induced a people to abandon its relations with monuments so majestic, symbols of its faith, and types of its power. Assuredly, then, the nation that had accustomed itself for ages to erect such costly structures for the sepulture of its kings did not spontaneously abandon that custom to hew out of the rocks mausolea of a quite other character. Custom in Egypt was like custom in China, a force which the nation itself had no power to break through, and the burial of the dead was so solemn a portion of the national creed, and court ceremonial is everywhere so regulated by ancient precedent, that the transition from the pyramid to the cavern can be viewed in no other light than an evidence of conquest, and a change in the national faith.

But if the pyramids were simply tombs, what were the temples of a nation which could build such tombs? The pyramids are confessedly the oldest monuments of Egyptian civilization ; if they were built as tombs, Egypt had no temples when they were built, or every vestige of those temples has perished. But Egypt, a great nation, and yet without temples, is an idea which no one will think of maintaining ; and no people will ever devote to the memory of dead-kings monuments surpassing in grandeur those assigned to the worship of living gods. When these, then, were the tombs, the temples must have been surpassingly grand. Where are their vestiges? Not a fragment exists, and not a breath of tradition alludes to them. Such works could not have been utterly swept away while so many inferior ones have defied the ravages of time.

Shall we reverse, then, the obviously rational decision of antiquarians, and say that the existing temples are coeval with the pyramids? How, then, account for the utter want of analogy between the two classes of monuments; for the entire absence of writing, of columns, pilasters, and ornaments of every kind in the one case, with their lavish profusion in the other? As well might we assume that a nation which had erected the palaces and cathedrals of modern England, would be satisfied with burying its kings and heroes in great rude mounds like Silbury Hill, without name, or date, or record. Such violent and needless contrasts are not in the nature of things, and no nation has ever been known to indulge in them.

But, assuredly, the pyramids were never built as tombs; there is no sort of proportion between the object and the enormity of the cost. Any one of the greater of these works would be a serious undertaking for even the wealthiest empire; the liability to have such works repeated in every generation, perhaps several times, is what no nation could possibly think of assuming, or carry out if assumed. Some one has calculated that the great pyramid, which originally covered an area of thirteen acres, could not be built, at the present day, for less than thirty millions sterling; and Mr. Gliddon* gives it as the opinion of a particular builder, that if the materials of the great pyramid were converted into brick, they would build the entire city of Philadelphia. What, then, must such a struc-

---

* Otia Ægyptiaca, pp. 26–29.

ture have cost at the period of its actual erection ! for
however numerous the population, and however cheap
the labor, a modern steam-engine and its concomitants
might easily do the work of hundreds, or even of thousands of Egyptians, with their rude appliances. A
monument of this costliness would be a somewhat
serious compliment to departed worth or royal imbe-
cility.

Lepsius has proposed an ingenious theory in explanation of some of the difficulties involved in this tomb-
theory of the pyramids. According to this theory, the
the size of the monument was always proportioned to
the duration of the reign which it was intended to commemorate. Every monarch, at his accession, began to
build his tomb ; a rather sombre amusement, it must
be confessed, for a royal mind. He erected a nucleus
in the shape of a small pyramid ; every year he built a
a layer of blocks round and above it ; the longer he
lived, the larger it grew ; as he descended, his tomb
arose ; as he grew feeble, his monument waxed strong ;
till the plaything of his early days became, at last, the
devouring monster of his later years, swallowing up
his resources, and devastating his kingdom   No wonder we find a tradition in Egypt which tells us that its
ancient kings were allowed, by law, to live and reign
only a certain number of years. When the period ex-
pired, a priest announced the fact, and the accommo-
dating ruler of millions went straightway forth, took
his cup of poison. and was gathered to his fathers. In
these economical days, the reigns of pyramid-building
kings would be of very moderate duration. for it is a
matter of consequence to settle accounts as speedily as
may be, with claims which annually increase at a rate
so fearfully rapid as this theory implies. How, under
such circumstances, old Phiops, or Cheops, managed to

evade the law, and reign some ninety-four years, is somewhat of a marvel.

Seriously, however, and were there no other grounds of rejection, it would be impossible, without the most unequivocal evidence, to believe in the existence of a system which practically measured glory by age, which was a premium upon regicide and revolt, and which bound a great nation to the liability of building a monument like that of Cheops, for some superannuated fool, while forced to content itself with commemorating, by some ridiculously disproportionate structure, a youthful hero, the pride, perhaps the savior, of his country. Or is it possible to believe that a people so prone to monument-writing as the Egyptians, and who took such pains to perpetuate the names and deeds of their heroes, would leave their tombs, and such tombs, without any record whatever? We shall be told, perhaps, that it was intended to conceal the place of burial, or render it difficult of access, in order to prevent the chances of profanation. But what is the meaning of a monument which seeks to conceal what it was intended to proclaim, or of a secrecy which takes such infinite pains to reveal itself? Better, surely, bury within the rock, than above it, or hew out the mountain's side, as in later times. It is impossible to believe that a nation which had such a passion for writing on everything, would have left the pyramids without inscriptions, had they been erected at a time when this passion had developed itself. They are plainly anterior to this time.

The difficulties of archæology are often due to causes fully within our own control. In the first place, we have studied in too sectional a spirit. We have been Egyptologists, Indianists, Classical antiquarians, British antiquarians, and so forth, instead of being simply

Archæologists. In point of fact, archæology is as much one indivisible science as geology is, and it is as impossible to understand any important section of it in detail, without a general knowledge of the whole, as it would be for geology to fix the succession of strata and the forms of life by an exclusive study of some one region of the globe

In the next place, we have placed an undue reliance on the statements of history, a reliance entirely inconsistent with the requirements of science. The object of all genuine science is the attainment of certainty ; all certainty of deduction must be based on certainty of evidence, and no evidence can legitimately be called certain which cannot be proved to be such. It is but rare, comparatively, that the statements of history admit of any proof, and, therefore, a science, based to any considerable extent on such statements, is but a science in name. Such, unfortunately, is too much the case with archæology even at the present day, whenever it rises beyond simple description. The systematizer and reasoner have to squander away fruitlessly their time, talent, ingenuity, and learning, in finding proofs and explanations for facts which have no existence, and never had.

When we look beyond Egypt, every important idea connected with the pyramids finds its counterpart or explanation in one or other of the great centers of monumental archæology. In Mexico and Central America, for instance, we see by existing evidence that the main, if not only, use made of pyramidal structures was to support a sacred shrine, a temple, or a sacerdotal palace.

Several of the American pyramids, if divested of their crowning shrines and finished to an apex, would differ in no respect from the Egyptian model. We

simply find a greater variety and the evidences of a
longer history in the   Cis-atlantic monuments. A
pyramid at Ocosingo, in Central America, figured in
Mr. Stephens' work,* has very nearly the same inclination as the great pyramid at Ghizeh, while two analogous monuments at Palenque† resemble, in their more
extended base, several monuments at Sakkarah and
Dashour,‡ and are almost identical, in inclination, with
one of the group at Metanyeh. These American pyramids, like most of those of Egypt, are graded and terraced. In other cases we have, in both countries, terraced monuments. There is a very striking general
analogy between one of the terraced pyramids of Mexico, described and figured by Dupaix, in his Monuments
of New Spain,§ and a terraced pyramid at Meydoun,
described in the great French work just referred to.¶
The Mexican structure is found near the town of Quer-
navaca; it has three stages; on the top is a ruined
building, doubtless a temple, or shrine, to which leads
up, from the base of the pyramid, a broad flight of steps,
a very frequent concomitant of the American monuments. The Egyptian structure has also three stages,
and chiefly differs in the middle one being twice the size
of the upper. In both countries we find pyramids with
four, five, and even more stages; the pyramid of Pa-
pantla, in Mexico, had six, if not seven stages, which
number was rarely exceeded. Many of the Egyptian
pyramids which are now carried to an apex have every
appearance of having once been terraced and truncated,

* Incidents of Travel in Central America. London, 1842, Vol. II
pp. 258-9.
† Ibid, pp. 339, 344.
‡ Description de l'Egypte, tom. 4, pl. 72, fig. 4.
§ See Lord Kingsborough's Antiquities of Mexico, Vol. IV., part
1st, pl. 7, fig. 16, and for text V. VI.
¶ Description de l'Egypte, tom. iv., pl. 72, No. 3.

for they have a double inclination. If the lines that spring from the base were carried up till they met, the present height of the pyramid would be nearly doubled, and the inclination of its sides would present a degree of acuteness of which we believe there is no parallel in either country. This form is easily accounted for if we suppose these structures to have been originally terraced, the first inclination representing their lowest stage, and their actual condition, the change made in them when pyramids began to be converted into tombs.

There has always been a close connection between the temple and the tomb. In every age, and in almost every creed, there has been a tendency to deposit, in consecrated spots, the remains of the illustrious dead ; sometimes in the temple or sanctuary itself, sometimes in its immediate vicinity. We see what our own tendencies are in this respect ; we find that the gigantic, though rude mounds and Cromlechs of North-Western Europe, to which it is impossible, on any rational grounds, to attribute a sepulchral origin, as it is to attribute such an origin to the pyramids of Egypt, were, nevertheless, in numerous instances, subsequently used as places of sepulture ; and we also find from the Spanish writers on Mexico, that not only was the idea of sepulture always connected in the national traditions with their pyramids, which were all *Teocalli*, that is temples or *Houses of God*, but that even in the little sanctuaries which crowned the great pyramidal temple of the city of Mexico, and which were respectively dedicated to the two principal deities of the nation, there were deposited, in one of the upper stories. the ashes of some kings and lords who, from special devotion, wished their remains to be so disposed of.* The plain in which the pyramids of *Teotihuacan* were situated, was called

* Clavigero, Storia Antica del Messico, lib. vi , sec. x.

Micxatl, or " the path of the dead," and the hundreds of
small pyramids which surrounded the two principal
monuments were said, by tradition, to contain the ashes
of the princes and nobles of the race which erected
those structures—the ancient Toltecs.

We must remember, too, that the gods of the ancients
were generally believed to have once been terrestrial
and mortal rulers of the nations which principally worshiped them ; this was especially the case in Egypt,
and it was natural, consequently, that their principal
temple should be regarded as their tomb, and in such a
case, an empty sarcophagus in the chamber of a pyramid, or in the sanctuary of a cavern or other temple,
would be a natural and appropriate symbol. Add to
this, that ancient kings, even when most human looking,
are, in numberless instances, nothing else but the gods
of perished creeds, and it will be easy to account for
all the facts, and even for all the traditions connected
with the pyramids of Egypt.

It is easy, too, to understand how, after creeds had
been superseded for ages by rival faiths, and had perhaps even been forgotten, that the great monuments
which they had left behind them should be converted
to other purposes. It is also intelligible how even a
modification of an ancient creed, introduced in connection with a more advanced civilization, might entail a
modification of the ancient temples of a nation without
detracting from their sacredness, and that what was
once both temple and tomb, should subsequently be
tomb only, when the deity to whom that temple and
tomb were dedicated, was now worshiped in temples,
and with ceremonies, of an entirely different order.

From one or other of these causes, the pyramids of
Egypt have, in many cases, undergone modifications.
Some of the graded pyramids have been carried on to

an apex, and their steps filled in so as to make them
present smooth, unbroken, and polished sides, from
base to summit ; some of the truncated pyramids would
seem to have had their stages similarly filled in, but as
many of them were very broad in base. while relatively
inconsiderable in height, like some of the Mexican
structures, instead of going to the heavy cost of com-
pleting the monument from the slightly inclined lines
of the lower terrace, that terrace would seem to have
been treated as a foundation, new lines being struck
from its upper extremities.   Thus filled up, the pyramid
was thenceforth a tomb exclusively, and the final resting-place of the god or king was secured, as far as possible, from the injuries of the elements and the profanation of the impious.

In the archæology of America we may almost trace
the entire history of the pyramid, from the rude earth-
mounds of the Mississippi valley, to the magnificent
structures of Palenque, Uxmal, and the other great
cities of Central America.   We have mounds of various descriptions and constructions, pyramidal terraces
and platforms supporting magnificent temples and palaces, and regular pyramids of almost every character—
some simply graded. others smooth, and others presenting a succession of stages.   The pyramid of Cholula,
one of the oldest monuments of Mexico, had a base
twice as large as the great pyramid of Egypt, being,
according to the measurements of Humboldt,* a perfect square, each side at the base measuring four hundred and thirty-nine metres, though its height was
only fifty-four, little more than that of the pyramid
of Mycerinus.   Like all the American monuments of
its class,† its sides, as in Egypt, faced the cardinal

---

* Vues des Cordillères, Vol. VII., p. 24, &c., folio.

† Antiquities of Mexico.

points; and, according to Dupaix, it was ascended, on the western side, by a flight of steps, which advanced diagonally, and in a zig-zag manner, from terrace to terrace. A similar mode of ascent may be seen in the pyramid of San Cristobal *Teopantepec*.‡ All the pyramidal structures of Mexico had their ascents, approaches, and the openings of their sanctuaries, facing the west.

The pyramid of Cholula had four equal terraces or stages, and its summit commanded a magnificent view of the great plain in which it was situated. It was built of layers of unbaked brick, alternating with strata of clay. The two great pyramids of Teotihuacan were built on the same model, but with a less extended base. The larger of these monuments was fifty-five metres in height and two hundred and eight in breadth of base, the second being of somewhat smaller dimensions. They were formed of clay mixed with small stones, and cased with a thick wall of stone, resembling in these respects one of the pyramids of Sakkara described by Pococke,† as a mass of small thin stones and yellow gravelly mortar enclosed with a wall of hewn stone. This pyramid has six stages, the Mexican monuments in question had four.

The great temple of Mexico, on the arrival of the Spaniards, was a pyramid of five stages. It was in the midst of an enclosure, large enough, according to Cortez, to contain a town of five hundred houses. This enclosure was formed by a thick wall of stone and lime, and contained the residence of the priests, seminaries for youth, &c., together with upwards of forty lesser temples, all, with one exception, likewise pyramidal, and dedicated to different deities.

---

* Antiquities of Mexico, Vol. IV., part 1st, folio 8.
† Description of the East   Vol. I, p. 50.

As the stages of the pyramid receded but slightly, the upper terrace was very extensive, and on it were represented the principle ceremonials of religion in the sight of assembled thousands below. At its eastern extremity were two small sanctuaries, in the shape of towers, dedicated to the two principal deities of the nation—*Tezcatlipoca* and *Huitzilopochtli*. In front of each was a stove, in which the sacred fire was kept perpetually burning, and similar stoves, to the number, it is said, of over six hundred, were, in like manner, kept burning in the court below.

At Teotihuacan, the two principal pyramids, dedicated respectively to the Sun and Moon, were surrounded by several hundreds of small pyramids, forming streets running north and south, east and west. In like manner we find the pyramids of Egypt arranged in groups. Those of Ghizeh present three great structures in decreasing ratio, with many small ones in their immediate vicinity.

The Mexican Temple gives us the key of these variations, as well as that of the pyramidal worship generally. We see that difference of size represents the relative rank of the deities worshiped, and has nothing to do with the varying lengths of kingly reigns. In the one case we have a great duality worshiped on a single temple, in the other a duality, of which each member has its own temple. If in Egypt we find this duality replaced by a trinity, the fact is in full accordance with what we know of its ancient creeds. It would be strange if, among so many analogies, all should be accidental.

The structures that crowned the American pyramids were often of imposing dimensions and great solidity, but in other cases—and this was evidently the older idea of the American monuments—they were insignifi-

cant in size and fragile in material. In the temple of
Mexico the sanctuaries were not only small, but their
two upper stories were formed of wood. No vestige
of a temple or shrine is found on Cholula, nor do we
hear of any at Teotihuacan, though we are told that
these monuments were surmounted by two colossal statues of the sun and moon covered with plates of gold,
and, of course, long since plundered and destroyed.
It is not surprising that monuments so ancient as the
Egyptian pyramids should represent, in this respect,
the older ideas of the American continent, rather than
the far less ancient ones represented chiefly in Central America, as well as in many of the Mexican structures also.

Under every aspect, then, the pyramids are clearly
the oldest monuments of Egypt. The entire absence
of hieroglyphics, their utter simplicity of structure,
the rude materials of which many of them are composed
—viz., unburnt bricks, and even mixtures of rough
gravelly mortar and small flat stones — all these are circumstances so utterly discordant with the associations
of the other monuments of the land, that it is impossible to assign both to the same era, and if so, it is impossible that the pyramids should have been other than
temples originally. If we want, then, to trace the earlier stages of pyramidal architecture, we must look for
them out of Egypt; the very rudest of its monuments
are works far too serious for the infancy of civilization.

The same may be said of the cavern-temples and
tombs. They belong to a distinct phase of thought
and creed ; they represent a distinct era of civilization,
the antecedents of which must be similarly looked for
out of Egypt, for there they do not exist.

Still more emphatically is all this true of the general

architecture of the country. It bursts upon us in meridian splendor; we look around in vain for its earlier and ruder stages.

What is true of the monuments is equally true of the arts and learning of Egypt. Its creeds are neither primitive nor original; its writing is a perfected system from first to last; its implements are hardened copper; there is no "stone age" in its archæology, no real beginnings in any direction: we must look elsewhere for the origin of its civilizations. Let us stretch its antiquity to any extent we please, there must still be other antiquities beyond it. What we see, is relative maturity, what we do not see is the youth and infancy of this maturity.

As with Egypt so with Assyria, Chaldea, Babylon, India, China. China has, properly speaking, no *monumental* antiquities of remote date, none, at all events, known to European research. In Southern India, we find some rude structures of the same class as the Cromlechs and stone circles of North Western Europe, and in Northern Asia we have specimens of the mounds of the same region; but, with these exceptions, all that we know of the great centers of Asiatic dominion and civilization, speaks only of relative maturity.

It is in vain, then, that we search Africa or Asia for the early eras of monumental history. It is still more in vain that we question written history for any information relative to the Primeval World of man. The earliest lispings of history give us but the names of perished empires. She speaks of the East only, and the East, everywhere, bears the unmistakable stamp of a Recipient, not that of a Creator. We must look elsewhere for the Master and Teacher.

CHAPTER II.

CYCLOPEAN STRUCTURES OF SOUTHERN EUROPE AND ASIA MINOR.

AND so Greece and Italy were dark and barbarian when Egypt and Assyria were basking in the meridian splendors of empire and civilization, building pyramids, and towers, and palaces, and temples, spreading their conquests far and wide, and carrying the appliances of advanced knowledge into the recesses of Negro forests, or taming down the Tartar nomad to the usages of stationary existence! So says History, and so says Hypothetical Criticism, endorsing her statement; but there are witnesses to be examined on the other side, also—we have yet to hear what Science and actual Fact have to say upon this matter.

Egypt and Assyria had made bricks for ages; Babylon and Nimroud had stamped theirs with written characters—an elaborated and perfected system. Palaces and temples had grown up upon the soil of Asia, and sculptured slabs had handed over to posterity, in the language of advanced art, the story of national greatness and the symbols of highly developed creeds. On the banks of the Nile, architecture and sculpture had achieved their highest triumphs; polished granite faced the pyramids, forests of gorgeous columns supported the temples, colossal sculptures had risen on every side, and every vacant spot bore a legend or a painting recording some scene of battle or of triumph, some invocation of the gods, or some picture of domestic life. Yet all this while Italy and Greece were unborn as nations; commerce approached not their shores, religion deigned not to think of them, even the accidents of barbarian barter had never revealed to these benighted lands the marvel of a brazen scymitar, or the utility of a metal axe or chisel. Nay, the very waves of the Great Sea, which had a thousand times strewn other shores with wrecks, had never awakened in Græco-Italic minds the least suspicion that, beyond those waters lay the land of the pyramids—the venerable Egypt of unborn Solons and Platos. This is what we have to believe, if history be true—nay, even worse than this.

Many centuries after the times of which we now speak, when the Shepherds had been expelled from Egypt, and the Great Eighteenth Dynasty had repaired the ravages of ages of confusion and foreign despotism, an Egyptian prince, the brother of the reigning monarch, having violated the trust reposed in him, was compelled to fly the land, and with a band of followers reached the shores of Greece, where he was hospitably received, and subsequently became the founder of a line of Argive kings. A century later, the Egyptian Cecrops led a colony from Sais, founded Athens, humanized the rude natives, taught them to worship the gods of Egypt, and made them, in a word, partakers of the fruits of centuries of foreign culture.

Thus was Greece first civilized, and thus did she become the pupil and the imitator of Egypt. So, again, says history.

Upon this statement, the record of monumental facts makes a curious commentary. It tells us that these civilized invaders or colonists, in leaving their native land, left behind them—not their hearts, but their *brains*. In their new homes they raised no temples, they sculptured no statues, they engraved no writing, *they cut no stones*. They neither buried in lofty pyramids, nor worshiped in pillared halls, nor dwelt in granite palaces, nor told the tale of their achievements by

graver or by pencil ; but with marvelous humility and
oblivion, they were content to shelter themselves in
wooden dwellings, rudely shaped by means of stone
axes, pointing their javelins with flint, exchanging their
brazen swords for wooden clubs, and surrounding their
cities with huge walls of unshaped rocks—walls which
one would have thought would have been a very horror to an Egyptian eye. So completely must the bil-
lows of the Middle Sea have washed out of their minds
every idea bearing an Egyptian stamp, that as far as
monumental connection is concerned, they might as well
have dropped from the moon as have sailed from the
Nile. Gentle, indeed, must have been the sway of
these Southern invaders, airy the tread of the Genius
of the Nile, for the current of monumental thought
flows on from first to last in one unbroken stream, and
not a vestige remains to testify that an Eastern teacher
had ever here spoken, or an Eastern ruler ever trodden
this classic soil, until we come to late and evil times.
Such are the thoughts which *monumental* history suggests, and such the kind of commentaries she is ever
making on our traditional legends.

It is quite true, indeed, that the gods of Greece and
Egypt are, in the main, identical, and the same may be
said of the gods of India also ; but this fact does not
prove that either Egypt or India must necessarily have
been the teacher or originator, rather than Greece or
some fourth power. To establish the true order of sequence, in this transmission of ideas, requires an extensive induction and a profound analysis of mythic
facts ; while criticism, hitherto, has usually begged the
question at issue, in accordance with the lights or prepossessions of each individual writer. The ground has,
therefore, to be gone over again, and in a very different spirit. Hypothetical criticism has done its best

and its worst, and the question is no more settled than it was ages ago. It is high time that we should perceive that such questions are only to be settled by a direct appeal to the laws and appliances of inductive science.

The monuments of Greece and Italy have not only a native aspect, but they even present a progressive and unbroken sequence from first to last, and the few specialities which do not belong to the general stream of thought have an exclusively European, never an African or Asiatic character. It is only in comparatively late times, as in one or two paintings in Etruscan tombs, that we see anything in the least calculated to remind us of Egyptian art. But such could not be the case, had Greece or Italy ever derived any considerable amount of instruction from the civilizations of the East, or been to any serious extent subjected to the sway of its monumental empires.

With Asia Minor, indeed, the relations of the Græco-Italic races have always been most intimate. This region, in fact, is essentially European, ethnically as well as monumentally. Eastern Syria, too, is semi-European, and has been repeatedly influenced by European conquest and commercial relations. If the Western wave has sometimes been rolled back—if Phœnicia, in its turn, has acted upon Europe—this is only like saying that Constantinople has acted upon Rome. We see how, out of the civilization spread abroad by Greek and Roman conquest, Asiatic empires, Persian, Saracenic, and Turkish, have subsequently arisen, two of which have seriously re-acted on parts of Europe, and we also see that whatever light belonged to these empires was but a planetary reflection from the Sun of the West. The Turkish rule is actually before us, and it is obvious that while its heart is Asiatic, its brain is

Greek. Might not similar remarks have been equally true when the Moor was in Spain, and the Caliphs in Bagdad? Might they not also have been similarly applicable in the old times of Egyptian and Assyrian dominion? It is just as if, two centuries hence, a British India should invade Britain itself. Before such an event could be possible, the soul would have to be European, however Asiatic might be the body.

Had Egypt or Assyria, then, ruled or colonized in ancient Greece or Italy, they would necessarily have left their mark there. A nation can no more divest itself of its associations than an individual can lay aside his character. A creed can no more migrate without its *impedimenta* of ceremonial, than an army can travel without its baggage. The laws of antiquity are the laws of to-day, and the movements of present humanity the best key to the obscurities of the past. We see that wherever Rome held dominion or planted colonies, we can trace her presence monumentally; and so also with Greece before her; nor do we need historic evidence to assure us that the Saracen has ruled in Spain, or the Turk in the city of Constantine How could the case have been otherwise with the Egyptian, the Assyrian, or the Persian, had they ever been here as rulers or teachers? As little, in fact, could an ancient Egyptian colony have avoided engraving its hieroglyphics or carving out statues of its gods, as a modern Anglo-Saxon colony can migrate into the wilderness without presently setting about the erection of a church, a school-house, and a tavern.

To form, then, a correct estimate of the past, we must begin by ascertaining the facts and laws of the present. Geology has recognized this truth, and benefited accordingly. Before we can become archæologists to any serious purpose, we must first become

ethnologists. As little could geology have preceded
natural history as scientific antiquarianism can pre-
cede the ethnological study of actual man. Our *de
facto* antiquarianism has taken this precedence, and,
as might have been expected, it turns out to be, in the
main, a dream.

How stands the case with actual humanity? Simply
thus, that the noon-day sun, in a cloudless sky, is
scarcely more evident than is the intellectual supremacy of the European races in the present era of the
world. No matter what the cause, the fact is beyond
all rational question. The moderate intellectuality of
the American races either wholly perished or vanished
by eclipse at the first touch of Spanish energy; Africa,
when not barbarian, is simply the reflex of Europe or
of Asia; Central and Eastern Asia are as fixed as
their mountains, or wherever there is an intellectual
movement, it obeys an impulse from without. Even
Western Asia, though mentally higher, has, at the
present day, almost as little spontaneity of advance as
the more eastern regions. Europe alone is inherently
mobile, restless, progressive, enterprising, cosmopolitan. The theatre of Asia is Asia; the theatre of
Africa, Africa; the theatre of America, America; but
the theatre of Europe is the world, and the theatre of
its higher thoughts the very universe itself. This is
more or less true of every one of its nationalities,
emphatically so of several of them. It is more or less
true of every educated man, in every one of these
nationalities. We wake from our slumbers, descend
to our breakfast tables, and there as naturally expect
to find spread out before us the record of what is doing
at the ends of the earth, as we expect to see the physical comforts necessary for repairing the wear and tear
of the previous day. It is simply a matter of circum

stances, whether we look more eagerly to home or to foreign news. Some transaction at the antipodes may be that which absorbs all our thoughts; it may mean for us happiness or misery, wealth or beggary, life or death. We make but little difference as to place; it is often but the turn of a hand whether we erect our dwelling on ancestral soil, or settle down in the woods of America or the plains of Australia.

Every *body* must have its *head;* and beyond all question, the body of present humanity has no head but Europe; that is to say, of course, the *races* of Europe, wherever they may dwell. Every living body, also. is expected to grow or to have grown, and we know it to be a general law that the higher portions of any growth are the latest in reaching their ultimate development. It would not, therefore, be anything strange if, at certain periods, the chest or abdomen was found to be more advanced in development than the head; but it would do violence to all analogies were we to find the different regions of any body periodically interchanging functions—were we to find that the head of to-day was the stomach of yesterday, and would be the lungs of to-morrow. But such must have been the case if Egypt, as Egyptian, or Assyria, as Assyrian, or India, as Indian, was ever the real center of intellectual life and movement—the brain of humanity. Analogy here rises up against history, and opposes fact to fables. Ethnical research equally does so, and shows us that the present superiority of Europe is not a thing of accident—not the mere fortune of war, or the transfer of material resources, but a thing innate, organic—a superiority of structure and function, a superiority of temperament and material, a supe-. riority of blood and race. If this be the character of European supremacy, then, humanity must obey other laws than those of zoology, or Europe has always been the place of its head. But we are not thrown exclusively upon zoological evidence in this case. History, indeed, knows nothing of Europe as the head of humanity, until it comes down to the times of classic Greece und Rome ; but archæology lights up the darkness of the past, and reveals to us the fossils and the footprints of an older Europe—*of a Europe which also was cosmopolitan.*

The nations of the earth may have their rotation in development and decay, in organic action or remission ; but they have no rotation in natural authority or power, and where they seem to have, there is illusion. We are looking on the surface of things ; we are dazzled by reflected light ; and the great under-current of realities escapes our notice. We look, for instance, upon ancient Rome, and we talk of it as if it were all Roman, and forget, for the moment, that Italy was in those days a great vortex which drew into itself large accessions of the native talent, enterprise, and energy of all surrounding regions, even of many which history calls barbarian. We look upon modern England, and think ourselves all English, and forget, for the time, that that land is the refuge for the persecuted brave, the ark of political deluges, the mart of every form of intellectuality. We forget how Italy sends us her artists, Germany her musicians, France her patriots, and even distant Phœnicia her merchants ; and how all of these pay us back with interest, and often when we least know of it, whatever of benefits our protection or wealth has conferred. We look upon America, and think ourselves American, totally oblivious of the fact that we are a concrete people, and that we have been made what we are by the force of circumstances, of blood-minglings, and our central position on the globe ;

for we are mid-way between old Europe, and still
older Asia and Africa. Even viewed from within,
we are not one but many; at least, three distinct and
important nationalities converging into a focus their
united energies and talents. Under common or familiar names, under undistinguishable features or accent,
we are perpetually appropriating to our own glory the
patient industry, the clear practical sense, the indomitable energy and force of character which Scotland is
ever sending us, as well as the dash, the enthusiasm,
the varied talent, the eloquence, and the genius of
Ireland. True it is, all three form one consistent—
one natural aggregate, despite political conflicts and
theories; but are not one race or nation. And if
we can thus so easily overlook, in our reasonings, present and familiar facts, how much easier is it for us to
attribute to the native races of ancient empire, qualities
which may not at all have belonged to them—qualities
which may have been wholly an importation from without, which may have belonged exclusively to the masters who ruled them, and who, while bearing historically their name, may, nevertheless, be of very different
blood and lineage.

While, therefore, it is unquestionable that there is a
succession in empires, an ebb and flow, a transfer and
a journeying in the movements of civilization, it is not
the less true that nations and races have their inherent
specialities of character, and a fixity of hierarchical
position which, while perfectly consistent with development and progress, entirely negatives that rotation of
attribute and rank which a superficial view of history
may countenance, and which popular theories are so
fond of insisting upon. The growth of humanity, as a
whole, is as much an affair of zoological law as the
growth of its individual elements. There must be re

gularity and control in its masses, however chaotic may
seem the relations of its constituent atoms; for without such regularity and control these atoms could not
maintain their existence.

This hierarchy in race and nationality is not an isolated fact in zoology; on the contrary, it is a general
rule. This rule is but gradually dawning on the minds
of naturalists, but they have long been preparing for it
by the facts they have collected relative to the different
fauna and flora of the earth. If these facts be carefully
collated, they will be found to show that natural provinces vary in rank as well as in general character;
and that just as we may speak of the region of Australia as among the lowest of these provinces, Europe
possesses claims to a marked superiority over all of
them. Excluding things unfitted for the climate as
regards mere temperature, it may confidently be asserted that in no other region of the earth have so many
of the higher types of vegetable and animal life attained so high a status as in Europe, and that in no
other have introduced plants and animals manifested
so little tendency to degenerate, so frequent a tendency
actually to improve. All this is as true of man as of
the inferior animals. The Jew, for instance. has not
degenerated in Europe or America. On the contrary,
he has advanced in mental expansion and general intellectuality; and this, seemingly, exclusive of anything that may be due to an occasional mixture of
blood.

Except, then, as regards traditional legends, and the
criticisms based on them, there is nothing incongruous
in the idea of the pre-historic superiority of the European races. The laws of the present necessitate it, the
facts of zoology harmonize with it, monumental evidence admits of no other conclusion without doing

violence to the laws of inductive reasoning. Europe, therefore, is now civilized and dominant, not because fortune has so determined it, or because it has come to its turn to be so; but it is so because it has come to its turn to take a new and greater leap than ever in development—to be, in a more complete sense than ever, the master of this earth, the brain and intellect of humanity. The *New Zealander* may, indeed, one day stand upon the ruins of a perished London; but when he looks around him, he will not find savages in the land. He may, possibly, find a country torn by civil discord, or slumbering in relative torpidity, or held down by the strong arm of a foreign despotism; but assuredly the arm that holds down a British or American race will have European blood in its veins, and though there *has* been savageism here as well as elsewhere, yet the entire sweep of terrestrial development emphatically proclaims that the days of European and American savageism have vanished never to return. As well might you expect the Megatherium and Iguanodon back again, as a seriously retrograde Europe, or America.

CHAPTER III.

PRIMEVAL EUROPE.

There is a sense in which yesterday is younger than to day, and in which the "wisdom of antiquity" is but the voice of Childhood.

There was a time, and no distant time either, when a mountain gorge revealed nothing to the eye but a mass of rocks irregularly broken through, and when every bone of unusual size, or fossil of unusual shape, was the remnant of a giant, a freak of Nature, or a monument of the deluge. For the history of the earth, that time

has passed, never to return ; for the history of man, that
time is still the present.

Touched by the spell of Science, the mountain gorge
is now a written book, every line pregnant with meaning, every stratum the history of an epoch, every fossil
the record of a vanished race. The bone, indeed, is the
bone of a giant still, but of a giant of quite another
mould from the monster of human credulity ; and the
strange-looking fossil, though thrown into being in a
mood of Nature, very different from any which she now
puts on, was yet planned and fashioned with the same
seriousness and care as the very latest of her productions. There are, too, here, records of a flood, and of
many floods, but they are floods on whose waters no
mystic ark ever floated, and for whose devastations no
crime of man's commission is responsible. They are
floods which speak of millions of years : floods which
had become rocks countless ages before the date which
human story had fixed for their rise and ebb.

And thus the veil has fallen, and man at last sees
that ancient books knew nothing of the history of this
universe.

But every generation must purchase its own experience, and pay for its special wisdom the price of its
special folly. And thus the generation that has dared
to face even the worst anathemas of theology, still trem-
bles before the harmless frowns of a few literary critics,
and still devoutly believes in the civil story of ancient
Italy, after having ventured to confront with doubt the
sacred records of Judea.

But the veil has begun to fall here also, and if in
these pages we presume to lower it still further, and
with no ceremonious hand, the reader should remember
that we but do for the present time, and for a special
subject, things which he has long learned to rejoice at

and commend in other persons, and times, and topics.
If we look at a ruined temple, or at the remnant of
an ancient wall, without forethought or preparation, or
plan of study, or law of reasoning, and then decide or
speculate about its founders, its era, or its purpose, just
as chance, or the accidents of our previous knowledge
and prepossessions may determine, are we not simply
in the position of the pre-geological critic discoursing
learned folly about the flood, and the giant, and the
freak, or spinning world-theories out of the vacuum of
a fancy without facts? If we wish to evolve a stable
deduction, if we wish to build up a system which the
next observer will have to add to, instead of pulling
down, we must give up the idea of building until we
have made some progress in the collection and selection
of our materials, learned the fundamental rules of our
trade, and acquired due facility in the use of our tools.
The age, indeed, has awakened to the clear consciousness of the first of these requisites, and has worthily exerted itself in the collection and sifting of facts, but it
is still much in arrears as regards the second, and still
builds very much at hazard, or by the aid of rules, which
however sanctioned by tradition, have never yet produced any really substantial result.

If we want to understand the character and place of
a fossil, must we not previously understand the structure and physical history of existing animals? Or how
shall we correctly estimate the laws of action which
have governed past humanity, while leaving out of consideration the laws and facts of the present? What,
then, can a pre-ethnological archæology possibly be but
a direct equivalent of a pre-zoological geology? In
these pages, then, the reader must not expect to find
any deference shown, or any special attention given to
reasonings which have preceded, or which ignore, the

ascertained facts and laws of the physical history of man.

In previous chapters it has been shown that the monuments of Egypt, though for the most part bearing an unequivocally native aspect in general style and workmanship, have nevertheless, in their sudden transitions and entire absence of preparatory stages, a very exotic character as to origin. But nothing of this can be said of the region of facts into which we are now about to penetrate. The archæology of Italy, Greece, and Asia Minor, presents us with a history without breaks, with a maturity whose early stages may be traced almost to the birth. For although there be far older monuments in Europe than any which this classic soil can show, they belong to wholly other spheres of thought, and have in no way served as types to the styles or the structures on which repose the beautiful creations of Græco-Italic genius.

The oldest and rudest monuments which meet us in this part of Europe, have received the name of Cyclopean, from the gigantic character of their structure. Popular ignorance found an easy refuge from doubt in attributing to mythic monsters of superhuman strength and size, erections which seemed incommensurate with the powers of current humanity ; and learned credulity found it easier or safer to refine on the popular traditio than to supplant it with more accurate thought, and so the name has come down, and may now very well be preserved, since it distinguishes the group, without creating any risk of error for the modern inquirer, for we are as little in danger of believing in the Cyclops at the present day, as of worshiping the gods against whom they warred.

The Cyclopean structures, as they present themselves in Greece, Italy, and Asia Minor, consist, mainly, in their earlier form, almost exclusively of works of a defensive character. They are walls, or fragments of walls, which originally encompassed cities or citadels, or helped to increase the strength of some place already strong by nature. Their essential characteristic is their strength and massiveness, and the contract between their rude simplicity, and the skill, labor, and appliances, which they otherwise evince. This contrast is especially marked in the older ranges of these monuments.

Three distinct styles of construction are discernable in the Cyclopean works, and these styles plainly imply three distinct eras in their erection. The first and second styles are especially distinct, the third rises by easy gradations from the second, and thence passes into the later or Post-Cyclopean styles of classic times.

In consonance with these distinctions, we name the Cyclopean structures as Primitive, Secondary, and Tertiary, as to style and era.

The Primitive Cyclopean walls are composed, exclusively, of blocks of stone entirely rude, but of so great a size that their mere weight, conjoined with the skill with which they are laid, and the general thickness of the wall, constitutes an erection of immense strength.

Whoever has passed over a stony country, and noticed the rude walls which, instead of hedges, separate field from field, has had before him the rudimentary idea of a Cyclopean wall. To understand the reality, he must imagine that wall some twenty feet thick, and some thirty, forty, or even sixty feet high, the general size of its stones from three to seven feet, the largest being rocks of ten feet in length, with a corresponding breadth and thickness; and, finally, he must imagine these materials placed with consummate care and skill, and the interstices filled up with small stones, and he

will have an image before his mind of one of those
gigantic structures, which have resisted, for thousands
of years, the ravages of time, and which nothing but
the earthquake's shock, or the cannon's play, or the deliberate dismantling of a victorious enemy, would seem
adequate to disturb.

A brief description of one of these works will give
a sufficient idea of the general character of all, the
variations being little more than differences in the extent of the space enclosed, or in the general thickness
or height of the walls.

Hamilton,* one of the travelers who has examined
these structures in Greece with great care, thus speaks
of the walls of Tiryns, one of the very oldest of the
Grecian cities. The walls of Tiryns "present a stupendous specimen of the most ancient mode of military
building in Greece : even among the ancients it was
reported, as well as Mycene, to have been the work of
the Cyclops. It would seem from the dimensions of
the space enclosed within these gigantic masses, which
is no more than two hundred yards long and fifty wide,
that the remains now seen, formed only the acropolis of
the ancient city ; though the words of Pausanias hardly
warrant the supposition. His description of the walls
can only be explained by an inspection of them. They
consist of vast irregular masses of rock, some of them
equal in solid contents to a cube of six feet, and the
least of which, Pausanias says, could not be moved by
a yoke of oxen. The intervals between them are filled
up, or as the same geographer calls it, harmonized by
smaller masses, without any cement. The walls are
twenty-five feet thick, of solid masonry. and where the
upper part has not fallen, are forty feet in height."

* Remarks on the Fortresses of Ancient Greece. Archæologia, Vol.
XV., pp. 320, 321.

Dodwell, who has given exact drawings of these ruins as they now stand, states the dimensions of the space enclosed as 244 yards by 54, and the general thickness of the walls as twenty-one feet—in some cases twenty-five. Their present height, where most perfect, is forty-three feet, and their original height, probably, was not less than sixty feet. The largest stones are between nine and ten feet long, by four in thickness, the usual size being from three to seven feet.*

Walls of this kind, some of them enclosing extensive spaces, as at Norba, in the ancient Latium, are found in various parts of Greece, Italy, and Asia Minor, and even beyond these centers in individual instances. In some cases they form considerable ruins, still in most they are now nothing more than the lower portions of walls of more recent date, which have obviously been erected on the site of ancient strongholds. But wherever they are found, in connection with other styles, they are never superposed. Like the granite, they underlie all other strata, sometimes pushing up, as it were, between them, but in this case, more rigid than the granite, never resting on them.

The second style differs from the first in a very remarkable manner. The stones are, as before, irregular and large, but now they are accurately cut and fitted—so that this second style consists of irregular polygons carefully cut and fitted, *without cement*. So careful is the workmanship in many instances, that numerous travelers have spoken of these walls with astonishment, and have described the working of the stones as so accurate that the point of a pen-knife could not be inserted between them. Small stones are naturally excluded from

* Views in Greece. Pl. II. to IV., pp. 3 and 4.

these secondary walls, as they would but needlessly add to the labor, while diminishing the strength of the structure.

This secondary style is more extensively diffused than the primary, is often superposed upon it, or is otherwise used in repairing, especially in gateways, the dilapidations made by war or time in walls of the primary style.

In these two styles nothing like successive courses or strata in the laying of the stones is at all possible, and therefore they are distinguished from later styles as being *unstratified*.

A greater or less amount of stratification is the distinguishing feature of the third Cyclopean style. In walls of this kind there is always a tendency to have the upper and lower faces of the blocks more or less parallel, while the lateral faces form with them angles of every degree of acuteness or obliquity. In this manner we see—first, a progressive tendency to form genuine strata ; and parallel with this, though slower in development, a tendency towards the formation of regular rectangular parallelograms. This latter is the usual style in the classical era of purely Greek constructions. Roman works present the further advance of being often formed of absolutely cubical blocks. Thus we have in Graeco-Italic art four eras and styles of construction, Primitive, Secondary, Tertiary, and Recent ; for classic architecture is truly but recent, when compared with the remote stretch of the older Cyclopean structures.

Thus far, however, we have stated merely the general facts and results—we must now endeavor to show the special evidence which justifies the deductions implied by these results.

First, then, it is obvious that the rude style here named primary, is the older of the four—first, because

it is the one which would most naturally present itself
to the mind in the infancy of art and knowledge, the
more especially as it fully accomplishes the purpose intended ; secondly, because it often underlies the second
style, while never overlying it, nor ever co-existing with
it without implying priority in the circumstances of that
co-existence ; thirdly, because it implies ignorance of
the use of metal tools fitted for conveniently shaping
and working blocks of stone, while the works of the
secondary, and all subsequent styles, necessitate the
knowledge and use of such tools ; and fourthly, because
the secondary style acknowledges the pre-existence of
the primary, by imitating its arrangements without necessity, and often at great inconvenience, thus showing
that it was an encroachment on pre-existing ideas, and
that, like all such encroachments, it was a compromise
between the new thought and the old or a mere development of the latter.

The first of these categories needs no special remark.
Abstractly considered, the rudeness of this primary
style would be little more than a simple presumption
in favor of its antiquity, but it becomes an argument of
high importance when taken into connection with ulte-
rior considerations.

The second category speaks for i'self. Hundreds
of these monuments have been ex mined and described of late years, and we are not aware of the existence of any fact that would even tend to militate
against the statements here made.

[The only traveler we know of wh even seems to
have spoken adversely to the sequence here insisted on,
is Sir Charles Fellows, and he speaks vaguely, and
under the bias of pre-existing views. for he was opposed
to the Pelasgian theory of Petit-Radel which first fixed
modern attention on these Cyclopea structures and
therefore drawing no clear distinctions between the

different styles, he often uses the words Cyclopean and
Pelasgian in such a manner as to leave it uncertain
whether he is speaking of the rudest or of the most
advanced of them, or whether he is speaking of a
Cyclopean style at all, for this term is often with him,
as with several other writers, simply synonymous with
gigantic. He seldom, for instance, distinguishes between an original wall and subsequent repairs or im-
provements. A Cyclopean wall of secondary or tertiary
style, with gateways or buttresses of a more modern
character, are with him simple contemporaneousness,
while an old erection on a rock with more recent fillings in beneath, in the side of that rock, would be a
sequence of the ruder over the more advanced, as would
likewise be the case, if in a wall of regular polygons
we found some gigantic masses of stone, less regular in
shape, placed over gateways or other points where
solidity was a higher consideration than regularity.
Thus, valuable and precise as are the researches of Sir
Charles Fellows, in the main, they very often want both
precision and detail when he speaks of the present class
of structures. The passage to which we have special
reference, occurs in his description of the ruins of
Pinara, in Lycia, and is as follows :

"The walls and several buildings of the city were of
the Cyclopean style, with massive gateways formed of
three immense stones. I measured one over the portal,
which was fourteen feet in length ; the buttresses of
the same walls were of regularly squared stones.

"These modes of building were both used in the
same works, and certainly at the same time ; the Cyclopean, which is generally supposed to be the older made,
I have often seen surmounting the regular Greek squared
stone walls. The whole city appears to be of one date
and people, and, from its innumerable tombs, must have
existed for a long series of generations, and from a
very early period."—*Discoveries in Lycia;* 1840. pp.
140, 141.

With all deference, these are *pre-geological* statements, deficient in classification, ignoring the laws of
sequence in thought, and the known phenomena of
existing life. But even were they true, they do not

touch the point actually under consideration—viz., the invariable priority of the style here named primary.]

The third category involves very important considerations, and must be considered in some detail.

The primary style presents itself under circumstances of a wholly unequivocal character. It is found exclusively in great public works, and those of a defensive kind—viz., walls of towns, citadels, or other strongholds. No rude, scattered, ignorant, or poor populations, could need, erect, or even defend the generality of these constructions. They speak exclusively of populous, settled, organized, industrial, wealthy and intelligent nations, and, if so, they necessarily speak of the infancy of art and knowledge. These structures are very numerous, far too numerous to be needed by any but populous nations. They are widely distributed in Greece, numerous in Middle Italy, and met with in all the principal States of Asia Minor, as well as in several of the islands of the Archipelago, and they have the aspect of belonging to a distinct era, and that of long duration, as well as of clearly implying foreign intercourse and conquest. They rapidly thin off, and soon cease altogether, as .we advance to the north, either in Greece or Italy. In Italy, the Po seems to be their boundary. To the South, the African shore is their limit; here they are known in a single spot only—viz., in the vicinity of Tunis, a very old monumental site. In the west, they have possibly reached the eastern coast of Spain;* but the statements given on

---

* Most unfortunately, the celebrated Louis Petit-Radel, who may be said to have created all our knowledge of the Cyclopean monuments by first directing attention to their specialities, devoting his whole life to their study, and inspiring with a portion of his own enthusiasm, numerous travelers and learned men, adopted the theory of their being all monuments of one era and people, the Pelasgian; and this unlucky assumption has introduced great vagueness. not only into his

this point in Petit-Radel's work are vague, and we have
not been able to obtain access to the original accounts.
The sites spoken of are Saguntum (now Murviedro),
Tarrogona, and Toledo ; and on the coast of France,
Marseiles and Aix are also mentioned. Eastward,
they have probably reached Syria, if not even Persia.*

This central multiplicity and progressive thinning off
speaks unequivocally of empire and conquest, and all
other circumstances confirm the indication.   But a
population requiring a multitude of walled cities thus
distributed, means one which has something to preserve,
which is warlike in character, and surrounded by warlike neighbors ; which is wealthy enough to devote a
considerable share of its time, labor, and resources, to
great public works ; which has distant communications
by sea and land ; which has sufficient talent in its ruling
races to select the sites of its fortresses with consummate skill, and to transport and elevate immense quantities and heavy masses of stone in a manner that would
considerably tax even the ingenuity and resources of
modern times ; while a perfect uniformity of style and
circumstances, in the great public works of several different races and nations, is only intelligible under the
circumstances of a unity in rule and era.   We have
here before us then, in these primary Cyclopean structures, the vestiges of an Empire, not of distinct national, still less provincial, rules.   But an empire situated in this part of the world, and erecting such works
as these, yet leaving behind no sign of temple or of

---

own statements and observations, but also into those of most of the
writers who have adopted his views. We are, therefore, often unable
to determine to which of two, or even three styles a particular monument may belong. The principal work of Petit-Radel is his *Recher-
cher sur les Monuments Cyclopéens.* Par. 1841.

* Petit-Radel. Ibid. pp. 84, 98, 99 and 102.

palace, and no indication of ever having touched a metal tool, could not possibly be otherwise than very ancient.

National wealth and power mean agriculture, social organization, intelligence, enterprise, commerce, traveling. Great wealth and power mean all these things intensified. They also mean curiosity, and the power of giving and receiving knowledge. They mean a people acquainted with all its neighbors, visiting them, buying from them, selling to them, prying into their concerns, sending and receiving embassies, quarrelling with them, fighting with them, invading and despoiling them, making peace, exchanging presents, interchanging curiosities, borrowing advantages and giving them ; and in a word, doing all those things which neighboring nations now do, and ever have done, since nations came into existence.

But the idea of a nation of any kind under these circumstances, to say nothing of a great empire, building walls like these when they could, with infinitely less labor, have built far better ones, or remaining ignorant of the use of metal instruments with the advanced civilizations of Egypt and Assyria blazing at their very doors, is simply ridiculous. Such conjunctions have no precedent, and would necessitate mental and physical phenomena that cannot co-exist, since they directly negative each other.

We already know that, somehow or other, metal tools found their way into the rude sepulchres of Northern and Western Europe, and Eastern Asia, and that, with a uniformity of alloy which speaks of singleness of origin, they meet us in Greece as in Egypt, in Britain as in India, in Mexico as in Assyria. Do we not see, too, that our own manufactures, our axes, and knives, and guns, now travel to every corner of the

earth, and to every recess of the great continents, pene-
trating forests, crossing mountain chains, passing from
hand to hand, and tribe to tribe, by the accidents of
of war or barter, into regions' where the white man's
foot has never trodden, or a civilized voice been heard
for ages?

Besides, what could have prevented men, acquainted
with the use of metal tools, from at least partially
shaping their materials, especially in their gateways,
which they have been forced to construct in a very inferior style—small, narrow, and with sides sloping in-
wards till they meet at a point? They could, too,
have attained increased strength with less ponderous
weights, and obviated the necessity of those fillings in
of small stones. They could not have been indifferent,
where they have taken so much pains, nor have minded
trouble or expense, where they have encountered such
an enormous amount of both, nor have been stupid,
while displaying so much skill and resource, nor ignorant, while the knowledge required, had it existed
among their neighbors, must have forced itself upon
their attention in a thousand different ways. They
were, therefore, ignorant, solely by anteceding the era
of that knowledge.

Or what could have induced those who erected the
secondary structures from squaring their blocks, as
later times have done, and thus obviating that infinitude of lines, and that minuteness of fitting, which the
style necessitates. were it not that their eyes were fa-
miliarized with unstratified walls, while they had never
beheld a regular one; that their fathers had built with
irregular blocks, and that it was some amount of presumption to differ at all from heroes and sages who
had erected such mighty works as Tiryns, and Lyco-
sura, and Mycene, and Norba, and the hundred other

wonders of these early times? The ever living laws of development, association, and conservatism, can alone account for these things, and they account for them fully.

Here, then, rises before us a great primeval Europe, growing and conquering, and passing away, while Egypt was still a blank, and Assyria a desert— while temple, and palace, and column, and granite statue, and sculptured slab, were ideas unborn, and the ring of a metal tool a sound which had never yet been heard upon this planet, and we go on believing in a history which ignores this grand old Europe, and heaps upon its venerable fossils the rubbish of its myriad fables. High time we should open our eyes, and question the guides that have led us into these abysses of gloom, these quagmires of inextricable contradictions. High time to remember that common sense is needed in history as well as in science, and that common sense has but one mode of working, whether it work in science, or in history, or in creed, or in business.

TOPIC SECOND.

THE FICTIONS OF CHRONOLOGY, ANCIENT AND MEDIEVAL.

CHAPTER IV.

In the chapters now presented to the reader under the above heading, we shall have to present a range of deductions which, if announced without preparation, would necessarily be received as not merely very rash, but even as altogether wild conclusions. We have all of us been so accustomed, in this direction, to move in beaten tracks, historical scepticism, even where it exists,

has usually assumed such mild and cautious forms, that
the demands here made upon the reader's good sense,
simple and natural as they are in themselves, will nevertheless alarm him by their magnitude, as much as they
startle him by their novelty.

Yet such ought not to be the case. A moment's reflection ought to prove to him that his faith in history
rests on no solid foundation. He accepted it as a
child, when his credulity was eager, his knowledge imperfect, his judgment immature, and his experience un-
purchased; and he has continued to acquiesce in it as
a man, not because he has since proved its truth,'but
simply because custom, association, or the want of
special stimulants have left him without any motive for
doubt, or without one sufficiently powerful to overcome
the *vis inertiæ* which these circumstances are calculated
to produce.

The results here offered are certainly very strange,
when viewed in connection with the actual state of
opinion, but then they have been produced by mental
processes the direct reverse of those usually employed
in historical inquiries. Historic criticism has hitherto
been, in the main, hypothetical criticism, and hypothetical criticism can produce no better result than hypothetical certainty, which is no certainty at all. Whatever has gone beyond this has been the result of entirely different processes, but these processes have
hitherto been applied only fractionally and incidentally, and the great body of historic data still rests,
after centuries of research and criticism, on no better
foundation than a tradition of which the stages cannot be traced, and of which the statements cannot be
verified.

It will readily be admitted that history is something
more than an amusement for a leisure hour or a field

of exertion for literary curiosity. It is either an important truth, or a mischievous fallacy. In so far as it is true, it tends to give us correct ideas, not only of remote events, but also of human nature itself. In so far as it is false. it is an illusion in the one case, a snare in the other. The politician draws from it his illustrations, and bases upon it his arguments : the teacher deduces from it rules of conduct for the formation of character and the guidance of the young : and the philanthropist builds upon it schemes of progress or regeneration, which are to change the present and predetermine the future. It is, therefore, a very serious matter whether the materials of all these workings be substantial truths or idle dreams—the sports of fancy and the blunders of criticism.

At the very outset, it must be observed, that there is one grave inconvenience attached to ancient history which is far too little appreciated, and much too generally ignored altogether. It is this : ancient history is mainly based upon statements which, even when true, cannot be proved to be true, as they do not admit of any present verification. This fact alone makes it obviously illogical to base upon such statements any argument aiming at certainty.

Many of the oldest known materials of both medieval and ancient history are rude chronicles, in which events are recorded without any attempt at proof, or any reference even to authorities. The more formal histories, with partial exceptions, add little in the way of evidence to the bald statements of the chronicles, beyond the surmises or conjectural criticism of the writer. Even the very existence and era of the writers, or supposed writers of these histories, are rarely matters of demonstrable fact, but points decided upon inferential evidence, often of the slightest and most ques

tionable character ; so that what is generally viewed
as contemporaneous history is usually as hypothetical
as any other.   Nay, even when statements are tested by
a reference to actual monuments, the era of those monuments has usually been previously settled by the very
history which they are subsequently called upon to test,
so that the historical argument is usually an argument
in a vicious circle, supporting one unproved statement
by another unproved statement.

This is, in all respects, a false position, and there is
but one possible escape from it—that is, by cutting the
Gordian knot, abandoning hypothetical reasoning altogether, and working exclusively with demonstrable
facts : in a word, by substituting science for credulity,
and rational deduction for insane attempts to reach
certainty by means which cannot by any possibility lead
to it.

The moment we determine upon this course, we have
no longer to complain of any dearth of genuine evidence.   All the statements of history become at once,
under this aspect, available and unquestionable facts.
Whatever their character otherwise, they are facts in so
far as their simple existence is concerned ; they are the
wrecks and fossils of ancient thought ; they bear the
impress of more or less ancient events ; let us use them
as the geologist uses his wrecks and fossils, and, like
him, we shall reproduce a history which requires no
credulity in its acceptance, and needs offer no statement
unsusceptible of strict verification.

We shall not tantalize the reader's patience by carrying him, in the first instance, through those preliminary explanations and evidences which will be finally
necessary for the full comprehension of the general argument, but endeavor, at once, to enlist his interest in
the inquiry, by laying before him a specimen of the

results which this new mode of viewing an old subject has already produced in the department of chronology.

He is certainly not prepared, by his knowledge of
real life, to expect that the important events of history
—the rise and fall of empires, and states, and dynasties,
and creeds—are arranged by chance or Providence into
minute accordance with certain standard periods, always the same, however times and circumstances may
vary, still less that these events often contrive to obey the
laws of two or more conflicting periodicities. In modern times, certainly, such things do not occur; but if
ancient and mediæval history be true, they have occurred formerly innumerable times—almost, indeed, as
a universal rule.   Either, then, the course of Nature has
entirely changed within the last few centuries, or the
far greater portion of general chronology is a system
and a theory, not a fact.

The following details will give some idea of the evidences on which the foregoing statements are based,
and of the degree to which they are likely to admit of
verification.   We have taken for illustration the Roman
annals, as being familiar to most educated readers, and
as offering one of the most continuous, sober, and mat-
ter-of-fact-looking narratives which antiquity presents.
What, in fact, can be expected to stand, if Roman story
be found to mock our trust?

The following quotation from the illustrious Niebuhr,
with which we preface our exposition, has a special interest on this occasion, and we would remind those
whose nature and habit of thought lead them to attach
great weight to authority and precedent, that we have
merely endeavored to do universally—in regard to all
epochs and all histories—what Niebuhr has so well accomplished in those instances in which he has been able

to persuade himself, not only to reject baseless authorities and listen to the instincts of his own clear common sense, but also to curb that impetuosity of mind which has so often led him, while justly rejecting the assumptions and conjectures of his predecessors, to supply their place with assumptions and conjectures of his own :—

" Wherever in history." says Niebuhr, " we see numbers capable of being resolved into arithmetical proportions, we may say, with the greatest certainty, that they are artificial arrangements to which the history has been adapted, as the philosopher exclaimed when he saw mathematical diagrams on the sand, 'I see traces of man.' The course of human affairs is not directed by numerical proportions, and wherever they are found, we may, according to a law which Leibnitz would have laid down as an axiom, declare unhesitatingly that there is an arrangement according to a certain plan. Such artificial arrangements we find in the Indian and Babylonian eras; large spaces are divided according to certain numerical proportions. Such, also, is the case with the history of Rome, from its foundation down to the burning of the city by the Gauls. For this period 360 years were assumed, which number was taken for granted by Fabius and Polybius, who copied it from a table (Greek, *pinas*). Of these 360 years, 240 were allowed to the kings, and 120 to the commonwealth. In all Roman institutions the numbers ten, thirty, and twelve, play an important part; all numerical combinations connected with Rome arise out of multiples of three, which is most frequently multiplied by ten, as 30, 300, 3,000. Such, also, is the number of the 360 houses of Athens in its ancient constitution. Of the 240 years assigned to the kings, 120 is the half, and hence the middle of the reign of Ancus Martius, the fourth king, falls in 120. He is the creator of the plebeian order, and, consequently, 120 is the date of the origin of the plebeians. Thus we have three periods, each containing ten times twelve years; 120 years previous to the existence of the plebeian order, 120 with plebeians, and 120 without kings. How could it ever have happened that of seven kings, the fourth

should just fall in the middle of the period assigned
them; and that the period should be divided into two
halves by the middle of the reign of the fourth king?
Here is evidence for those who will judge with reason
and without prejudice; even if there were not other
circumstances in the history, which involve impossibi-
lities, such as the statement that Tarquinius Superbus
was a grandson of Tarquinius Priscus. For this whole
period, then, down to the Gallic conquest, we have a
made-up history, at least, with regard to chronology."[*]

The following facts will plainly show that the fabri-
cation has not stopped short at the period in question :—

The Roman annals always commence from the fall
of Troy, as their natural starting-point, and the great
epochs of the history are clearly these—the building of
the city—its destruction by the Gauls—the establishment of the empire—and the removal of the seat of
government from Rome to Constantinople. Now this
same 360 years is the exact interval which separates
these five great events. From the fall of Troy to the
building of the city, according to one of two main
dates, is three hundred and sixty years,[†] and we have
already seen that three hundred and sixty years is
also the date of the Gallic catastrophe. The establishment of the empire is usually reckoned from the year
of Rome 723, when Octavius triumphed over Antony
and Cleopatra, at Actium. This event is just 360
years from the destruction of the city, for the super
fluous three years belong to the pre-Gallic era, and depend on differences, among the authorities, relative to
the exact date of the foundation of the city. Finally,
from the establishment of the empire to the solemn dedi-

---

[*] Lectures on the Hist. of Rome. Ed. by Schmitz, Vol. I., pp. 15–16.
Lect. III. Introduction.
[†] Servius, "Commentary on the Æneid," Lib. I., v. 267.

cation of Constantinople as the new seat of empire, in
A. C. 330, is also exactly 360 years ; for 830 of Christ
is 360 of the era of Actium. Besides, the " Paschal
Chronicle," one of the most respectable of the Byzantine records, not only places this event in the year of
Christ 330, but also in the year of Rome 1080 (three
times 360), thus virtually rejecting the superfluous
three years, and leaving 720 as the date of the empire,
and 360 as that óf the destruction of the city.*

Thus, then, for 1080 years, Rome is a seat of dominion ; for 1080 years its old creeds rule the State ;
then empire deserts the Eternal City, and a new creed
tramples on the primeval faith. In this year of the
dedication of Constantinople, Paganism was abolished
by Imperial edict, and Christianity established as the
religion of the State.† Nor is this all ; 1080 years is
also the duration of the Consular dignity as a distinct
magistracy. It began in 240 of Rome ; it was finally
merged into the Imperial privileges, and ceased as a
distinct magistracy on the 1st of January, A. C. 566,
according to one set of reckonings, and 567 according
to another, that is in 1319 or 1320 of Rome.‡ If we
take 240 from 1320, the result is 1080. And even the
number 1319 does not appear to be an accidental variation, for it meets other coincidences which cannot be
now touched upon. Thus Rome existed 240 years before the creation of the Consular dignity, and this dignity continued 240 years after Rome had ceased to

---

* "From the building of Rome to the year in which Constantinople
was dedicated, are reckoned MLXXX years," is the formal statement
of the " Paschal Chronicle." Vol. I., pp. 529–30, in the " Corpus
Scrip. Hist. Byzantinæ."

† Cf. " Paschal Chronicle," ibid.,p. 525 ; and Cedrenus, Hist. Com-
pendium, in the Corpus Scriptorum, ibid. Vol. I, pp. 495–500.

‡ Art de Vérifier les Dates dupuis Jésus-Christ," tom. IV., p. 170 ;
and Clinton, " Fasti Romani." Vol. I., pp. 818–22.

exist as a seat of empire. Neither do these adjustments stop even here.

Neibuhr seems to have viewed the number 360 as arbitrarily chosen, or as resulting simply from the multiplication of certain favorite elements; but there is far more in the matter than this, for we are now able to speak upon this point with a degree of evidence and precision which no one could have foreseen at the time when Niebuhr wrote.

Most of my readers are doubtless familiar with the extravagantly long periods involved in the mythic chronologies of the principal nations of antiquity, and many of them are also aware that modern research has thrown an unexpected light on the character and constitution of those periods, showing them to be as far removed from arbitrary extravagance, on the one hand, as they are from genuine chronology on the other. We find them, in fact, to be very regular and systematic formations, without any shadow of historical basis, but suggested, nevertheless, by important facts of another kind.

Their fundamental idea, as well as that of the legends with which they are almost always associated, is the belief, almost universal in antiquity, that the events of the universe, by the laws of destiny, or the arrangements of the Divine will, are constantly passing through great and perfectly regular cycles of change, commencing with creation or renovation, and ending with destruction or annihilation; and it has been found that the subdivisions and numbers involved in these cycles always recognize the adjustments of the ordinary year, in one or other of the many forms which they have assumed in different periods of human history.

The most interesting of the numbers made use of in these cycles are the roots 360 and 432, with their triplicates 1080 and 1296 ; 120 and 12,000 are also important periods, and 365 is a frequent, and 354 an occasional, substitute for 360. To these numbers, more or fewer ciphers are added, according to the grandeur or extravagance of the notions entertained by the framers or adaptors of these legendary creations.

Thus, for instance, the great cycle of China contains 129,600 years, divided into 12 great months, each containing 10,800 years ; and, of course, the four great seasons of such a year contain each 43,200 ordinary years, while each of its months contain three times 3,600 years.[*] The Persian cycle of the followers of Zoroaster contains 12,000 years, and such also was the duration of one of the cycles of ancient Etruria referred to by Suidas,[†] 120 *Sari*, or 432,000 years was the period contained in the antediluvian history of Chaldea, and this was also the measure of the *Kali yuga* of the Hindoo cycle, while the *Maha yuga*, or great age, contained 4,320,000 years, considered as 12,000 divine years, the *Kalpa*, or great cycle of all, containing 432,000,000 years.[‡] And, finally, not to enter into superfluous details, the cycle of ancient Mexico contained 18,000 years and a fraction (18,028), as the ordinary year contained 18 months and a fraction (18, multiplied by 20, plus 5), while the great cycle of Egypt comprised 36,500, or 36,525 years, 25 times the ordinary cycle of 1,460, or 1,461 years, formed by the accumulation of the unallowed-for quarter day, in a year of 365 days only.

These few facts will give a sufficient idea, for the moment, of the real character of the number 360, and of the *mythic* reason of its playing so important a part in the chronology of ancient Rome.

* Livres Sacrés de l'Orient (Pantheon Litteraire), p. 20.
† Lexicon, v. Tyrrhenia.
‡ According to one authority.

We must now give some evidence of the working of the great element 432, with its triplicate 1,296, and the reader will at once see that the only real difference between the great mythic chronologies and these sober-looking periods of Roman story is that, in the one case, we have the intervals amplified by the addition of imposing trains of ciphers, to speak in the language of modern numeration, while in the other these are rigidly lopped off as unsuitable to the facts of human experience. The natural inference suggested by the prevalence of such periods in any history is, that we have before us not genuine annals, but old mythic creeds, gradually criticised down into a semblance of realities, and ultimately mixed up with all that tradition or record had preserved of the real deeds of the nation. Criticised down, in fact, by those self-same processes of arbitrary assumption and metaphysical finessing, with which modern conservatism, in its often well-meant, but always most foolish, struggle with advancing science, is constantly defacing, perverting, and mutilating the grand old tales of remote antiquity.

To return then to our main subject : it will be found, as regards the number 360, that, in the first cycle of Roman history, nearly all the divergencies of opinion, among the different ancient historians, lie between that number and its cyclical equivalent 365, and that of the two main dates assigned to the interval between the building of the city and the fall of Troy, the one is 360, as already shown, and the other 432, as elaborately contended for by Dionysius of Halicarnassus, on the authority of Portius Cato, the tables of Eratosthenes, and the chronology of the Alban kings.† 432 years after the building of the city, occurred one of the

† Lib. 1., cap. 74.

greatest, calamities in the early annals of the state,
when the entire Roman army passed under the yoke of
the Samnites ; 432 years was also the duration of the
Republic, as measured from the expulsion of the kings
to the deaths of Marius and Sylla, its principal des-
troyers ; and it was likewise the interval during which
the Temple of Janus stood constantly open, from the
death of Numa, to the close of the First Punic War.
This number, however, though it thus maintains its
ground in special instances, is generally sacrificed to
the period 360, the dominant element of the chronology, but in medieval times it often comes into considerable prominence.

We have seen that 360 years is the duration of the
Empire as measured from the era of Actium to the
dedication of Constantinople. It is also its duration
as commencing with Julius Cæsar, and the era of Phar-
salia, B.C. 48, and coming down to the death of Dioclesian, the last of the supreme emperors in the purely
Roman series. This event occurred in A.C. 312, and
in this year Constantine, the founder of the new empire, entered Rome in triumph, and published edicts in
favor of the Christians, of whom Dioclesian was the
great persecutor.

In like manner, the duration of the Empire, taken
absolutely, that is, extended to the close of the Western Empire in A.C. 476, is similarly cyclical ; 476 of
Christ is 1229 of Rome, according to the usual reckonings. which range, for the building of the city, from
the 4th year of the 6th to the 1st of the 8th Olympiad.
But Timæus the Sicilian, referred to by Dionysius,[†]
places the founding of Rome 38 years before the Olym-
piads, which is 67 years before the 1st of the 8th.

---

* Lib. I., cap. 74.

Now, 67 added to 1229 gives 1296, making the duration of the Roman dominion, in this sense, a great triplicate of three times 432 years, just as in another it is
a parallel triplicate of three times 360. ' And again, if
we deduct from 1229, the first cycle of Rome, taken as
365 years, we get, as the period from the destruction of
the city to the destruction of the Western Empire, 864
years, twice 432 ; while, finally, 476 of Augustus, counting his reign. as many do, from the death of Julius,
B.- C. 44, is just 432 of Christ.   It is manifest that such
precise and manifold coincidences as these bear no relation to the accidents of genuine chronology, and are
only possible in artificial schemes based upon common
principles of adjustment.   ·

The elements of medieval chronology are so numerous and conflicting that it would be impossible, even
within far wider limits than those to which I now re-
strict myself, to give any satisfactory account of the
cyclical combinations which everywhere present themselves in the latter section of the Roman annals ; but
one or two illustrations of the manner in which conflicting dates may not only be accounted for, but often
also fully reconciled, by the application of these mythic
data, will probably have some interest at the moment,
as showing that these fictious combinations are by no
means confined to the remoter history, but are equally
an inherent portion of medieval story.

The destruction of Rome by Alaric, King of the
Goths, is usually placed in A.C. 409, and its destruction by Genseric, King of the Vandals, in A. C. 455.
The former date is 23 years less, and the latter 23 years
more than 432, and, as will presently be noticed, 23
years is one of the rectifying numbers in medieval
chronology ; 409 of Christ is 1162 of Rome, and 1162
is twice 365 plus 432.

Again : 1140 of Rome and 410, 425, and 426 A.C. are also dates of the capture of the city by Alaric; 1144 is equal to 712 plus 432, and 712 is the date of the battle of Philippi, one of the natural starting-points of the Augustan era; while 410 of Christ is 455 of the Julian era, as 425 of Christ is 455 of the ordinary Augustan era; 410, besides, differs 22 years from 432, which is the difference between the system of Marianus Scotus and the ordinary Dyonysian era, while the differences of the other two dates from 432 are trivial.

Thus all these discrepancies of date accommodate themselves to determinate and important epochs, while most of them yield, with more or less of precision, the cyclical element 432. These interchanges, too, between 409 and 455 seem plainly to imply that the two destructions of Rome are but different versions of one story; and, in point of fact, one of them is completely ignored by one set of writers, and the other by another. The British chronicles, universally we believe, ignore the destruction by Genseric, while some, at all events, of the Byzantine writers, equally ignore that by Alaric. Yet the British chronicles constantly synchronize the leading native events with Roman epochs, and especially emphasize the year 455 as that in which perished the last of the British kings, and in which the first of the Saxon invaders ascended the throne.

These facts will sufficiently show the extent to which chronological discrepancies admit of reconciliation, but such reconciliations are, in the main, altogether fatal to the historic worth of the materials. Yet these are the results which constantly meet us in all departments of medieval chronology, as far as the matter has been investigated from the present point of view. Everywhere we find the leading events manifesting a marked tendency to fall into cyclical combinations, and often

doing so with absolute precision. Many of the coincidences are, no doubt, accidental, but others are syste
matic beyond all rational doubt, and if so, is it not obvious that these seeming histories but cover the vacuity
which human forgetfulness has left in the story of ancient times, or that they overlie, conceal, and distort, a
more genuine record which, in part, may be still, perhaps, recoverable?

The learned reader who has been in the habit of looking at dates as they occur in our ordinary histories, or
as they present themselves incidentally in more ancient
writings, will naturally be startled by the coincidences
here pointed out, and naturally feel sceptical as to their
genuineness. He does not find these repeated succes-
sions of 360 and 1080, of 432 and 1296, on the surface
of chronology, and he will, therefore, be inclined to
fancy that the elements from which they are derived
have been arbitrarily selected among conflicting dates.
Such, however, is certainly not the case in the more important instances given ; and where there is room for
arbitrary selection the fact is either stated, or clearly
implied in the very terms of our description. Had the
Roman annals always dated, in all histories and chronicles, from one era—that of Rome, for instance—then
these repetitions would be manifest, with occasional
variations, even on the face of the history ; but when
authorities differ as to the precise date of the starting-
point, when, after the birth of Christ, the whole previous reckoning is changed, sometimes into the Christian era, variously reckoned, sometimes into the Imperial, viewed either as Julian or Augustan, with various
minor modifications, it is obvious that the cyclical
period may really exist, and even in perfection, without being in any way graphically expressed in the ordinary language of the chronology. It is only by a

careful study, and comparison of different eras and systems of reckoning, that superficial discrepancies can be made to vanish, and the underlying cyclical periodicity brought into clear view.

That numerous and tantalizing discordances in dates everywhere present themselves in classical and medieval history, is obvious, but these discordances are far less the result of accident than would at first appear. The minor discrepancies, as just intimated, chiefly depend on different modes of estimating the starting-points of eras ; more considerable ones are often satisfactorily accounted for by supposing an unconscious confusion on the part of writers or transcribers between one era and another, while others again are found in the most precise accordance with the workings of different cyclical numbers.

Thus the era of Rome may be viewed as commencing on the 11th of the Kalends of May, (April 21st,) on which day was commemorated the founding of the city, or on the preceding or succeeding first of January ; and according as one or the other is taken, a given event may fall in any one of three different years : and the same is true of many other eras. In the case of the Christian era the sources of ambiguity are especially numerous and important, for under this term we have four different eras included, that of the Incarnation, that of the Nativity, that of the Preaching, and that of the Passion. Here we have a source of confusion amounting to such considerable sums as thirty and thirty-three years, while even in the use of the vulgar, or Dionysian era, we are liable to an error of twenty-two or twenty-three years, as already intimated, owing to a theory adopted in the middle ages, and used by Marianus Scotus and his followers.

Similar elements of confusion present themselves in

the case of the Imperial era, which is sometimes dated
from Julius, the actual founder of the empire, but mostly
from the reign of Augustus, in whose person this new
system of rule became a settled institution. The usual
date of the Imperial era is the battle of Actium, in
which Octavius, afterwards Augustus, finally triumphed
over Anthony and Cleopatra, but other epochs in the
life of this monarch are also occasionally selected,
and, as a matter of course, most of them supply the
minor elements of discrepancy already alluded to in
the case of the era of Rome. We must, therefore, be
prepared to expect fractional deviations from accuracy in mythic coincidences, as well as in genuine
dates.

Two additional illustrations will bring this sketch
to a natural conclusion, and show, besides, that cyclical combinations, and artificial chronological systems,
are not matters which concern antiquity alone, but
things which come down even to late medieval times.

We have seen that one thousand and eighty years is
the measure of purely Roman sway over the Republic
and Empire; we have now to observe that one thousand and eighty years has evidently been also viewed as
the fitting duration of Roman dominion in its Eastern
seat.

The division of an empire into an Eastern and a
Western, is placed, as we have seen, by varying authorities, in 364 After Christ, under Valentinian and
Valens, or in 395 A. C., under Honorius and Arca-
dius; 364 A. C. may easily represent 365, and 365 of
Christ is 395 of Augustus, so that these two dates may
be altogether due to some confusion in the old authorities between the two eras, especially as there are many
reasons for believing that the Augustan and Christian
eras originally coincided in date.

Constantinople fell under the power of the Turks in A. C. 1453, which, according to the ordinary dates, is 2206 of Rome. This, from the division of the empire, gives 1089 and 1058, the former being nine years more, and the latter twenty-two less than 1080, and we have seen that twenty-two and twenty-three are rectifying periods in medieval history. And again, 2206 of Rome is forty-six years more than twice 1080, and forty-five or forty-six years is the difference between the Julian and Christian eras. In either case, then, we have 1080 years of dominion for Rome itself, and 1080 years of Eastern empire. There are conflicting systems at work, but they all bring out the cyclical coincidences.

Besides the destructions of Rome by Alaric and Genseric, another important calamity of the same kind, attributed to Totillas, king of the Goths, is placed in 546, A. C. 1299 of Rome. This latter number is three years more than 1296, and it will be remembered that the ordinary reckoning of the Imperial, and consequently of the Christian era, is three years more than what has already been shown to be the true cyclical date of the empire. This event, therefore, really falls in 1296 of Rome, three times 432.

Now, if we take the date of this destruction by Totillas, thus rectified to A. C. 543, and deduct it from 1453, the era of the destruction of the Eastern empire, we get for the interval between the two catastrophes 910 years, which is 46 years more than twice 432, and 46 years, as we have already seen, is the difference between the Julian and Christian eras. Thus while the general stream of the chronology is mainly based on the number 360, clear evidences of the working of the other great element are found both in remote and comparatively recent times ; and while from the foundation of the city to the advent of the Turks, we have two systems of 1080 years, so from the destruction of Troy, to the same event, we have two systems of 1296, and most of their elements coincide with events distinctly bearing the requirements of cyclical fable. From Troy to Rome, according to Dionysius, was 432 years; 432 years later the army was disgraced by the Samnites; 432 years more only exceed by 16 years, even according to the usual reckonings, the era of the death of Domitian, the last of the twelve Cæsars, a period presenting many striking characteristics of a mythic terminal epoch; then comes the catastrophe of Totillas giving a fourth 432, and, finally, a double period brings us to the fall of Constantinople.

Can all this be simple accident? Five-and-twenty centuries of historic tradition, from Troy to Constantinople, from Achilles to the Turk, thus falling into the rank and file of cyclical arrangement, often with the precision of a mathematical formula! From Troy to Rome, from Rome to the Gauls, from the Gauls to the empire, always 360 years; 1080 for Rome, 1080 for Constantinople, 1080 for the consuls, 1080 for the ancient creed, 1080 for Christianity, now, in its turn, trampled upon by a new faith! and then an analogous set of coincidences with the element 432. If all this be accident, what shall we call intention? If it be intention, what, then, is ancient history? For these coincidences do not apply to the Roman annals merely, but are equally presented by every ancient and medieval history which has been examined from the present point of view. There is surely enough, even in this first rude presentation of the facts, to fix attention, and call for scrutiny and reconsideration. If chronology be thus vitiated by mythic numbers, how vain the labor we bestow upon its rectifications and synchronisms!

If antiquity have thus filed down its grand old cycles into dimensions suitable to the realities of ordinary existence, may it not likewise have exerted its ingenuity in similarly reducing into human proportions the events and personages of those cycles? Or will any one, with those things before his eyes, be justified in rejecting the plain teachings of monumental facts, simply because they set aside the pretensions of chronological systems based upon dreams like these?

In studying nature, reverence should be the first of our feelings; in exploring human antiquity, the reverence of a modern is but manhood bowing to infancy. It is surely time for the world to remember that there is a sense in which yesterday is younger than to-day, and in which the "wisdom of antiquity" means little more than the prattle of childhood.

CHAPTER V.

TEN THOUSAND YEARS OF ITALIC TRADITION, OR THE ERRORS AND ADJUSTMENTS OF THE ROMAN YEAR AND CALENDAR FROM ROMULUS TO POPE GREGORY.

The history of the adjustments and aberrations of the Roman year and calendar, presents a series of facts of such curious and important interest, and one so intimately bearing on the topics discussed in another chapter, that I feel desirous of bringing it to the notice of my readers, for the same reasons that induced me to depart from strict regularity of treatment in the former case.

On a recent occasion I have endeavored to trace the gradual formation of the Roman year, in so far as the names of its months are concerned, and though I do not by any means pretend to cave given the precise

history of those names, still the general plan of formation, the laws of increasing complexity in the divisions
and symbolism of the year, may be fully relied upon.
since this plan is but an individual expression of
arrangements pervading the whole of antiquity, and
placed beyond the reach of doubt by the revelations
of mythonomy. That the primeval year of tradition
was one of four solar divisions only, and so continued
for a long series of ages. is a fact which admits of the
clearest proof, for the oldest mythic traditions are expressly based upon it, and owe their very origin to the
pictorial symbolism employed for its representation ;
and we know that these traditions *are* the oldest, from
the fact that all others acknowledge their priority in
various ways, and only become intelligible in proportion as they are understood ; indeed. the very first myth
which yielded to analysis, proved, also, to be the basis
of the whole superstructure, the fountain head of the
entire stream of mythology.

Upon similar evidence——an evidence infinitely
stronger than any amount of direct testimony, since it
is an evidence of demonstration—we also know that
this form of year was finally succeeded by one of five
divisions, then by one of seven, and subsequently by
others of eight, nine, ten, twelve, &c.

In the patch-work character of the Roman months,
considered as a series of names, we have seen some
curious evidences of most of these changes, evidences
supported by snatches of tradition, all the more reliable
from the fact that their transmitters totally misunderstood their character, and therefore did not invent
them. They merely gave the best expression they
could to current legends or fragments of legends, or
sought to explain by hypothetical reasoning traditional
usages which had lost their true import.

We know that the four fundamental names, Mar
tius, Aprilis, Maius and Junius, exactly correspond,
both as to name and sequence, and to some extent also.
as to actual symbolism, with the requirements of the
primary form of year, and with one special presentation of the planetary series, and that only as a series
of four could all these conditions have been complied
with.   This conjunction of facts gives a vast antiquity,
if not to the four names themselves, at all events to the
arrangements which they express, and absolutely negatives the idea of such arrangements being made in the
era to which tradition refers them: Roman history
has given us the legends of the Roman race, and these
legends, however recent in their ultimate forms, are
extremely ancient in their primary aspects, and this is
what we have here to consider.   As matters of historic
faith, these legends are, for the most part, beneath con-
tempt, notwithstanding the infinite pains bestowed
upon them by writers anxious to rationalize them, and
thus reconcile credulity with common sense: but as
wrecks of the past, as fossils of ancient thought, as
materials for science to work upon, these same absurdities become serious and important truths, and when
diligently studied and compared, throw a marvelous
light upon the darkness of antiquity.   We shall here
regard them under this two-fold aspect.   We shall see
them, as history, leading the narrators and critics into
endless and most ridiculous absurdities ; and, on the
other hand, we shall see them as science, instantly
falling into order and consistency, and yielding meanings which have no drawback but that of being sub-
versive of existing opinion.

We first learn from the traditions that the Roman
year received its original form from Romulus, the first
of the seven kings, and that it consisted of only ten

months ;* lunar months according to Ovid, but according to others† composed alternately of 30 and 31 days, making in all 304 days. Plutarch differs from the other authorities, in assigning 12 months and 360 days to the year of Romulus. This year, he says, had neither measure nor order, some months consisting of fewer than 20 days, while some were stretched to 35, and others even to more. People had no idea of the difference between the annual course of the sun and that of the moon, and only laid down this position, that the year consisted of 360 days !‡

Accounts so conflicting, and so individually inconsistent, do not represent the ordinary discrepancies of a common tradition, but rather inferences deduced from different materials, or from common materials viewed under different aspects. These months of 35 or more days, for instance, are just the sort of months to be expected in a solar year of 10 divisions, where ten times 36 would make the technical year of 360 days so general in remote antiquity, while these months of 20 days and more, seem to be but a distorted expression of those supplementary months, occurring at the end of regular cycles, by means of which the civil year was periodically brought into harmony with the natural year. Thus, at the end of the Mexican cycle of 52 years, there was an intercallary month of 13 days made up of the accumulation of the uncorrected quarter days. The civil year consisted of 360 days, divided into 18 months of 20 days each, 5 days being intercallated annually, and the quarter day being allowed to accumulate for 52 years, when it amounted to a month of the

---

* Ovid, *Fasti*, i., v. 27—Censorinus, cap. 20. Macrobius, *Saturnalia*, cap. 12—Solinus, cap. 1.

† Censorinus, Macrobius, Solinus, Ibid.

‡ Life of Numa.

same length as those of the sacerdotal years. These
arrangements were all based on technical conveniences
and symbolic associations, and so far from being the
patchwork of blundering ignorance, they exhibit the
most precise and ingenious contrivances. They formed
part of a cycle of four great divisions, representing the
four seasons and the four ages of the great cosmic cycle,
each division containing thirteen years, under the pre-
sidency, so to speak, of one of four traditional symbols,
Tochtli, the Rabbit, *Acatl*, the Cane, *Tecpatl*, the Flint
(arrow-head,) and *Calli*, the House (or temple.) The
five supplementary days were not considered as belonging to the year, but as an interval between two distinct
years. They were *Nemontemi*, empty days, unlucky
days ; nothing of consequence was done upon them.
They were an exact counterpart, in fact, of the Egyptian *Epagomenæ*. Thus there were four divisions like
those of the great cycle, each containing thirteen years,
like the thirteen days of the sacerdotal year, with five
superadded days, in some sense recalling the five divisions of the month of twenty days, which were also represented by the same *Tochtli*, *Acatl*, *Tecpatl*, *Calli*, and
a supplementary month of thirteen days, representing
both the thirteen years of the cyclical divisions, and
the ordinary months of the sacerdotal year.*

In presence of these adjustments so ingenious, elaborate, and perfect in their way, invented, or at all events
thoroughly understood, and rigidly maintained for ages,
by an American and semi-civilized race, what are we to
say of those absurdities transmitted to us by the classical writers, and gravely re-echoed by modern commen-

---

* These curious adjustments will be found described in most of the
principal works on Mexican history and antiquities, especially by
Clavigero, Storia Antica del Messico ; Humboldt, Vues des Cordillières;
Prescott, Conquest of Mexico, &c., &c.

tators, relative to the impossible ignorance and blunderings of the framers, correctors, guardians, and users of the Roman year and calendar? Romulus, we are told, was so ignorant of the length of the year, that he made his year consist of ten months of thirty or thirty-one days each. The Albans had similar years, and some other nations had years of six, four, three, or even two lunar months only! Numa, in introducing his lunar year, made it consist of three hundred and fifty-five days instead of three hundred and fifty-four, simply because odd numbers were lucky, yet in managing his biennial intercallations he overlooked this added day, and made his intercallary month too long, and then to conceal his blunder from the nation, he had recourse to a clumsy periodic contrivance for rectifying it; but after his death the Pontiffs so managed the matter that they made the year sometimes longer and sometimes shorter, occasionally introducing an entire month when nobody expected it, so that by the time Julius Cæsar became Pontifex Maximus, the year was in discordance with the seasons to the amount of two months. These are some of the absurdities offered to us as history, absurdities which would require the Roman people to have been a nation of slaves and idiots, instead of one of high-spirited and intelligent men.

A year of ten lunar months has no conceivable advantage, while it has all sorts of inconveniences; and to attribute its institution to the gross ignorance of a European nation in that period of the world, and in an ancient seat of civilization, and ruled by a man who, even according to the hypothesis of the history itself, was a great and enlightened ruler, the descendant of a long line of civilized kings, the contemporary and immediate neighbor of the advanced intelligence of Greece and Etruria, is altogether preposterous. No nation, much less a civilized one, can remain ignorant of the true length of the year, within a moderate fraction, nor use any form of year not regularly and frequently adjusted to the natural one. It is the natural year alone which regulates the entire business of life ; agriculture, commerce, war, all receive the laws of their periodicity from the sequence and variations of the seasons, and the prospects of the rude hunter, or nomadic herdsman are as much involved in the precision of return of annual phenomena as those of the civilized farmer, speculator, or warrior. Nor is the problem to be solved a difficult one till we descend into fractional details. The moon gives a convenient divisor, and a few rough averages, extending over a moderate number of years, would soon point out the number of the superfluous days. To an intelligent nation even the quarter day would not be long in revealing itself. The addition of a day in four years, would amount to a month in one hundred and twenty years, or to an entire season in three hundred and sixty, and a nation with a fixed calendar and its apparatus of festivals and ceremonies, would soon be made conscious of an error of this amount. Imagine a nation celebrating the commencement of the spring, the budding of the trees, the opening of the flowers, and the loves of bird and beast : imagine it chanting snatches of ancient songs in which its forefathers spoke of the labors of agriculture, or the pleasures of the chase, or the dangers and glory of war in connection with these phenomena, and then suppose that these songs have to be sung and these festivals celebrated with all their apparatus of religious rites and social amusements, year after year, in the depths of winter, with the trees shivering leafless in the blast, the rivers bound in ice, forest and plain in a robe of snow, and bird and beast struggling only for food and shelter; would not the contrast between Present and Past be vividly impressed upon the attention, and continue to excite curiosity, and to demand a solution, until the truth was at last reached, a due correction made, and the calendar again placed as of old, in harmony with the seasons?

But in the case before us, there is far more than this to be said. At the era which history assigns to Romulus, Italy had been for thousands of years a center of civilization. Three great strata of Cyclopean structures reared their venerable ruins upon its soil, marking the sites of perished cities, telling the tale of vanished greatness and wide-spread empire, and almost justifying the popular boast that the progenitors of the race had been gods and demigods. No rude gap breaks the sequence of these monuments: nothing tells that supervening barbarisms had ever done more for eclipsing civilization, than subsequent barbarisms have done. The inference is, rather that even when power had passed away, intelligence and its acquisitions were still preserved, in some form or other, clouded and diminished doubtless, but not destroyed.

At the era in question, Etruria was the great Italic power; her dominions embraced the greater part of northern Italy; on the south, they were in the immediate vicinity of the Roman territory; and we know by direct evidence, still better than by tradition, what Etruscan civilization amounted to. In the painted chambers of the sepulchres of this race, we see a polished people surrounded by all the appliances of an advanced ancient civilization. We see them at their banquets elegantly attired, reclining on couches, waited upon by their attendants, served in those graceful cups and vases, which even at the present day are justly re-

garded as models of elegance, as well in their forms as
in the outline paintings which decorate them.   We also
see them witnessing the athletic sports of wrestling,
boxing, and equestrianism, and in various other scenes,
civil and religious, all bespeaking an advanced social
organization, and no mean measure of acquired knowledge.   They had arts and a literature ; for there are
their implements, their arms, vases, statuettes, paintings,
and written characters, alluding in various ways to an
elaborate mythology.   They had the most intimate relations with Greece, for the legends of Greece are
depicted on these graceful vases, and often given with
the names of the personages in Greek letters.   Nor
were they ignorant of Egypt—as a commercial nation
they could not be—for in some few instances these
sepulchral frescoes plainly remind us of the Egyptian
style.   In a word, when we read early Roman history
in presence of these facts, the utter absurdity of many
of its statements becomes at once transparent.

The writers on the calendar, then, have given us
facts of which they knew not the import, and reasons
of which we need not dispute the paternity.   These
years of ten, and six, and four, and three, and even
two months, are simply the dying echoes of perished
solar adjustments, and the only wonder is, that even
an echo of such long-superseded systems should have
been heard in classic times.

In view of these explanations, we can easily understand these contradictory and inconsistent statements
of Plutarch on the one hand, and of Ovid and Censorinus on the other.   A year of 360 days, with some of
its months containing thirty-five days and more, and
others twenty and less, evidently refers to a solar year,
not, as Plutarch says, of twelve, but of ten divisions.
Such a year would naturally have equal months of

thirty-six days, while the supplementary five days would
every four years amount to an intercallary month of
twenty days, or to one of twenty-one days, if we take
into account the extra quarter day. Analogous results
might be produced by other combinations, but this is a
simple and natural adjustment, and fully meets the requirements of the tradition, the statements of which
are of too vague and general a form to demand a literal
interpretation.

On the other hand, a year with alternating months
of thirty and thirty-one days, evidently means one of
twelve, not of ten divisions; in fact, a year of three
hundred and sixty-five days, like that subsequently attributed to Cæsar. Thus Plutarch ought to have spoken of a year of ten months, and these authorities of
a year of twelve, and the two accounts would then have
been more self-consistent; but as they stand, it is as if
two traditions had been beheaded, and the heads replaced on the wrong shoulders.

The year of Romulus, as it has been called, should
have begun with March, and ended with December, as
this is the tenth month, counting from March. But the
statements given in our last chapter make it evident
that all we have a right to conclude from such a tradition is, that a year of twelve divisions, beginning with
the vernal equinox, and the month of March was superadded to a year of eight, beginning with January and
the winter solstice, and the account of Plutarch exactly
meets the requirements of this superaddition, when we
substitute twelve for ten as the number of the months.
The order of these systems has evidently been inverted,
for the months of January and February are obviously
of older date in the Roman calendar, than those of
September, October, November, and December; otherwise, how should the former months exist in the calen-

dar of the Romano-Britons, which contains no trace of the latter? Thus it is the year of seven divisions which represent the regal period of Roman history, the year of eight the Republican, and the year of twelve the Imperial. But in this view the record ceases to be anything beyond an amalgamation of zodiacal myths, and other like materials, mingled with leading events of real occurrence, and gradually criticized and rationalized, as it is termed, into a quasi-history. And this is the view that will meet us at every turn in the course of these inquiries, until it be ultimately placed beyond the reach of doubt.

The next step in the tradition informs us that the year of Romulus being found erroneous and inconvenient, was reformed by Numa, the second of the kings, who made it lunar, and added to it the months of January and February, or rather February and January, as February is stated to have come between December and January, as the last month of the year, January, being now made the first. To this tradition I have sufficiently alluded already.

The year of Numa, then, as lunar, ought to have consisted of three hundred and fifty-four days, with an alternating intercallation of twenty-two and twenty-three days every second year ; but Numa, to make it of more fortunate omen, added an extra day, making it consist of three hundred and fifty-five days. It would seem, however, that he had not the good fortune to perceive that, in adding his extra day, he was bound to subtract it from the intercallation ; so that towards the close of his reign, he had to introduce a contrivance for getting rid of it, and not having the honesty to confess his error, and his subjects being too stupid and ignorant to perceive it, he so managed matters as to invent a cycle of twenty-four years, in the latter inter-

callations of which he regularly dropped the superfluous days, which were always accumulated in the early
ones. Thus, according to the commentators, he killed
two birds with one stone, concealing his blunder, while
removing its consequences. And all this trouble and
complexity for a matter which a schoolboy could have
settled, and about a blunder which an ordinary schoolboy would have been ashamed to make! In fact, the
commentators are in a worse predicament with the
calendar of Numa, than even with that of Romulus.

To argue against the possibility of such occurrences
as these, seems like an insult to the reader's judgment,
yet they are related by the classical writers, and repeated by modern commentators with the most earnest
gravity, and without the faintest suspicion of their inherent absurdity. In the actual world, we think it a
lucky occurrence when kings and legislators are even
up to the highest level of the intelligence and learning
of their age ; as to their going immensely beyond it, it
is an event which we never contemplate, even in the
case of the most distinguished monarchs ; but here, it
is Romulus, and Numa, and Cæsar, and Augustus, and
so on, who know everything and do everything, while
their subjects merely look on with stupid wonder, and
accept the letter of their arrangements without any
consciousness of their spirit.

The adjustment of the calendar was a matter which
concerned every intelligent man in the nation, and the
adjustment in question was sufficiently simple to be
universally understood. A man who knew the length
of the lunar and solar years, and expressly added a
day to the former for the sake of good fortune, could
not have forgotten the necessity of allowing for that
day, when settling his intercallation ; or had he done
so, those about him, who must have been cognizant of

all the facts, as well as of their motives, for the whole
matter was necessarily patent and public, would naturally have pointed out the error. The whole nation
could not have made the same oversight, still less could
they have failed to perceive that the later arrangements were intended as a correction of the initial error;
nor could they have failed to be indignant at the absurdity and insult implied in a cycle, which constantly repeated in its earlier arrangements an error which had
as often to be corrected towards its close; and all
this for the petty vanity of concealing an oversight,
and with a dishonesty which, for such a motive, could
cheat and inconvenience an entire nation; and this,
too, done by the good and venerable and enlightened
Numa! Such are the inconsistencies which credulous
chroniclers and equally credulous critics are perpetually creating or repeating, in their attempts to amalgamate incongruous facts, and explain by conjecture
what they cannot touch by analysis. And yet, many
will deem it an impertinent presumption in a modern
to drag into the light of day such venerable follies.

The calendar of Numa, though, according to hypothesis, finally adjusted to the year of 365 days and a
quarter, did not, however, keep in harmony with the
seasons. In the time of Cæsar, the latter were in advance of the civil year to the amount of 67 days, and
the correction of this error is stated to have been the
object of his reformation. If we consult the historians
as to the cause of this error, we get nothing but gratuitous and contradictory statements like those already
alluded to. The charge of the calendar and the man-
agement of the biennial intercallation was, we are told,
in the hands of the College of Pontiffs, and the Pontifex
Maximus of the day added or curtailed, inserted or
omitted, at his pleasure, sometimes a portion, sometimes

the whole of the intercallation, either because the times were prosperous or the reverse, or because he wished to spite or favor some particular magistrate, by shortening or lengthening the period of his office, the nation all the while knowing nothing at all about the matter. And all this is gravely uttered relative to a people, like the old Romans, free, restless, clear-seeing, manly, and always engaged in ·political antagonisms ; and relative to an intercallation which a child might understand ; which took place every second year, generation after generation, and century after century ; which always amounted to twenty-two or twenty-three days, and that every man in the country was obliged to take into special account in the arrangement of his affairs. The ancient nations of America could keep in perfect order calendars immeasurably more elaborate and intricate than that of Rome, and yet we must believe that in this great focus of European intelligence and independence, the Pontiff of the day could lengthen or shorten the year, at his pleasure, for such motives as those just stated, and without senate or people being in the least the wiser ! The Pontifex Maximus could as easily have stolen, unperceived, a letter from the alphabet as a day from the calendar.

The calendar of a people is part and parcel of the religion of a people, part and parcel of the daily life of a nation. To disturb it in the least is to derange all festivals and interfere with all business concerns, and a chief Pontiff is one of the most unlikely persons in the world to trifle with religion or established usage, und the republican Romans, as described in history, were the least likely people to permit such interference.

We have only to consider the opposition made almost everywhere to the introduction of the Gregorian rectification to see how impossible was the occurrence of such tamperings as those in question. This correction dropped 11 days in one year, so as to bring the equinoxes and solstices to their ancient position in the calendar; but in doing this it necessarily disturbed all chronological calculations, and evoked all the antagonisms of party spirit. Catholic countries, for the most part, readily adopted it as an arrangement decreed by the head of their church, but it met with the utmost opposition in the Protestant States. Its introduction into England was resisted for nearly two centuries, nor has Russia even yet accepted it. A recent writer well describes the inconveniencies occasioned by this change, necessary as it was in other respects:

" A measure, of which the effect was to overturn the long established landmarks of time, and to substitute for them others, new and altogether strange to tradition and use, could not be supposed to pass without exciting many reclamations among persons of all classes from the peer to the peasant. Personal feelings were excited at the unceremonious perturbation of birth-days and of marriage anniversaries. Religious exasperation was produced by the arbitrary transposition of the most solemn festivals. Even the movable feasts already surrounded with some confusion, became, for the moment, confusion worse confounded. Political celebrations and the dates of historical events shared in the general disturbance."*

And yet the writer of these lines follows, mechanically, in the track of his predecessors when speaking of the year of Numa.

"The supplementary month called Mercedonius," he remarks, "had been the subject of constant maltreatment by the Pontiffs, having been abridged and extended in the most capricious and arbitrary manner, so as completely to derange the position of the seasons, relative to the commencement and close of the year." (p. 162.)

* Lardner's Museum of Science, No. 64, p. 172.

And all this without the shadow of necessity or utility, for petty party or even individual purposes, and by the very guardian of traditional usages! done, too, in the face of conflicting factions, or worse still, done without any man among an intelligent, and, in later times, an enlightened people being, in the least, aware of the cheat!

But the reader does not yet comprehend the full measure of absurdity implied in these random statements. February appears to have been for a long series of ages the month of the intercallations, and judging from the placing of the supplementary day in the Julian calendar, as well as from the terminal associations implied in the feasts of the Terminalia and Regifugium, the place of the intercallary month, like that of the intercallary day, was between the 23d and 24th of February. Every second year, then, these two dates had to be separated by an entire month of twenty-two or twenty three days. We will suppose this separation to have taken place last year; this year, consequently, the people expect to commemorate the flight of their kings on the day after the Terminalia, but just as they are thinking of these matters, and making their preparations accordingly, an order comes from the Pontifex Maximus directing that the intercallation shall take place as usual. Would not the response to such an order be the universal cry "We intercallated last year?" Could an entire people forget such a fact? Or know nothing about the matter, as the historians would phrase it? Or, if the Pontiff pretended to have reasons for an irregular intercallation, would not these reasons be demanded and canvassed by a people like the old Romans?

The result would be the same at whatever period of the year the intercallation was made, for the Roman

calendar was full of festivals.   What should we say at
the present day if assured that the Archbishop of Paris,
in France, or the Pope in Italy, were accustomed to
intercallate slyly, from time to time, some twenty-two
or twenty-three days between a certain Saturday and
the succeeding Sunday, or rather say between Good
Friday and Easter Sunday, or between the 24th of December and Christmas Day, or between the 31st of
January and New Year's Day, no one but himself being
the wiser?   Or suppose, that in America, the Secretary of the Interior, to spite Mr. Welles, and oblige
Gen. Fremont, were to lengthen the year by twenty-
three days, just when Congress was about to dissolve,
or some important debate to come on!   Let any of
these things be fancied, and the reader will understand
the supreme absurdity of these historical statements.
Every day in the Roman year had a particular name;
every month was divided into three parts, by the
Calends, Ides, and Nones, and every day on which one
of these did not fall was either the first before them, or
the second, third, fourth, and so on, before them.   .It is
plain, then, that to displace or misname a Roman day,
would be just the same thing as, with us, to put a Sunday before a Saturday, or separate Tuesday and Wed-
nesday by some such interval as *Baldursday*, or *Niurds-
day*.

And now we come to the climax of this chapter of
asserted blunderings and tamperings.   The calendar
of Numa, we are told. was reformed by Julius Cæsar,
at a period when it was in discord with the seasons to
the amount of sixty-seven days.   Cæsar substituted the
solar for the lunar reckoning, and made the year consist of 365 days, distributed as in modern times, while
the extra quarter-day was allowed for by intercallating
one day in every four years, between the 5th and 6th

of the Calends of March, the 23d and 24th of February. And to bring back the festivals into accordance with the seasons, he made one special year consist of 445 days, being 365 for the year itself, the intercallary 'month of twenty-three days then due, and two months of thirty-three and thirty-four days each, being the amount of the aberration just spoken of—in all fifteen months and 445 days. This anomalous year was called *"the year of Confusion."*

Now the year of 365 days and a quarter, had been known for ages in Egypt: it must equally have been known to the Romans, for the cycle of Numa took cognizance of it. Besides, had it not been allowed for in the intercallations, the seasons would have been constantly, and comparatively speaking, rapidly receding on the calendar, as in Egypt, at the rate of a month in 120 years, a fact which could not have been left unrecorded among a people possessing such records as the Romans possessed, and which, nevertheless, has left no impression on the traditions, but, on the contrary, all the recorded aberrations of the Roman Calendar have been in one invariable direction, and that the opposite of the one in question. The seasons have always been in advance of the calendar, not the calendar in advance of the seasons. Yet in the face of these evidences, positive and negative, we are gravely told that the entire Roman Empire blundered for six-and-thirty years in reference to this very plain matter, nay, that they even contrived to misunderstand the simple numerical phrase, *one day in every four years*, and, while fancying themselves to be complying with it, were actually intercallating *one day in every* THREE *years!*[*]

Cæsar died the year after his rectification of the

---

[*] Macroblus, l. l., c. 14; Solinus, c. 3; Pliny, l. xviii., c. 25; Suetonius, Life of Octavius, c. xxxi.

calendar, and though he was assisted by the Egyptian Philosopher, Sossigenes, and might naturally be supposed to have fully explained to all concerned, and especially to his subordinates in the College of Pontines, the nature of his new arrangements, yet we are told that his successor in the Pontificate managed to blunder in the manner stated. The apology for this blunder is thus expressed in the little work already quoted :

The mistake is known to have arisen thus—in Roman counting, every *fourth* is our *third*.

1 2 3 4   1 2

A. B, C, D, E, F, G, H, I, J, K, &c.

1 2 3 4   1 2 3 4

" Livy describes the cycle of 19 years as one which begins every *twentieth* year." (P. 164.)

Now the Romans must indeed have been a strange people if every fourth with them is a third with us, and it is somewhat singular that we have not had more specimens of their doings in this new style of arithmetic. But no ; it was not the Romans who blundered, but the historians and critics, modern and ancient, who have recorded facts which they did not understand, and invented absurd reasons where they ought to have confessed ignorance. This " fourth year incipient," as others have expressed it, is a real third, and can only be called a fourth once in a series, unless indeed a man be nearly idiotic on the point of numbers, or have his head bewildered by a theory ; for unfortunately a head full of a false theory, even if placed on the shoulders of a philosopher, may think and speak any amount of nonsense on the subject of that theory.

A Frenchman calls a week of seven days *huit jours*, because he includes the octave Sunday; but he does not call a fortnight *seize jours*, but *quinze jours*, fifteen, not sixteen days ; neither does a musician when speak-ing of octaves, count sixteen notes in two octaves. twenty-four in three, thirty-two in four, and so on ; but he gives either fourteen, twenty-one, and twenty-eight, as the nnmbers, or fifteen, twenty-two, and twenty-nine, just as he implies the repetition or otherwise of the oc-tave note ; and as to this illustration from Livy, it is a very unfortunate one, for it tells the reverse of what the writer meant by it. Of course the cycle of nine-teen years begins every twentieth year ; had Livy made it begin every nineteenth, the reference would have been in point.

Historians and commentators usually speak of the single city of Rome, as if it were everything, and all the rest of the empire a mere passive, powerless mass. In the present case it is Rome only that is thought of in connection with this intercallation, and the Pontifex Maximus of the day is the only person who has to make the intercallation, or is supposed to understand any-thing about it. The historians, forget for the moment, that the Julian rectification was an enormous innova-tion on the ancient usages, permanently distributing ten days among the months, introducing an intercallary day every fourth year, instead of the intercallary month of Numa every second year, and making one year—the year of confusion, consist of fifteen months and four hundred and forty-five days. Every man in the empire was personally interested in a change like this ; every intelligent man in the empire must have been familiar with its nature, causes, and concomitants. Rome at that era was the great focus of European—nay, of Mun-dane civilization ; it must have held representatives of all the subject races, and of all the States in amity with it, and its intellectual classes must have been familiar with the corresponding institutions of all the enligh-

tened nations around them.   Precise orders relative to
the change of system, the year of confusion, and the intercallation, must have been sent to all parts of the empire, wherever the State had a soldier or commerce a
representative.   It was not the Pontiff Lepidus alone
who had to give an additional day to the month of February every four years ; but this had to be done in
every temple and office in the empire, and by every intelligent man who happened to have ears and eyes, or
any business arrangements with his neighbor.   The
blunder of Lepidus, therefore, to have been effectual,
must have been made spontaneously and simultaneously
over the entire empire.   Is it not manifest that the attempt to carry out such a blunder, even in a single instance, would have made the unlucky Pontiff the laugh
ing-stock of the whole Roman world ?   Here then, obviously, is another of those cases in which an important
fact has been utterly stultified and misunderstood, because its true explanation is irreconcileable with the
history which records it.

The next time we hear of any error in the calendar
is at the period of the Nicene Council in A. C. 325 or
330.   It was then found that the vernal equinox had
advanced from the 25th of March to the 21st, which
occasioned irregularities in the celebration of Easter.
The Council fixed the equinox to the 21st, but the equinox, nevertheless, would not stay there.   It still advanced, until it had gained ten other days, when its
course was finally checked by the Gregorian rectification, introduced A. C. 1582, but, as already noticed,
not adopted in England till 1752, it having required
more than a century and a half of discussion before our
sagely conservative ancestors could persuade themselves
to accept of common sense from the Pope.   We laugh
at them for this, of course ; but we ourselves are all

the while enacting similar absurdities. for the amusement of our grand-children.

And now we come to the *denouement* of this drama, which, whether to call farce or tragedy, we know not, for it has its sad, as well as its ridiculous aspects. We hear not of the tamperings of Pontiffs, or of the stupidity of peoples in connection with these latter rectifications, although the year went wrong, and went wrong in the old direction, and without a shadow of difference in the results—but then, in this last case of the series, men had found out a good reason for the fact, and, therefore, had no occasion to beat about for a bad one, and in the case immediately preceding, though no such reason was known, yet the Pontiffs of those times were the early Christian Fathers, who, of course, could not tamper; while the peoples of those times were the Faithful of the Church, who, of course, could not be stupid; and so the chroniclers, and historians, and commentators, and critics, having no good reason to offer, for once held their peace, and gave none. But Pagans were not so reverent. They looked upon their ancestors as men, not as religionists, and, therefore, when they thought them stupid, they said so.

And why had the calendar been thus getting into disorder since the days of Augustus? Simply because the civil year of three hundred and sixty-five days six hours, is eleven minutes and 10.46 seconds longer than the mean solar year, and the latter, consequently, was continually advancing on the calendar, at the rate of a day in about one hundred and twenty-nine years. Here is a perfectly satisfactory answer. The error was inherent in the calendar; it wanted nothing but time for its development: one thousand five hundred and eighty-two years were allowed it, and the minutes grew into fourteen days, without any aid from tamperings or stupidities.

But this error was inherent in the Roman year, from first to last ; in the Imperial as in Christian times, in the Republican as in the Imperial, in the Regal as in the Republican—from Romulus to Pope Gregory. And has it not left its footprints on tradition ? Five great re-adjustments ; sixty-seven days gained by the time of Cæsar, three others by the time of Augustus, four more by the time of the Nicene Council, ten additional ones by the era of Pope Gregory—eighty-four in all ; which, multiplied by one hundred and twenty-nine, give ten thousand eight hundred and thirty-six years of recorded Italic tradition ! And this, probably, since the introduction of the year of eight divisions ; leaving untouched the depths of antiquity implied in the previous years of seven, five, and four divisions.

The reader no longer requires to wonder at the nonsenses uttered by ancients and moderns, relative to the adjustments and aberrations of the ancient Roman year and calendar. How were they to recognize this grand sweep of ages in a history of some seven or eight centuries ? eight thousand six hundred and forty-three years between Numa and Cæsar ; three hundred and eighty-seven years between Julius and Augustus ! How could they dream of facts like these ? Will the reader himself receive them even when thus emphatically announced and explained ? or will he not, rather than receive such startling results, throw himself back again into the arms of those wise and venerable teachers who have told him these pretty tales about tampering Pontiffs and stupid nations ?

At all events he will ask how it has happened that these adjustments and rectifications were attributed to the particular personages and times in question, rather than to others, if there were not some historic foundation for the attribution. The following conjunction of facts will, I think, satisfactorily answer this, by no means unreasonable, query.

Romulus was the first of the kings, Julius the first of the emperors. Numa was the second of the kings, Augustus the second of the emperors. Romulus was the founder of the State, and of its leading institutions; Julius the founder of the empire and of its special forms. Numa improved all that was incomplete, reformed all that was defective, and created all that was still wanting in the institutions of the kingdom. Such did Augustus in the case of the empire. Romulus was a wise king, but, above all things, a distinguished warrior. Julius was, similarly, one of the most accomplished men of his age, and one of the greatest warriors and conquerors of antiquity. Numa, on the other hand, was pre-eminently pacific, he was the type of religion as Romulus was of war, and all the fundamental religious institutions of the country are attributed to him. Augustus, though from the elaborate and complicated character of the later traditions, he figures as a warrior in the early portion of his career, is, nevertheless, as an emperor, the type of the pacific, the religious, and the intellectual. As Numa was the Venerable, Octavius is the August, and his name has become a designation for a specially intellectual period, while he further represents Numa by the multiplicity of reforms and innovations which he introduced, both in civil and religious institutions. And, finally, as Romulus was slain and cut in pieces by his senators, while reviewing his army, Julius fell pierced by the daggers of his senators, in the midst of the great council of the nation.

In view of these coincidences, what more natural than to attribute the adjustments and re-adjustments of the year and calendar to those personages who are the types of all analogous phenomena?

As Romulus then first arranges the year and calendar which Numa re-adjusts and perfects, so Julius introduces the solar year, which Augustus re-establishes after it had fallen into disorder. Thirty-six years was the typical duration of the reign of Romulus, and it may be viewed as the space of time which intervened between his adjustment and that of Numa, and thirty-six years is similarly the interval which separates the adjustment of Julius from the correction of Augustus. Nor is this all.

The first of the chapters of the second part of this volume has exhibited the grouping of the great events of the history into cycles of three hundred and sixty and four hundred and thirty-two years, with an occasional substitution of three hundred and sixty-five for the former number. Now the year of Numa was lunar, and a lunar year consists of three hundred and fifty-four days. As, then, two solar cycles of three hundred and sixty years are allowed from the building of the city to the establishment of the empire under Augustus in the year of Rome, 720, so just two lunar cycles of three hundred and fifty-four years are allowed from the same point, to the establishment of the new calendar by Julius, in the year of Rome, 708! Surely no one will be so infatuated as to cling to the notion of a genuine chronology in the face of such facts as these. Nor has the spirit of system stopped even here.

The first allusion to the disorder of the calendar in Christian times, is made in connection with the Council of Nice, the first general Council of the Church. The equinox had then advanced from the 25th to the 21st of March, thus again gaining four days on the civil year. Now as this advance of the seasons is at the rate of a day in somewhat more than 129 years, four times 129 make 516 years, while the council is placed in 325 or 330, nearly two centuries earlier than it ought to be according to this astronomical coincidence. Here is something for chronologists to settle, and for astronomers to pause upon, when they think of introducing these wild fictions of legendary dates into the sacred precincts of physical science—when they think of benefiting astronomy by the study of ancient eclipses and such like materials of a chronology always conjectural, even when not purely mythic.

What concerns us, however, now, is the fact that the year 330 of Christ, is the year 360 of Augustus, the year of the solemn dedication of Constantinople as the seat of empire, by the first of the Christian emperors, the year in which Christianity was established by imperial edict as the religion of the State, the year which completed the great cycle of Rome's existence as a seat of dominion, the great 1080—three times 360—the year of the death of Paganism as a State creed, and of the birth of Christianity in the same character. It is in full consistency then with the system of these adjustments, that the first Christian fixing of the equinox should be assigned to a distinguished epoch, although the synchronism be wholly discordant; but what are we to say of our early Christian chronology, if it has erred by nearly two centuries in fixing the date of the first of the great councils?

And now to crown this history of systematic arrangements, we are finally told that the cause of the aberration of the seasons relative to the calendar, was first pointed out by the Venerable Bede, in the year of Christ 730, twice the solar cycle of 365 (the variant of 360), as the Julian arrangement was twice the lunar cycle of 354 !*

Here surely is a series of results which no one could have anticipated, and which no one can misunderstand. They are fatal to the history, such as ignorance and credulity have given it; but they open out vistas of a far grander story, which it will be the business of Science to restore.

In speaking of Ten Thousand years of Italian tradition, I simply offer a question to be examined, not a thesis to be proved. It is enough for the moment that an imposing theory is shaken to its very foundations, and the necessity of subjecting history to a new order of criticism made plain to every mind capable of rising above the prejudices of party and education.

CHAPTER VI.

So completely has the mind of the age been borne along by the current of tradition, that the most glaring historical inconsistencies lie perpetually before it without awakening the slightest suspicion of their presence, or if a doubt does at any time present itself, it is instantly dismissed as one of the difficulties inherent in the subject, or explained away by the best conjecture that happens to offer itself for the occasion.

Who, for instance, has noticed, except with a feeling of passing and unprofitable wonder, the unaccountable omissions which History presents in so-called contemporaneous events; its marvelous silence sometimes, its gross ignorance at others, in regard to matters of the utmost interest and importance, matters that could not be unknown to contemporaries, or left unnoticed by historians cognizant of their existence?

* Brewster's Encyclopædia, article Chronology, p. 406.

Let us look, for example, at the case of Egypt. Between that country on the one hand, and Greece and Italy on the other, there must have existed from remote times a constant commercial intercourse. A rich, powerful, and civilized kingdom like Egypt, could not be otherwise than a commercial country, and therefore well acquainted with all its neighbors; nor could such neighbors as enlightened Greece and Italy be other than well acquainted with the history, creeds, literature, languages, and institutions of a country so remarkable as Egypt. Besides, we are specially told that Solon and Herodotus, and other Grecian sages and writers, visited Egypt for the express purpose of study and observation; and to crown all, a Grecian monarch conquered the country, and a dynasty of Greek sovereigns ruled there for nearly three hundred years, in the golden age of Hellenic enlightenment, and in part also in the meridian splendor of the Roman mind. During all this time Greeks poured into the country; their language was current there by the side of the native tongues; their lineaments and their styles of architecture meet us among the monuments, and their mummies are turned up in the catacombs sometimes pure in feature, sometimes more or less Egyptianized.

But more important still, during all this period Egypt had not ceased to be Egyptian. Its gods were the gods of old, its creeds the native faith, its hierarchies and forms of government were all modeled upon ancient standards, its language was the immemorial tongue of the people, and that tongue was written, as in the remotest times, in the sacred characters peculiar to the race.

All the monuments of the country, except the Pyramids, are covered with that character. There is no secret in a style of writing

sands of years, and alike impressed on the temples of
the gods, the mausolea of the kings, and the coffin of
the private citizen ; nor could the priests of the country
keep such a secret from the masters of the country,
especially when those masters were themselves among
the conservators and rulers of all sacred rites. The
Greek sovereigns of Egypt appear on the monuments
as priests and terrestrial gods, just as appeared the
monarchs of old, and utter their invocations and offer
their prayers and sacrifices in the native language and
writing.

It is utterly impossible, then, that contemporaneous
Greece could have been ignorant in anything of consequence relating to Egypt, and yet that which we call
contemporaneous Greece, has told us nothing, or next to
nothing, on the very points on which curiosity would
have been sure to be most excited.

A catalogue of kingly names is not a history, neither
do temples and statues and emblems and innovations,
however great their numbers, constitute a religion. It
is in its creed and its legends that a religion truly consists ; remove these, and all else may be little better
than meaningless or delusive symbols. Judging by
these rules, what do we know of the religion of ancient
Egypt ? Scarcely anything beyond what might be inferred at any time from the monuments themselves.
With the exception of a few fragments of myths that
have reached us through comparatively late sources,
the entire mythology of Egypt may be said to have
perished. The speculations of the later Greeks are but
dreams and philosophies. They speak of ancient Egypt,
much as we speak of the Druids or Chaldeans, and only
prove how complete was the destruction, at the period
in which they were written, of the faith which they attempt to commemorate.

A seat of civilization so ancient, with a people so superstitious, and a religious apparatus so elaborate, must have had a body of traditions of proportionate magnitude. Egypt could not be an exception to a universal rule, and we have only to cast our eyes on Greece or Italy themselves, on modern India, Brahminical or Budhistic, on China, Japan, Ceylon, Burmah, Thibet Tartary, Persia, Scandinavia, Japan, Mexico, Peru, or Mediæval Europe, to see how necessary is the connection between an elaborate creed and an elaborate religious history.

How, then, has it come to pass that the mythology of ancient Egypt has found no echo in the writings of classic Greece or Rome? The historian has not described it, the fabulist has not drawn from it, the poet has not made it the subject of metaphor or allusion. When Egypt is named it is spoken of as a thing of the past—great and mysterious; and even when it is said to be described by an eye-witness, there is nothing told us that might not be written at a long subsequent period, while there is a total absence of that speciality and life which a work of actual observation always presents. Often, too, there is an ignorance which modern research has found it impossible to account for with any degree of satisfaction.

How has it come to pass that, in the days of the Ptolemies, with the Greek city of Alexandria in meridian splendor, and filled with learned men of various nations, that no one has thought of giving us a *bona fide* translation of any of the curious myths or historical traditions of Egypt? If the work of Manetho were such a work, why do we not hear of it till Christian times? And why, even then, does it come to us in a form which leaves it little better than a barren catalogue of names and dates? Names and dates, too,

which it requires no small amount of special pleading
and critical torture to bring into anything like agree-
ment with the monumental records, as deciphered by
modern ingenuity.

How comes it, too, that we are left in total ignorance
of the language of Egypt, that we know no more of its
manners and customs, than the monuments themselves
reveal, that, as far as books are concerned, it is a
grand dispute whether the people were black or fair,
and that were it not for these same monuments the entire ethnological character of the nation would be a
complete blank for us?

But above all, and before all, how comes it that we
are left in entire ignorance of the mystery of Hieroglyphics? Not a word, not a hint, till we reach the
bald *deductions* of Harapollo Nilous, or the passing notice of the Christian writer, Clemens Alexandrinus, a
notice not understood till the secret had been otherwise
attained. Yet what so calculated to excite intelligent
curiosity as this elaborate and peculiar style so utterly
unlike the graphic system of every neighboring nation?

Let any one try to imagine such things occurring at
the present day, or at any time within the last four centuries, in any portion of Europe. Every one must feel
that such results would be entirely impossible. And
yet we are required to believe that they were possible
in Greece and Italy in their most enlightened days.

We are told, indeed, as a sort of explanation of this
mystery, that the Greeks and Romans were incurious,
and despised barbarians. But the classic writers
never despised Egypt; on the contrary, they always
speak of it with an almost superstitious respect, but
they speak of it much as we speak of the Palestine or
Mesopotamia of Biblical history. The Greeks and Romans incurious? Curiosity is the very barometer of

intellect and civilization. It is only another term for
the desire of knowledge, and every page of classic literature, fabricated though it be, still bears intrinsic
evidence of the inherent literary inquisitiveness of the
Græco-Italic mind. Yet neither Solon, nor Socrates,
nor Plato, nor Aristotle, nor the prying Herodotus, nor
the all-learned Cicero, has a word to say on this curious topic, for had they had such a word, one or other
of them would infallibly have said it And when we
mention names like these, the mind does not present to
itself either the childish exclusiveness of China or the
stolidity of Mahometanism ; but it sees before it European genius and taste, and eagerness, and enterprise,
and cannot reconcile them with the silence and ignorance in question.

There is but one means of untying the Gordian knot
of this difficulty ; it will only yield to the sword. Call
the entire classic literature a gigantic swindle, as far as
history is concerned, and facts will speedily explain
themselves.

In the first chapter of the second part of this book,
we have seen Roman history regularly arranging itself into great epochs exactly measured by the cyclical
numbers 360 and 432, and their triplicates 1080 and
1296 ; and in the second we have seen the records of
the calendar, with its aberrations and corrections, revealing facts of a still more extraordinary nature, facts
which stretch out Italic tradition till even a portion of
it spans the vast interval of some Ten Thousand years.
The facts before us are a third emphatic indictment
against the legacy of tradition, and they are but a
small portion of those which go to make up the charge.

How comes it, for instance, that history knows nothing of the wonderful civilization of Etruria, which, if
records be true, must have existed in meridian splen-

dor centuries after the foundation of Rome? Until the researches and accidents of modern times had laid bare its painted tombs and identified the sites of its cities, it was impossible to form the least idea of the real character of this important phase of Italic life. Greece has told us nothing : Rome, next to nothing. Yet these painted tombs furnish unequivocal evidence of the existence of the most intimate commercial relations between Etruria and the Greece of its day; for not only do we see clear evidence of a community of manners, but so similar, in all respects, are many of the productions of art, that antiquaries have been sorely puzzled to determine whether the beautiful vases discovered in these tombs be of native or Greek manufacture, so entirely Greek are they in material, form, painting, taste, etc., even to the mythic personages represented on them, and the names in Greek characters which occasionally accompany these representations.

The Italy which the legend of early Rome brings before the mind is much like the Palestine of Abrahamic times, while the Etruria of the tombs and monuments is a powerful and wealthy republic with the social organization, the luxury and refinements of an advanced civilization. If our histories be genuine, how comes it that they not only give no intimation of this state of facts, but are cast in a mold entirely inconsistent with it? How was it possible that a petty territory like Rome should contend successfully with a confederacy which reached from its vicinity almost, if not quite, to the foot of the Alps? And that even in its early infancy this single city, with its handful of men, should successfully wrest town after town from the grasp of such an antagonist? When in the tales of the nursery the pigmy slays the giant, we have at least cunning and intellect matched against muscle and bone; but here it is the half civilized which conquers the highly civilized, without any advantage that could compensate for the enormous disproportion of the forces. Rome, indeed, except in the legend of Porsena, is never represented as contending with Etruria. The contest is always a contest of city with city, petty State with petty State, and there is nothing whatever to intimate that Etruria, during these wars, was the Etruria of the sepulchers. Yet if dates count for anything, this must have been the case. They evidently, therefore, in this instance, do not count for anything but that which they really are, elements of mythic cycles, to which tradition has been accommodated.

Etruria had a peculiar language; Rome has given us no account of it. The country is spoken of as eminently religious, and must therefore have had an elaborate mythology. Rome has suffered it all to perish. It had power and enlightenment, and must have had a history—that history has not left a wreck amid the annals of Rome, neither has it among those of Greece, if we except some vague conjectures as to the origin of the race. What prevented Rome from preserving the writings of Etruria—or what prevented the Etruscan cities from preserving them—as the Greece of the same era preserved its writings, and traditions, and customs, and as it preserved them equally under Roman dominion? It is absurd to suppose that all could have perished utterly in the midst of the very circumstances that would have aided in their preservation—viz., the close proximity of intellectual neighbors. Who ever heard of a cultivated language spread over a considerable extent of territory, yet perishing wholly in the course of a century or two, without any extermination of the people speaking it, or any known efforts to suppress it? How many centuries of conquest have passed over Wales, Ireland, Brittany, Greece, and many other regions, whose languages still survive, sometimes without the aid of literatures, and sometimes in the face of the most energetic attempts to suppress them? Is it not manifest that the sun of Etruria had set for ages before the star of Rome appeared upon the horizon, and that a deluge of conquest and barbarism had swept away thus completely the landmarks of ancient power, before the new one had commenced its special development? Between Etruria and Rome as a power, must stretch an interval long enough for the entire life of classic Greece, and other such intervals appear in various directions, although history has been at such pains to bridge them over

What, too, does Grecian history know about Tyre, beyond its destruction by Alexander, the legend of Dido, the names of a few kings, and a faint echo of its power? Yet it ought to have known everything worth transmitting to posterity. And it ought to have had a similar knowledge of Carthage, too. respecting which its notices are still more meager. Even Rome has given us little in this direction beyond a record of battles.

The relations of Greece with Persia, if we are to believe history, must have been sufficiently important to have awakened a vivid curiosity in regard to all that was singular in the condition or institutions of this powerful and baffled foe. Yet, though the army of Alexander swept over Persia, and established Grecian kingdoms on the ruins of that great empire, though Aristotle, from Greece, was exchanging epistolary courtesies with his royal pupil, then sitting on the throne of Darius, though Ctesias wrote Persian histories, and Xenophon historic novels on the same theme, yet no one has thought of telling us anything about the cuneiform writing, although information on so singular a system must have been infinitely more acceptable to an intellectual Greek than a catalogue of long perished kings, or the details of an ordinary campaign. There is but one rational interpretation for this unanimity in silence and ignorance, and that has already been given.

According to history, no deluge of barbarism, no casualties destructive to civilization, passed over Greece from the days of Alexander to the advent of the Turks, and yet Greek literature knows next to nothing of the specialities of countries that Greek armies had overrun, and in which Greek kingdoms were established for centuries; nothing of hieroglyphics, nothing of those wedge-shaped characters that covered the palaces of Persepolis and the slabs of Nimroud, and the bricks of Babylon, of those very things which have so vehemently excited the curiosity of modern times! It is just as if the England of the present day should transmit to posterity large sections of its literature, of its poems, songs, histories, plays, travels, tales, religious records, philosophical treatises, &c., &c., and yet leave in all this no intelligible account of the creeds or literature of India, no allusion to the peculiar writing of the Chinese, to the pictorial symbols of the Mexicans, or to a host of other curious facts which the present is always ready to chronicle, and the future always thankful to receive.

Let not the reader point, in reply, to the occurrences of mediæval times, for they have to be subjected to the same criticism as antiquity, and yield results of an analogous kind; nor to the doings of Asiatic, African, or other non-European races, among which mind is usually stationary, and curiosity usually low. We are here criticising European races, and, in phases of national life, only second to the civilization of the actual hour. They had not the press, it is true, but they had the pen, and they used it freely, as is obvious from innumerable references and lists of works. India had not the press either, and yet its literature, Brahminical and Budhistic, is absolutely vast; so, also with China, Arabia, and many other countries, in various degrees.

Of course, when Egypt, and Persia, and Tyre, and Carthage, have been thus treated, we cannot wonder that Palestine has been left unnoticed, or that we know nothing of the creeds or languages of Spain, or that we have such meagre accounts of Gaul and Britain. Yet Rome was master of Spain in its palmiest days, and the Spaniards are inherently an intelligent and manly race, while their relation with Cyclopean Italy, with Tyre, Carthage, and Rome itself, must have called forth their native powers at various periods of their history. Languages and monuments testify to all this; it is history alone which is silent.

Gaul and Britain had been, for unknown ages, the seats of elaborate creeds and powerful hierarchies—nay, they even had their times. as existing monuments unequivocally testify, of wide-spread empire and relative civilization, and yet all we have obtained from contemporaneous Rome is the meagre notice in *Cæsar's Commentaries*, and two or three other allusions of less note. All of which imply a social condition wholly inconsistent with the antecedents of the race, while some of the details given, by their distinctly mythological character, show that the accounts in question have nothing about them of genuine contemporaneousness. These war-chariot and naked savages. painted blue, are but readings off from mythic picture-writing—a portion of the symbolic imagery of the north-west quarter of the universe. Contemporaneous Rome is represented as speaking of the conquest of Britain as that of a new world, as if Roman commerce could have been to this extent unacquainted with the outer sea, or as if Phœnicia had never conquered Ireland, or traded with the Casseterides, to say nothing of the fact that the Cyclopean styles of the so-called early Christian architecture of Ireland, and the absolute identity in model and construction of the Round Towers, with similar monuments recently discovered in the Grecian Isles, plainly speak of an ancient Greek conquest also, thus confirming the national traditions.

What, too, are we to say of the curious fact that the calendar of the Cornish Britons has taken the names of the first eight months from that of Rome, while it has supplied the simply numerical names—September, October, November, December, with an entirely different series, proving manifestly that it received this calendar at a time when the Roman year had but eight (solar) months, a fact in full harmony with the generally archaic character of Roman remains in Britain, and with their depth beneath the present surface of the soil? Showing, in fact, two different and widely separated Italic conquests, the first attributed to the mythic head of the empire, the second to more recent times. Rome has not given us the real histories of her northwestern conquests; but old tales criticised into history, and such materials could not be given by contemporaries.

Of like character are those narratives in which we read of barbarian hosts overturning the mighty Roman empire; of countless hordes of savages, or semi-savages, cohering without organization, living and doing well, carrying on war and siege, conquering, and sustaining reverses, campaign also after campaign, year after year, without money, without established supplies, without national resources to fall back upon, without even the idea of a commissariat—but all at the sole expense of the enemy! Such a thing as a barbarian army does not exist on the face of the earth at the present day ; with a moment's reflection every man of sense must see that the thing is a physical impossibility ; and yet with all this before our eyes, we can go on believing in Brennus, and Attila, and Alaric, and Genseric, and the Germans, and Gauls, and the painted and naked Britons, and the Kimbri, *and the overflowing swarms of the frozen and barbarian north*, and all that sort of thing! We have seen the giant power of Russia tottering with approaching exhaustion after two campaigns, and yet believe in Roman history, which is one eternal campaign from beginning to end! We have been children, cheated right and left—-effectually, because at all points.

These extraordinary omissions, and these impossible narratives, cease to be mysteries the moment we cease to believe in written history. Let us allow facts room, and all becomes plain. Great gulfs of barbarism must have separated the principal civilizations of antiquity. Etruria, Athens, Macedon, Ptolemaic Egypt, Republican Rome, Imperial Rome, Constantinople—all must represent distinct and widely separated epochs. There must have been ample time for forgetfulness.

It will naturally be asked how, under such circumstances, classic literature came to exist? But it may be asked, in turn, why should not Greek and Latin poems and histories, and speeches and letters and philosophic treatises, grow according to the same laws by which Vedas, and Puranas, and Mahabarrhatas, and Homeric ballads, and books of Zoroaster, and books of Confucius, and Eddas, Chronicles, and Mediæval legends, grow and are transmitted fron and become melted down, and transformed, and polished up, according to circumstances and national genius; and why the one as well as the other should not ultimately be fathered upon mythic and legendary names?

These are but hints, and the subject is inexhaustible; but these hints will gradually become demonstrations, and ere long will change the entire aspect of antiquity, and leave our legends and our beliefs, and our criticisms and our learning, in much the same relation with the real history of man, which the exploded dreams of Neptunists and Plutonists and Mosaical philosophers bear to the great truths of our present geology.

The day is not far distant, wherein the common sense of civilized man will turn loathingly from the idle tales and ridiculous nonsense which unwise teachers have so long and so successfully imposed upon him under the borrowed garb of divine truth; and in that day he will have emerged from childhood to thinking man's estate. The story of Adam will be set down like all the other grand old Myths and pretty, ancient Dreamery, at its proper value; true religion achieve her final and everlasting triumph, and—

> "In that new childhood of the world,
> Life of itself shall dance and play;
> Fresh blood through Time's shrunk veins be hurled,
> And Labor meet Delight half-way.

TOPIC THIRD.

THE GENESIS OF NATIONS.

CHAPTER VII

THE progress of organization is progress in *Individualization* or *Specialization*. All progress, all life is an advance from the vague to the regular, from the chaotic to the elaborately arranged. The germ of even the highest life is a vagueness, in which we detect but a few faint shadows of future distinctions, but as growth advances, functions which at first were generalized, common to the entire mass, become progressively specialized, and committed to the charge of distinct organs, and the number of these specializations is the measure of the rank and importance of the general organism. It is the economic law of the *division of labor* carried out in organic mechanism, for here, as elsewhere, Nature has taken precedence of man, as well in application as in discovery.

Such is the law of Individual life, and the law of individual life is the law of all life ; the law of the race and species, the law of the genus and class, the law of the world and universe : for the plan of existence is everywhere the same. Low types develop few specialities, and reach their ultimate growth at relatively low stages ; high types become more and more complex, and ascend farther and farther in proportion to their destined rank, and *young* types also, as low in their own spheres, similarly exhibit less complexity than their correlative maturities.

Man is a high organism,* but a young life, hence he

---

* The question of the specific unity or diversity of the human family will be found admirably and learnedly discussed in the recent work of M. de Quatrefages on the "Unity of the Human Species," [Unite de l'Espece Humaine, Par A. de Quatrefages, Membre de l'Institut, (Academie des Sciences) 128 Par. 1861,] decidedly the most masterly, lucid, and well-sustained argument which Ethnology has yet produced. Still, though unanswerable on its own ground, this work is far from being decisive on the main points at issue, for, like almost all other writers on this subject, M. de Quatrefages has depended too exclusively on the study of details, and thus has lost sight of those great primary laws which alone can decide such a question, and which peremptorily settle in a moment the greater portion of its difficulties.

shows neither classic, generic, nor even specific differences, but an enormous amount of racial and subordinate distinctions, especially in his mental nature ; and the diversity is exactly proportionate to his social status.

When he is but one, when he is distinctionless. or only shows infinitessimal and unclassifiable differences, when, in a word, he enjoys the theoretic felicity of complete equality, of being naturally, as well as socially, on an exact level with all around him, he is a *savage,* and a savage of the lowest stamp, in proportion as he separates into distinct realms and nationalities, in proportion as each nationality develops distinction of type and class and capacity, in proportion as we can talk of artist and mechanist, of peasant and artisan, of merchant and manufacturer, of poet and orator, of statesman and soldier, of scientific and literary, &c., &c., and in proportion as these names become distinctions, not of scattered individuals merely, but of social groups, bound together by sympathies of instinct as well as considerations of interest, so does the nation rise in rank, in mind, in general nature, in civilization, in mundane influence, in genuine power.   All other elevations are but shams in the presence of this real rank, mere artificial aggregations, whose principle is oppression. whose coherence force, whose stability is that of the mushroom, rising or vanishing with the individual despot, or the shifting interests of the dominant *clique.* It is in vain to think of *creating* nationalities, *they must grow,* and grow in accordance with time and plan and special character, and grow, too, like all other growths, *from the very germ,* from a low, unspecialized type, from primitive savageism, in a word, and not from the fragments or the eclecticisms of any form of civilization. A nation must grow as one of the prescribed facts of mundane development, as a correlated phenomenon, as a portion of an organism, as one of a fixed number which can neither be increased nor diminished. The origin of nations belongs to the days of old, it is a geological event, an accomplished fact, which cannot again be repeated until, in due time, this planet enters into new cosmic conditions.

All genuine research carries us back to the savage ; the so-called historic migrations of nations are little better than hypothetic dreams, based upon fable in the the first place, and conjectural criticism in the second. Monuments, implements, ornaments, bones, fossils—these give us genuine facts, and only demand genuine reasoning to give us also genuine conclusions. As we go back, we move towards infancy, as we approach infancy we approach lowness, simplicity, relative homogeneousness. What is this in the case of aggregate man, but an approach to unspecialized barbarism ?

Beyond this point, it is not yet safe to go, but out of the fractional diversities of this early humanity must necessarily have arisen all existing nationalities, *and in their present centers also*, making due allowance for geological changes, and the occasional pressure of border nations, for soil and climate are necessary conditions in national growth. [*See Part III. present Volume.*]

These statements are the inevitabilities of law and plan, and when we turn to the sphere of special facts, we find nothing to contradict. but everything to bear them out. No nation has ever been known to repeat itself, nor are there two nations alike on the face of the globe ; yet dominant nations have constantly sought to repeat themselves, by colonization on the one hand and conquest on the other. As far, however, as any genuine evidence reaches, no conquest has ever yet perpetuated a type, nor has any colony been enduring. The

Persian, the Greek, and the Roman have vanished out of Egypt, without having left a living wreck behind them. The Ottoman but waits the advent of the next conqueror, and unless he presents himself soon, he will disappear of himself. There is no Moor or Saracen in Spain, no Roman in Gaul or Britain. Neither is there a Saxon, Scandinavian or Norman in the so-called Anglo-Saxon nation, in the so-called Norman nobility, else why such entire difference in genius, character, and destiny between the respective nationalities as now existing? Thus has it been everywhere and always, as far as the testimony of genuine facts can carry us.

As with conquest, so with colonization. It has nowhere reproduced the likeness of its parent—it has nowhere remained as an enduring aggregate. I do not now speak of the spread of savage tribes; they are more or less germal, and we are at present discussing the movements of civilization. In various regions of the earth we find monuments which clearly point to foreign sources—sources which, in many cases, can be distinctly identified—but for any living memento of what must once have been a powerful sway, and a life of many centuries, we look around in vain. Egypt, Northern Africa, Western Europe, Syria, Arabia, Southern India, Java, Borneo, Peru, Central America, Mexico, the valley of the Mississippi, and many other spots, furnish testimony of this kind, unequivocal and instructive. Could conquest or colonization have perpetuated types, many a proud race would have been blotted out, and many a nation would be found repeated. Savage *tribes*, indeed, have been exterminated even within living memory, but never *nations*, in the sense here implied, for many forms of savageism have fulfilled their destined functions, and die out before our

eyes even when we are most anxious to preserve them.
But no national types perish without leaving successors
somewhere; outlying tribes may be swept away, but
their centers of formation keep up a ceaseless life, which
defy alike the conqueror and the colonist. You may
sweep Egypt, from the Delta to the Cataracts, but you
cannot clear Abyssinia, try as you please. The Indian
of the northern woods and prairies makes way for you
in all directions, but the Mexican and Central American stands his ground. He will not vanish, and you
cannot do without him. So it is everywhere; courage,
climate, local circumstances—even the very interests of
conquerors make certain spots sacred to certain races.
To be conquered is one of the conditions of their
growth; it gives new blood, new thoughts, the acquisitions of other labors and experiences, and out of the
commingling springs a renovated and advanced nationality, and in the process, the conqueror gradually vanishes—vanishes even when his name, his language, and
his institutions remain.

There are, however, human aggregations which cling
to life with a strange tenacity, and which at first sight
might seem to contradict the principles here laid down;
but the discrepancy is apparent only. The Jew is pre-
eminently one of these; the Parsee may be cited as another. But the Jew is not a nation, but a *class*—he is a
merchant, and a merchant is no more a nation than an
eye or an ear is an animal. The merchant is pre-
eminently one of the floating elements of humanity. He
moves hither and thither, he marries here and there, he
renovates his blood in various directions and degrees,
and however far distant he may be, as a body, from the
parent stock, he is constantly coming into contact with
it through one or other of his members. All the Jewish communities, not divided by some schism in creed,

thus intercommunicate, while all look to the parent land. The type is preserved, but there is no national growth, or if there be, it is so faint as to be altogether equivocal.*

Similar remarks are applicable to the Parsee. He likewise is a merchant, a traveler; he similarly communicates with his native stock. Any fragment of nationality, kept pure in blood by stringent laws of creed or cast, living in a climate reasonably congenial, and keeping up communication with the parent race, might possibly exist indefinitely, while these conditions were duly maintained, but there is no reason for supposing that, on any other terms, the phenomena in question could be exhibited.

A nation, then, may be called an organism composed of locomotive elements; an organism whose bonds are mental, whose particles are held together by common sympathies and wants, springing from a common nature. It cannot, therefore, be a fortuitous aggregation; it cannot be a fraction or a selection; it must be a totality of one order or other; and though foreign ingredients may mingle with it, not only without injury, but often with the highest advantage, still they must not be too many to interfere with the aggregate power of control and absorption, otherwise the nation is in one of its convulsive periods.

---

* A strange interest has of late been given to the question of Jewish Nationality. Dr. James Hunt, in an able and instructive paper on the "Acclimatization of Man," read at a late meeting of the British Association, and recently again before the Ethnological Society, has called in question the Asiatic origin of the existing Jews, contending that they are rather representatives of old European conquests in Syria than actual aborigines of that land. This seems at present an extreme opinion, but it has fixed attention on a very curious fact, for it is formally asserted that the Jew cannot live permanently in Palestine, but would die out there if the population were not kept up by immigrations from the Jewish communities in other countries.

Could a nation so colonize as to represent in due proportion all the social elements of the mother country, then, indeed, it might repeat itself, for a time at least, but this cannot be done, for many of the social elements are too stationary to be thus displaced in sufficient quantity. The aristocracy of a land have no occasion to expatriate themselves, the masses generally have their local and class attachments ; it is mainly the restless, the ambitious, the enterprising, and those pressed by circumstances, who sacrifice their home affinities to the allurements of some great counterbalancing advantage. All colonization, therefore, amounts in the end to a practical eclecticism which is far from representing the full requirements of organic life and development.

While a colony continues under the rule of the mother country, it partakes of its life, and grows with its growth ; it is simply in the condition of an outlying province, and the common blood flows through it, and it thinks and feels with the common thought and feeling; but the moment it is severed from the parent stem all is changed. If there be growth that growth is abnormal, for the growth of a fragmentary organism is necessarily such, and abnormal growth continued is disorganization.

Among the many illustrations that might be given of these statements, two may be selected as having special interest at the present moment. Lower Canada had the advantage of representing, with some approximate fidelity, the social groupings of old France. Its population consisted of gentlemen, peasants, and a *bourgeoisie* in tolerably natural proportions. It has always cohered as one mass, without effort, and under considerable temptations to dispersal, because there was between all its members the irresistible sympathy of race, and of institutions born of race. But while old France has developed into the magnificent diversity of new France, Canada, cut off, remains precisely old France still, notwithstanding its advantages of space, neighborhood and freedom. Yet is it, in every ethnic sense, far more a nation than are these American States, which were founded under different conditions, as well as by different races. While the original States of the Republic were colonies, they had national attributes and coherence, but the moment they ceased to be such, that moment' the Republic felt a life of its own. It grew, indeed, but not as nations grow—slowly and organically—but rapidly, suddenly, by the mere absorption and multiplication of individualities—grew, in a word, as mercantile companies grow, where the bond of union is simply interest, and the *esprit du corps* not that subtle tie whose power is over the heart. This, of course, was not wholly wanting; but it could not be a prominent feeling, where there was neither community of origin, nor distinction of class ; and, therefore, in the very pride of its early strength, when the young giant seemed destined to overshadow half the globe, when its spirits were most elastic, and its dreams the brightest, the first intestine pang has snapped the thread of its feeble life, and it divides—how ? Not organically, as a real nation would divide, but simply conventionally—by the line of a mercantile interest, and of a thermometrical range ? The United States have never been truly such—have never been a really consolidated nation ; and never could or can be, so long as their Constitutional parchment admits of diverse renderings and interpretations ; never could or can be so long as the interests of one section antagonizes the interests of another. The country is now passing through the ordeal that all nations must

pass through, on their way from adolescence to maturity.
It is being tried by fire —it is undergoing the baptism
of blood ; but that it will successfully make the passage, no sane mind, no man with the least practical
statesmanlike faculty, can for a moment doubt.   Human
Slavery has unquestionably been the dividing acid that
has hitherto prevented interfusion, and retarded the
growth of a *national* spirit. Remove that, and forthwith
will begin America's real Unity—for that of the past
has been only such in seeming ; remove that, and forthwith will begin a chemico-national process, whose result
will be the consolidation of these States, whose power
may safely challenge the civilized world ; remove that,
and a national youth will go on toward a maturity yet
lying among the Possibilities of future centuries, and our
country will reach an eminence whence she may dic-
tate laws to the habitable globe, and dictating, be
obeyed !   This is our destiny ; I feel it—I know it !
Were Great Britain to fall to pieces, every one would
see that its divisions would necessarily be what they
have been all along—Ireland, Scotland, Wales, England, even down to the heptarchy or the county, if
needs were ; but they would be ethnic to the last, and
force alone could make them mercantile.

And such is the natural history of the great experiment ; and thus must human hopes be dashed when
they outrun experience ; and thus must the most elaborate calculations of the politician and the philanthropist be scattered to the winds when they choose to
assume a knowledge of humanity in advance of the
teachings of Science.

The events of the day, as well as the experience of
the past, read a lesson of profound significance to all
outlying sections and colonies.   Cut off from the heart,
their doom is irrevocably fixed ; events may delay it,

may even light up for the moment a deceptive splendor, and give a progress that shall simulate genuine
growth, but the day of trial must come at last, and
then will be seen the difference between a nation and
a heterogenous mass. Anarchy or insignificance—these
are the Scylla and Charibdis of every severed country,
and to one or other must all such ever float ; and the
end of both is extinction. This, indeed, is a fate which
cannot be escaped in any case, for the mutability of
human affairs will ultimately break the connection in
one way or other, and then what climate does not
effect, will be accomplished by the moral surround-
ings ; the intruder will be gradually absorbed by some
indigenous race which he has helped to elevate. If
this be not the history of the past, then monuments,
languages, creeds and traditions are things without a
meaning.

But if nations cannot be created by conventional
arrangements, so neither can they be destroyed; they
are parts of a plan over which man can only obtain
even the most limited and indirect control by understanding and respecting it. An oppressed nationality
is a canker for which there is no cure but freedom, and
that cure must come sooner or later, for it is inherent
in the oppression itself. By infusing new blood into
the vanquished, the conqueror restores the wasted energies of the fallen, and in the end, the prostrate nation
awakes into renovated life, and flings off the incubus
which crushed and disgraced it. Even in the union of
cognate races, even in the consolidation of the various
sections of a common country, the local tribes still keep
up their individuality of nature. Costume, language,
forms of Government, all the accidents of nationality
may vanish or amalgamate; but *time, instead of obliter-
ating, only deepens and multiplies all genuine ethnic traits.*

Britany is still Breton, and Wales, Welsh, and even to the end of the chapter, Ireland will be Irish, and Scotland Scotch. And why should we wish things otherwise? Progress is specialization, unorganized commingling, chaos. In these seemingly useless or mischievous distinctions, nature is working for distant futurities even when she is not working for the actual moment. We may as well let her work in peace, for she will not be thwarted, do what we may.

But whatever may be the evils which attend their progress, colonization and conquest are among the inevitabilities of national development. Population must have room, energy must have a theater of action. Humanity is an organism, and its blood must circulate; all its chief portions must, in due course, be centers of special action and development, and hence the fluctuations of power and the sequences of empire. While humanity is young, and reason feeble, the conflict of interests must arouse fierce passions; but a knowledge of the laws of life, and attention to the teachings of science, will enable us to minimize evil, and make the most of good.

My limits will not permit me to pursue this interesting subject farther on this occasion. My object will be sufficiently attained if I fix attention on an important truth, though not with all the precision and distinctness that can be given to it. This great ethnic truth is the *growth* of nations in the *organic* sense of the term; their systematic and correlated growth; their growth in a sense which implies definiteness in number, determinate affinities and contrasts in character, and hierarchy in attribute and power. The terms of this growth may be thus summed up:—

1st. That humanity divides into an Organic and an Inorganic section. The former comprises a determinate

number of great groups or ethnic realms, each having a
fixed number of distinctly characterized nationalities.
These realms though, in the main, those pointed out in
this work, have now to be presented in a different arrangement. Of course, a nationality, in the sense in
which the term is here used, does not mean a single
tribe, whether large or small, but an aggregate of cognate tribes all more or less differing in character. The
inorganic section does not occupy a series of special
realms like the organic, but partially surrounds and
partially divides off the organic groups, each portion of
it having special affinities to the particular realms which
it thus encloses or separates. Thus the Esquimaux,
Laps, Samoides, Fuegians, and Hottentots, may be mentioned as extreme outside races of the inorganic section, while the races of Northern Africa separate the
European from the Negro realm, as those of Western
Africa—the Nubian, Abyssinian, &c., divide the latter
from the Asiatic, and as the native tribes of Syria,
Caucasus, and the Ural divide Europe and Asia.

2d. That every true nationality has had its origin in
a remote, and probably geologic epoch, and has gradually developed in such a manner as will ultimately
give it a degree of subdivision and specialization proportionate to the rank of its scale, and to its own place
in that scale, so that the highest nations are those
which will be the most diversified, especially in their
mental attributes; and such is the fact even already.

3d. That neither conquest nor colonization, nor any
other national interblendings, ever produce permanent
mixed races, in the usual acceptation of the term,
though they are aids, and seemingly indispensable aids
in the production of *new* races and varieties within the
bounds of nationality; in other words, in the production of national specialization.

4th. That all realms and nationalities originally, and all specializations of nationality subsequently, have been, and are produced by the regular action of chemical laws, and that their production obeys the great primary chemical necessity of *determinate, harmonic, unequal proportions*. By this law, vague or indefinite interblending is absolutely impossible; partially congruous mixtures tend to destruction by disease, monstrosity, or barrenness, while only fully congruous combinations have an enduring vitality.

All our knowledge of organic existence, whether vegetable or animal, will be found in the strictest accordance with these statements, while all other modes of explanation have but made confusion worse confounded, and difficulties more formidable than before.

CHAPTER VIII.

THE GORILLA *vs*. MAN.

HIS TRUE PLACE IN THE ANIMATE SCALE—IS HE BUT A
GENUS AND ORDER OF THE CLASS MAMMALIA ?—OR IS
HE THE INITIAL TYPE OF A VASTLY HIGHER ORDER
THAN HE YET IMAGINES?

It is not pleasant to have it proved that one is in error, to be told that a discernment of which, perhaps, we are not a little proud, has been signally at fault; neither is it agreeable to be moved from positions in which we find ourselves comfortable, and bidden to adjust ourselves to new and imperfectly understood relations. Hence, in the sphere of mind, *Innovation* is always an ominous and hated word, and he who bears it on his standard is ever viewed as the disturber of repose, the censurer of the present, and the calumniator of the past.

No one objects to novelty as novelty ; only let it accord and fraternize with what has gone before—only let it come with a friendly smile, shaking hands and making itself at home, and it will be an ever-welcome guest, always received with open arms.   But let it come with a frown and a reproof, as a censor and a master, ejecting and displacing, and what wonder that its approach should be viewed as that of an intruder and a foe?   Now the novelties of Science are very apt to be of this latter character—its great truths always are. Hence its progress is necessarily a warfare, and the ground it gains has often to be disputed, inch by inch.

He who is engaged in a contest and feels himself weak, naturally looks around for an auxiliary, hence the invariable appeal to authority, feeling, prejudice, interest, and, above all, and before all, to Religion, whenever a new truth claims recognition, and is felt to be strong.

Religion, which, in these cases, rarely means anything more than Theology, is sufficiently plastic to yield to the torture of each individual interpreter, and sufficiently extensive in its relations to meet the ever-changing aspects of advancing knowledge.   Creeds are so numerous, their modifications so innumerable, that no truth has ever been uttered by Science which does not contradict, either in itself or in its consequences, some form of creed, some modification of religious opinion. Hence the most sacred feelings of our nature are ever arrayed against the laws and facts of the universe, and a perpetual feud is kept up between the Word and the Works of God.

And yet Science, when real, is but another term for Truth, and the sole aim of its genuine votaries is its pursuit by the best and most legitimate means.   How then can it ever antagonize with religion, except on the assumption that religion is false?   But Religion is the

law of the heart, as Science is the law of the understanding, and the one can no more err than the other.
Normal feeling is as infallible as normal perception,
and both are as unerring as the great laws which have
called them into being—as the Supreme Mind which has
set those laws in operation. There never has been,
then, and never can be, any real feud between Science
and Religion. But Theology is another matter, and
there are few who do not practically confound theology
with religion. Yet theology is but the *dress* of religion,
not the reality ; and while one is eternal and ever the
same, the other is constantly changing with time, and
circumstance, and grade of knowledge, and even with
the whims and vices of men. Creeds rise and perish,
the Revelation of to-day is the scorn of to-morrow, the
gods of one faith the demons of another ; but the same
object, the same feelings, the same aspirations and
yearnings underlie all the myriad aspects of this kalei-
descope of opinion, and the pure heart is ever right,
however wrong may be the head.

Science cannot change law or fact to accommodate
theology ; it is for Theology to suit herself to the requirements of advancing knowledge, as she has done
with reference to Astronomy and Geology—as she will
inevitably be compelled to do with reference to Miracles and the Human Origines. She may struggle for
a while, only to yield in the end! Time out of mind
she has had to do so ; she will ever have to do so until
she merges her interests in those of Science, and makes
one with it. And why should not this happy union
take place ? Why must the heart be severed from the
head, intellect from feeling ? Not he who made both,
and divinely fitted them to interact as minister and
ruler, as counsellor and queen—not he, but the pride

and petulance and ignorance of man, have willed their unnatural severance.

There have been men in every age who have clearly perceived these fundamental truths, and who, therefore, in all seeming discords, have quietly pursued their course, fully persuaded that time and patience would bring everything into harmony. But these, unfortunately, are the exceptions to the rule, and, as far as the public is concerned, there has always been some current feud between theology and advancing knowledge.

It is no more our duty to give adhesion to the crudities and rashnesses of science, than it is to listen to the prejudices of feeling, but where science has calmly studied, and maturely weighed ; where facts are abundant and unequivocal, and inferences clear and irresistible, even to prejudice itself, then opposition becomes not only folly but worse than folly, for it is a rebellion against the authority which God himself has given for our guidance—an authority, too, which must, after all, be obeyed, and from which there lies no possible appeal. Only with his own mouth can a man eat, only with his own eye can he see, only with his own brain can he think or reason ; is it not then the merest infatuation to pretend to have a higher standard of reason than that furnished by the only powers with which we can reason, or better means of perception than those furnished by the only instruments with which it is possible to perceive ?

The great Battle of Science, in our own days has been that which Geology has had to wage with the Cosmogony set forth in the book of Genesis. That battle is now virtually over ; all that geology has claimed has been fully surrendered, and it would be ungracious to the struggle while victors and vanquished are still upon the scene, were it not that the latter, untaught by experience, still present a defiant front, and refuse to acknowledge defeat, even while conceding every point contested by their opponents. As Science would not come to the book of Genesis, the book of Genesis has been brought to Science, and heaven and earth set in motion to prove that the two records are not, and never have been, at real variance. Thus, though yielding in one direction, prejudice has not surrendered her weapons either of attack or defence, but stands prepared to encounter every fresh innovation with the very same arms with which she made so vehement an effort to crush the rising strength of geology. These are my reasons for alluding to the subject in a formal manner, for while sophistry remains unexposed and fanaticism unchecked, the battle of science is simply removed from one field of action to another : from Astronomy to Geology, from Geology to Ethnology, Archæology, Mythonomy, and above all, to the Science of sciences, Cosmology.

In the language of common life, in all the arrangements of practical existence, a wide gulf separates man from all other terrestrial beings : In the language of zoology, and in the classifications of the naturalist, man enjoys no pre-eminence beyond that of simply heading the long chain of organic types. Which is the correcter view of his nature and position—which brings him nearer to his true place in the animate scale—that which regards him as " Lord of the Creation " and Ruler of the Earth, pre-eminent and apart, or that which treats him as a mere animal, a member of a group, every other member of which is a *beast*, and separated from these beasts by no broader line of demarcation than that which separates one group of beasts from another—a cat from a dog, a monkey from a squirrel, or a cow from a horse—the line of an *order?* Which of these views is the more natural and accurate? This is the question which we have here to discuss.

In the first place, it is obvious that the language of common life is simply the expression of unquestionable facts. Man *is* the lord of the creation ; he *does* stand pre-eminent and apart ; there *is* a wide impassible gulf between him and all other creatures on this globe. It is not, then, the language of ordinary life, or the universal sentiment of humanity, that is here called upon for a defence ; it is Science itself that we have to take to task—it is from the zoologist we have to demand how it happens that his arrangements as a naturalist do not accord with his acts and sentiments as a man, that he speaks one language in his closet, and a wholly different one in every other relation of life ?

His books thrown aside, his study closed, the naturalist walks forth into the world as keenly alive to the dignity and pre-eminence of his nature as the least scientific of his brethren. He no more thinks of bringing himself down to the proximate level of the monkey or the dog, than he thinks of connecting himself with a bramble-bush. He looks around and beholds the already great achievements of his race, infantile though it be—civilization, arts and sciences, mechanism, learning ; he looks within, and feels the swellings of lofty aspirations, the yearnings for something brighter and grander still, the half glimpses, the looming shadows of glories and achievements yet to come ; and then from the proud heights to which his thoughts have borne him, he looks down upon the lowly subjects of his zoological realm, and asks what are their deeds and aspirations ? The answer is— none ; no creation, no aspiration, no change : it is the contrast of magnificent reality with the blank vacuity of negation.

But his walk ended, his mind refreshed by air, and exercise, and change, the man of Science once more re-enters his study. Instantly the splendid vision has vanished, as if touched by the wand of an enchanter, and the refreshed brain is again busily at work, tortur-ing itself to discover some sufficient point of distinction in the hand, or leg, or arm, or face, or cranium, of some chattering monkey or hideous ape, to warrant the sepa-ration of the creature from man by some broader damarcation than the line of a genus! What is the meaning of this great contrast between theory and practice—between one phase of thought and another? There must be some serious error here, for truth is con-sistency, and this conduct is not consistent.

The answer of the naturalist to these questions will be something to this effect. Anatomically, he will say, man differs little from the beast—less, in fact, from some beasts, than they differ from many others. Man, too, is but a single genus—nay, even a single species : where can he be put if not in the group which he most resembles? We cannot make a great primary division, or a separate class in any sense, for a single species ; there is no precedent for such an adjustment within the entire range of the organic world. Besides, everywhere else structure is the guide and criterion of classification ; why should it not be so here?

This reply seems plausible, but it will not bear ex-amination. If man differ but little from the beast structurally, how does it happen that he differs much from him functionally? Function is but structure in action ; superior function but the action of superior structure. To say that there may be vast superiority in the one, and little or none in the other, would be to say that an effect might be wholly disproportionate to its cause, which would be absurd.

It matters nothing to this argument whether man's superiority be partial or general, in one portion of his nature or in all. It is perfectly indifferent whether it lie in his hand or in his foot, in his brain or in his soul; it equally demands recognition in classification, and recognition to the fullest extent.

Apart from function, structure is valueless. How, then, can a classification be rational which practically ignores that which is important, while duly emphasizing that which, without it, would be worthless; or which ignores the superior portion of a nature or structure, while giving infinitesimal attention to the inferior?

Let it be assumed that man is wholly material in his nature; then the whole, or some portion of his structure, must be immeasurably superior to that of all other terrestrial existences, since it produces functions immeasurably superior. Let it be granted, on the other hand, that man is, in part, of a spiritual nature, and that his superiority entirely depends upon this portion of his being; such an admission can furnish no reason for the neglect of so important a circumstance in our estimate of his relative position in the scale of existence.

Whatever, then, be our theory as to the immediate source of man's intellectual superiority, we are equally bound to recognize in our arrangements the fact of this superiority. If anatomy fails us in the study of mental structure, we must look to physiology for light. If we cannot appreciate either the machinery itself, or its more immediate effects, we must look to remoter effects. Function is a reality as well as structure, for it is structure in action; it has, therefore, to be estimated. Where anatomy is powerless, we must look to results, however remote, and judge of the nature and value of the cause by the nature and value of the effects. But such one-sided arrangements as those in question—arrangements which virtually ignore the superior half of a nature and structure, while giving infinitesimal attention to the inferior, are not only wholly indefensible, but would be wholly unaccountable, if we did not take into consideration the influence of association and routine, especially in infantile sciences, in which the mind is absorbed in the study of details, and the functions of the reasoner are discharged by the mere observer.

We should hardly deem it a very brilliant feat of classification were an upholsterer gravely to persist in grouping upright pianofortes with chiffonniers, and horizontal ones with tables, on the simple ground of external form and material; yet this is precisely what we have all done or acquiesced in as naturalists and anatomists. We have duly estimated the mahogany and rosewood, but quite forgotten all about the music. If we have not omitted the character of Hamlet, " by express desire," yet Hamlet has forgotten to appear, and the audience has forgotten to call for him.

It is quite true that, in external structure, a man differs far less from a monkey than a monkey does from an elephant; but it is equally true that a square pianoforte differs far less, in external structure, from a table, than a table differs from a harp or flute; yet the harp, flute, and piano belong to the same category of existences, and the table to quite another. Could we duly estimate the finer chords of the living instrument, we should find that its superiority in tone, power, and character, was the simple result of its superiority and specialty, in material or in structure, one or both. On what else could it depend? Why, then, fail to recognize, in classification, this superiority when the very ob-

ject of classification is to group things in due relation
with the nature and amount of their resemblances and
differences, their affinities and discrepancies, their approximations and recessions in material, structure,
function, rank, and all other qualities and aspects of
their being ?

But, it will be said, man is a single genus nay, even
a single species; where then can he be put, if not in the
group which he most nearly resembles ?   Supposing we
had ten thousand silver and copper coins, and only a
single gold eagle, should we not recognize that eagle
as something distinct and apart in nature and value,
however near its approach in size and shape to a quarter
dollar ?   Or would the fact of its being one, and not
many, make the least difference in our estimate ?   Man
is the sovereign of the organic world, distinct and
apart.   Why confound him with baser metal, because
of resemblances in mere form and stamp ?

If man be a single type he is also the most recent of
all the great types ; have we allowed him sufficient
time to grow into complexity ?   The universal law of
growth is from the low to the high, from the simple to
the complex, from the one to the many.   The entire
stream of geological evidence leads to the conclusion
that every great group in the animal kingdom was once
represented by a single type.   This evidence is far
from being complete, as a matter of positive observation, but this is its entire tendency in every direction ;
in all groups, great and small ; in kingdom and in class,
as in genus and in species ; *and, in principle, it could
not be otherwise.*

Man, is younger, by millions of years, than the initial type of the beast, to say nothing of the bird, reptile,
fish, insect, etc.   He is younger by hundreds of thousands of years than the mammalian type to which he

most approximates—the monkey; we cannot then expect him to be much diversified. It is impossible that he should form an exception in the plan of the universe, or in the inevitable laws of development; let us then clearly recognize his *initial* position, and allow time for his progress. And certainly, if we are to judge from the innumerable minor groups into which his species has already been split up, we must admit that he is at all events traveling on the high road to diversity.

The errors of early science are less due to simple ignorance or precipitancy of deduction than they are to unsystematic reasoning. When there are no rules of guidance, and no criteria of accuracy, it is not only easy to err, but easy to err needlessly. Had naturalists commenced their labors by distinctly formulating the obvious requirements of scientific classification, or had they subsequently placed before their eyes such a formula for testing the propriety of their adjustments, so serious an error as the one under consideration could never have been committed. What is it that we aim at in scientific arrangement? Simply to place the objects to be classed in such conjunctions as shall correctly represent their relative rank, and their several relations of affinity and difference. Consequently :—

In every consistent arrangement, all objects will be so placed as to approach to, or recede from, each other, in exact proportion to the number, nature, and importance of their affinities and differences.

This simple and obvious law is primary, and, so to speak, innate. It belongs to the very nature of things, and applies with equal force to the highest generalizations of science and the most familiar arrangements of every-day life. It requires us to consider the rank and importance of attributes, the number and character of affinities and differences; it requires us to embrace all

and exclude none ; and, finally, it requires us to gra-
duate strictly the rank of our divisions, so as to make
them a clear mirror of the rank of our differences, because every oversight or carelessness, in such cases, is
a distortion of the true relations of things, and not only
an error, but a source of errors. .

With such a law as this before his eyes, it would
have been impossible for the naturalist to have placed
man in a group from which he is more widely severed,
in all the higher attributes of his being, than that group
is severed from any other, high or low, within the
bounds of the animal kingdom.

When we make the rank of our divisions a clear
mirror of the rank of our differences, we shall not base
important lines of division on trivialities of structure,
nor represent important differences of nature by dividing lines of minor rank.   We shall not feel bound to
expend volumes of learned controversy, and endless details of minute anatomy, in emphasising the differences
between the hand and foot of the monkey and the hand
and foot of man, in order to justify our separation of
these two animals by the line of an order, nor shall we
feel bound, on the ground of relatively trivial resemblances, to destroy the consistency of a great primary
group, by forcing into it an element of an entirely different rank.

It is quite true that nature is so consistent in all her
operations, and that mechanism of a high order requires such minute relative adaptations in all its parts,
that, absolutely speaking, the knowledge of the part is
a key to the knowledge of the whole.   But then we
must have adequate intelligence, and patience to make
the profound and careful deductions which this mode
of procedure often demands ; nor must we confound
the means with the end, and come to view our key as

the very object we are in pursuit of, instead of being its simple index. Anatomy and physiology are confessedly most important guides and criteria in zoological classification ; all important, in fact, as far as they are fully available ; but then it must be remembered that there may be two grand departments of anatomy and physiology, the material and the spiritual, and that even if there be not, there is that which is equivalent to them. Now, spiritual structure is beyond our reach ; but if we believe it to exist, it is a fundamental error to ignore it in our arrangements ; and if we do not believe it to exist, we must, at least, believe in an equivalent—namely, a refinement of material structure, capable of producing all the phenomena of mind ; and to ignore such a portion of our organization as this, is an error equally fundamental. Where anatomy fails us, we ought to seek aid from physiology, and the reverse. Physiology can aid us here ; if we cannot dissect with the knife and see with the eye those ultimate textures and fluids on which mental phenomena immediately depend, we can study the phenomena themselves in their external manifestations, and judge of the general nature and value of the cause by the nature and value of the effects. By practically neglecting all this, in the case before us, the naturalist has fallen into one of the gravest errors which it was well possible for a classifier to make ; he has brought into incongruous conjunction, and separated only by the mere line of an order, a being who, in all the higher attributes of his nature, demands not merely the separation of a great class, but even that of an entire kingdom.

True, the affinities, the resemblances, must not be neglected, but such affinities everywhere present themselves in the case of *initial* types. It is difficult to dis-

tinguish from vegetable structures the lowest animal
forms, yet the humblest of these forms has a something
in its nature of such vast superiority, that it lifts it not
only into a new class, but even into a new kingdom.
The lowest existing mammals approach, in many important attributes, to the structure of the bird ; others,
still lower, and more bird-like, have doubtless passed
away.   The lowest type of the bird may be now known
as a saurian, the oldest reptile as a fish, and so on.   At
all events, even the lowest existing orders, in every
class, have striking affinities with the next lowest class.
All this speaks of plan and growth ; but it does not
justify the confounding of high and low, still less the
entire neglect of the former.

The present is one of those many questions which
present serious difficulties when viewed simply on the
ground of mere observation and detail ; none when
examined on the higher ground of principle.   All hesi-
tation vanishes the moment we look to the necessities
of rational arrangement.   The cause must be proportionate to the effect : if the effect be superior, so must
be the cause.   Function is the product of structure and
nature : the superiority of the one is the superiority of
the other.   These truths are plain and immutable, and
equally certain, whether our knowledge of causation
be direct or inferential.   The fundamental laws of arrangement require that objects should be grouped or
separated in exact relation with the number and importance of their resemblances and differences ; therefore, with reference to the totality of their nature ;
therefore, in such a manner that the lines of separation
shall be narrow or broad, just as are the differences
little or great.   Now, the most important attributes
of animal existences are mental attributes ; all others
are valueless, except in so far as they can minister

directly or indirectly to these ; therefore, all the major divisions of zoology, not to say all divisions whatever, must be based on mental attributes, and be broad or narrow as these are great and many, or few and trivial. These are the laws ; the application is simple.

Man differs from the monkey and every other mammal by more numerous and vastly higher mental differences than any one group of mammals differs from any other ; therefore the line that separates him from the monkey is not that of an order, but one much broader.

Man differs as much mentally from every beast as the beast differs from the bird, the bird from the reptile, the reptile from the fish, and so on—as much, in fact, as any great primary group in the animal kingdom differs from the next in rank ascending or descending ; therefore, he cannot be separated from the beast by any narrower line than that of a great class. Whether his destiny be to continue one, or to develop into many types, matters nothing to this argument—he equally forms, *de jure* and *de facto*, one of the great primary divisions of the animate world.

But man differs far more from the beast in mind than the beast differs from the bird, or the bird from the reptile—more, in fact, than the beast differs from the worm. It is not, then, even the line of a great class which must separate him from the monkey, but one far broader and more important. From the mammalian to the articulate type is a descent of four great classic stages, yet no one will pretend that man, in his intellectual and moral nature, does not rise far higher above every other mammalian type than the highest of these types rises above the highest insect ; and, if so, his separation is not one of class simply. If we consider man in his very highest aspects, such as he appears in his highest races, and in the highest portions of those races, and then remember that he is an *Initial* and an advancing type—if we view him as the highest poet, the highest orator, the highest artist, mechanist, statesman, ruler, warrior—as the highest naturalist, mathematician, astronomer, etc., one and all, and then compare him with the lowest existing mammalian types, such as the opossum or ornithorhynchus, can we say that he differs less from these than they differ from the very lowest radiates ?

But man's nature is as yet but very partially developed. He is very young, even as a genus, even as a species. We probably know little of what he is yet really capable. We are judging him as if he were the real man, when he is but the tiny infant of humanity, just awakening into the first shadowy consciousness of himself, and of the great universe around him. Yesterday he was but the savage ; the day before he was unborn. Let us wait, at least for his childhood, before we judge of his maturity. The ornithorhyncus, on the other hand, is a very old animal, long past its maturity, just preparing, according to all appearances, to add the yet few remaining links to the fossils of its race. The comparison, therefore, is wholly unfair to man. We compare him not with the infancy of the first beast, but in all probability with the maturity of types several generic grades above the initial beast.

We will not pursue this subject farther in the present work, but may have occasion to again resume it ; nor shall we seek to evade the difficulties, nor shrink from the logical consequences which the present view of the matter entails. The reader will see at a glance that this view opens out a great and exciting theme. A new *Kingdom* in nature is no trivial term. A kingdom whose lowest type is man, is something to rouse the dullest, and animate the coldest. It is either an argumentative dream, or one of those great facts which from time to time startle Science into a new consciousness, opening out new spheres of thought and new fields of research

A new kingdom, in the ascending scale of being means nothing less, according to all the known analogies of nature, than a series of great classic groups rising one above the other, mentally and physically, each with its numerous orders, genera, species, and individualities. When we compare the extremes of the animal kingdom—the infusorial monad or a particle of sponge, with the elephant or the dog—what are we to say of a grand sweep of existences whose lowliest form, whose infusorial monad, whose first bit of sponge is MAN! There is something here to confound as well as to dazzle, and yet is it not the old story? The realities of nature immeasurably transcend the highest and the strangest dreams of man, and the progress of knowledge is ever from marvel to marvel.

A new kingdom in nature means millions of ages yet to come : a kingdom of this rank means a sphere of existence appropriate to both its dignity and importance. It means the infancy of the present and the past, the immeasurable stretch of the future ; progress everywhere, inorganic, vegetable, animal, *Intellectual.* It means, in a word, the turning over of a new page in the great book—the drawing aside of another fold of the mystic veil. Let us then neither delude ourselves with a dream, if this be a dream, nor frighten ourselves out of a great reality, if it be such, but let us calmly and resolutely scrutinize the conditions and necessities of this great problem, and then decide, in accordance with law and evidence. We have to consider whether an *initial type* does not necessarily mean a new growth, and whether a new growth does not mean a regular and pre-arranged advance to maturity and decay. We have to settle whether man's type of structure rises above the nearest mammalian grade, by the stage of a genus or an order only, or by that of a class or a kingdom ; and whether an initiated genus must not necessarily mean one which is destined to develop into many species ; an initiated class, one which in due course present numerous genera and orders ; and an initiated kingdom, one which must, in time, exhibit a grand sweep of classic groups with their elaborate apparatus of subdivisions ; and, finally, whether an initiated world can be other than in its merest infancy, when the very first of its intellectual inhabitants has but just budded into being. These are the questions which we have to determine, and there are more resources for their settlement within reach than the reader is yet aware of.

The three subjoined articles are quoted from the columns of newspapers, and are here presented, not for their fullness, or even suggestiveness, but as mere waifs from the literary atmosphere, showing clearly which way the wind is blowing, and demonstrating that there is a great and unappeasable appetite in the public mind for stronger food than it has hitherto subsisted upon. Indeed, it is plain that even the unread masses of the people are beginning to doubt the Adamic theory, and to demand a different explanation of the human genesis.

One of the most exciting and interesting discussions of the session followed the reading of a paper, by Richard Owen, D.C.L., F.R.S., " On the Zoological Significance of the Brain and Limb Characters of Man, with Remarks on the Cast of the Brain of the Gorilla."

The position which Mr. Owen endeavored to establish was, that there is, between the brain and limbs of the gorilla and man, a much greater structural distinction than there is between the gorilla and the animal

next below it—the orang, for example—in the scale of
creation. He argued that, in the ascending scale, from
the lowest animal to the highest, there is a regular and
gradual development of brain structure, but that between the highest animal and man there is a remarkable and sudden enlargement of the brain, manifested
more particularly in the extension of the cerebrum
over the cerebellum ; whereas in the gorilla, orang,
ape, baboon, and monkey tribes, the cerebellar portion
of the brain projects posteriorly far beyond the cerebral
portion. The cerebellum is also proportionally larger
in those animals than in man, and this disproportion is
much greater between man and the gorilla than between
the gorilla and the above-named animals. Other anatomical distinctions, though less noteworthy, were also
pointed out.

The positions advanced by Prof. Owen were warmly
contested by Prof. Huxley, President of the Geological
Section. Others took part in the debate, and there was
much disagreement in relation to the anatomical facts
as set forth by Prof. Owen. Prof. Huxley contended
that the great difference between man and animals
was psychical and moral, not anatomical, and that the
alleged remarkable structural difference between the
brain of man and that of the gorilla had no existence.

The subject was discussed at much length, and seemed
to involve the issue, whether man was a developed
monkey, or whether monkey was a degraded man. It
was amusing to hear learned professors of Comparative
Anatomy, Physiology, Zoology, and Ethnology—M.D 's,
F.R.S.'s, D.D.'s, etc., discuss for a whole hour the nature of the distinction between the man immortal and
the brute that perishes, without one of them looking in
the right direction for a solution of the problem.

Instead of disputing about the posterior prolongation
of the cerebrum, the relative development of the cerebellum, the posterior cornu, the hippocampi, etc., they
should have looked at the phrenological organs. There
they would have found a structural difference and development quite sufficient to satisfy Prof. Owen, and a
psychical and moral difference as immense as Prof.
Huxley could desire. They would have seen that the

real distinction is in kind, not in degree. Man is endowed with certain mental organs or powers which no animal possesses the least trace of—hope, ideality, conscientiousness, and spirituality. These are the moral organs, and constitute the religious element of humanity; and it is this element which prompts the human being to look forward to a future existence, to improve his condition here from generation to generation, and to believe in and worship a Supreme Being. It is true that in the reflective portion of the intellectual faculties the difference between man and the gorilla is immense both as to size and quality of brain structure; and this, were it ten times as great, would only render man a " superior animal." But the superaddition of new organs renders him another being entirely, and raises him quite out of the domain of the animal kingdom. " In the image of God" was man created. This is not true of mere animals.

The *Irish Times* of October 10, 1862, reports a meeting of the far-famed British Association for the Advancement of Science, then holding its sittings at Cambridge, England. The proceedings of Section D, Zoology and Botany, gave rise to a discussion on the gorilla and man. Among those present were the Duke of Devonshire, Mr. Walpole, M. P., Mr. Napier, and Mr. Whiteside, M. P. Some remarks having been made with reference to " spontaneous generation"—

Professor Owen exhibited two casts, one of the human brain, which had been hardened in spirits, and had therefore not preserved its exact form, but to all intents and purposes, it would serve as an illustration of the human brain. The other cast was taken from the interior of the cranium of the gorilla. From an examination of these, the difference between the brain of man and that of monkeys was at once perceptible. In the brain of man, the posterior lobes of the cerebrum overlapped, to a considerable extent, the small brain or cerebellum, whereas, in the gorilla, the posterior lobes of the cerebrum did not project beyond the lobes of the cerebellum. The posterior lobes in the one were prominent and well marked, in the other deficient. These peculiarities had been referred to by Todd and Bowman. From a very prolonged investigation into the characters of animals, he felt persuaded that the characters of the brain were the most steadfast; and he was thus induced, after many years of study, to propose his classification of the mammalia, based upon the differences in the development in their brain structure. He had placed man—owing to the prominence of the posterior lobes of his brain, the existence of a posterior cornu in the lateral ventricles, and the presence of a hippocampus minor in the posterior cornu—in a distinct sub-kingdom, which he had called archancephala, between which and the other members of the mammalia the distinctions are very marked, and the rise was a very abrupt one. The brain, in his estimation, was a far better guide in classifying animals than the foot; but the same difference that existed between their brains was also observable between their feet. The lecturer referred to diagram which represented the feet of the aye-aye, the gorilla, and man, pointing out the chief difference in the structure of the skeleton. The difference he considered sufficiently great to elevate man from the sub-kingdom from which the monkeys belonged, and to place him in a distinct sub-kingdom by himself.

Professor Huxley observed that the paper just laid before the Section appeared to him in no way to represent the real nature of the problem under discussion. He would therefore put the problem in another way. The question was partly one of facts, and partly one of reasoning. The question of fact was, what are the structural differences between man and the highest apes? The question of reasoning, what is the systematic value of those differences? Several years ago Professor Owen had made three distinct assertions respecting the differences which obtain between the brain of man and that of the highest apes. He asserted that three structures were " peculiar to and characteristic" of man's brains—these being the " posterior lobe," the " posterior cornu," and the " hippocampus minor." In a

controversy which had lasted for some years, Mr. Owen
had not qualified these assertions, but had repeatedly
reiterated them.

Professor Huxley, on- the other hand, had contro-
verted these statements, and affirmed, on the contrary,
that the three structures mentioned not only exist, but
are often better developed than in man, in all the higher
apes. He, (Professor Huxley,) now appealed to the
anatomists present in the Section, to say whether the
universal voice of Continental and British anatomists
had not entirely borne out his statements, and refuted
those of Professor Owen. The Professor then discussed
the relations of the foot of man with those of the apes,
and showed that the same argument could be based
upon them as on the brain—that argument being, that
the structural differences between man and the highest
ape are of the same order, and only slightly different
in degree from those which separate the apes, one from
another. In conclusion, he expressed his opinion of the
futility of discussions like the present. In his opinion,
the differences between man and the lower animals are
not to be expressed by his toes or his brain, but are
moral and intellectual.

Professor Rolleston said he would try to supply the
members of the Association with the points of positive
difference between the human and the ape's brain. For
doing this we had been abundantly shown that the
hippocampus minor and the posterior lobe were insufficient. As differentive they must be given up at last.
But as much had recently been done for the descriptive
anatomy of the brain by Gratiolet and others, as had
been done for astronomy by Stokes and Adams, for language by Max Müller, and that this had been ignored
in this discussion was little creditable to British science.
This analysis of the brain's structure had established, as
differentive between man and the ape, four great differences—two morphological, two quantitative. The two
quantitative are the great absolute weight and the great
height of the human brain ; the two morphological, the
multifidity of the frontal lobes corresponding to the
forehead, usually, popularly, and, as this analysis shows,
correctly, taken as a fair exponent of man's intelligence,

and the absence of the external perpendicular figure.
This had been abundantly shown by Gratiolet. No
reference to these most important matters had been
made by Professor Owen, and this omission could not
fail to put the British Association's repute for acquaintance with the work of foreign fellow-laborers at great
disadvantage in the eyes of such foreigners as might be
present. Professor Rolleston concluded by saying that
if he had expressed himself with any unnecessary vehemence he was sorry for it, but that he felt there were
things less excusable than vehemence, and that the laws
of ethics and love of truth were things higher and better than were the rules of etiquette or decorous reti-
cence.

Mr. W. H. Flower, looking at the subject solely in
an anatomical view as a question of fact, stated that
the result of a considerable number of dissections of
brains of various monkeys, was that the distinction between the brain of man and monkeys did not lie in the
posterior lobe or the hippocampus minor, which parts
were proportionately more largely developed in many
monkeys than in man, and that if these parts were used
in the classification of man and the monkeys, the series
would be, first, the little South American marmosets,
then would follow the baboons, the cercopithea, mac-
aque, then man must be placed, followed by the antro-
poid apes, the orang-outang, chimpanzee, and gorilla,
and, last, the American howling monkey.

Professor Owen replied. Professor Rolleston had led
the meeting to conclude that he had not paid any attention to the convolutions of the brain of mammals, and that
the investigation of this subject was the exclusive property of the German anatomists, whereas he might be
permitted to state that almost at the very time that Leu-
ret wrote his memoir on this subject he had delivered a
course of lectures on the convolutions of the brain, which
he regretted had not been published, owing to the pressure of other labors ; but the diagrams were still in existence, as his successor could testify, in the Museum of
the Royal College of Surgeons.

Much has been said, and very loosely, on the subject
of a connecting link between man and animals. In

fact, there is no such thing as a connecting link between
man and animals. Linking means interlocking, each
taking in a part of the other, which, applied to the subject before us, is a fallacy, a misnomer. Strata of
being, like courses of brick in a wall, one above another, is a truth, and therefore a better simile. The
" What Is It ?" for years past on exhibition at Barnum's
Museum, has been seriously described to us by clergy-
men and other educated men as a connecting link, as if
it were half man and half beast. True, Barnum's ad-
vertisement used to read, " Is it man ? is it beast? or is
it both ?"   But the acute showman had the sagacity not
to make the assertion.   The gorilla, many specimens
of which were on exhibition in New York, some years
since, brought from Africa by M. Du Chaillu, was a
subject of much speculation by persons who were not
physicians, anthropologists, or ethnologists.

Though monkeys, baboons, orang-outangs, and gorillas have clenching power to the hands (most of them
also have the same to the feet) ; though some of these
animals are in body, particularly in skeleton, considerably like the human, and though some apes have the
rudiments of a nose, they differ in so many other points
that the only verdict possible relative to them is *animal*,
BEAST.   As mind, including the higher reason and moral sentiments, constitutes the strictly human peculiarity ; the faculties which animals do not possess being
added to those which are common to the lower animals,
constitute human nature.   When we examine the wide
range of animated life and find perception and instinct
in various degrees of development and perfection in the
lower animals, and find nothing in them which can properly be called reason or moral sentiment, we regard
this as the true line which divides forever and thoroughly animals from man.   On this point the old *Edinburgh
Review*, which more than thirty years ago took ground
against Phrenology, has of late indorsed the principle
for which we now contend, as follows: "The brain is
observed progressively to be improved in its structure
and augmented in volume more and more, until in man
we behold it possessing some parts of which animals are
destitute and wanting none which they possess."

We have seen two views of the skull of the male gorilla. The animal was over five feet in height, and in figure had the semblance of a man. He weighed nearly three hundred pounds, measured fifty-one inches round the breast under the arms, and, without a weapon, was probably able to master the unarmed assault of fifty common men. Nearly all the brain is above and about the opening of the ear. From it we can learn of the power of the gorilla; and, judging from his tremendous jaws, we doubt not he would be able to grapple successfully with the bear. Is there anything human about these teeth? Those tusks look more like a tiger's. The grinding teeth resemble those of a bear, adapted to crush fruits and nuts, and we see nothing human in that face. Behold those bony ridges about the eyes, and that ridge running backward from the center of the top of the skull, adapted to the attachment of muscles! All these are indices of a most powerful muscular system.

A child three months old has more brain than the largest gorilla the world has seen, and nearly all the brain the gorilla has, is devoted to mere animal propensity.

It is an interesting fact, and, to these "connecting-link" people, we think is a "stunner," that this terrible beast, this human-shaped terror of the African forest, has less intellectual abilities, less instinctive skill, than several of the ape tribe that are not one-tenth his size; and it is interesting to phrenologists, and ought to be to everybody, that these more skillful and intelligent chimpanzees have a more highly organized brain. Indeed, we have seen a chimpanzee that did not weigh over forty pounds, perhaps less, whose brain was more than three-fourths as large as that of the largest gorilla, and, what is more, it was better developed in the frontal or intellectual portion, but without moral sentiment.

The skull of an Australian dog indicates a much greater likeness to the gorilla than the gorilla does to the human. Indeed, we utterly repudiate the idea that the gorilla skull has anything resembling humanity about it. The Australian dog is low, fierce, and has a small brain, as may be seen by the bulbous portion above and back of the under jaw.

Whether the gorilla could be tamed and domesticated like the dog is doubted by those who have had most to do with him, though doubtless he might be improved. Notwithstanding his apparently human form, his teeth, face, and brain indicate him to be in all respects a beast—ferocious and savage in the last degree.

Luke Burke says, in reference to this general subject, and I perfectly agree with him, that " he has seen with much pleasure that he does not stand alone in assigning to man, *zoologically*, the supremacy which the common sense of mankind has universally and always assigned to him, on every other ground." He finds in fact that he has even been anticipated on this point.

In Professor Huxley's paper, *On the Relations of Man to the Lower Animals* (Natural History Review. No. 1, January, 1861), after referring to Professor Owen, who raises man to the rank of a sub-class in the animal kingdom, he adds—"M. Terres* vindicates the dignity of man still more strongly, by demanding for the human family the rank of a kingdom equal to the Animalia or Plantæ; while a countryman of our own arrogates to his fellows so high a place in the aristocracy of nature as to deny that mankind can be thought of zoologically at all." (p. 69)

---

* "L'homme ne forme ni une espèce in une genre comparable aux Primate. L'homme a lui seul constitue un regne à part—le Regne humain." Resumé des Legons sur l'Embryologie Anthropologique, Comptes Rendus, 1851.

Part Third.

FOSSIL MAN.

CHAPTER I.

TESTIMONY OF THE ROCKS TO THE EXISTENCE OF PRE-ADAMITE MAN ONE HUNDRED THOUSAND YEARS AGO.

Louis Agassiz, in speaking of geological time, says : " Among the astounding discoveries of modern science is that of the immense periods that have passed in the gradual formation of the earth. So vast were the cycles of the time preceding even the appearance of man on the surface of our globe, that our own period seems as yesterday when compared with the epochs that have gone before it. Had we only the evidence of the deposits of rocks heaped above each other in regular strata by the slow accumulation of materials, they alone would convince us of the long and slow maturing of God's work on earth ; but when we add to these successive populations of whose life this world has been the theater, and whose remains are hidden in the rocks into which the mud of sand or soil of whatever kind on which they lived has hardened in the course of time—or the enormous chains of mountains whose upheaval divided these periods of quiet accumulation by great convulsions—or the changes of a different nature in the configuration of our globe, as the sinking of lands beneath the ocean, or the gradual rising of continents and islands above ; or the slow growth of the coral reefs. those wonderful sea-walks, raised by the little ocean architects whose own bodies furnish both the building stone and cement that binds them together, and who have worked so busily during the long centuries, that there are extensive countries, mountain chains, islands, and long lines of coast, consisting solely of their remains—or the countless forests that have grown up, flourished, died, and decayed, to fill the storehouses of coal that feed the fires of the human race—if we consider all these records of the past, the intellect fails to grasp a chronology of which our experience furnishes no data, and time that flies behind us seems as much an eternity to our conception as the future that stretches indefinitely before us."

As with Agassiz, so with a host of others, not only in his own chosen, but other fields of inquiry and research. Nott, Glydon, Calvert, De Wette, Gesenius, Eichorn, Ammon, Herder, Kavanagh, Rousseau, Taylor, and a host of equally brilliant suns in the scientific firmament, all testify to the same end and purpose, and declare that man is not the creature of a mere six thousand brief years, as the world has been accustomed to believe, and that, too, not on solid evidence, but upon the *ipse dixit* of some unlearned and prejudiced man. I say "unlearned," because I deem that man truly so who has studied only in one direction, and mastered but a single principle of education.

> "One science can but one single genius fit,
> So vast is art—so narrow human wit,"

Is a wise old saw, according to the wisdom of the past, and it may have once been true, but if so, such is not the case in these days. No man is competent to give a final and decisive opinion on a science or point which he may have studied for a lifetime, unless he be acquainted with its various cognates. For instance, we would think but little of the opinion of an astronomer—a mere Boston-Common star-gazer—who had no acquaintance with optics, or of that of a political economist not familiar with climatology and agriculture. For the same reason ought we to be cautious of accepting the teachings of a preacher, whether lay or clerical, who, departing from his legitimate sphere, ignorantly attempts to settle any question of chronology psychology, ethnology, or geology, with a text of Scripture or citation from the " Fathers," having no more real connection with his legitimate business -- soul-saving -- than Tiglath Pilaser had with Horace Greeley's overland journey to California, or Speaker Raymond's to Solferino.

In preparing this, as well as the other parts of my book, I have freely availed myself of all material, of whatever kind, from whatever source, that suited me, or had a legitimate bearing on the topic under treatment, consequently I claim no especial originality as regards the matter, but only in its application and arrangement; for my book is only for the purpose of shedding light on a subject heretofore involved in obscurity.

      *   *   *   *   *

The course of science is ever onward. Discoveries are continually being made, which are not only in themselves startling and calculated to revolutionize all our previous opinions, but which prepare the way for revelations even more marvelous than themselves, and such as, had they been but hinted at a few centuries ago, would have been treated as the most extravagant speculations of a madman, or the dream of an Arab poet reveling in the regions of fancy and romance. So many long-cherished theories have already given place to sounder and more correct views of nature, through the instrumentality of experiment and induction, that the human mind becomes in a manner prepared at any moment to unlearn the results of years of tuition, at the signal given by some known worshiper in the temple of Science.

A few years ago, when the grand truths of geology first made themselves felt amongst the students of nature, the non-scientific world stood aghast at the boldness of the theories propounded, and the novelty of the facts upon which those theories were based. A quarter of a century later those doctrines had become universally recognized ; all previous opinions regarding the chronology of the earth had been hurried away into the limbo of exploded hypotheses ; and geology had found its way into the education lists of the most elementary schools. Young ladies talked learnedly of rocks and fossils, and geological implements became as well-known as children's toys. The pulpits resounded with the new truths of the great antiquity of the world, and the press lent its aid in the diffusion of scientific knowledge. The statement of the Rev. Dr. Lightfoot, that the heavens and the earth were created exactly at six o'clock on Sunday morning, in the month of September, at the equinox of the year B. C. 4004, was very correctly looked upon as being quite akin to some of the whimsical theories with which schoolmen amused themselves by discussing during the middle ages. The astronomer had said that there were stars so distant in the infinity of space, that since their creation a sufficient time had not elapsed to bring their light to our own small planet, and the geologist now proclaimed that the human imagination might wander back over periods vieing in duration with the distances of the heavenly bodies, and still be myriads of ages from that point in eternity when creation woke into being. The firm old earth upon which we tread, all recognize now as having commenced her career in a period so remote that human thought is paralyzed in its contemplation. Nor does it apply simply to the inorganic part of nature. The organic kingdoms, with their superiority of form, and their wondrous endowment of life, are now known to stretch back in their existence through periods which even imagination fails to fathom. Animals of various kinds have lived and died myriads of ages ago, and the vestiges of their mortality are still preserved in those old rocks that have recently disclosed so many secrets. Plants of every grade and every shape have filled the earth with a luxurious vegetation thousands of times over, each to flourish in its turn, and at last to return to the soil, and fix its impress there for the generations of men to observe and philosophize upon a million of ages afterwards. Sea, and air, and earth have each been inhabited. innumerable times over, with various forms of living things, whose whole race has perished in the lapse of ages, to give place to others, who, in their turn, should also disappear. All this the merest tyro in science now knows, and no one can be found bold enough to dispute it. One reserve, and one only, has been, up to the present, placed upon this doctrine. Among organic beings, man, it has been held, is of recent origin. Between six and seven thousand years ago his superior organization made its appearance on the globe after an indefinite series of centuries had been spent in preparing the way for his coming, and the earth for his habitation.

Within the last few years facts have been brought to light, however, which, if insufficient to demonstrate that the human race has existed on the earth for a longer period than is generally imagined, at least are calculated to somewhat modify the views at present entertained with respect to this matter. Statements have recently been put forth on this subject which, although they may not be deemed conclusive, are certainly deserving of candid investigation and mature consideration, both from the well-known standing of the men from whom they have issued, and also from the number and magnitude of the facts upon which they appear to be based. That man is the very last creation that has yet appeared, there can be no kind of doubt; the perfection of his organization, his position at the very top of the scale of animate beings, and the absence of his remains at least from the early rocks—all point to a comparatively modern origin ; but that no traces of him existed until within six or seven thousand years ago may fairly be open to question.

The principal argument relied upon in support of the commonly accepted theory has been the entire absence of human fossils, even from the most recently formed deposits. Bones of human beings, it is admitted, have been often found, but nearly always under such circumstances as allowed of their having found their way to the spot where they are discovered, at a very recent date, by some sudden and violent change taking place in the locality. Even as early as 1748, a human body in a fossilized condition was discovered at Gibraltar by some miners employed in blowing up "rocks, for the purpose of raising batteries, about fifty feet above the level of the sea." It is not at all surprising that, at that time, it excited no interest. Much more recently, a fossil human pelvis was picked up by Dr. Dickeson, at Natchez ; but any argument, based upon it, for the antiquity of the race, was at once disposed of by Sir Charles Lyell, who suggested that it had fallen from an Indian graveyard at the summit of the cliff. The same explanation was given of the discovery of a human skull, with other fossils, in a sandstone rock at Brazil ; though, in this case, the difficulty of such a supposition was greater, *because the place where it was found must have sunk to the bottom of the sea subsequently, and again have been raised to the position in which it was then observed.*

Supposing an entire absence, as far as our knowledge extends, of human fossils from the most recent deposits, it still becomes a very important question whether the assumption that man did not live at the period when these deposits were formed, be not somewhat illogical and unjustifiable. It must be remembered that, in the days of Cuvier, no fossil remains of monkeys had been discovered, and that the great naturalist himself looked upon their absence as a proof of recent origin. Now, fossil quadrumanes have since been found in England, France, India, and South America; and although the number at present brought to light is certainly not large, yet it is clearly sufficient to prove that these animals existed at a period much earlier than was previously imagined. Those discovered in England are stated by Sir Charles Lyell to belong to the genus *Macacus*, and to an extinct species, and have been exhumed from the London clay, associated with crocodiles. turtle and nautili. Cuvier's conclusions were probably correctly drawn from his data, but his premises were wrong. So that if no human fossils had been at present discovered, it still would not follow that there are none such deposited in the wide range of unexplored strata, to be brought to light by future industry and perseverance.

Moreover, there can be little doubt that large numbers of animals have lived on the earth and have passed away, leaving behind them no trace of their ever having been in existence. But for the plastic nature of the sand on the river's brink in the Connecticut Vale, the colossal birds which, at one period, wandered up and down beside the stream, would have disappeared, without leaving to subsequent generations the slightest record of their being. Some of these birds were at least twelve or fifteen feet high ; their footprints on the sand are all that remain of them.

Still, as no deductions can be drawn but from what is known, it may not be amiss to glance at the discoveries that are believed by many to contain positive evidence of the existence of the human race, at an earlier period than has been generally recognized. This evidence may be divided into two kinds. In the first place, there are the direct remains of man himself, said to have been met with in different parts of the world; and, secondly, the traces of human labor, in the form of knives, arrows, and other productions of art, manufactured generally from flints. To these a third kind of proof has been added by some, more as a support to the others than as containing much evidence in itself, viz., that derived from the study of monuments, inscriptions, etc., many of which date their origin prior to the commencement of the historic period.

Generally speaking, human fossils have been found in large caves which occur in the calcareous strata. These ossuaries or bone caverns, are met with in the *diluvium* or drift. Their floors are covered with a layer of diluvial clay, and over this a crust of stalagmite has become deposited subsequently. Under this two-fold covering of lime and clay, the bones of innumerable animals, some of which have long since disappeared from among the living tribes, are met with; and, intermingled with these, have been found the fossil remains of man. The Kirkdale cave, discovered in 1821, about twenty-five miles from York, and referred to by Dr. Buckland in his *Reliquiæ Diluvianæ*. affords an excellent illustration. It is situated on the declivity of a valley, and occurs in the formation called *oolite*. It opens by an irregular, narrow passage, for a distance of 250 feet into the hill, and at the end, expands into small chambers. The layer of stalagmite which covered the floors, and which has been formed by drippings from the roof, has beneath it a bed of sandy micaceous loam, of about two or three feet in thickness. In the lower

part of this layer, innumerable bones were discovered,
belonging to the tiger, bear, wolf, weasel, elephant,
rhinoceros, hippopotamus, horse, ox, deer, water-rat,
and mouse, most of them of extinct species.   Dr. Buckland concluded that this cave had been inhabited by
hyenas, and that the greater number of the remains of
animals found there had•been dragged in to serve the
occupants of the cave as food ; and that in some cases,
the hyenas had even preyed upon each other.   Other
bones, especially the smaller ones, he supposed to have
drifted in by the current, or to have fallen into the
chasm through fissures since closed up by the incrusta-
tions of stalactite.   This may serve as a general description of a bone cavern ; and the explanation hazarded by the late lamented Dean of Westminster, if accepted as satisfactory, effectually gets rid of any evidence
of the great antiquity of the human race arising from
the discovery of fossil remains of man in such a place.
In the cave of Durfoil, in the Jura, situated in a calcareous mountain three hundred feet above the level of
the sea, human bones were discovered by Mascel de
Serres, in a true state of fossil, and embedded in a calcareous matrix.   The Rev. Mr. M'Enery collected flint
knives and human bones from the caves of Torquay,
where he discovered them among the remains of many
extinct animals.   In the Brixham cavern, Devonshire,
human bones were found which had been evidently
gnawed by hyenas.   M. de Cuslobles discovered, and
M. de Serres afterwards examined, remains of humanity
intermingled with those of the rhinoceros, bear, hyena,
and other animals, embedded in mud whinstone rock,
at Pondres.   A fossil human skeleton, dug out of the
schist rock at Quebec, is still preserved in the museum
of that town ; while the Guadaloupe skeleton, in the
British Museum is familiar to every one.   In the " Ca-

verne de Engihoul," examined by Dr. Schmerling, the
bones of man occurred with those of extinct species of
animals, and appeared to have found their way there at
the same period and under similar circumstances. Tied-
mann exhumed human bones from the caverns in Belgium, mixed with those of bears, hyenas, elephants, wild
boars, and horses. The cave of Gailenruth, in Fran-
conia, and those of Zahuloch and Kuloch, yielded the
same products; and their great elevation places them
beyond the reach of partial inundations. Many other
cases of a similar kind might be quoted, all seeming to
prove the same fact. To the whole of them it is, however, objected, that notwithstanding the circumstances
under which these human remains appeared to have
been deposited, still they were of recent date.

There is one method by means of which some slight
clue may be obtained to the age of a bone, not perhaps
a very decisive one when we have to deal with such extended periods as geology brings before us, but one
which still may be of some value; at all events it may
be taken for what it is worth. It consists in treating
the bone with dilute muriatic acid, which has the effect
of dissolving the earthy portion, and leaving behind
simply the gelatinous, or animal part. If a very recent
bone be subjected to the action of this agent, the earthy
matter is removed, and the animal part, which comprises
about one-third of the whole bone, still preserves the
original shape, but is flexible and elastic; so much so,
that in the case of a rib, a knot may be tied in it. If,
on the other hand, the bone be fossil, and, from the
length of time it has been exposed, has lost its gelatinous matter, the muriatic acid will dissolve it entirely
away, with effervescence. Now, in some of the cases
already quoted, this test was applied both to the human
and the other bones, the result arrived at being, that

the time of deposit of both was as nearly the same
as could be discovered. Numerous instances are recorded by Lieutenant-Colonel Hamilton Smith, in which
the bones of man were discovered, broken and worked
up with those of the lower animals in the same breccia,
where the strictest chemical examination could detect
no difference in age.

In America, some very remarkable discoveries have
taken place, which, if not conclusive, are, at all events,
deserving of the most unbiased consideration. There
is one in particular, described in Nott and Gliddon's
Types of Mankind, of the skeleton of a man found in
the delta of the Mississippi, where, according to the
conclusion arrived at in that work, it must have been
reposing for a period of about fifty-seven thousand
years. This supposition is arrived at as follows :—In
excavating on the plain upon which the city of New
Orleans is built, successive growths of cypress trees are
met with. Such obstacles do these present to digging
to any depth, that on one occasion the Irish spadesmen
relinquished their work, and the Kentucky axe-men had
to be employed to hew their way downwards. Ten distinct cypress forests have been traced, by Messrs.
Dickeson and Brown, at different levels below the present surface, they are arranged vertically above each
other, and on the surface over them all stand stately
oaks, that have flourished for centuries. Between the
growth of each of these ten cypress forests the plain
must have been submerged, the soil on which the next
forest was to grow being deposited during the submer-
sion. Dr. Bennet Dowler makes a calculation as to the
period which must have elapsed since the last submer-
sion of the site of the city :—" He divides the history of
this period into three eras: 1. The era of colossal

grasses, trembling prairies, &c., as seen in the lagoons,*
lakes, and sea-coast.   2. The era of the cypress basins.
3. The era of the present live oak platform."   Existing
trees, he maintains, show that the development occurred in this order.   It is, then, supposed that the elevation has taken place at about five inches in a century,
that being the most rapid rate at which the accumulation of detritus in the Nile has ever been computed to
have taken place.   This will give 1,500 years for the
era of aquatic plants, before the appearance of the first
cypress forest.   Estimating the cypress trees at ten feet
in diameter, Dr. Dowler concludes that their age would
be about 5,700 years.   " Though many generations of
such trees may have grown and perished in each cypress
period," he "has assumed only two consecutive growths,"
giving 11,400 years.   " The maximum age of the oldest
tree growing on the live oak platform is estimated at
1,500 years."   The following table is arrived at :—

Era of aquatic plants, years......................	1,500
Era of cypress basin, years.......................	11,400
Era of live oak platform, years...................	1,500
Total	14,400

Dr. Dowler then goes on to reckon ten other such
elevations, which he supposes may have taken place,
each of equal duration, yielding 158,400 years.   The
skeleton of a man, together with burnt wood, was discovered at the excavations for the gas works, " at the
depth of eighteen feet," and "beneath the roots of a
cypress tree belonging to the fourth forest level."   " The
type of the cranium was that of the aboriginal American race."   Reckoning, then, the present era at 14,400
years, and allowing for three other eras of equal dura-

* The lagoons of this part of America, which is for the most part
little better than one huge swamp, are usually so covered with aquatic
plants and tall grasses as to resemble prairies.

tion, that skeleton must have been deposited 57,600 years ago, while a luxuriant flora must have adorned the country 100,000 years earlier.

Exception will reasonably be taken to this calculation, as it seems to be based on so much that is hypothetical ; still, the bare fact of human remains being found at such a depth, and under the roots of the cypress trees, —where they could not have found their way by means of a current, or any other accidental agency, at least except at a very remote period—will go far towards proving the great antiquity of the human race, even to those who may feel disposed to dispute the statistics of Dr. Dowler. A far more satisfactory, and more moderate, calculation has been made by the celebrated Agassiz, with regard to human "jaws with perfect teeth, and portions of a foot," discovered by Count F. de Pourtales, upon the shores of Lake Monroe, in Florida. Professor Agassiz entered elaborately into the matter in a lecture delivered at Mobile, in 1853, and arrived at the conclusion that 10,000 years ago, at the lowest computation, mankind peopled that large continent.

The second argument is, perhaps, equally important, and is certainly not less conclusive, being based on the discovery of the workmanship of man in positions that indicate its having been buried at a period prior to the historical epoch. As early as 1797, a memoir was published by Mr. John Frere, in which there is mention made of the discovery of some flint implements, in a bed of gravel, at Floxen, Suffolk, together with the bones of an animal now presumed to have been the mammoth. A series of most important discoveries of this kind were afterwards made by M. Boucher de Perthos. This celebrated archæologist pursued his researches for a great number of years at St. Acheul, near Abbeville, in the South of France, and succeeded in satisfying himself that in the flint implements he discovered, there came to light the last vestige of the handiwork of a people who inhabited Western Europe at a period antecedent to that to which any written record refers. No doubt can now possibly be felt, by any one investigating the matter, that the workmanship of man has been met with in the diluvian drifts among the detritus of older rocks, masses of sand and gravel, and bones of those extinct quadrupeds generally supposed to belong to an epoch prior to the creation of the human race.   M. Boucher made numerous excavations in the departments of the Somme, the Pas de Calais, the Oise, the Seine, and the Seine Inferieure ; and although no human fossil rewarded his researches, he found what were, perhaps, equally important—utensils, weapons, figures, symbols, and other traces of human ingenuity—buried with the remains of elephants and mastodons, at a depth where no traces of man had been previously suspected.   In Celtic and Gaulish burial-places he discovered successive beds of bones and ashes, with cinerary urns, belonging to a period immensely remote. Nor do these discoveries now depend simply on the judgment of M. Boucher, who, although a man of great scientific knowledge, patient investigation, and strict veracity, yet might, perhaps, be suspected of leaning too much to his favorite hobby.   Others have now followed him into the same field.   Dr. Rigollot, a celebrated French geologist, after a careful investigation of the whole subject, expressed his concurrence in the views of his predecessor in the inquiry as to the age of the gravel—the only point open to doubt, since the fact that the implements were found there, was universally admitted.   Dr. Rigollot, in a letter to M. Boucher, dated the 26th of November, 1853, declares his assent to the opinion of the latter—that it was now clearly

proved that the country had been inhabited by human
beings before "the grand disturbance that caused the
destruction of the elephants and rhinoceroses that lived
there." Others followed in the same field; and no
longer ago than the 26th of May, last year, Mr. Prestwich read a memoir before the Royal Society, upon the
results of his own examinations. He confesses that he
entered upon the subject full of doubt, but that, having
examined the matter, his conclusions were the same as
those of M. Boucher. The gravel beds of St. Acheul
he describes as "capping a low chalk hill"—"one hundred feet above the level of the Somme." At the top
were ten or fifteen feet of brick-earth, containing coins,
old tombs, etc., but destitute of organic remains. Then
came from two to eight feet of whitish marl and sand,
full of recent shells, etc., and underneath this, a layer
of coarse, flint gravel, of from six to twelve feet in
thickness, the whole deposit resting on chalk. Now, it
was in neither of the upper layers, but in the gravel be
low, that these flint implements were found in great
numbers, and intermingled with the teeth and bones of
the elephant, ox, deer, and horse.

As to the age of this gravel there is no dispute. It
is of the same period as that at East Croydon, Wands-
worth, and many other places surrounding London. and
dates back to a time long antecedent to that at which
it is usually supposed the human race commenced its
career upon the earth. MM. Herbert and Bateaux,
French geologists, who have made the tertiary deposits
a subject of special study, examined carefully the position of these beds, and reported that the implements
were found "exclusively in the true diluvian—that is,
the deposit which contains the remains of species belonging to the epoch immediately preceding the cata-

clysm by which they were destroyed. "There cannot," they add, "be the smallest doubt as to the point."

These implements consist of arrow-heads, knives, spear-heads, axes, religious emblems, symbols, etc., and bear a very striking resemblance to those discovered by Mr. Squier in the western mounds of America. Many of them appear to have been so slightly fixed to their cases as to become detached whenever a blow was struck, and would, therefore, have been left in the wound. They are not always made of flint, but sometimes of granite, porphyry, basalt, serpentine jaspar, and almost every kind of hard stone.

The conclusion, then, appears obvious, unless some other explanation of these facts should hereafter be suggested, that man has existed on the earth much longer than we had been hitherto led to suppose. After all, this is but bringing us to the Chevalier Bunsen's theory, derived from sources of an entirely different character, " that a concurrence of facts and traditions demands for the Noachian period about ten millenia before our era, and for the beginning of our race another ten thousand years, or very little more." It is very difficult to ascertain upon exactly what grounds the Chevalier has arrived at this conclusion : but it is a conclusion very much in accordance with the results to which science seems to be leading us.

A third class of evidence was alluded to above, namely, that arising from a study of monuments and other works of art. This is, perhaps, more valuable, taken in conjunction with the geological facts than as an independent guide. Stonehenge stands as a familiar example of a record of a very remote past—no one knows how remote ; but the lesson that it teaches is anything but definite and clear. Throughout Europe

many other monuments of a similar character exist.
Call them Celtic or Druidical—but what does that
mean? That they were erected by those races? They
were not. The ancient Druids may have used them for
religious worship, but were, in all probability, as ignorant of their origin as we of the present generation
are. Their early history is shrouded in obscurity, and
we can learn little of them, further than that they have
withstood the ravages of time for many centuries.

In Egypt perhaps the prospect is clearer, clouds having recently broken and passed away; but even there
we can learn little except by the aid of physical science.
True, there stand those mighty monuments of the past,
seemingly as eternal as the globe itself—the Pyramids;
but a long interval must have elapsed after Egypt became inhabited by human beings ere such works as
these could have been erected. It must have taken
many centuries before a race of savage or nomadic
tribes could have reached by self-tuition such a degree
of civilization as would enable them to raise such enduring proofs of their skill. There is, therefore, a wide
blank in chronology between the date at which Egypt
was first inhabited by man, and that of the origin of
the pyramids and tombs in the fourth Memphite dynasty
—according to Lepsius, thirty-five hundred years B. C.
From the year three thousand eight hundred and ninety-
three B. C., everything appears tolerably clear from
the monuments and hieroglyphics; but before that time
there is nothing but physical science to guide us.*

Mr. Leonard Horner has thrown much light upon
this subject. He made nineteen borings into the Nile
mud near the site of the ancient city of Memphis, and
seventy-eight other borings in other parts of the delta
of the Nile. It had been previously computed that the

---

* It will be seen that Lepsius differs with us on some points.

deposit of Nile sediment had taken place at the rate of
about five inches in a century ; but, by measuring carefully the depth at which a certain statue of known date
was buried, Mr. Horner found that the rate must be reduced to three and a-half inches per century, at least for
the neighborhood of Memphis—and yet in this neighborhood fragments of burnt pottery, pieces of carved
stone, and other human remains, were brought up from
a depth of thirty-nine feet, and must thus, on Mr. Horner's calculation, have been buried not less than 13,500
years.   In other parts of the delta of the Nile similar
remains have been found at all depths down to seventy
feet, borings deeper than seventy feet not having then
been made.   Many of these fragments of human workmanship were obtained from levels below the low-water
mark of the Mediterranean, and must therefore have
been "brought down by the river from the higher and
inhabited part of the valley, *at a time previous to the
formation of that part of the delta,*" thus seeming to
prove that the higher parts of the valley of the Nile
were inhabited by civilized men before the sites of some
of what we have been accustomed to regard as among
the most ancient of the Egyptian cities, had yet emerged
from beneath the waters of the Mediterranean!   After
all, therefore, the assertion of Plato, put into the mouth
of an Egyptian priest, may underrate rather than over-
rate the antiquity of the Egyptian nation :—" And the
annals even of our own city (Sais) have been preserved
8,000 years in our sacred writing.   I will briefly describe the laws and most illustrious actions of those
States which have existed 9,000 years."—*The Timæus.*
" And you will, by observing, discover that what have
been painted and sculptured there (in Egypt) 10,000
years ago—and I say 10,000 years not as a word, but
as a fact—are neither more beautiful nor more ugly

than those turned out of hand at the present day, but are worked off according to the same art."— *The Laws.* Plato's assertions on this point have long been disregarded, in consequence of their supposed extravagance. Time may prove them to be quite within the bounds of truth, as I, the author of this book, most assuredly believe they are.

CHAPTER II.

PROFESSOR WILSON, of Toronto, in his recent work on "Pre-historic Man," and to whom I am indebted for several things in this volume, says: We call this western hemisphere the New World, and fancy that, in its savage Indians, whom we designate aborigines, we are looking on a primitive condition of life. But the Indian of the American wilds is no more primeval than his forests. Beneath the roots of their oldest giants lie chronicled the memorials of older phases of a native civilization; and while the naturalists of this continent dwell with peculiar interest on the persistency of a common type, and of specific and almost instinctive habits throughout all its widely-scattered tribes, they have been studying only the temporary supplanter of nations strange to us as the generations of extinct life in geological periods older than our own . . . Abrupt mountain chains divide and subdivide the elevated table lands of Central Asia into regions which have been for unrecorded ages the great hives of wild pastoral tribes, which were, by unknown causes, made to overflow and pour themselves southward over the seats of a still more primitive Asiatic civilization, or westward into the continent of Europe. . . . We trace him (the nomade) back three thousand years; but had

we no other knowledge to guide us, it would be quite
as easy to believe that these nomades had wandered
over their desert homes for *thirty thousand* as for three
thousand years.

It appears to the writer of this work that we have
that "other knowledge" to guide us, and that, too,
without looking very far. The Professor's own book
effectually settles any lingering doubt as to man's antiquity, that might perchance arise in timid minds.
These proofs I proceed to present to the reader. And,
first, he gives us an account of a fossil man taken from
concrete limestone, from the solid rock, in the Island
of Gaudaloupe, one of the West Indian group. True,
the Professor, in his Scotch Presbyterian zeal, afterwards tells us that this rock is but the hardened detritus of corals and shells of recent formation, but he
forgets that a "recent" geological change may mean
one hundred thousand or five hundred thousand years
ago !

In the Museum of the Philadelphia Academy of Sciences is the *os innominatum* of a human skeleton, taken
from *beneath* the skeletons of the megalonyx and other
fossil mammals ; and that the latter may safely claim an
age of one hundred and twenty thousand years, I think
no true geologist will pretend to dispute.

The Danish naturalist, Dr. Lund, describes fossil human bones, of vast antiquity, found with the remains of
extinct species in the calcareous caves of Brazil.

At the foot of the Grampian Hills, which no tide
has laved for many a thousand years, discoveries have
recently been made, that quite effectually settles the
question concerning Pre-Adamite man ; and flint arrow-
heads, stone battle-axes, horn lances and harpoons,
turned up on the Carse of Sterling, give additional
testimony to the same point. In the year 1819, there

was disclosed in the alluvium of the carse-land, where the River Forth winds its circuitous course, the skeleton of a gigantic whale, with a perforated lance or harpoon of deer's-horn beside it. They lay together near the base of Dunmyat, one of the Ochil hills, and twenty feet above the highest tide of the neighboring estuary. Over this was an accumulation of five feet of alluvial soil, covered with a thin bed of moss. The locality was examined at the time, and the levels noted by scientific observers, peculiarly competent to the task. Nor was the example a solitary one, for remains of those gigantic Balænæ have been repeatedly found, and one skeleton discovered in 1824—*seven miles further inland* than the first example—now lies in the Natural-History Museum of Edinburgh University, along with another primitive deer's-horn harpoon found beside it.

What becomes of Adam and Moses in face of facts like these? When it is remembered that the recession of the sea, in this part of Scotland, was manifestly due, not to a sudden volcanic action, but to a gradual and slow upheaval of the ocean bed, and with it the land where its beach once was, it is patent that we must add at least two cyphers to the accustomed six thousand years, before we reach the period when those whales were run ashore, and butchered at leisure, by the piscatory Nimrods of Scotia's early days. With these examples alone before us, we are perfectly justified in assigning the human race, in that part of the world, an antiquity compared to which that of Egypt, Chaldea, China and Tartary, are but as of last week, and yet these are not the oldest by any means.

Has the reader ever heard of the monstrous fossil elks found in Ireland, at the Curragh ; at Walton, in Essex ; and in Folkstone, in Kent, England? If not, then I assure him that such there are, and myself have seen them, especially a gigantic one now set up complete in the British Museum—an animal which, when living, was as much larger than our common deer, as a full-sized goat is larger than a common cat. I had the exact dimensions of the animal, but since my return from England have, unfortunately. lost it. These skeletons were found associated with those of the fossil ox, rhinorceros, hippopotamus and hyena, every one of which animals of course must have existed alive where their dead bones are now found ; and the question is, How long is it since the British Islands were possessed of a tropical climate ? for, be it known, all these animals belong to hot climates. The answer is, a period so distant that it must be counted by centuries and not by simple years. Well, as long ago as when British forests sheltered and nourished these extinct beasts. so long ago was man also an inhabitant of those islands ; for his remains are found along with theirs ; and along with them are also seen flint arrow-heads, stone hatchets and fragmentary pottery. One of these monster elks was found with an arrow-wound in one of its ribs. The evidence of this fact is good, notwithstanding that Dr. Hart's assertion that the fact was so, has been disputed by Professor Owen, in his *British Fossil Mammals*. Professor Jamieson and Dr. Mantell have seen and reported on a human body exhumed from under a peat-bog, eleven feet thick, in the county of Cork ; and it was wrapped in the skin of one of those enormous elks, both having been preserved by the peat from decay, just as the ices of the Northern seas preserved the entire body of a mastodon, concerning which we read so much a few years ago.

Human remains have been found along with those of the great fossil ox—*Bos primigenius* the skull of one of which, in the British Museum, measures a yard in length, and the span of the horns forty-two inches—an animal that would shame the prize oxen of these days.

Mr. Frere, in 1797, discovered, in Suffolk, flint weapons—unmistakable human weapons, along with the remains of elephants, imbedded in gravel, overlaid by sand and brick earth, at a depth of eleven or twelve feet from the surface; and some of these may be seen at this day in the Museum, in Great Russell Street, London. It is a very long time since elephants roamed wild over British soil, or rather what now is such.

Fossil human remains have also been found on this continent, along with those of the extinct *Elephant, Mastodon, Megalonyx, Megalodon, Ereptodon,* and *Equus Curvidens*—an extinct species of American horse; and Professor Holmes, in exhibiting a collection of fossils from the post-pliocene of South Carolina, before the Philadelphia Academy of Natural Sciences, said that: Dr. Klipstein, who resides near Charleston, in digging a ditch to drain a swamp, discovered a Mastodon's tooth. He, (Professor Holmes,) with a select party of scientific friends, went there, and not only obtained other teeth and bones of the huge beast, but also an entire tusk, and, alongside of it, a beautiful fragment of pottery. Was that piece of pottery fashioned by the hand of an Adamite man? Verily, I think not.

In the State of Kentucky there is a very extensive morass, know as the Big-bone Lick. Deep down in the blue clay bed of this great and ancient bog, was found the partial and complete skeletons of not less than one hundred Mastodons, and twenty Mammoths, besides remains of the Megalonyx, and, it is asserted, human skulls also; though the evidence to that effect is not satisfactory. But whether the story be well founded or not, certain it is that, in the British Museum, is now a skeleton of a mastodon, found, along with many others, near the banks of Potatoe River, (*La Pomme du Terre*,) a tributary of the Osage, Missouri. These last were discovered by Mr. Albert Koch, and were examined, in his presence, by Mr. Mantell, their describer, who says that the bones were found in a brown sandy deposit, full of vegetable matter, with recognizable remains of the cypress, tropical cane, palmetto stems, and swamp mosses, all of which were beneath a superimposed bed of blue clay and gravel, quite fifteen feet in thickness. Mr. Koch found a flint arrow-head beneath the leg-bones of the great skeleton, and several similar weapons in the same stratum. Another mastodon, and part of its hide, was found in Missouri, associated with stone spear-heads, axes, knives, and arrows, under circumstances that rendered it almost certain that the huge beast had been entangled in the bog, and there not only stoned and worried to death by its human foes, but also partially consumed by fire, as if they had piled flaming wood against the poor brute, and thus roasted him, probably before he was dead.

In 1712 certain gigantic fossil remains were found in Claverack, in Massachusetts, probably those of the mastodon, but which the notorious Dr. Increase Mather described in his report thereon to the Royal Society of London, as being decidedly human ; and giving it as his profound opinion that in the antediluvian world there lived men of prodigious stature, " as incontestibly proved by these remains, particularly a tooth, which was a very large grinder, weighing four pounds and three-quarters, with a thigh-bone seventeen feet long."[*] The New England Doctor must have been reading Talmudian descriptions of the venerable " Ogg, King of Bashan !"

Along with the fossil mammals, including those of

[*] Philosophical Transactions. Vol. XXIV.

the scelidotherium, glyptodon, and chlamydotherium, as well as those of extinct carnivora, found in limestone caverns. in Brazil, by Lund and Claussen, human remains were discovered. The relics were taken from a bed of reddish loam, covered over with a thick stalagmitic flooring. Dr. Lund found there relics of human skeletons, that must have belonged to men who flourished when those monsters did—that is, from one to two hundred and fifty thousand years ago.

From a depth of fourteen feet beneath the surface, among the rolled gravel and gold-bearing quartz of the Grinell Leads, in Kansas, Mr. P. A. Scott, an intelligent Canadian, exhumed a flint knife, an unquestionable relic of human art. The locality is in the Blue Range of the Rocky Mountains In digging for gold, a shaft was sunk through four feet of rich, black soil, and then through ten more feet of compact gravel, reddish clay, and rounded quartz, and there the knife was found. The question is, not how it came there, but when ? and the answer is, certainly not less than ninety thousand years ago, taking geological indications as the data of judgment.

In sinking a coal-pit at Misk, in Ayrshire, a tobacco-pipe was found a great many feet beneath the surface of the ground. I have already quoted Dr. Bennett Dowler's discovery, in the delta of the Mississippi, from the " *Types of Mankind,*" by which he concludes that men existed there fully 57,000 years ago.

In a place in Scotland, called St. Enoch's Croft, in 1780, when digging for the foundation of a church, a " Clyde canoe," hewn out of a single oak. was found twenty-five feet beneath the soil. This primitive vessel rested horizontally upon its keel, and in it, near the bow, there was found a beautifully finished stone axe ; thus, again, proving that beneath the ancient of Scotia's old people, rests the records of a vastly older human story.

According to the statistical accounts, in the vicinity of Falkirk, an ancient boat was found thirty feet below the surface of the same carse, whence a fossil-elephant was exhumed in 1821. In the earlier part of the previous century, a sudden rise of the river Carron undermined a portion of its banks, and exposed to view an ancient canoe, of unusually large dimensions, lying imbedded in the alluvial soil, at a depth of fifteen feet, and covered by successive strata of clay, shells, moss, sand, and gravel. Sir John Clerk has described it with great minuteness, in the *Bibliotheca Topographica Brittanica*, as an antediluvian boat. This ancient barque was finely polished, and perfectly smooth, both inside and out, and was formed from a single oak-tree, with pointed stem and square stern. In the same locality, on the authority of Dr. G. Hamilton, a human skull was found, along with ancient canoes and fossil bones of the *Elephas primigenius*, twenty feet below the surface, in a bed of shell and gravel, by those who were digging the area of the large Grangemouth lock of the Union Canal, on the 29th of June, 1843.

The bones of the *Bos primigenius*, *Bos longifrons*, and fossil carnivora have been found marked with javelin wounds, and accompanied with human remains. Indeed, I might multiply such instances by the thousand. to say nothing of human skulls, and pottery of undoubted Pre-Adamite origin, now in my possession. But these instances will suffice. We now pass to the consideration of " Flints in the Drift," now agitating the European mind.

CHAPTER III.

"FLINTS IN THE DRIFT"—HUMAN REMAINS.

JOHN ELLIOT, Esq., an able contributor to the *Geologist*, London, in a recent number of that excellent journal, remarks that in a deep ravine, surrounded by trees and brushwood growing in wild profusion, was, until lately, a cave, in that member of the carboniferous formation locally called the "Great Limestone," and situated about one mile and a quarter north from the town of Stanhope, in the county of Durham. The limestone is now being worked for the purpose of supplying the Weardale Iron Company with a flux used in the operation of smelting their iron stone ; and consequently the cave has been laid bare to the light of day.

The cave was much visited a few years ago, both by strangers and persons living in the locality, but probably few of the visitors ever studied the excavating forces by means of which the cave was hollowed out of the solid limestone, and fewer still, if any, would think, that they were treading on a primeval burial-place.

Doubtless the excavation must be mainly due to aqueous agency, but a reference to Sir Charles Lyell's "Principles of Geology," Professor Phillips's "Treatise on Geology," and Richardson's "Geology," shows that our leading writers on this subject consider that the *first* cause of a cavern must have been a fracture in the limestone rock, consequent on the upheaval of the strata, and that water then finding access to the crack, would wear it out to its present dimensions.

Fractures in this case would most probably take

place when the "Red Vein" was formed, which is only between two hundred and three hundred yards distant from the cave, and crosses the ravine nearly at right angles. This vein, which contains lead ore, iron-stone, etc., is a wide one, requiring a wide fissure, and the force necessary to produce such a fissure would be sufficient to cause rents and small dislocations in the rocks at considerable distances. Besides this, there are two other veins crossing the ravine at lesser distances from the cave, and these would still further increase the probability of an original fissure.

The cave must be very old if we suppose it to have been formed by the water running down the ravine, when on a level with its mouth or opening, seeing that the water-course is now worn down ten or twelve feet below the cave's bottom. Again, if we suppose it to have been excavated by the attrition of the waves of the sea during some remote period, when the waters of the ocean stood on a level with the cave, it must still have a very ancient origin, for the cave is situated upwards of thirty miles from the sea, and upwards of eight hundred feet above its present level. This locality must have been submerged during the glacial period, as we have evidence of, by the deposits of boulder-clay; and if the sea on receding should have remained on a level with the limestone for a great length of time, the result would have been the wearing down of the rock, or the hollowing out of crevices and caves in the exposed strata.

In a certain place of the cave-flooring, the workmen recently came upon a large sheet of stalagmite of varying thickness, but averaging about four inches. This calcareous incrustation has been formed by the ceaseless dropping of water holding lime in solution, from the roof of the cave. On removing this crust and a

small portion of fine sand and silt, the workmen exhumed a human skull and a quantity of bones, some
undoubtedly human, and others belonging to the lower
animals. The human skull, according to its phrenological development, seems to indicate a low intellectual capacity, the forehead being low, and the circumference under the average standard. There is also a
fragment of a skull which seems to have belonged to a
tolerably large animal, as it measures three and a quarter inches from the medial line to the outside beside
the ear, giving a breadth of six and a half inches for
the whole skull ; then if the integuments, hair. etc., be
added, we should have a physiognomy little short of
nine inches wide, and this creature may have been
one of the principal tenants of the cave, and which
probably devoured the others. Intermixed with the
remains are very small pieces of bone, etc., partially
cemented together by calcareous matter, and occurring
in patches at different places ; these have the appearance of coprolites. The bones are nearly all fragmentary, and much broken ; the fractures being of an ancient date, thereby showing that the remains had been
subject to violence and fracture *before* they were imbedded in their calcareous tomb.

How long these remains have lain in the cave? by
what means they had been carried and entombed
there ? whether the animal-remains belong to existing
or to extinct species ? and how the fractured bones are
to be accounted for ? are all very interesting palæon-
tological problems.

The cave has, in all probability, been occasionally
inhabited by wolves, foxes, etc., which would sally
forth, seize their prey, and return to devour it, leaving
the bones to be covered over by the stalagmite as we
find them ; the coprolites before mentioned seem to

point to this conclusion. There seems to be not so much mystery about the animal bones being found there; but the case is quite different as regards the human. There is always something strange and startling in such occurrences, when human remains are found otherwise than reposing in the silent and hallowed precincts of a regular burying-place.

During the interment of these relics of some of the perhaps earliest members of our race, the rippling of running water on the cavern floor, the monotonous drippings from the roof, the growling perhaps of wolves, or the barking of foxes, and the bellowing of the wind through the gloomy chambers of the cavern, would form the only requiem.

It ought to be observed, that the remains are deposited in a certain wing or chamber of the cave, about two feet above the floor where the water runs, so that they would lie dry, with the exception of the calcareous droppings from the roof, or in the case of the cavern water being swollen above the capacity of the lower channel to contain it.

Although a considerable portion of the cave has been destroyed by the quarrying operations, which are still going on, there remains yet a much larger extent undisturbed, so that more remains will most likely be discovered.

In carrying on the quarrying operations from the point where they were suspended when the first discovered relics were sent to London, the workmen found numerous fragments of bones, also bone pins and knives, fragments of very rude pottery, portion of an armlet, boar-tusks, bronze spear-head, pins, celts, and armlet, two coins, some marine shells, cockle, limpet, and mussels, and large quantities of charcoal, etc., all deposited under an incrustation of stalagmite, varying from two to four, or at some places to eight inches in thickness, with the exception of one or two manufactured articles, which were found in the sand not covered by stalagmite. The whole of the cave-deposits, with this trifling exception, were covered by a thick sheet of stalagmite, varying from a very dense, compact structure, to a highly crystalline, or to a more or less porous substance ; some portions easily fractured by the stroke of a hammer, others yielding only to most energetic blows.

The bronze armlet and the two coins were found in sand uncovered by stalagmite ; but as they were deposited in what had, not long ago, been the water-course, the stalagmite had either been denuded, or had been prevented from forming, at that particular place, by the action of the stream ; the *coins were under very little cover*, and might have been imbedded very recently.

The stream of water through the cave has evidently changed its course many times since the cave was excavated to its present size, as we find accumulations of sand and gravel about three feet above the present water-level, and about two feet above the ancient water-course.

There was also a hillock of angular blocks, covered by stalagmite, and upon this stalagmitic hillock were deposited bones, tusks, bone knives and pins, large and small snail shells, fragments of pottery, piece of an armlet, a cockle-shell, and large quantities of charcoal, cemented together by calcareous matter. No sand or gravel was observed among them ; there being considerable interstices in some parts of the bed, plainly showing they had not been drifted there by water, but pointing to the conclusion that they had been *purposely* placed there by the animals or men that inhabited the cave.

In this cave bones, bone pins, tusks, pottery, and

charcoal were found in coarse sand and smooth pebbles, and might have been drifted while *in* the cave ; but it is not at all probable that they were drifted *into* it, for every appearance connected with the deposits, such as the large quantities of charcoal found, and the numerous burnt stones, etc., lead to the belief that the cave had been inhabited for a considerable length of time ; and that fires had been burned at different places, the thick deposits of charcoal testify.

The bronze implements found, were associated with a few bones, a limpet-shell, some mussel-shells, and a large quantity of charcoal, and were deposited in sand and gravel.

The deposits throughout the cave are nearly on the same relative level, with the exception of the hillock already mentioned ; and the greatest part of them have only one stalagmitic covering.

The " Communion Table," as it was called by the visitors to the cave, was a large pillar of the rock, around which the water had washed until it had undermined the base, when the pillar fell down, leaving a considerable space between its top and the roof of the cave, which had afterwards been partially refilled by pendulous stalactites from the roof, forming a junction with the stalagmitic bosses on the " table," and on the top of the " table" there was found a tusk, some bones, some large snail-shells, and pieces of charcoal, under an incrustation of stalagmite.   One of the workmen wondering what thickness the incrustation had attained on the " table," struck his back into it, and exhumed the above-mentioned relics to his no small astonishment. Perhaps this is the first time that such a discovery has been made "on removing the cover."

The appearances of the deposit and the great thickness of the stalagmite—in places six and even eight

inches thick—shows that portion must have taken a
greater length of time to form than the rest, which was
only two to four inches, while from the absence of any
bronze implements, I am led to consider it of more ancient date ; the probability also is, that bone implements, would cease to be used when metal ones were
introduced.

The general appearance, on entering the cave before
it was demolished, was very interesting and grand.
The fine pendent stalactites from the roof ; the various
round bosses of stalagmite undulating over the floor ;
the gurgling of the cave-stream ; and the momentary
droppings of water from the crevices and joints of the
rock, gave the place a very solemn and enchanting
aspect. What changes in the manners and customs of
the human race have taken place since the date of the
cave-men ! Were we to take a poetical or an imaginative view of the case, and picture to ourselves a few
naked or half-naked human beings in the gloomy cavern,
standing or sitting round a fire made of wood, and enveloped in its stinking smoke, with perhaps an animal's
skin flung round their bodies and secured by one of
these very bone-pins we have found ; making their rude
repast of a boar which they had hunted down in the
surrounding forest, and the flesh of which they may
have boiled in one of these coarse earthen pots, of
which we have found such numerous fragments, flayed
too, probably, with those bone-knives which have thus
strangely come down to us ; poor creatures, who lived
and died so long ago, that no Hume has chronicled the
career of their race, and who probably had perished
long ages ago : picture their condition of want, priva-
tion, and hardships, as compared with the plenty, the
luxurious mode of living, and the high state of civilization which *we* now enjoy. What a contrast there is !

But Science does not sanction the play of the imagination, which is ever an unsafe guide.   Well-ascertained
facts and reliable observations are the data on which
Science rears the structures on which she plants her
standards.   But one can scarce refrain from speculation
on a theme like this.

Professor Huxley, F.R.S., a British geologist of
very high standing, in a brief article in the same journal whence the foregoing account was taken, in speaking of the famed Muskham Skull, says that it is, like the
animal bones discovered along with it, stained of a
dark brown color ; the whole of these parts of the
cranial bones which bound the cranial cavity were
well preserved; but the facial bones, with the exception of a small portion of the nasals, were broken
away, so as to expose the whole of the under surface
of the base of the skull

The considerable development of the frontal sinuses
and of the different ridges and processes of the skull.
shows it to be that of an adult, and the same charac
ters lead me to believe that it belonged to a male.
Otherwise, it is small enough for a female, as its extreme length does not exceed 7·2 inches, its extreme
breadth 5·4 inches, and its horizontal circumference
20½ inches.

The skull has a very peculiar form.   If a line drawn
from the glabella to the superior curved line of the
occiput be made horizontal, the highest point of the
longitudinal median contour of the skull will be seen
to be situated about the middle of the length of the
sagittal suture, and from this point the contour shelves
rapidly downwards, to the brow on the one hand, and
to the center of the space between the apex of the
lambdoidal suture and the occipital protuberance on
the other.   This last is the most prominent portion of

the back part of the skull, the median contour below
it bending forwards to the occipital protuberance,
which is a very strong, projecting, triangular process.
It follows from this description, that a line taken from
the glabella to the occipital protuberance is shorter
than one from the glabella to a point midway between
this and the lambdoidal suture. The difference between
the two is about 0·3 of an inch. I find that crania
differ a good deal in this respect, the occipital protuberance being in many, especially the lower races of
mankind, the most backwardly situated part of the
skull, when the glabello-occipital line is made horizontal, while in others, as in the present instance, the most
posterior part of the skull is situated much higher up.

The line of greatest breadth of the skull is situated
nearly in the same plane as that of its greatest height,
in the position indicated, and the auditory foramina
may also be said, roughly, to be intersected by that
plane. The forehead is low and narrow, but not retreating. The supraciliary prominences are very well
developed, and, by their form, indicate the existence
of large frontal sinuses. The space between the glabella and the nasal suture is not really very depressed,
though on the side view of the skull it appears to be
so, by reason of the projection of the supraorbital
prominences.

The vertical height of the skull from the center of
the auditory foramen to the vertex is 4.8 inches, and
the center of the auditory foramen lies about 0·8 of an
inch below the level of the glabello-occipital line.

The mastoid and styloid processes are well developed.

The base of this skull is remarkable in several respects. The occipital foramen is placed far back, and
its plane is directed more backwards than is usual in

human skulls. When the base of the skull is turned
upwards, and the glabello-occipital line is horizontal
(its length being 6·7 inches), the anterior edge of the
occipital foramen lies 1·5 inch above the line, and a
perpendicular let fall from it would cut the line 3·9
inches from its anterior end. A similar line let fall
from the posterior edge would cut the glabello-occipital
line at 5·3 inches from its anterior end, and that edge
is only 0·9 of an inch above it. In a length of 1·4,
the plane of the occipital foramen, therefore, has a fall
of 0·6 towards the glabello-occipital line.

In a well-formed European skull, whose glabello-
occipital line measures 7·0 inches, while its extreme
length is 7·25, the distance of the anterior edge of the
occipital foramen from the glabella, measured in the
same way along the glabello-occipital line, is 3·8 ; of
its posterior edge, 5·3. The anterior edge is 1·1 vertically above the line, and the posterior edge, 1·0 above
it. Thus. in a length of 1·5, the occipital foramen has
a slope of only 0.1 inch, so that, instead of being greatly
inclined backwards, it is nearly horizontal.

The skull from the Valley of the Trent belongs to a
cranial type which seems at one time to have been
widely distributed over the British Islands. I have
seen skulls from rude stone tombs in Scotland with
similar characters, and others obtained from the Valley
of the Thames. There are skulls in the Museum of the
Royal College of Surgeons, exhibiting like proportions,
from the remarkable tumulus at Towyn-y-Capel, Angle-
sea, described by the Hon. W. O. Stanley, M. P., in
the *Archæological Journal* (Institute) for 1846 ; and
my friend, Mr. Busk, has shown me others from Cornwall. But the skulls which most clearly resemble the
Trent cranium are some, also from river beds, which
I saw in the Museum of the Royal Irish Academy, and

in the collection at Trinity College, Dublin, and of which my friend, Dr. E. P. Wright, the curator of that collection, has been good enough to supply me with excellent casts. Two of these skulls are from the bed of the Nore, in Queen's county, and two from that of the Blackwater River, in Armagh, and one of the latter has the most extraordinary resemblance to the Trent skull, as the following table of measurements will show:

	Trent.	Blackwater
Maximum length	7·0	7·2
Length of glabello-occipital line	6·7	7·0
Greatest vertical height from center of auditory foramen, the glabello-occipital line being horizontal	4·8	4·7
Distance of auditory foramen below glabello-occipital line	0·8	0·7
Greatest transverse diameter	5·4	5·65
Transverse diameter at the lower edge of the coronal suture	4·4	4·75
Horizontal circumference	20·5	20·75
Transverse arc from one auditory foramen to the other	13·25	13·0
Antero-posterior arc from glabella to occipital protuberance	12·5	12·5
Antero posterior arc from glabella to posterior edge of the occipital foramen	14·25	14·4

The plane of the occipital foramen of the Blackwater skull, however, is less inclined, so that this feature may be accidental in the Trent skull. The frontal sinuses are also less developed in the Blackwater skull, but, in all other respects, the resemblance is very close. The other Blackwater skull, and one of the Nore skulls, are also very like the Trent skull, but the remaining Irish skull from the Nore is much larger (having a length of 7·8 inches), and more depressed. It exhibits, in a very marked manner, however, the projection of the superior part of the occipital bone beyond the occipital protuberance which characterizes the other skulls, and it retains a strong resemblance to them in its other peculiarities.

The Trent skull was found associated with bones of the *Bos longifrons*, goat, red deer, wolf and dog.

I have dwelt thus long upon the Trent skull, because of its comparatively perfect condition, and because, so far as the imperfect condition of the fragments from Heathery Burn Cave allow me to judge, they appear to belong to the same race of rather small and lightly-made men, with prominent superciliary ridges and projecting nasal bones.

In a paper devoted to the crania of the most ancient races of men, Charles Carter Blake, Esq., another high authority on questions of this nature, says, in the *Geologist* of June, 1862, that the authenticated discovery of human remains in strata of high historical antiquity in the Heathery Burn Cave, near Stanhope, and at Muskham, in the Valley of the Trent, and the approaching discussion which "looms in the distance" of Palæontology, induces me to offer a few observations on the osteological nature of the evidences at present afforded to us of man contemporary with the mammoths, with a view, if possible, to determine the grade of the individuals whose remains have been preserved in suprapliocene strata.

The deposits on the banks of the Somme, (Abbeville, St. Acheul, St. Roch,) at Grenelle, near Paris, at Hoxne, in Suffolk, at Brixham and Kent's Hole, in the south-west of England, under Gray's-Inn-Lane, in Middlesex, at Macagnone, in Sicily, the Kjökkenmöddings, in Denmark, and at Wookey Hole, in the Mendips, indicate to us the existence of man in a low state of civilization, as proved by his weapons, but of whom the osteological evidences have not yet been discovered. In these deposits the bones of extinct mammalia are found, as well as a more or less per centage of animals of existing species.

At Engis, in Belgium, Massat, in France, Aurignac, in Gascony, Muskham, in the Valley of the Trent, the Lake habitations, in Switzerland, proofs of man have been found in strata contemporaneous with the most recently extinct animals.

Human remains have also been obtained from the Neanderthal, from Plau, in Mecklenburg, Mewslade, in Glamorganshire, Sennen, in Cornwall, Montrose, Nether Urquhart, in Fifeshire, Plymouth, East Ham, and Heathery Burn Cave, Stanhope, of which the antiquity, however undemonstrated by the association of extinct animals, has been advocated upon more or less amount of geological evidence. Many other instances, but of less authentic value, might be added to the above.

I shall discusss *seriatim*, as briefly as possible, the recorded instances, before drawing those conclusions which seem to be capable of deduction from the facts before us.

With respect to the Neanderthal cranium,[*] unquestionably the most interesting of the evidences before us, I have briefly discussed in the *Geologist*, Vol. IV. p. 395, the question of its grade of organization. I hoped that English geologists would have thrown light upon the question of its age, and that a discussion might have arisen which would have established it either as a skull of comparatively modern antiquity, or as possibly coeval with the deposits of the Somme valley.[†] The

---

[*] This skull is figured in the London *Geologist*, Vol. IV., (1861,) plate xi., p. 396.

[†] While obtaining material for this work, Professor Huxley, F.R.S., kindly permitted me to inspect the cast of the Neanderthal skull in his possession. I see sufficient grounds to infer its representing a distinct race of men.

apparent ape like, but really mal-developed idiotic character of its conformation is so hideous, and its alleged
proximity to the anthropoid *Simiæ* of such importance,
that every effort should be made to determine its probable date in time. That such efforts have not been
made, and that the evidence at present in possession of
English palæontologists, is wholly inadequate to enable
us to draw any conclusion as to its being the representative of any given type of mankind, living or extinct,
is the object of the following observations.

The fact has not yet been conclusively demonstrated
to the satisfaction of English geologists that the Neanderthal skull is of high antiquity. The time required
for the deposition of the four or five feet of mud in the
cave *might* have been accomplished in a comparatively
short space of time. It is not stated at what height in
the deposit the bones were found.

Dr. Schauffhausen's statement, " that the bones adhere strongly to the tongue. although, as proved by the
use of hydrochloric acid, the greater part of the carti-
lage is still retained in them, which appears, however,
to have undergone that transformation into gelatine
which has been observed by Von Bibra in fossil bones,"
is hardly precise enough to convince practical geologists
of the antiquity of the skull. But of the Engis cranium no such evidence is afforded us. It is hardly necessary to repeat the arguments made use of by Buckland against Schmerling, at the meeting of German
naturalists at Bonn, which proved the less degree of
gelatine in the fossil hyæna bones than in the human
remains from the Belgian cave deposits. The condition
of the Vale of the Trent skull, which has been apparently
immersed in glue or some analagous liquid since its dis-
interment, has deprived us of the only chemical evidence
which could have decided the question of its antiquity.

Prof. Huxley admitted to his audience at the Royal Institution (Feb. 7, 1862,) that, with respect to the Neanderthal cranium, " its great antiquity was not *directly* proved, although its date was undoubtedly very early."* Professor Huxley said, that in the Museum of the College of Surgeons there are Australian skulls which closely correspond in configuration and development with those of the caverns of Engis and the Neanderthal, the differences between which latter were " hardly greater than occurred between individuals of that race, while in form the ancient and Australian skulls presented many analogies."

Engis (Belgium.)—This skull was found by Dr. Schmerling, in the year 1833, in a cave, with the cave bear, cave hyæna, elephant, etc., and has since proved the *teterrima causa belli* of palæontologists from the days of Buckland and Schmerling down to our own, exhibits a type of *cranium* which, if attention had not been specially called to it, as that of an alleged contemporary of the cave bear and mammoth, would have been the last to attract the attention of a craniologist.

This most ordinary type exhibits a fairly-developed forehead, a full and high, but not shelving, occiput, supraorbital ridges not prominent, and, generally speaking, analogous to dozens of Indo-European crania. In the Nepal collection, in the British Museum, there are several skulls which resemble the Engis cranium in their configuration. It is dolichocephalic, but does not approach to any of the boat-shaped (kumbecephalic,) skulls which have been afforded to us from graves in Scotland of the early " Stone period."

Massat.—The remains from this bone-cave do not afford us any evidences which would lead us to distinguish their cranial type. Only a few teeth have been

* 'London Medical Times,' Feb. 15, 1862.

discovered associated with remains of *Felis spelæa,
Ursus spelæus, Hyæna spelæa,* etc.

Plau (Mecklenburg.)—The skeleton to which this
skull belonged was found in silicious sand, six feet below the surface, associated with bone implements made
out of the osseous remains of stag and boar.   Dr.
Schauffhausen says : "A very high antiquity was assigned to this grave, as it was wholly unprotected by
any masonry, and afforded no trace of cremation having
been practiced, nor any implements of stone, clay, or
metal."   Similar arguments might be adduced in favor
of the high antiquity of the soldiers buried at Antietam, who, tossed into a pit naked, or with a blanket
round them, would afford no evidences of masonry, cremation, stone, or metallic implements.   The cranial
appearance of the skull is, however, truly remarkable,
although it approaches very much to the configuration
of the cranium from Montrose, to which I shall presently allude.   It is brachycephalic,* the occiput being
high, and the supraorbital ridges well developed.   The
length from the glabella to the occiput is 6" 5'", the
breadth across the parietal tubers 5" 5'".   Dr. Schauffhausen states : "Notwithstanding the great similarity
in the form of the forehead between this skull and that
from the Neanderthal, the prominence of the supraorbital ridges in the latter is more marked, and they are
completely continuous with the orbital margin, which is
not the case in the former.   But the skulls are essentially distinguished by their general form, which in the
one is long-elliptical, and in the other rounded."   A
portion of the upper jaw, with the teeth, and the entire
lower jaw, have been preserved, indicating that the
Plau man was orthognathous.   As in most of these

* Brachycephalic—Flat, broad, retreating type of head
Dolichocephalic—Elongated crania, receding type of head.

cases, the sole chemical evidence of the antiquity of the Plau skeleton is, that " the bones are thick, but very light, and adhere strongly to the tongue." More exact analysis of their component parts is unrecorded by Dr. Schauffhausen.

Aurignac (*Gascony*).—The human remains from this cavern, which were associated, but in a way not known, with those of *Elephas primigenius, Rhinoceros tichorhinus, Megaceros*, etc., after their discovery, fell into the hands of the mayor of Aurignac. Not regarding the interests of science, and in order to prevent the dissemination of any hypotheses on the subject among the Gascons, he carefully collected all the bones together, amounting to seventeen individuals, and caused them to be reinterred in the parish burial-ground. Eight years afterwards, "not even the sexton retained any recollection of the precise spot at which these human remains had been deposited in a common trench." Future palæontologists will rank Dr. Amiel, the mayor of Aurignac, with the trustees of the Ashmolean Museum, who destroyed the last specimen of the Dodo, in Oxford. His ignorance, or superstition, has deprived Palæontology of one of the most important links of evidence ever discovered. No information consequently exists of the appearance of the bones, as denoting the race to which they might possibly appertain.

Mewslade (*Glamorganshire*).—This cranium Professor Busk describes as " probably that of a female, found together with less perfect skulls and numerous other bones belonging to six or seven individuals of different ages, from sixty or seventy down to three or four years, in a narrow fissure in a limestone quarry at Mewslade in Glamorganshire, and *not improbably* of the same period as the bones of animals. etc., found in the neighboring caverns in Gower, which have been described by

Dr. Falconer and others.　This cranium is obviously of a wholly distinct type from that of the others, though still in some respects peculiar." The frontal region is elevated, the supraorbital ridge being only moderately prominent. The alisphenoid and the parietal join. The skull belongs markedly to the dolichocephalic type, and slightly reminds us of the Engis cranium.

Sennen (Cornwall).—In this cranium, which was discovered in a subterranean peat-bog or forest, thirty feet below the present level of the sea, at Sennen, near the Land's End, Cornwall, and of which Prof. Busk remarks that it "bears some resemblance to the Engis cranium of Dr. Schmerling," the dolichocephalic character is strongly marked. The frontal region is retrocedent; the occiput shelving backwards. The alisphenoid and the parietal bones join for a greater extent than in most Caucasian skulls. The supraorbital ridges are less prominent than in the Plau, more so than in the Mewslade crania. The *meatus auditorius externus* is large; the zygomatic arch strong and powerful.

Montrose.—This, the most typical example of a British brachycephalic skull, was found in a tumulus, supposed to belong to the later part of the Stone period. In the words of Professor Wilson, it "is square and compact in form, broad and short, but well balanced, and with a good frontal development. The supraciliaries are moderately elevated."

Nether Urquhart (Fifeshire).—This is one of the *kumbecephalic* or boat-shaped skulls which were found in a cairn in Fifeshire in 1835. It is supposed to belong to the early part of the Stone period. This period might be called the protolithic (from *prótos*, first, and *lithos*, stone). The long, narrow and shelving occiput, the retrocedent frontals and the prominent supraciliaries, indicate the similarity of this skull to that from Sennen, to which I have already alluded.

The researches of Professor Wilson lead him to the result that the kumbecephalic (dolichocephalic) races in Great Britain antedated the brachycephalic races in time ; those of Professor Nilsson, that the brachycephalic men in Scandinavia flourished before the dolichocephalic races.

Plymouth.—In this small portion of a cranium, "found in a limestone quarry at Plymouth, at a depth of about six feet below the present turf," the retrocedence of the forehead is very remarkable. The supra-orbital ridges project but slightly, and are discontinuous over the nasal bone. The fractured condition of the cranium precludes any observation on the form of the occiput or the length of the sphenoido-parietal suture.

East Ham (*Valley of Thames*).—Mr. Cresy, at the meeting of the Geologists' Association on April 7, 1862, exhibited this skull, as well as two others, of supposed less geological antiquity. The conditions under which it was found were detailed by him. The "skull was found in excavating for the foundations of the Northern Outfall Sewer, in East Ham Marshes, at a depth of fifteen feet below the surface, the strata being—

```
2 feet grass and mould.
5  "   yellow clay.
5  "   peat.
3  "   sand and gravel in which it was found.
--
15 feet."
```

With it were discovered two "celts" (stone axes) chipped on the surface, excepting the trenchant edges, which were ground, and the lower jaw of a cetacean animal. Having had the opportunity, through the kindness of Mr. Mackie, of examining this skull, I give the following table of measurements, taken with tape and rule, in the ordinary manner :

INCHES.

Longitudinal diameter from between supraorbitals to inion..... 6¼

Parietal diameter between parietal tubers.................... 5¼

Frontal diameter, between anterior and inferior angles of parietal bones.. 4¾

Vertical diameter from fossa, between occipital condyles to top of skull.. 4¾

Intermastoid arch, from one mastoid to the other, over the calvarium.. 14¼

Intermastoid line, measured in a straight line, between the points of the mastoid processes........... 4

Occipito-frontal arch, measured by a tape on the surface of the cranium, from the nasal suture to the posterior margin of the foramen magnum.............. 14

Horizontal periphery, by a tape round the cranium, so as to touch the os frontis immediately above the superciliary ridges, and the most prominent part of the occipital bone............. 20¾

In the above table, I have used the system of measurement proposed by Dr. George Williamson.[*]

It appears from the proportion of this (a female) skull, that the breadth was to the length as $7\frac{5}{10}$: 10, and that it was consequently "dolichocephalic." The type is oval, the frontal being rounded, with a flat calvarium, and the parietal tubers moderately developed. The occiput is oval, the inion being slightly protuberant ; the lower half of the supraoccipital shelves gently downwards to the *foramen magnum*. The occipital condyles are flattened. The alisphenoid and the parietal join on both sides of the head, with small *ossa wormiana* intercalated in the suture. The frontal

* "Observations on the Human Crania contained in the Museum of the Army Medical Department, Chatham." 8vo. Dublin, 1857, p. 73.

suture is obliterated. Above the interorbital space is
a slight projection. possibly coincident with, though not
necessarily an indication of, the frontal sinus. Behind
the coronal suture, the calvarium is slightly depressed.
perhaps indicating the use of a constricting bandage
compressing the cranium. From these characters it appears that no distinctive points can be predicated of this
cranium, as differentiating it from the skulls of the ex
isting individuals who inhabit the valley of the Thames.
To this skull was adherent a small amount of fine mud.
apparently of the same chemical constituency as the
clay-bed of the river Thames or Lea. The whole of
the animal matter was present in the skull, which did
not adhere when applied to the tongue.

Borris (bed of Nore,) Ireland.—The supraorbitals
here are slightly more prominent than in the Blackwater, less so than in the Valley of the Trent skull.
The lambdoidal suture is very complex, and develops
many *ossa wormiana* on both sides. The fractured condition of the skull precludes any observation as to the
junction of the parietals and alisphenoids, or as to the
presence of a paroccipital tubercle. The opportunity
of inspecting this skull at leisure has been afforded to
me by Prof. Huxley.

Bed of Blackwater River, Armagh (Ireland).—In
this skull, which has been kindly lent to me by Prof.
Huxley, the alisphenoid and the parietal join on the
right side ; the apex, however. of the parietal impinges
on the alisphenoid on the left : the supraorbitals are
scarcely, if at all. prominent ; the retrocedent frontal,
and the calvarium sloping gently upwards to the center
of the parietal bone, repeat here the characters of the
Borris skull and the skull from the Valley of the Trent.
In the cast, the paroccipital tubercle is slightly prominent on the right side.

Valley of the Trent.—This skull repeats many of the characters of the Borris and Blackwater skulls, from which, however, it is markedly distinct. The alisphenoid and the parietal join on both sides. On the right the jugular eminence is pronouncedly distinct, and indicates a well-defined paroccipital tubercle. The left jugular eminence is, however, broken away. The digastric fossa is deep ; the inion is protuberant. Over each orbit is a ridge, discontinuous over the nasal suture, and which projects forwards. This contains, on each side, large, distinct, and well-defined supraorbital foramina. Along the sagittal suture is a slight elevation, or crest, analogous to that often observed in the Australian races. The low frontal bone reminds the observer forcibly of the Andaman skull,[*] which it does not exceed in regard to its frontal development.

One of the most important differences which the cranium of the *Troglodytes Gorilla* presents to the human skull has been defined by Prof. Owen (Osteological Catalogue of the College of Surgeons) to be the more backward position of the *foramen magnum*, and its more oblique plane in relation to the base of the skull in the gorilla, than in man. The almost horizontal direction of the *foramen magnum* in the human species, co-related with the character *(situs erectus)* applied by the Linnæan definition to man, is modified in the Valley of the Trent skull, and such modification is in the direction of the inferior type. The angle made by a line drawn from the anterior to the posterior margins of the *foramen magnum*, with the plane of the basioccipital, is more oblique than I have observed in any human skull, and markedly more so than in the so-called "lowest" races of mankind, as *e. g.* the Australians and Andaman Islanders. This character, coupled

[*] Owen, Trans. Ethn. Soc. 1862.

with the powerful occipital spine, the ridged and crested surface of the lower half of the superoccipital, indicative of the action of powerful nuchal ligaments to keep the head from falling forwards, the presence of a " par-occipital" process for the firmer attachment of the *rectus capitis lateralis*, and the slightly more backward position of the occipital condyles, seem to indicate that an entirely erect position was not the normal attitude of the pre-historical contemporary of *Bos primigenius* in the Valley of the Trent.

The skull from the Valley of the Trent exhibits, on the right side of the upper half of the superoccipital bone, a partial retention of the suture dividing the *squama occipitalis* from the lower half of the superoccipital bone. This character, the " *os Incæ*," was first observed by Dr. Bellamy, in the skulls of the early Peruvians. Prof. Tschudi* considered it as a mark of the primeval distinction of the Peruvian race, the skulls of which, according to him, manifested this alleged "embryonic character" as in the lower mammalia. Morton observed it in a Chimu (called by him Chimu-yan), and in a Cayuga skull. In the British Museum is a large handsome skull, belonging to the " Chincha" type, in which the interparietal bone is manifest. In Mr. Edward Gerrard's most useful and valuable catalogue, recently published, the locality is marked as from Pasadama (*i. e.* Pachacamac), near Lima.

In the collection of the Royal College of Surgeons, on No. 5711 (a Laplander), Prof. Owen remarks, " the suture between the exoccipital and supraoccipital is retained on the right side, and partially so on the left." Here, however, there are numerous Wormian bones in the lambdoidal suture. On No. 5390 (a New Zealander), he says, " the upper half of the supraoccipital

---

* Rivero and Tschudi, 'Antiguedades Peruanas.'

has been developed as an interparietal from a separate
center, and has united by a complex dentated suture
with the lower half of the supraoccipital." A similar
conformation exists in a skull from the Roman burial-
place at Felixstow, preserved in the Anatomical Museum at Cambridge,* and in the cranium of a Bengalee.
The law which regulates the repetition of similar characters in skulls of nations aboriginally distinct is termed
by Prof. J. Aitken Meigs,† of Philadelphia "homoioke-
phalic representation." Analogous congenital varieties or imperfections may be seen in almost every ethnic
type. Dr. Williamson has described them in the Al-
banian, Singhalese, Timmani, Kosso, Krooman, Fanti,
Ashantee, Calabar, Burmese (Malay), and Esquimaux;
whilst in the Limbu tribe from Nepâl, an instance has
been described by Prof. Owen, in which the "interparietal" is divided into three distinct *quasi*-symmetrical
portions. Dr. Spencer Cobbold has seen a true interparietal bone in a skull in the Edinburgh Museum; and
I have recently observed it in a skull belonging to the
Ethnological Society's collection, of which I am not yet
satisfied as to the precise nation to which it belonged.

A cursory examination of the bones found with the
human skull, at the Valley of Trent, has afforded to me
evidence of *Bos longifrons*, *Bos primigenius*, stag, wolf,
goat and horse. Some of the horn cores of *Bos longifrons* appeared to me to be more curved than usual, but
the majority exhibited the normal form.

ETRURIA.—In the osteological department of the
British Museum are four skulls, of presumed high his-
torical antiquity, which were derived from caves in
Etruria. I give the following table of their measure-

* Davis and Thurnam, p. 29.

† Meigs, 'Description of Fragmentary Human Skull from Jerus-
salem' 8vo. Philad. p. 279.

ments, taken in the same way as I have measured the East Ham skull. This table is necessarily defective, as in the skulls marked I. M. N. and +, the apical extremities of the mastoid processes are broken away, and the horizontal periphery of the skull marked + cannot be computed exactly, by reason of the left squamosal having posthumously bulged out from the parietals.

MEASUREMENTS.	Etrurian. O	Blackwater.	Etrurian. I.M.M.	Etrurian. I.M.N.	Borris.	Valley of the Trent.	Etrurian. +
Longitudinal diameter..	6¾	7¼	7	7½	7½	7¼	7½
Parietal diameter......	5¾	5⅞	5⅛	5¼	5¼	5	5
Frontal diameter.......	5	4½	4½	4½	—	4¼	4⅝
Vertical diameter......	4¼	5¾	4¾	5	–	6⅜	6
Intermastoid arch......	14¾	14¼	14¾	14½	—	14½	14½
Intermastoid line......	4¾	4½	4	4½	—	4	4⅜
Occipitofrontal arch....	14¼	14½	14½	14½	15 ¾	14	15¼
Horizontal periphery...	20⅜	20¾	20	20½	21	20	20⅜
Proportion of breadth to length, the latter being estimated as 10...	8.518	8.103	7.321	7	7	6.879	6.666

In I. M. M. and I. M. N. the occiput is globular, and shelving gently downwards. In + it is full and oval, the lower half of the supraoccipital being flattened. No undue prominence of the supraorbital ridge, or of the paroccipital tubercles, is observable. Small *ossa wormiana* are present in the lambdoid suture of I. M. M., but in I. M N. the sutures are obliterated; nor does + exhibit any peculiarity in this respect. The frontal suture, however, in I. M. N. is present. The inion is distinctly marked in I. M. M. and in +; not so, however, in I. M. N. In all three skulls the alisphenoid and parietal join. A slight depression of the vertex is indicated behind the coronal suture in the three skulls, and especially in I. M. M. No history of the specimens has been preserved, nor is there any

geological or antiquarian evidence demonstrating their
antiquity. The contrast between the brachycephalic
skull marked O, and the dolichocephalic one marked
†, from the same locality, is significant.

Switzerland.—Mr. Lubbock, in his memoir on the
subject, has told us " Human bones occur in the Pile-
works *(Pfahlbauten)* but very seldom, and may no
doubt be referred to accidents, especially as we find
that those of children are most numerous. One mature
skull was, however, discovered at Meilen, and has been
described by Professor Hiss, who considers that it does
not differ much from the ordinary Swiss type. And
while his work was in the press, M. Rütimeyer received
from M. Schwab four more skulls, two of which were
obtained at Nidau-Steinberg, one at Sutz, and one from
Biel." Mr. Lubbock proceeds to say: " Whether the
Drift race of men were really the aboriginal inhabitants of Europe, still remains to be ascertained. M.
Rütmeyer hints that our geographical distribution
indicates a still greater antiquity of the human race."
No general statement of facts is, however, adduced in
support of M. Rütmeyer's theory, while the negative
evidence, which proves that human bones are as capable
of preservation as those of mammalia, tends to refute,
until observation and demonstration shall establish the
greater antiquity of man.

A human cranium belonging to the first age of iron,
from Tiefenau, exhibited exactly the same profile as
the cranium from Sanderumgaard. M. Morlot states
that the height of the Swiss cranium is identically the
same, and the length is a little (5 *millimètres*) longer
than that of the Danish cranium. (Morlot, ' Etudes
Géologico-Archéologiques,' p. 317.)

Objects of human art have been found at various
depths in a tumulus near the Tinière rivulet, which

flows into the Lake of Geneva near Villeneuve. In order that my readers may understand more clearly M. Morlot's reasoning, I transcribe his diagram and references.

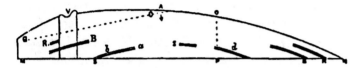

ACTUAL SECTION OF THE " CONE DE DÉJECTION TORRENTIELLE DE LA TINIERE."

From A. Morlot, 'Leçon d'ouverture d'un Cours sur la haute Antiquité, fait à l'Académie de Lausanne en Novembre et Décembre 1860.' 8vo. Lausanne, 1861.

R. *Bed of Roman age.*

B. *Bed of the Bronze age,* date 3000 to 4000 years ago.

S. *Bed of the Stone age,* date 5000 to 7000 years, in which were found, at *a,* a piece of pottery ; at *b,* a human skeleton, which appeared to have been laid in a tomb, and of which the very small, round, and remarkably thick head presented the Mongolian or Turanian " brachycephalic" type, strongly marked ; at *d,* many fragments of very coarse pottery, much charcoal, and broken pieces of the bones of various animals—a proof that man had inhabited that precise spot.

A. *Central axis of the cone,* transversely bisected by the railway. It is here that the torrent flowed in ordinary times, before the dykes had been constructed.

C C. *Surface of the cone,* when the torrent was commenced to be dyked. This line is, to a certain extent, ideal ; all the others are real, and have been actually observed as they are represented in the section.

M N. The iron road.

V. Bridge acting as aqueduct to the torrent which crosses the railway.

O P N. In this space exclusively all those distances are included which have served to establish chronological calculations. These distances, often repeated, are capable of being taken here very exactly ; they can be considered as exact almost to half an inch.

The section has been interrupted at M, because it became indistinct here. Its southern extremity was complete in every relation.

Kjökkenmöddings (Denmark).—Numerous human

skeletons from the ancient deposits of Denmark, in
which the remains of extinct animals, with one exception *(Bos primigenius)*, have not been found, have been
afforded to us. The skulls are brachycephalic, and possess well-defined supraorbital ridges. M. Morlot says
" that their front teeth did not overlap as ours do, but
met one another, as those of the Greenlanders of the
present day. This evidently indicates a peculiar manner of eating." The value of this assumption could
only be estimated by the illustration of a drawing,
showing in what way such close juxtaposition of the
incisor teeth was effected. This evidence, however, is
not given to us, and those who are acquainted with the
range of dental variation in man, however they might
consider a conformation of this sort indicative of a
peculiar description of food, will hardly affirm that the
builders of the tumuli had " a peculiar manner of eating." M. Morlot, although he quotes the Greenlanders, Egyptians and other nations as exhibiting the same
dental peculiarity, the incisors being worn away so as
functionally to resemble molars, is evidently not aware
of the fact that this conformation has been observed
even among British sailors, and that it is due solely
to the triturating action of the hard substances used by
them as food. In the sepulchral edifices of the early
Danes, carefully constructed of large hewn stones, M.
Morlot has discovered numerous crania, of which, he
says, the type can be established. " It is a small head,
remarkably rounded in every way, but with a rather
large facial angle, and a forehead which does not bear
the mark of a slightly-developed intelligence. This
type reminds one of that of the Laplander, but it cannot be precisely affirmed to be identical with it." One
from Sanderumgaard, of the Iron period, in the island
of Fyen, is dolichocephalic, with a slightly retrocedent

frontal. Practical cranioscopists are aware that the range of variation in the skulls of the Indo-European races is such as to exhibit many crania of these two types among the existing races of Europe and Asia. Palæontologists are under a lasting debt of obligation to M. Morlot, who has, by his researches on the later geological strata of Switzerland, furnished us with an almost inexhaustible mine of information on the contemporaneity of man with the extinct animals at both the Kjökkenmöddings and Pfahlbauten.* Human osseous remains have not been demonstrated in the Kjökkenmöddings themselves, according to the testimony of the latest observers of these shell-deposits.

The broad ground may be admitted, that the earliest Briton skulls generally exhibit a supraorbital projection, which attains in its development, however, nothing like the size of the ridge in the Neanderthal cranium. The majority of the British, Hibernian and Caledonian skulls figured by Messrs. Davis and Thurnam,† exhibit a large supraorbital ridge. This character is also present in a few of the Saxon skulls.

---

* A. Morlot.

1. " Leçon d'ouverture d'un Cours sur la haute Autiquité, fait à la Académie de Lausanne en Novembre et Décembre, 1860." 8vo. Lausanne, 1861.

2. " Remarques sur les formations modernes dans le Canton de Vaud." (Bulletin de la Société Vaudoise des Sciences naturelles, tome v. No. 40.) 8vo. Lausanne, 1857.

3. ' Études Géologico-Archéologiques en Danemark et en Suisse." 8vo. Lausanne, 1860. (Bulletin, etc., tome v. No. 46.)

4. " On the Post-Tertiary and Quaternary Formations of Switzerland." 8vo.

5. " Recherches sur les Habitations lacustres des environs d'Estavayer," par M. Biot de Vevay et Henri Rey, rédigées par M. Morlot. (Extrait des Mémoires de la Société des Antiquaries de Zurich, tome xiii.) 4to.

† " Crania Britannica." 4to and folio. London: 1856

The supraorbital development of the Briton skull from Ballidon Moor* is fully equal to that of the Engis cranium. The Neanderthal skull, however, admittedly stands *sui generis*.

The Museum of Natural History at Copenhagen contains skulls of the "Stone Period" in Denmark, with an excessive supraorbital projection.

Aboriginal American races of high antiquity often exhibit a large supraorbital development. This may be seen on examining Morton's† plates of the Peruvian from Pachacamac ("Temple of the Sun"), plate 11ᴀ, and the skulls of mound-builders from the Upper Mississippi (plate 52), Tennessee (plate 55), and Steubenviile, in Ohio (plate 68).

The frontal development of the Australian race, accompanied by an absence of the frontal sinus, has been frequently noticed, and several Australian skulls have the supraorbital ridge overhanging the origin of the nasals to the degree shown in the skulls from Engis and the Valley of the Trent.

Supraorbital development in the Negro is far from being a constant character   It is undoubtedly present in many of the lower Negroes; but I have now before me a skull from Ashantee, which exhibits less supraorbital development than many of the skulls from the "Stone Period" in Denmark.

In India, the range of variation offered by the hill-tribes of Nepál exhibits the supraorbital ridge under a variety of aspects. The low-caste individuals, perhaps of all nations, have a greater tendency to repeat this character than the more elevated types. In Europeans, however, of high intellect, this conformation may fre-

---

* "Crania Brittannica." 4to and folio. London : 1856.

† ' Crania Americana." Philadelphia : 1839. In a Pachacamac skull before me, there is a very slight supraorbital development.

quently be remarked ; and I have observed it in more than one person with whom it was correlated, with a high degree of mental ability.

The words of Professor Owen, applied to the Nepâl crania, are also applicable to the remains from the Stone period. "There are not more than two or three skulls in the entire series which would have suggested, had they been presented to observation without previous knowledge of their country, that they belonged to any primary division of human kind distinct from that usually characterized by craniologists as Caucasian or Indo-European ; the majority might have been obtained from graveyards in London, Edinburgh, or Dublin, and have indicated a low condition of the Caucasian race. . . . They present varieties in the proportion of length and breadth of cranium, in the development of the nasal bones, in the divarication or prominence of the malar bones, in the shape of the forehead, in the degree of prominence of the frontal sinuses and projection of the supraciliary ridge, which would be found perhaps in as many promiscuously-collected skulls of the operatives of any of our large manufacturing towns, and which would be associated with corresponding diversities of features and physiognomy."[*]

The range of variation offered by the above skulls (the Neanderthal cranium excepted) is, on the whole, not greater than between a large series of the skulls of any given district—as e. g., Nepâl. Neither in the size of the supraorbital ridge; the extent of frontal development ; the form of the occiput, whether shelving, vertical, or globular ; the persistence of an interparietal bone ; the presence or absence of a sphenoidoparietal suture ; the position of the condyles ; the de-

---

[*] Owen, "Report on a series of Nepâlese Skulls." Transactions of the British Association, 1859.

velopment of sagittal or lambdoidal crests ; the size, shape, or position of the styloid or vaginal processes—have any of those differences—which so prominently characterize the *Homo sapiens* been departed from, nor any of the simial features superadded or retained as embryonal characters ; nor have the latest published demonstrations of the anatomical characters of these ancient crania by the ablest advocates of the hypothesis of direct selective transmutation, afforded us any satisfactory evidence to break down the broad bridge of demarcation which still separates us from the inferior animals.

The researches of Professor Steenstrup and others have led to the proposition of a series of periods, as exhibited in the annexed table, in which the propositions put forth by the advocates of the excessive antiquity of man are set forth in a tabular form. Direct contemporaneity of *e. g.* the denizens of the Kjökkenmöddings with the Natchez mound-builders is not inferred. "It would have been very much better for geology if so loose and ambiguous a word as ' contemporaneous ' had been excluded from her terminology, and if in its stead some term, expressing similarity of serial relation and excluding the notion of time altogether, had been employed to denote correspondence in position in two or more series of strata,"* and Professor Huxley uses the term *homotaxis* as expressing such relation. It has been further sought to show, that, as in Denmark and some other localities, a regular scale of division of the humatile strata into beech, oak, and pine-producing deposits prevails, each respectively coincident with iron, bronze, and stone remains, that an analogous distribution in time prevailed during the deposi-

---

* Huxley. Address to Geological Society, 21st February, 1862.

tion of the extra-European humatile strata. Neither
observation nor analogy, however, demonstrates this
assumption. In the whole American continent, although
we have the chipped flints and celts from Natchez and
Chiriqui,* the obsidian knives from Mexico, and the
arrow-heads from Tierra del Fuego, the copper and
gold implements from Peru and Chiriqui, the American mind never devised the plan of smelting iron from
the ore, and applying the metalliferous residue to a
useful purpose. The so-called " Iron Age" never existed in America.

Trees. Denmark.	Weapons.	Skulls. (Denmark.)	Instances.
Beech.	Workers in Iron.	Dolichocephalic.	
Oak.	Workers in Bronze.	Dolichocephalic.	Switzerland.
Pine.	Hatchets not chipped, but ground in Stone.	Brachycephalic.	Switzerland. Köjkkenmöddings Natchez.
	Hatchets not ground but chipped in Stone.		Somme Valley.
	PLIOCENE.		
	MIOCENE.		
	EOCENE		

The division of human crania into " brachycephalic"
and " dolichocephalic" originated with the late Professor Retzius. Like the arbitrary and conventional divisions of other anthropologists into " orthognathous"
and " prognathous," it was convenient as affording easy
and intelligible descriptive terms for crania of diverse
races. As a test of distinction of race, however, it is

* W Bollaert and C. C. Blake on Antiquities from Chiriqui : Ethnological Society, March 18, 1862.

an insufficient mark of distinction. The supporters of
the theory have based on it the following classification.*

As types of these two varieties of crania. Professor
Huxley adduced the West Coast African Negro and
the Turk. The typical cranium of the West Coast African Negro is long and narrow, its transverse measurement being only six or seven tenths of the longitudinal,
while the side to side diameter of the Turk's skull is
as much as eight or nine tenths of the fore and aft
measurement. The facial angle of the skulls also was
different, owing to the projection of the jaws in the Negro : the dolichocephalic skull was prognathic, while
the brachycephalic skull was orthognathic The most
striking developments of these diversities were associated with the greatest differences of climate and situa-
tion. If a line be drawn from the center of Russian Tartary to the Bight of Benin, the north-eastern extremity
of the line would represent the center or pole of the brachycephalic orthognathic variety, the south-western
would be the center of the dolichocephalic prognathic
type. The center of Russian Tartary was distinguished by an arid climate and great diversities of
heat and cold, and presented the strongest contrast
with the hot, moist, reeking swamps of the Western
Coast of Africa. Now, in whatever direction we di-
verge from these dolichocephalic and brachycephalic
centers, we find the type beginning to fade and to pass
into the opposite. Thus diverging from the brachycephalic pole, if we pass eastward into China, we notice the population becoming more dolichocephalic and
prognathic ; if we travel northward to the Aleutian
Islanders, Esquimaux, and Greenlanders, we observe

---

* On Fossil Man. Royal Institution. February 7, 1862.

them more or less long-headed, as compared with the
Tartar type.   The same divergence of type is seen on
leaving the dolichocephalic center ; the peculiarities
of the Western African cranial conformation gradually subside and approach in proportion the other type.
Another line drawn across the center of the former
from the British Islands to India, would mark a population whose skulls may be said to be oval, presenting
a medium between the dolichocepalic and brachycephalic conformation."   The question was then raised
" whether the distribution of cranial forms had been
the same in all periods of the world's history, or whether the older races in any locality, possessed a different cranial character from their successors."

The induction that, on the whole, the brachycephalic type of cranium is more ancient than the dolichocephalic is capable only of a limited application.   The
skulls from Sennen, Plymouth, and Mewslade, said to
be of antiquity transcending human historical records,
all, belong, as Professor Busk has stated, to the dolichocephalic type.   If brachycephalic-skulled men existed before these, their remains have not been vouch-
safed to us, here or in England at least.   In the Continent, on the contrary, the Engis skull, said to be " the
oldest relic of man on record," exhibits a dolichocephalic
type.   So does the Neanderthal sknll, " the lowest in
rank of any human being," exhibit. as well as can be
ascertained from its fragmentary state, a long-headed
or dolichocephalic type.   These two types, therefore,
" the oldest" and " the most degraded," according to
the preconceived theory, belong to the so-called modern or dolichocephalic type, said to be coeval with the
bronze and iron periods of man.   So far their craniological nature *per se* fails to demonstrate their anti
quity.

General biological analogy would not lead us to suppose that short-headed races of men first existed on this planet. We almost invariably find the "lowest" races of animals first. The " dark races of man,"* comprehending the Negroes and Australians, are the lowest in our classification. They, if any, offer most affinity to the anthropoid apes. They are dolichocephalic. It would be far more consonant with analogy to suppose that the " dark races" once stretched over the tropical regions of the globe, and have left their modified descendants in Africa, Australia, and the Andaman Islands,† long previous to the introduction, origin, or derivation of the lighter races of the Old World, than to infer the existence of a supposititious race of short-headed men with or without simial supraorbital ridges, who flourished over the whole earth (America inclusive) antecedent to historical time. Speculation on this subject must be checked till we know what are the most ancient crania of the autochthonous tribes of the earth. In America, the mound-builders of the Mississippi valley are probably not the most ancient aborigines of North America. They are certainly brachycephalic to a degree transcending the existing American races. But the modern Quichua skull‡ (often termed Inca) is almost as short-headed, and the Quichua race has not the slightest claim to ethnological antiquity. Antecedent to the Quichua races, the " Flat-heads" of Titicaca (not satisfactorily identified with the Aymarás) who peopled Bolivia and Southern Peru for ages of unrecorded duration, even giving due allowance for

* Knox. Races of Men.

† Possibly in Ceylon, according to Mr. Brayley, F.R.S.; Medical Times, May 10, 1862.

‡ Vide Ethnological Society's Transactions, May 6, 1862, for C. C. Blake's paper " On the Cranial Characters of the Peruvian Races."

distortion by artificial pressure, exhibit a long-headed or dolichocephalic type. A plausible hypothesis has even been mooted, that the Titicacan Flat-heads distorted their crania with a view to perpetuate the remembrance of the dolichocephalic character of their ancestors. Retzius has attempted to identify the "Ancient Peruvians" of Morton, and the so-called "Huancas" of Tschudi, with the eastern dolichocephalic races of South America. This writer by no means coincided with those authors who consider the brachycephalic mound-builders of Mississippi as the remains of the typical American stock. He pointed out that in the eastern part of the American continent, from north to south, the dolichocephalic type predominated. The remains from the Brazilian bone-caves, described by Castelnau and Lund, with retrocedent and possibly flattened crania, are dolichocephalic, and according to Retzius, represent the primæval population of Brazil. Whether the flattening of their skulls was artificial or natural, may well be doubted. If natural, the succession of crania in Bolivia, Eastern Brazil, and Peru, would be as follows:

1st. Natural Dolichocephali.
       Brazilian bone-caves.
       Oldest builders of Tia-huanaco (?)
2d Artificial Dolichocephali.
       Titicacans, Aymarás.
3d. Artificial Brachycephali.
       Pachacamac Quichuas, Incas, Atacamans.
       Changos.

The mounds termed *Koorgan* or *Bongor* in the Government of Tomsk, of which the antiquity is unascertained, containing brachycephalic skulls, afford no evidence of bronze or chipped stone implements.

TABLE SHOWING THE ASSOCIATION OF THE EARLIEST EVIDENCES OF THE HUMAN RACE WITH THE REMAINS OF EXTINCT AND RECENT MAMMALIA.

Fossil species in italics. Bones x. Works o. Pliocene Mammalia †. Pleistocene ‡. Domesticated Animals ¶.

	Neanderthal.	Engis.	Abbeville.	St. Acheul.	St. Roch.	Grenelle.	Massat.	Plau.	Aurignac.	Hoxne.	Brixham.	Kent's Hole.	Gray's Inn Lane.	Mewslade.	Sennen.	Montrose.	Nether Urquhart.	Plymouth.	Valley of the Trent.	Heathery Burn.	Switzerland.	Maccagnone.	Kjökkenmödd'gs,&c.	Wookey Hole.
Man	x	x	o	o	o	o	o	x	x	o	o	o	o	x	x	x	x	x		'	'	o	o	o
Felis spelæa		x	x			x			x		x	x										x		x
Ursus spelæus		x	x			x			x		x	x										x		x
Ursus priscus			x	x					x			x												x
Hyæna spelæa ‡											x	x										x		x
Machairodus latidens ‡												x												x
Machair. megantereon †												x												
Bos primigenius ‡			x	x	x	x	x?		x?	x?	x	x	x						x				x?	x?
Bos longifrons ‡																			x		x		x	x
Bos frontosus (?) ‡																			x		x			
Bison priscus ‡			x	x		x			x		x	x									x	x		x
Ovibos moschatus ‡												x									x			
Elephas primigenius ‡		x	x	x	x	x	x	x	x	x?	x	x	x						x			x		x
Elephas antiquus ‡																								
Rhinoceros tichorhinus ‡		x	x	x	x		x	x	x		x	x							x			x		x
Rhinoceros leptorhinus ‡					x							x												
Hippopot. major †																								
Equus fossilis		x	x	x	x	x		x	x	x?	x	x							x			x		x
Cervus megaceros ‡												x												x
Cervus strongyloceros												x									x			x
Cerv. pseudovirginianus												x									x			
Cervus Somonensis ‡												x									x			
Cervus Guettardi		x	x	x	x	x	x		x	x		x							x			x		x
Cervus Bucklandi						x						x										x		x

Cervus tarandus ....
Cervus elaphus ....
Cervus alces ....
Cervus capreolus ....
Cervus dama ....
Sus scrofa¶ ....
Phoca gryphus ....
Lutra vulgaris ....
Canis lupus ....
Canis vulpes ....
Canis familiaris¶ ....
Felis catus¶ ....
Felis lynx ....
Mustela putorius ....
Mustela erminea ....
Mustela martes ....
Mustela foina ....
Sorex vulgaris ....
Erinaceus europeus ....
Hypudæus amphibius ....
Capra ibex ....
Capra hircus¶ ....
Antilope rupicapra ....
Ovis aries¶ ....
Ursus arctos ....
Meles taxus ....
Mus sylvaticus ....
Lagomys spelæus ....
Lepus timidus ....
Rhinolophus f. equinum ....
Arvicola agrestis ....
Arvicola pratensis ....
Lepus variabilis ....
Lepus cuniculus ....
Castor fiber ....
Sciurus vulgaris ....
Equus caballus¶ ....
Equus asinus¶ ....

The foregoing table may be epitomized as follows:

The dolichocephalic skulls are here marked D ; the brachycephalic, B

Locality.	No of extinct species.	No. of recent species.	Total.
Neanderthal. D........................	0	0	0
Engis. D.............................	5	0	5
Abbeville..............................	8	1	9
St. Acheul.............................	5	0	5
St. Roch,..............................	7	0	7
Grenelle...............................	4	0	4
Massat. ?.............................	7	1	8
Plau. B...............................	0	3	3
Aurignac. ?......	7	12	19
Hoxne.................................	3	1	4
Brixham...............................	5	1	6
Kent's Hole............................	12	19	31
Gray's Inn Lane........................	1	0	1
Mewslade. D...........................	0	0	0
Sennen. D.............................	0	0	0
Montrose. B...........................	0	0	0
Nether Urquhart. D....................	0	0	0
Plymouth. D?..........................	0	0	0
Vale of Belvoir. D....................	3	4	7
Heathery Burn. D......................	0	7	7
Switzerland. B.	4	27	31
Maccagnone	7	1	8
Kjökkenmöddings, &c. B..............	2	14	16
Wookey Hole...........................	10	4	14

The weapons and other objects found by Meynier and Eichthal, in the tumuli, are either of bone or iron; the ornaments are of bone, melted silicate, polished quartz, or copper; there were, moreover, in one of the tumuli fragments of pottery; in another the remains of a wooden vessel. All the tumuli, without exception, had some remnants of iron tools or weapons, but none of bronze, the metallic ornaments found being cast in copper, exactly like all others our travelers have met with in Siberia in the collections of dilettanti. The cranium bears in all the skeletons strong marks of relationship with those which Retzius has designated under the name of 'Brachycephali,' their chief feature [*sic in orig.*] being the rectangular form of the orbital cavity, a form common to all Mongolian races. MM. Meynier and d'Eichthal are, nevertheless, inclined to believe that several different kinds of tumuli must be distinguished in Siberia, and that it would be premature to consider all these tombs as pertaining exclutively to a single race.*

Supporters of a derivative hypothesis of the human race from existing species of anthropoid apes, have drawn a parallel between the dolichocephalic chimpanzee, and the dolichocephalic Negro of Western Africa, and also between the brachycephalic orang-outang of Borneo and the brachycephalic Malay of the same locality. Ethnic centers of specific dispersion in time have been inferred from this geographical distribution. The remarkable alleged coincidence of the long-headed ape with the most long-headed man, and the short-headed ape with his short-headed human representative, and inferred descendant, certainly seemed a fact which might lead anthropologists to admit a possible transmutation. Reference, however, to the simple facts of the case gives a totally different aspect to this surmise. When we examine the skulls of the young orang-outang and chimpanzee, side by side, before their typical characters have been masked by superadded peculiarities connected with their functional needs, we see that the young orang-outang, gorilla, and chimpanzee have the transverse diameter of the skull proportionately equal,* and that the apparent length of the head in the chimpanzee is produced by the greater development of the supraciliary ridges than in the orang-outang. In the young gorilla, also an African ape, coincident in its geographical distribution with races of dolichocephalic

* Comptes Rendus, Acad. Sciences, 1862.

† Sur le Gorilla, par Professeur Owen, avec six planches ajoutées par Eudés Deslongchamps. 8vo. Caen. 1861.

Negroes, the transverse diameter actually slightly ex
ceeds in Deslongchamps' 5th plate that of the orang
outang. For all practical purposes of classification,
however, it may be said that in youth, before the action
of the biting muscles has altered the typical outward
aspect of the brain-case, the orang-outang, gorilla, and
chimpanzee exhibit skulls of which it cannot be predicated that each exceeds the others in the proportion
of its transverse diameter.

Professor Deslongchamps says, " Pour bien saisir les
rapports souvent cachés, des êtres, entr'eux, l'état adulte
ne suffit pas toujours ; dans cet état, ce sont surtout les
différences qui se prononcent ; dans les premiers âges,
les ressemblances sont plus accusées, les affinités sont
moins masquées.   Il est utile, dans l'étude des animaux,
d'imiter les botanistes, qui vont chercher les affinités
des genres et des familles des végétaux dans les premiers rudiments des fruits de la graine, de l'embryon, etc.
Le groupe des singes anthropoïdes est remarquable
entre tous par les changements, je dirais presque par
les métamporphoses, que subissent leurs têtes."*   The
comparison of the skulls of the anthropoid simiæ in their
young state, made by the cautious and philosophical
Dean of the Faculty of Sciences at Caen, therefore,
may be accepted as evidence against the hypothesis of
the coincidence and derivation of the short and long-
headed races of men with and from the alleged brachy-
and dolichocephalic genera of Asiatic and African apes.

The foregoing table is drawn up with a view to exhibit generally the number and proportions of extinct
and existing mammalia which have been found in a
fossil state in deposits where the remains of man have
also been discovered. With no pretensions to com-

---

* See note on preceding page.

pleteness, it may yet serve as a convenient record, and
may, to a certain extent, demonstrate the greater antiquity of~e. g. the Abbeville beds as compared with the
Danish Kjökkenmöddings, evinced by the greater proportion of extinct species in the former deposit. It
must, however, be borne in mind that the mammalia of
the Somme valley may not have attained a more northern range during the post-pliocene age, while boreal
species existing in England and Denmark at the same
time, might leave no remains in post-pliocene strata in
Gascony or Sicily. We know too little respecting the
distribution of mammalia over limited areas in the
later tertiary strata to entitle us to form any compre-
hensive generalization.

In the table, I have made use of the researches of
M. Lartet (*Geol. Journal*, 1860, p. 471 and 491, and
Natural History Review, 1862, p. 53;) Mr. Prestwich
(*Geol. Journal*, 1860, p. 189, and *Philos. Transact.* 1860,
p. 277;) Dr. Falconer (*Geol. Journal*, 1860, p. 99;)
Dr. Schauffhausen (*Nat. Hist. Review*, 1861, p. 155;)
Mr. Busk (*Nat. Hist. Review*, 1861, p. 172;) Mr. Lub-
bock (*Nat. Hist. Review*, 1861, p. 489, and *N. H. Re-
view*, 1862, p. 26;) and Mr. Dawkins (*Proceedings of the
Geological Society*, 1862.)

In the diagram which accompanies Part Third, I have
indicated the locality of some of the most authentic remains, the antiquity of which has been strongly advocated. It is not, however, intended to be conveyed
that any of the remains, here indicated were contemporaneous. The contemporaneity of some of them with
the extinct mammalia is hitherto undemonstrated. It
is certainly significant that so many instances should
occur in the extreme south-west of England, to which
the early Britons were driven by their Saxon conquerors, and where the traditions of British local history

and the Cornubian dialect still survive. The remains
from the Land's End, Plymouth, and Mewslade, may
have been those of early Britons, and their antiquity,
unproven by any chemical or geological evidence, may
not date further back than the period of the Saxon
conquest.

Not the least point of interest in the table on pp. 340–
341, is the fact that in Gascony and Devonshire we
have evidence of the contemporaneity of the horse and
the ass, both animals domesticated by man, with the
extinct mammoths, rhinoceri, cave lions, bears, and
hyænas. The question then arises whether the fossil
horses and asses are specifically distinct from the existing, as, if identical, the commonly-received doctrine
that the horses and asses were introduced from a
warmer climate must be essentially modified. It might
be supposed that the horses and asses of the post-pliocene might have been domesticated by the early pre-
Gascon or pre-Devonian, and have possibly aided them
to exterminate the elephants and rhinoceri. The association of human remains with those of *Machairodus*
at Kent's Hole is not a more remarkable fact than his
association with *Elephas antiquus* and *Hippopotamus-
major* in the Somme valley and in Sicily. Remains of
Hippopotamus-major have also been found in Kent's
Hole.

Switzerland and the Kjökkenmöddings, belonging
to a later epoch in the so-called "Stone Period,"
afford us first evidence of man's faithful companion,
the domestic dog; and the former locality indicates
also the proof of goats and sheep, specifically indistin-
guishable from the existing species. With these in
Switzerland are associated remains of the *Bos primigenius*, the *Bos frontosus* of Nilsson, and the *Bos longifrons*. The latter species was domesticated by the

early Europeans, and probably formed the *souche primitive* of our domestic oxen. Whether some *primigenius* blood may not possibly exist in our breeds, may be reasonably doubted ; but the conclusions of Professor Nilsson, who derives an existing breed of oxen from the *Bos frontosus*, will need further discussion before their acceptance by palæontologists. With these domesticated or domesticable species of ox, flourished in Switzerland the *Bison priscus*, a species which the most strenuous efforts of the early Europeans would not have rendered capable of serving as a docile, milk-producing beast. The musk-buffalo *Bubalus (Ovibos) moschatus*, which lived in glacial clay and drift in England contemporary with the elephant and tichorhine rhinoceros, has not hitherto been found associated with the remains of man.

Morton, in his posthumous manuscripts,[*] said, " Why may we not discover the remains of man in the tertiary deposits, in the cretaceous beds, or even in the oolites ?"—a supposition which, considering we have quite proved his existence in the post-pliocene, is probable. For the real origin of man we must go immeasurably further back from the time of the existence of man among the mammoths, and far into the great Pliocene *or Miocene* ages.

That we shall find abundant human remains in the tertiary or secondary strata, I, the writer hereof, have no doubt ; although till then, perhaps, the negative evidence which disproves the existence of monkeys, the ancestors of man on the derivative hypothesis, in any stratum below the eocene rocks, may have a tendency to check our desire to · anticipate the conclusions which future palæontologists may arrive at, through

---

[*] Usher, in Nott and Gliddon, " Types of Mankind," p. 343.

a slow and cautious process of induction and observation.

With the broad question of the antiquity of the human race, the foregoing remarks have no necessary, or even contingent, connection. A higher and more satisfactory evidence than any which the geologist or the cranioscopist can bring to bear, is furnished us by the researches of those ethnologists and philologists who have most studied the affiliations and relations of the most ancient languages of the globe. Upon the supposition that such languages as the Sanscrit, Græco-Latin, Teutonic, Keltic and Lithuanian, have been derived from a once primeval "Arian" stock, a vast lapse of time is necessary, during which their derivation and divergence from such parent stem took place. Upon the rejection of the "Arian" hypothesis,* and the acceptance of the doctrine of diverse ethnic centers of linguistic origin, an equal or greater lapse of time is necessary during which such a language as the Greek could have improved by ascensive development from the simple utterances of a barbarous early tongue to the high grade of philological civilization when Homer wrote. Such a supposition would corroborate the conclusions to which à priori analogy would lead the geologist ; but it would leave the problem of the origin of the inferior non-"Arian" races of men still unsolved. The great question of the origin of these races, whether as our representatives in a state of arrested moral and mental development ; whether as the scanty remnants of inferior types which, called into being ages before the advent of the "Arian" race, have passed the fore-ordained limit which "species" can attain, and are slowly succumbing before the superior

* Crawfurd, "Antiquity of Man on the Evidence of Language." Trans. Ethnological Society, 1862.

mental force of their exterminators, " the most exalted object of which we are capable of conceiving, namely, the production of the higher animals directly following"[*] the extirpation of the lower race, are speculations which cannot be solved by the inspection or measurement of any series of skulls, still less from so limited a number as those which I have noticed above.

The question of the nature and date of anthropogenesis, like that of cosmogenesis, will perchance not be solved for many generations yet to come, if indeed they ever will. There are many difficulties in the way of the solution, and future research, and new tools to work with, can alone enable us to surmount the obstacles that beset our path at present, and may dissipate the prevailing or the proposed theories respecting the recent creation, or the vast antiquity of man. Till then, the constant observer of recorded facts follows his track through the devious labyrinth of anthropology, conscious that by a steadfast adherence to exactitude, he may possibly succeed in throwing some small light on the nature of the earliest evidences of the human race.

CHAPTER IV.

ADDITIONAL TESTIMONY.

PROCEEDINGS OF VARIOUS GEOLOGICAL SOCIETIES.

LIVERPOOL GEOLOGICAL SOCIETY.—*March 24th.*— The President, Henry Duckworth, F. L. S., F. G. S., read a paper " On Flint Implements from the Drift ;

---

[*] Darwin, " Origin of Species," 1st edition, p. 480.

being a description of a visit to Amiens and Abbeville during the summer of 1861."

Mr. Duckworth did not discover any worked flints himself, but he exhibited several very characteristic specimens, some of them being obtained from the quarrymen, and others presented to him by Monsieur Boucher de Perthes and Monsieur Pinsard. Mr. Duckworth also exhibited a human skull, which he disinterred from the brick earth-bed, in what was stated to be a somewhat unusual position. The paper was illustrated by drawings of sections, etc. In conclusion, Mr. Duckworth remarked, that in examining these Drift-beds both at Amiens and Abbeville, but more especially at the former place, it seemed to him that they must have been deposited very rapidly. There is no evidence whatever, so far as he could judge, of any very slow or gradual formation ; and the impression left upon his mind was that they have been produced by some sharp and sudden catastrophe.

———

GEOLOGISTS' ASSOCIATION.—*April* 7, 1862.—Mr. Cresy read a paper " On some ancient skulls and flint-implements found in the Essex marshes during the progress of the Northern Outfall Sewer of the Metropolitan Main Drainage Works."

The three skulls exhibited were found along the line of the sewer, one on the east, and another on the west side of the River Lea, and the third, to which the greatest interest attached, in the East Ham marshes. A diagram was exhibited showing sections of the strata at various points.

From one to two feet of surface soil, chiefly vegetable mould, was first penetrated, then a bed of yellow or brown clay, three to five feet, then blue clay, two to four feet, this sometimes alternated with beds of peat, and then the gravel was reached. No shells of any kind have yet been found, nor is there any other evidence by which the age of the several deposits can be determined.

The author did not assign the highest antiquity to any of the skulls exhibited, as the flint-tools found near them were not of the earliest or drift type; those exhibited were both polished and chipped.

Previously to describing the skulls, the author enumerated the most marked characteristics of the Orcadian, Scandinavian, Ancient British, Roman, and Saxon skulls, comparing the one with the other, at the same time admitting the difficulty of an absolute classification, and pointing out the wide differences existing among individuals of the same race. Still, the causes of modification being fewer and less active among ancient than among modern races, it was easier to arrive at more certainty of determination in ancient skulls than of those of our present mixed races.

The author pointed out that the three skulls exhibited separate and well-marked types. That from the west side of the river Lea was comparatively small, and well-proportioned, and apparently of a young person.

The second, from the east of the river Lea, was of large size, with immense posterior development, and was evidently that of a man past middle life. The large bony crest of the occipital bone was extremely marked by the former attachment of large and powerful muscles. Altogether this skull showed great animal development and had marked affinities with many of the skulls of the Celtic period.

The third skull, from East Ham marshes, presented the greatest interest; in its vicinity were found two flint-implements, and it was probably the earliest of the three. The frontal development was very low, the vertical aspect narrowing rapidly anteriorly, the occipital region predominating considerably over the frontal ; the bony ridge of the occiput, too, was very marked ; the sutures were nearly obliterated, so it was an aged skull. The author compared it with a cast of the Engis skull, and believed there were points of resemblance.

Professor Busk, F.R.S., gave elaborate descriptions of the peculiarities of the skull.

Mr. C. C. Blake pointed out the discrepancies between the observations of those craniologists who had assigned particular crania to particular periods, as *e. g.* between Steenstrup and Wilson, the former having, by his observations in Scandinavia, correlated the brachycephalic skulls with the date of the earliest known stone deposits in Denmark, while Wilson had demonstrated the existence of a long-headed (kumbecephalic) race of men from cairns at Nether Urquhart in Fifeshire and elsewhere, prior to the brachycephalic races who have left their remains in the later Stone period at Montrose. He hoped that some solution might be offered for this apparent discrepancy.

Mr. S. J. Mackie, F.G.S., remarked that the geological conditions in the present case seemed to have been somewhat overlooked. The sections in some places exhibited three beds of peat, and these ought to be carefully examined to see whether any vegetation existed in this country at the periods of their formation different from that which is now indigenous.

He did not think attention should be solely given to the form and other craniological characters of the exhumed skulls, for craniologists seemed to be by no means certain of the distinctions they had drawn being typical. He thought it rather rested with geologists to prove by *stratigraphical* evidence the *antiquity* of such remains, and thus furnish a stable basis for the inferences of the craniologist and ethnologist.

ROYAL SOCIETY.—*March* 27.—" Theoretical Considerations on the Conditions under which Drift Deposits containing the remains of Extinct Mammalia and Flint Implements were accumulated, and on their Geological Time." By Joseph Prestwich, Esq. In the paper which the author read before the Society in 1859, it was demonstrated that the flint implements occurred in undisturbed gravels, commingled with the remains of extinct mammalia ; but the theoretical considerations of the subject were then omitted. The author now showed that in existing river-valleys, in parts of England and France, two lines or zones of gravels or drift deposits are met with ; one at from fifty to two hundred feet above the present streams, and usually forming a terrace : the other ranging along the bottom of the valleys. The elevated terraces are portions of former valleys, wider and more shallow than the present ones, scooped out by other and different causes than ordinary river-action. They are above the reach of the highest floods, and no other mass of water than that flowing up an arm of the sea could fill them. The Seine, at its highest flood, has not exceeded twenty-nine feet, but it would require the present rivers to be of a hundred times that volume to fill the existing valley. That the terraces were originally connected is proved by the isolated patches of their gravels still lying at elevated spots between them. The author believed that the gravels were brought and distributed by ice and by the melting of the winter snows in spring pouring down great bodies of water, the gravels enclosing boulders of hard rock, brought often from long distances. He also attributed much importance to the action of ground

ice. He pointed out contortions in the drift-bed at St.
Acheul, as formed by the pressure and squeezing force
of massive ice. The characters of the gravels were
then considered, in reference to the climatal condition
of the drift period, which the author argued were those
of a more intense cold, by 20° or 25°, than the average of our present winters. The bearings of the geographical distribution of the animals of that period,
and its comparison with those of existing forms of life,
were also assumed to confirm this inference. The use
assigned for some of the largest flint implements was
that of making holes in the ice—the men of the drift-
age, like the North American Indians and the Esquimaux, being very often dependent upon winter supplies
of fish. Since the formation of the high-level gravels,
an elevation of the land has taken place, and the present valleys excavated, and the lower gravels deposited.
The tendency of existing rivers was to cut deep gorges,
and not valleys, with sloping sides, such as those containing the gravels. The large flint implements were
nowhere so abundant in the valleys, as in the terrace-
gravels. Flint-flakes, on the contrary, were most common in the valley-gravels—the climate of the valley-
period being more lenient, there was a diminished need
of great flint chisels for breaking the ice. These dis-
tributions, at two periods, of different forms of implements, indicated a difference in the habits of the tribes
by whom they were respectively used.

In the questions of time and succession the value of
probabilities must be considered. The antiquity of the
flints was carried back through three geological ages—
the loëss, terrace, and valley-gravels ; all long periods
except the loëss, the duration of which was comparatively
short. The sand-pipes in the valley of the Somme were
first considered as a standard of time-measurement ; and

then the author commented npon the probable condition, at those periods, of the British Channel, the formation of which, while a late geological event, he was not prepared to admit to be one of the last. Even in the Pleistocene period the British Channel existed, although much narrower, and there was a line of cliffs running parallel with the present coasts. The sea being narrower, was frozen over every winter, permitting the passage of men and animals. Some of the great effects of such a cold period might already be conceived, although it might not be in our power as yet to accurately define them. In looking at a distant mountain-chain we could judge of its great magnitude without waiting for a trigonometrical survey to be assured of its exact dimensions. The author then suggested as a possible measure of time the perturbations in the increasement of heat at various depths in the earth's crust, arising from disturbances originating with the glacial period; and he concluded by giving his impression that in the existence of this remarkable cold period preceding our own, we might possibly trace evidence of great and all-wise design by the circumstance that, in this long glacial era, the earth's crust would tend to acquire an earlier adjustment in its equilibrium, and obtain a rigidity and stability which should make it more fitting for the habitation and pursuits of civilized man. So thinks Carter Blake; so think we all!

The prominent part which Mr. John Evans took, in a brave and consistent manner, at the beginning of the discussion on the important topic of the antiquity of the human race, which the early fossil flint-implements evoked, gave him justly the leadership of British antiquaries in this warfare against deeply-rooted prejudices and inculcated opinions, in the same way as Mr. Prest-

wich took the lead among British geologists ; and, as
we look to the latter for the narration and reduction
of new geological facts, we look to receive from the
former periodically the antiquarian view of all fresh
details and novelties. I do not propose to use my
pages, in expressing my sense of the valuable services
rendered by Mr. Evans, however justly such enconiums
may be due, but I do prefer to economize my space by
giving, without comment, a summary of the " finds" not
hitherto recorded, or but slightly noticed.

Paris.—Flint-implements have been found by M.
Gosse, of Geneva. The pits in which they were discovered are two—that of M. Bernard, Avenue de la
Motte Piquet, No. 61–63 (Champ de Mars), and that
of M. Etienne Bielle, Rue de Grenelle, No. 15 ; in
beds of sand and gravel analogous to those of Menchecourt, near Abbeville ; the beds are not disturbed,
their average thickness is twenty feet. The implements
and flint-flakes were found in a bed at the base of the
gravel from three to five inches in thickness, associated
with bones of *Bos primigenius*, *Elephas primigenius*,
deer allied to reindeer, and a large carnivorous animal,
probably the cave-tiger. These observations have been
confirmed by M. Lartet and Mr. Myline. This place
was signalized as a probable locality previous to M.
Gosse's discovery by M. Boucher de Perthes, At
Clichy, also, one implement has been found by M.
Lartet.

Creil.—A flint-implement *(hatchette)* has been found,
under similar circumstances, in a gravel-pit at Précy,
near Creil, in the Valley of the Oise (between Amiens
and Paris), with a tooth of an elephant. Exhibited to
the French Society of Antiquaries, 16th May, 1860, by
M. Peigné Delacourt.

Rouen.—The Abbé Cochet reports two flint-implements in the museum there, which the curator, M. Pottier, states to have come from the sandpits of Sotteville in the neighborhood. This requires confirmation, as Mr. Evans could not find these implements in the museum, and M. Pouchet, the director, was not aware of their existence. Mr. Evans states, however, the pits at Sotteville to be of " precisely the character that renders it probable that flint-implements may be discovered in them."

Clermont.—In a valley leading into that of the Ariège, there is a deposit of gravel underlying brick-earth, at five hundred and forty feet above sea-level and thirty-three feet above the stream which now waters the valley. In this gravel, mixed with bones of *Elephas primigenius, Rhinoceros tichorhinus, Felis spelæa, Cervus megaceros, Equus*, and *Bos*, have been found manufactured "pieces of quartzite." Dr. Noulet says, " One of them is four inches in length, two and a half inches wide, and its greatest thickness one inch. It has been formed into shape by chipping it on only one of its faces. The second is much more important ; both its faces have been modified to bring it to the shape it now presents. The side and point, which is truncated, present a beveled edge; but the base, which is cut obliquely, has *evidently been polished even with care.* This is also about four inches long, two and three-quarter inches wide, and one and one-quarter inch thick.' * Mr. Evans passes a comment on this statement. " if it be," he says, " really the case that this is in part polished, and that this polish is not due to the natural fracture, it is certainly a singular fact in

---

* See also an account of a very curious discovery, somewhat of the same nature, in M. Lartet's " Researches respecting the Co-existence of Man with the the Great Fossil Mammalia," in the Ann. des Sciences Naturelles, 4th ser., tom. xv.

connection with the implements of the Drift period, which have hitherto always been *not* ground. Dr. Noulet, however, has paid some attention to this class of antiquities, as he draws a distinction, on account of their rude workmanship, between these implements and the *haches gauloises ou celtiques*. . . . Beside the chipped implements, round pebbles also occurred, which are considered by Dr. Noulet to have been used as hammers; and, though the account he gives of the whole discovery is not to my mind quite conclusive, it appears to be a proper case for further inquiry."

Swalecliffe (I. of Sheppey).—At the end of Stud Hill Cliffs, near the Swalecliffe Coast-guard Station, Mr. Evans picked up a flint-implement of the oval-pointed form, stained by ochreous colors, from having lain in the gravel; and in the Drift capping the highest point of the cliff, close to the farm-house at Stud Hill, a portion of a tooth of the *Elephas primigenius*.

Peasemarsh, Surrey.—One implement found by Mr. R. Whitbourn, F.S.A., of Godalming, twenty-five years ago, in a gravel-pit. "It was embedded in gravel, in a layer of sand about four or five feet from the surface, in apparently undisturbed ground." Mr. Whitbourn adds: "I have heard of remains of large animals having been discovered in the same beds, but not in very close proximity to the spot where it was found." The gravel-beds of this district have been examined and described by Mr. Godwin-Austen, in Quart. Journ. Geol. Soc. vol. vii., p. 278, in which communication he states that remains of *Elephas primigenius* are frequently found in this gravel, and that at Peasemarsh there are traces of an old land-surface, with branches of trees and the bones of these animals uninjured and lying together.

Horton Kirby, Kent.—An implement of the round-pointed form was found (November, 1861) on the surface of the ground at the top of the hill, on the east side of the River Darent, about a mile E.S.E. of Horton Kirby, by Mr. Whitaker, of the Geological Survey.

PAST LIFE IN SOUTH AMERICA.

Mr. C. Carter Blake says: Minds accustomed to review the complex phenomena of geology and palæontology in the Old, are apt to neglect the equally interesting evidence afforded to them of past life in the New World. American palæontology is distinguished, not because the mighty hemisphere has not passed through analogous phases of life-stages to those presented by the elder continent; nor because the extinct fauna of America is less interesting than that of Europe, Asia, or Australia; nor that the most-eminent men in both worlds have omitted to call attention to the stupendous monuments of bygone existence in the pampas of La Plata or on the shores of Patagonia; but because the public mind has not yet sufficiently realized the idea, that, during the period while Europe and Asia underwent the manifold and changing influences of geological time, like conditions were passed through in America.

A tradition exists in the minds of all the earliest aboriginal nations of America, on the banks of the Missouri, at Mantua, at Punta St. Elena, in Eucador, at Sauacha, in New Granada, at Tarija, on the eastern slopes of the Andes, and at Tagua-tagua in the South of Chile, that a vast nation of colossal human beings existed before the present inhabitants. These giants, the credulous and imaginative minds of the natives supposed were destroyed by the deities, like the old race of Titans by the Olympian gods, or the Hrimthursar—the frost-giants of ice and snow—by the supporters of Odin and Æsir in the Norse mythology. It is instructive to trace these unhistorical narratives back to their physical origin; it is suggestive to find that such origin is rational, and does not rest upon any purely mythical base. Such a colossal race of beings did exist in the old times; they were, however, the gigantic mastodons, etc., which man drove before him and exterminated. When M. Albert Koch, in the year 1842, carried the so-called *Missourium* skeleton to England, which afterwards was demonstrated to be identical with the *Mastodon Ohioticus*, and now forms a conspicuous object in the British Museum, among many other dubious anecdotes recounted by him, was one, that with the bones of the *Mastodon* had been found an arrow-head, proving apparently the existence of mankind in America contemporaneous with this great elephantine animal. This marvelous story was ridiculed by English geologists in 1842 as quite preposterous. Now, however, in 1863, we look at the subject with more cautious and less sceptical eyes. We know that both in France and England. mankind either lived so far ago as the period when the hair-clad elephants and rhinoceroses existed in Normandy and Gascony, or (which is nearly the same thing) the elephants and rhinoceroses lived down to the period when human life, in a state of barbarism, existed in Europe. It is not more preposterous to believe that man, at one time, hunted elephants in the United States, than to believe that he hunted rhinoceroses in Normandy, and was himself the prey of hyænas in Devonshire. At all the places where a tradition like this exists in America, evidence of the existence of a fossil *Mastodon* has been found.

In Brazil, proof has been afforded us of the existence

of a tradition amongst the Indians of a large ape, termed by them Caypore, which is the analogue of the gorilla and chimpanzee of Africa. As no man-like ape of any sort exists in South America at the present time, two theories may be suggested to account for this popular belief. The Negro slaves may have carried their faith in the existence of a huge ape from Sierre Leone and the Gaboon to Brazil, in the same manner as we recognize still among the half-Christianized slaves of America, the traces of the Obi-worship of their African forefathers. But the answer to this assumption is, that the tradition in question does not exist in the Negro, but in the Indian mind. None of the Indians, however, have actually seen a Caypore, or rather none of those Indians who profess to have seen them, have undergone satisfactorily, the ordeal of interrogation by such painstaking observers as Dr. Lund.

A signification is afforded us of the meaning of this tradition, when we learn that a colossal ape, approaching in size the human stature, once existed in Brazil, and that it was probably contemporaneous with the early human races. The *Protopithecus Brasiliensis* was four feet high, surpassing far the dimensions of any existing American monkey ; it nevertheless was a true platyrrhine, like all the simian forms of the New World. Found in the latter Pliocene, the possibility of its being contemporaneous with early man is rendered more probable when we reflect that on the borders of Lake Lagoa Santa, and at Minas Geraes, human remains have been found, coupled with those of forty-four extinct animals, among which was another large fossil ape, *Callithrix primævus.*

The extinct elephants and horses of America afford an interesting source of contemplation to the reflective palæontologist. Existing elephants, as is well known.

are but of three species, those of Africa, India, and
Sumatra. Professor Owen has, however, pointed out
that our knowledge has been expanded by fossil evidences, and that during the Pliocene period, elephants
existed in Africa, India, Europe, China, and Australia
Thus far there was little to surprise the practical observer, who was accustomed to find a wider distribution
of animal life in the later Tertiary times, than in the
present day. But when we learn that two species of
elephant (*Elephas primigenius* and *Texianus*) and one
species of *Mastodon* co-existed with each other, in warm,
temperate, and cold latitudes in North America, and
that two other so-called species of elephantine animal
(*Mastodon Andium* and *M. Humboldtii*) browsed on
the trees of South America, prior to the upheaval of
the vast Andian chain of mountains, astonishment almost verges to incredulity. "Well," it may be said,
"since we have thus evidence of American elephants,
why may we not have evidence of American rhinoceroses ?" We have such proof of an animal closely allied
to the rhinoceros and palæothere, discovered by Mr.
Darwin in Patagonia, and which at the same time bears
some points of analogy, but not of affinity, with the
llamas. This animal, the *Macrauchenia*, has also been
found on the eastern slopes of the Andes at Tarija, and
in the very heart of the Aymará country at Corocoro.
Imagination can scarcely conceive the period when this
bulky brute, with its long stiff neck, elevated straight
upright, as in the guanaco, contested the pastures of
Patagonia and Bolivia with the llamas and horses
around it. Some readers will say, "I understood that
horses were first introduced on the American continent
by the followers of Columbus, and that when the aboriginal Americans first viewed the mounted Spaniards,
they regarded them as centaur-like monsters, or almost

as divinities." The horse, however, of various species, had existed in the New World for countless centuries prior to the advent of the Spanish conquerors : whether its extinction dated previous to the human era is yet undemonstrated ; tradition even of its existence had passed away long before the Columbian epoch. Various species of these early American horses are known to us ; one from the States of North America ; another from Bolivia ; a third from Chile ; and a fourth from Patagonia. The last species (*Equus Curvidens,*) the best known, because the first discovered, indicates a species differing only from the European horse in the greater curvature of the molar teeth. These horses no doubt existed in herds, like the quaggas of South Africa, or like the wild asses of Central Asia. The same influences which promote the numerical increase of horses in South America at the present day, would have tended to promote a similar increase of the equine race in South America during the Pliocene period. The horse was first introduced in A. C. 1537, at Buenos Ayres ; forty-three years afterwards, in A. C. 1580, they were found at the Straits of Magellan. The cause why the horse, once numerous in America, became extinct centuries before the time of Columbus, at present baffles speculation. More significant is the fact, that we find in the Old World a three-toed fossil horse (*Hipparion,*) which, by its annectant affinities to the earlier odd-toed herbivoras, has been supposed to be absolutely the ancestor of the present *Equus caballus.* In the New World, however no such form exists. Whence, then, on a derivative hypothesis, the horses of America?

Two tapirs are found, the one in the North, the other in South America ; a dubious taperine form has also been found at St. Louis, in Missouri, associated with

fossils " of unquestionable Secondary date !" Pomel
has erected this very suspicious type into a new genus,
termed by him *Menodus*. It is not surprising that we
should find taperine forms in South America, when we
reflect that the existing tapir, or d'anta, is found over
the whole Brazilian and Argentine Confederation, and
from Guatemala to Patagonia. In the Panamá and
Chiriqui countries, the woolly taper of the Andes, or
Finchaqué, also exists, a species far more nearly allied
to the extinct races than the other American, or than
the Sumatran tapir. In the Andes of South America,
above the line of six thousand feet, the existing tapir
is not found.

When Castelnau was at Tarija, surrounded by fossil
remains of mastodons, horses, macrauchenes, schelido-
theres, llamas, and other mammalia, he was struck with
the state of " fat, contented ignorance " in which the
Franciscan monks had arrived in Geological knowledge.
The remains which he saw were all, according to them,
proofs of the existence of a gigantic race of men who
existed prior to the deluge. Padre Osario, a Jesuit of
Paraguay, had declared, in 1638, that he had seen with
his own eyes, in the Gran Chaco, a race of men of the
highest physical and mental cultivation, so tall that the
Jesuit, with his upraised arms, could hardly touch their
heads. Peradventure, these races belonged to the
same stock with those Indians of California, immortal-
ized by Padre Fray Pedro Simon, who had ears so large
that they served for canopies, and under each of them
five or six men could find ample shelter ; or they might
be allied to those of a neighboring province, who,
when in need of repose, used to go to sleep beneath
the waters of a lake on the banks of which they lived.
Even the giants whom Osario imagined, however, were
far too small to have produced the mastodon bones of

Tarija. When this argument was pressed on the monks, they replied, "that the bones had swelled since they were buried in the earth." Castlenau naïvely remarks, that a like proof might demonstrate that the mastodon bones of Tarija might have belonged to dwarfs. This singular superstition is by no means confined to the monks. Don Francisco Antonio Casello gravely tells his readers that "the soil of the town of Tarija possesses the virtue of making bones grow beyond measure. If a body of ordinary size is buried, and is disinterred after the lapse of some time, we find the bones excessively swollen." The American or English reader who scoffs at this ridiculous theory of the Tarijans may, however, recollect that, in the year 1863, there are still a few writers in America and England who speak of "an unknown mysterious force" which has kept the species of animals distinct from each other throughout all time. We are not yet so far removed from the trammels of an adherence to unproven and undemonstrable assumptions in science to entitle us to ridicule the hypothesis which our less gifted friends in Bolivia may suggest to the world.

MONKEY vs. MAN.

In England was lately published a letter from Professor King, of Galway, expressing the opinion to which that high authority has arrived, after years of due thought and consideration, on the probable method of operation of continuously-operating secondary laws, which have produced the species of animals successively or progressively throughout geological time. While paying the highest tribute to the candid manner in which this eminent geologist has treated his subject, I am led to suggest that the meaning of one passage in his admirable paper may be liable to misconstruction.

Professor King holds " that an organism, whether it typifies a species, a genus, a family, an order, or a class, is an autotheogen, if it possesses a series of characters which isolate it from other equivalent groups;" and that inherent and external forces may modify such organism, " thereby resulting in geneotheonomous forms." The limits within which autotheogeny can be predicated are, however, left unexplained by Professor King.

A writer in 1830, reasoning from the philosophical standpoint of the state of knowledge in the time of Cuvier, would have confidently pointed to the horse as an "autotheogen." Cuvier says, " If species have gradually changed, traces of these gradual modifications would be discovered; and between the *Palæotherium* and the recent species, some intermediate forms would be seen, a fact yet undemonstrated. Why have not the bowels of the earth preserved the monuments of so curious a genealogy ?" etc., etc., (Cuvier, " Discours, Préliminaire sur les Révolutions de la Surface du Globe," 6th edition, 8vo, Paris, 1830, p. 122.) Here the absence of intermediate organisms, previous to the discovery of *Paloplotherium, Anchitherium,* and *Hipparion,* is made the groundwork on which to base a theory of distinct specific origin. or " autotheogeny." That, " on psychological grounds alone, Man must be regarded as isolated from all other organisms," may be conceded. As psychological grounds, however, are unsafe bases for a zoological classification, and as the extent of man's isolation is the problem which biologists are attempting to decipher, whatever position we may assign to man, whether with Owen in a distinct sub-class *Archencephala,* or with Huxley in a family *Anthropini* of the order *Primates,* we must at least admit that the anatomical characters of man are not more unlike those of the higher *Gyrencephala* than the lower *Gyrencephala* are unlike the *Lissencephala* or *Lyencephala*, *i. e.*, that man is not more unlike the gorilla than the whale is like the rat or the opossum. I therefore would be slow to recognize that Man is an autotheogeneous species.

I coincide with Professor King's remarks, that "natural selection only holds the rank of a subordinate or ancillary agent," but I am far from identifying the "other and higher principles involved" with the doctrine of direct creation of animals through a fiat from a Primary Cause, even though such a fiat might operate through "a principle inherent in animated nature." Such phenomena as unity of plan, parthenogenesis, and successive development are far more probably accounted for on secondary laws alone. "He must be a half-hearted philosopher who, having watched the gigantic strides of the biological sciences during the past twenty years, doubts that science will sooner or later make this further step, so as to become possessed of the law of evolution of organic forms—of the unvarying order of that great chain of causes and effects of which all organic forms, ancient and modern, are the links."

In Professor King's ethnological remarks, no mention is made of the probabilities of a derivative origin of the lower races of man, as indicated by their physiological affinities to the higher apes. I commend the following extract from Dr. Büchner's "Kraft and Stoff" (8vo. Frank., p 75, 1858) to Professor King's consideration:

"An unbroken series of the most varied and multifarious transitions and analogies unites the whole animal kingdom together, from its lowest to its highest unit. Even man, who in his spiritual pride thinks him-

self raised high above the whole animal world, is far
removed from being an exception to this law. The
Ethiopic race unites him by a crowd of the most strik
ing analogies with the animal kingdom in a very unmistakable way. The long arms, the form of the foot,
the fleshless calf, the long slender hands, the general
lankness, the but slightly protuberant nose, the projecting teeth, the low retreating forehead, the narrow and
posteriorly protuberant head, the short neck, the con-
tracted pelvis, the pendulous belly, the want of beard,
the color of the skin, the disgusting odor, the unclean-
liness, the making of grimaces whilst speaking, the
clear shrill tone of voice, and the ape-like character of
the whole being, are just so many characteristic signs,
which in all the corporeal forms and relations of the
Negro unmistakably show the most decided approach
to the monkey genus." The same author goes on to
say. "Without doubt, man in his earlier periods approached, in his whole character, nearer to animals
than he does in his present condition : and the oldest
excavated human skulls indicate rough, undeveloped,
and animal-like forms."

Such conditions as these, agitating, and seething in
the minds of patient observers and reflective thinkers
in France and Germany, are being forced upon the
minds of scientists. Our best thinkers now refrain
from offering any theological or metaphysical explanation of geological facts

I trust that Professor King, whose valuable tables of
strata as recently published in the *Geologist* have had
so beneficial an effect on science, may be ultimately
led to reject the unphilosophical theory of "autotho-
ogeny."

The doctrine of "Geneotheonomy," or the "Derivative" hypothesis of animal causation, is now fast con-

verting the minds of all palæontologists. Among its
supporters can be numbered Lamarck, Geoffroy St.
Hilaire, Grant, Matthew, Rafinesque, Haldeman, the
author of the " Vestiges of Creation," D'Omalius d'Hal-
loy, Owen, Isidore Geoffroy St. Hilaire, Dr. Freke,
Herbert Spencer, Naudin, Keyserling, Schauffhausen,
Baden Powell, Wallace. Huxley, and Hooker. To these
may be now possibly added those of Lyell, Fawcett,
Lubbock, Mackie, Salter, Rupert Jones, Blake, Büch
ner, Schvarcz, Knox, Burke, Hutton, King, and many
others.

To accept, in 1863, the doctrine of the origin of species by creative fiat out of inorganic matter, is as unphilosophical as to believe in the theory of earthquakes
given out by the Muyscas of New Granada, that the
earth is supported by pillars of *guaiacum*. on the shoulders of the deity Chibchacum, who, being tired, shifts
the weight from one shoulder to another ; or, to the
Egyptian theory, that the earth, during earthquakes, is
tossed from one horn to another of a gigantic cow.
Such theories are fast disappearing in the minds of
those who, correctly "substitute the study of laws for
that of causes, the *how* for the *why*."

HUMAN REMAINS IN ALLUVIUM.—The alluvium of
the Kennet is a well-marked deposit, and forms large
and valuable water-meadows. Dr. Buckland, who records human remains in it, says it is " much mixed with
minute crystals of selenite and a small quantity of car-
bonate of lime, and abounds with the bones and horns
of oxen, red-deer, roebucks, horses, wild boars, and
beavers. A *human skull*, of high antiquity, has also
been found in it, at a depth of many feet, at the con-

tact of the peat with a substratum of shell-marl. It was accompanied by rude instruments of stone. Along the northern edge of this peat-bog, there is a considerable deposit of marl, mixed with calcareous tufa .. .... from two to ten feet in thickness, and frequently interstratified with beds of peat, varying from six inches to three or four feet in thickness." In the neighborhood of Newbury the lower marl contains mammalian remains, which are said to be more plentiful towards the edge of the valley. The list of these comprises :—*Bos primigenius, B. longifrons, Cervus capreolus. C. elaphus, Equus, Sus scrofa, Canis lupus, Lutra vulgaris, Ursus spelœus, Castor Europœus, Arvicola* (water-rat). The peat is dug in places for fuel, and, with shell-marl, but not for manure : in it are found remains of oak, alder, willow, fir, birch, hazel, and of mosses, reeds, and equiseta.

A few miles from Thetford, are a number of natural ponds, or meres, varying in size, from twenty roods to fifty acres. Many of these are situated in the parishes of East and West Wretham, and one of them, known as the West Mere, five or six acres in extent, was drained of the waters in 1851, by the proprietor, Mr. Birch, of Wretham Hall.

In this mere there was ordinarily about four feet of water, and beneath it about eight feet of soft black mud, partly held in suspension, and requiring to be removed in scoops. When this mud was being cleared out, a great number of bones were discovered, chiefly deposited, as from its semi-liquid nature might have been expected, at the bottom. They were nearly all those of the red deer (*Cervus elaphus*), and of the now extinct long-faced ox (*Bos longifrons*).

Near the center of the mere, lying below the black mud, was found a ring, or circular bank, of fine white

earth, outside of which, the bottom of the mere was so
soft and deep as to be impassable. This ring, or bank
was about twenty or thirty feet across, a foot wide, and
about four feet in height, and near its inner circumference a deep hole, or well, was marked out by a circle
of stout stakes. There was also, near by, the remains
of a flint wall and traces of a rude ladder.

The deer's antlers and other bones had many of them
cut-marks of rude tools. Many flint-disks, seemingly
resembling what the Danish antiquaries call sling-stones,
are said to have been found in this and other meres,
but none of them have been preserved.

A few years later, 1856, the largest of these meres,
having an area of forty-eight acres, was emptied and
cleaned out, and during the operation was visited by
Sir Charles Bunbury, who has recorded his observations in the Geological Society's Journal (vol. xii.) Sir
Charles incidentally states the presence of numerous
posts of oak-wood, shaped and pointed by human art,
standing erect in the mud.

M. Troyon, in his 'Habitations Lacustres,' recognizes
the similarity of these Norfolk antiquities to the Pile-
buildings of his own country—France.

HUMAN SKULLS—THE RIVER-BED SKELETON FROM LEICESTER.

I have been asked to give a few supplementary remarks on the fragmentary human remains from this
cave, in addition to those made by Professor Huxley,
('Geologist,' vol. v. p. 204). The observations made
by him led him to express an opinion that the Weardale remains belonged "to the same race of rather
small and lightly-made men, with prominent supercili-

ary ridges and projecting nasal bones," as the Musk-ham, Towyn-y-Capel, Sennen. Borris, and Blackwater skulls. In the spirit of these observations I cordially concur.

Particular description of the remains being, however, requisite, I proceed to remark that no perfect skull has hitherto been found in the Heathery Burn Cave. The most perfect, though not the most characteristic, is the one of which Mr. Mackie has given an excellent draw-ing (in *Geol.*) and which I shall denominate A. An-other skull is only represented by the *os frontis* and a small part of the parietal, and is far more striking. I name this B for facility of description.

The calvarium, or vertex of the skull, marked A. is not that of an aged individual. A large part of the frontal suture is persistent. The frontal region is low, but not markedly retrocedent. An even curve is continued backwards to immediately behind the coronal suture, when the same "post-coronal" depression is visible, as in the Mewslade and Eastham skulls. The points of attachment of the temporal muscle are scarcely visible. The coronal suture is, however, complex at the spot where it crosses the temporal attachments—a character on which Messrs. Thurnam and Davis have laid stress in British skulls. The parietal tubers are moderately prominent. The superciliary ridges are not unduly de-veloped, and the fractured condition of the skull war-rants us in affirming that the frontal sinuses were small. As far as measurement can be made, the length from the glabella to the apex of the lambdoidal suture is 7 inches; the breadth at the parietal tubers, $5\frac{1}{2}$ inches; at the coronal suture $4\frac{1}{2}$ inches; above the orbits, $3\frac{5}{8}$ inches. A fragment of right occipital condyle prob-ably belonged to the same young individual; a fragment of the mastoid bone appertained to an elder person.

The fragment marked B is a most striking relic of antiquity. It is the frontal bone, with much of the right parietal attached : the pieces of which I have succeeded in joining together. The close similarity of it to the fragmentary skull from Plymouth, which Professor Busk has described in the *Geologist.* is very striking. Unlike, however, the Plymouth skull, the superciliary ridges are markedly conspicuous. The retrocession of the forehead is very peculiar, and strongly resembles that in the skulls from Sennen and Muskham. Slight traces of the frontal suture can be seen. The frontal sinuses are present, though small. No traces of the post-coronal depression are visible. It is much to be regretted that no other pieces have been preserved of this curious skull. Many fragments, chiefly of parietal bones, were also obtained ; but their condition precludes an opinion as to their nature. The vertebræ and bones of the extremities did not offer any characters calling for especial notice.

I believe the fragment marked B was the skull which Mr. J. Elliott, the careful explorer of the cave, stated* " may have been that of one of the principal tenants of the cave, and which probably devoured the others." This evidence of " a tolerably large animal " rather appears to be that of a human being, with forehead " villainously low," and whose cranial characters were so striking as almost to excuse the error into which Mr. Elliott was unintentionally led.

The skull from Leicester is in good condition, and retains much of its animal matter. It exhibits the even oval contour characteristic of the existing type of Eng

---

* Geologist, Vol. V., p. 36. For cuts of fragments alluded to, see same journal.

374 PRE-ADAMITE MAN.

lishmen. By the smallness of the mastoid processes, the slenderness of the zygomata, and the slight degree in which the surface is pitted with muscular depressions, I conjecture it to have belonged to a female, and by the position of the wisdom-teeth in the alveoli, the individual probably did not exceed eighteen years of age. The following is a table of the principal admeasurements :—

	INCHES.
Longitudinal diameter	7
Parietal diameter	5
Frontal diameter	5¼
Vertical diameter	4¼
Intermastoid arch	13¼
Intermastoid line	3¼
Occipito-frontal arch	14
Horizontal periphery	19¼

The slope of the frontal and parietal bones is even and round, the occiput being full and globular, without any sign however of the "kumbecephalic" backward prolongation.

Comparison of the base of the skull with that of a well-formed European of about the same age, exhibits the prognathism of the maxilla more distinctly. The incisor teeth are rather more oblique, and the extero-internal breadth of the canines is greater than in the majority of existing European crania. The molar teeth do not exceed in size the average European proportions. Many of them were afflicted during life with caries to a large extent. The frontal bone is moderately arched, the glabella prominent, with no sign of the supraciliary ridges. All the sutures exhibit the normal configuration.

The ordinary junction of the alisphenoid with the parietal is present on both sides the skull. The mastoids are small, and the supramastoid ridge is undeveloped. No peculiarity exists in the form or position of the occipital foramen or of the condyles. The nasal bones are well developed and rather salient.

The lower jaw does not exhibit any marked peculiarity.

The appearance of the lower half of the supra-occipital bone is very different from that of the Muskham skull. The surfaces for attachment of muscles are less pronounced; the furrow for the insertion of the *obliquus superior* muscle is less deep; the crest, and the superior and inferior *lineæ semicirculares* are less developed, and the occipital protuberance, or inion, is less distinct. A small paroccipital tubercle is visible on the right side. The upper half of the supraoccipital is full and globular, and in the rather complex lambdoid suture are at least seven wormian bones, none of which, however, deserve the term interparietal.

An examination of the nearly perfect spinal column did not disclose any peculiar characteristic. The bones of the extremities indicate a youthful individual, the epiphyses being in many cases separate.

The animal remains said to be associated with this skull were *Bos primigenius* and *Equus caballus*.

The following table is merely offered as a temporary and provisional arrangement. Many of the sections do not represent distinct races, and all the skulls from the river-bed deposits offer many points of analogy with each other. The difficulty of laying down any general system can only be appreciated by the practical inquirer. In the meantime, the evidences appear to be capable of arrangement in something like the following order. [It will be seen that the "developments" of these skulls are such as to incontestibly prove that hundreds of thousands of years must have elapsed, even at the early day when those skulls encased human brains, since monkeys have merged into men. If the development theory be true, then millions of years have elapsed since " Man became a living soul"] :

1 Dolichocepbalic.
   A. Forehead retrocedent.
      a. Superciliary ri lges very large, continuous over nasal suture. *Neanderthal.*
      b. Superciliaries large. *a.* Foramen magnum abnormal. *Muskham.*
         B. Foramen magnum normal ?
            Sennen, Nether Urquhart.
            Heathery Burn, " B."
      c. Superciliaries small.
         Plymouth.
         Heathery Burn, " A."
         Blackwater.
         Borris (bed of Nore.)
         Engis.
   B. Forehead moderately developed.
      a. Superciliaries small.
         Mewslade.
         Eastham.
         Leicester.
2. Brachycephalic.
      a. Superciliaries large.
         Plau.
         Montrose.
      b. Superciliaries small.
         Etruria, O.

CHARLES CARTER BLAKE.

Says the London *Morning Star,* of February 22d, 1861, in its report of a meeting, held in London :

A meeting of the Ethnological Society was held on Tuesday evening for the purpose of discussing the subject of the flint implements found with the bones of extinct animals in the " drift." Many archæologists and geologists were specially invited to take part in the discussion, among whom were Sir Roderick Murchison, Professor Owen, Professor Quckett, Mr. Waterhouse Hawkins, Mr. Pengelly, Mr. Pettigrew, Mr. Planché, Mr. Savory, Dr. Lee, the Rev. J. Ridgway, Admiral Fitzroy, etc. Mr. Botfield, M.P, the President of the Archæological Association, took the chair, Mr. Craw-

ford, the President of the Ethnological Society, being
on his right hand, and Sir Roderick Murchison on his
left. The discussion was opened by Mr. Pettigrew,
who explained how the subject was originally brought
into consideration in this country by the presentation
to the Archæological Association, in 1848, of a number
of flint implements found in the drift near Amiens by
M. Boucher de Perthês. Those implements, and a
larger collection of others contributed by Dr. Hunt, by
Mr. Mackie and Mr. Christie, were displayed on the
tables. Mr. Wright said that he considered the flint
implements exhibited were intended for the chase or
for domestic use, and not for the purpose of war. Mr.
Evans explained the exact position of the stratum of
gravel from which he had extracted some of these implements. It was a stratum of coarse fresh-water gravel,
lying on chalk, and containing fossil bones of extinct
animals, among which was the entire skeleton of an extinct species of rhinoceros. Overlying the gravel was
a stratum of sandy marl, containing shells of existing
species, and above that was a thin stratum of brick
earth. The flint implements were extracted at a depth
varying from twenty to thirty feet from the surface,
and he felt convinced that the gravel in which they
were found had not been disturbed. The same opin
ion was formed by every one who had visited the spot,
and there seemed to be no doubt whatever that the
gravel and the flint implements were deposited at the
same time. It was possible that the animals supposed
to have become extinct before man was created might
have continued to exist to more recent periods than
had been supposed, otherwise it would appear that the
implements were fashioned by a race of men that had
also become extinct. Sir Roderick Murchison confirmed Mr. Evans's view of the great antiquity of the

stratum of gravel in which the implements were found, and observed that, without the presence of fossil bones of extinct animals, the surface of the country proved that there must have been an enormous lapse of time since the gravel, *beneath* which the human relics were found, was deposited. [It is the opinion of many of the most eminent scientific men of Europe, based on very careful examinations, that the race of "extinct men" alluded to, *could not have lived less than one hundred and thirty-five thousand years ago*, but probably more than double that length of time, or over two hundred thousand years ago.] The possibility of the continuance of species of animals supposed to have become extinct was, he said, rendered probable from the fact that there was now living in a forest in Poland, animals which had previously been considered extinct. In the subsequent discussion, in which Admiral Fitzroy, Mr. Christie, Mr. Pengelly, and other gentlemen took part, it was stated that flint implements of the same character as those on the table, had been found in various parts of the world. Mr. Botfield, in concluding the proceedings of the meeting, expressed his conviction that the cause of religion would have nothing to fear, but everything to hope, from scientific inquiry.

CHAPTER V.

M. GRAS' ATTACK ON THE EVIDENCE OF THE ANTIQUITY OF MAN.

[Lond. Geol., Aug. 1862.]

When the Antiquity of Man was first proclaimed from the discovery of the Abbeville flints by Boucher de Perthes, no one believed it. Everybody thought

him like the mad man who swore all the world was
mad ; and so it seemed, then, as if all the world had
mental obliquity of vision, which made them declare
the *savant* of Abbeville to be laboring under a delusion.
When, however, Rigollet, Prestwich, Flower, Lyell,
Evans, and others of the goodly company of geologists
—as unbelieving, however, as so many St. Thomases—
went, saw, and returned believing, the fame of Boucher
de Perthes' discoveries gained ground: Some there
were who hardened themselves in their unbelief, and
hazarded wild theories of ocean-waves chipping out
artificial forms, and of recent objects sinking down in
the ground, and burying themselves, and other equally
untenable notions, but these waxed fewer and fewer,
not by dying out, but by becoming converts to the novel
truths.   Others there were who enthusiastically grasped
at everything that came in their way, and attempted to
send back half the antiquities of the historic period,
to the Gravel age.   These still exist, and if their labors
be a little rash, they are not altogether useless. If
they make a great many mistakes, they now and then
drop on a new fact, and *that* covers a multitude of failures.   Others there are, and these are the best of all,
saving the real workers for science, who lose no chance
of collecting anything they think may afford *useful*
knowledge.   The people, so common at one time, with
the dreadful mental squint about the flint implements
of the gravel age are now, as we have said, few and
far between, but there are still some possessed of the
dangerous slight cast of mental obliquity, if we mistake
not—that is, if the obliquity does not lie with ourselves.   We do not think it can, nobody ever does
The London *Purthenon* lately printed a translation from
the French *Comptes-Rendus*, of a paper by M. Scipion
Gras, who brings up a question we had thought com-

pletely settled. We knew our best men had gone to
see; we knew they had come back testifying to the
facts. But M. Gras comes forward with an article
" On the Insufficiency of the Arguments drawn from
the Position of the Worked Flints of St. Acheul to
show the Existence of Man during the Quaternary
Period." There is mental obliquity somewhere, that
is certain; we fear it rests with M. Gras, for he says
he went to St. Acheul, " desirous of enlightening *his
doubts*" as to the conclusion drawn from the position
of the flint axes there. Of course we saw the notice
of M. Gras' paper in the *Comptes-Rendus*, where it appeared a short time before the *Parthenon* printed the
translation. As the *Parthenon* has brought the paper
before the public, which otherwise, perhaps, would never
have heard at all of it, we cannot let M. Gras' opinions
pass without comment. He shall, however, have fair
play. He begins:—

"There are found at St. Acheul and its neighborhood
(leaving out of question the more elevated plateaux)
two diluvial deposits, which appear to be quite distinct.
The more ancient one, immediately overlying the chalk,
is essentially composed of light yellowish, or brown
flints, for the most part rolled, disseminated through
a whitish-gray calcareous sand. The relative proportion of the sand and flints varies; sometimes veins
of almost pure sand alternate with flints, or cover
them. It is not uncommon to find in the sand fresh-
water shells, almost intact, in spite of their fragility
—a fact which indicates a slow process of accumulation. Ferruginous infiltrations from above have often stained the naturally clear color of this deposit.
This diluvium has a very unequal thickness, owing to
the numerous erosions which it has undergone. It
shows itself at St. Acheul at a height of from thirty to
forty mètres above the Somme; at the sand-pits of Mou-
tiers, at the western extremity of Amiens, it descends
all at once to the bottom of the valley; finally, at

Menchecourt, a suburb of Abbeville, it passes beneath the turf-beds. It results from this, that before the deposit of this transported bed, the Somme had already hollowed out its channel in the bosom of the chalk, which is seen rising right and left to a great height. The valley was even then deeper than it is now; it appears to have been entirely filled up at the time of the arrival of the rolled flints. The second diluvial bed in the neighborhood of St. Acheul is an argillaceous-sandy stratum of a dark brown, of which the thickness is usually from a mètre and a half to three mètres; it is almost everywhere dug for brickmaking. It shows usually at its base a thinnish layer of angular flints disseminated through a brown earth, rather more sandy than the rest of the mass. This argillaceous-sandy diluvium extends crosswise at once over the lower clear grey diluvium and over the chalk; it presents all the signs of complete independence. Its deposition probably coincided with the second excavation of the valley; it is observed, in fact, at different levels corresponding with those at which the Somme has successively flowed before withdrawing itself to its present bed."

In this account there are three topics which call forth observations. 1. *There are (at least) two diluvial deposits.*—There is nothing new in this. Mr. Prestwich, one of the most inquiring and capable investigators of the subject, and one of the strongest believers in the correctness of Boucher de Perthes' assignment of the chipped flint-implements to the Gravel age, has already shown that there is a "high-level gravel" and a low-level or "valley-gravel;" and in his papers before the Royal Society has shown, also, why there are these deposits, what are their relations to each other, the probable physical and meteorological conditions under which they were deposited, and their bearings in respect to the evidence of the flint-implements as a proof of the antiquity of man. 2. *That it is not uncommon to find in the sand fresh-water shells, almost intact, in spite of*

their fragility.—There is nothing extraordinary in this.
The wonder would be if we did *not* find them. Mr.
Prestwich has shown how much ice-action had to do
with the bringing down, during the early spring floods,
of the flints, rock boulders, and other heavy materials
— probably often also the bones of animals; and if
these heavier substances were frozen into the ice-floes,
masses of fine gravel, sand, and earth, enclosing fragile
shells, would also be brought down in the same way.
Moreover, the *gravel* deposits would chiefly be formed
during the period of spring floods caused by the melting of the ice; and consequently during the summer
there would be a period during which mollusca might
live under the influence of the quieter river-actions,
which actions would naturally intercalate beds and
streaks of sand and clay with fresh-water shells among
the coarser gravels. 3. *That the Valley of the Somme
was even then deeper than it is now; and appears to
have been filled up at the time of the arrival of the rolled
flints.*—All this has nothing to do with the question of
man's antiquity at all; besides there is no proof given
by M. Gras. What he states as to the various deposits and their conditions go for nothing in this respect;
they simply do not bear upon the point at all. It matters not whether the valley was hollowed out, whether
it was filled up or not, before the "rolled flints" were
brought in, so long as the gravel deposit containing the
flint-implements can be proved to be of *geological age*
—that is the point; and M. Gras, if we *do* not misunderstand him, admits the flint-implement-bearing beds
are *covered* by other diluvial or alluvial deposits—a
sufficient admission of their antiquity.

As to a previous complete excavation of a valley before any deposits collected in it, such a notion in the
main would be a very fallacious one, for the scouring

action of water and rain-falls is as great beneath a deposit as it is over its surface. Rains wash away visibly the fine soil on the surface, but the water that filters through, also washes away invisibly the fine disintegrated surface of the rock on which the deposit lies; so the whole mass of deposits gradually—slowly but surely—*sinks* into a greater and greater subterranean valley as age follows age.

But to return to M. Gras—for he himself admits the position that the flint-implement gravel *was* covered over in the following passage :—

" By the help of these details a clear idea may be formed of the position of the worked flints; they are found in the lower gray diluvium at variable depths, and often considerably below the surface of the soil. An attentive examination of the flinty mass which encloses them yields no re-arrangement of materials. Moreover, everywhere above these flints there is a thickness of two or three mètres of diluvium of the latest date, of a brown color. This itself appears to be perfectly intact, and sharply separated from the grey diluvium : which excludes the possibility of the introduction of foreign objects vertically through the argillaceous-sandy earth."

But here follows what certainly shows either M. Gras' obliquity of mental vision, or our own. If we err, however, fortunately we shall be in goodly company, for we shall be on the side of Prestwich. Rigollet, Lyell, Evans, and those many others who hold the like opinions with ourselves upon the subjects M. Gras attacks. Let M. Gras however, speak his own arguments :—

" These different circumstances, in appearance so conclusive, are not however irreconcilable with the idea of diggings having been made, at a certain epoch, in the soil. Before demonstrating this, I must dwell upon some important facts. The first is, the integrity and

perfectly excellent preservation of the axes; they look
as if just come from the hands of the workman. It has
been inferred (the inference was unavoidable) that they
were buried on the spot, or brought from very near localities. A second fact, not less remarkable, is the
truly astonishing multitude of these axes. The number
of them found at St. Acheul, in the compass, of about a
hectare (two acres). has been estimated at more than
three thousand. The rich collection of M. Boucher de
Perthes alone contains more than a thousand. M.
Albert Gaudry, who has caused diggings to be made,
has seen nine of them disinterred, one after another, in
close succession. The fact of the multitude of worked
flints, joined to the entireness of their edges, shows
clearly that there was formerly a considerable manufacture of these objects on the spot. If we adopt the hypothesis of those who would place this manufacture
beyond historic times, it must needs be admitted that
there existed on the banks of the ancient valley of the
Somme a people of the quaternary epoch occupied in
cutting axes by thousands. As evidently it could not
use them all, it must doubtless have supplied them to
other quaternary races of the neighboring countries.
But if this were so, why has this industrial population
of the ancient world left no other trace of its existence
except these rudely-fashioned flints? Why, above all,
do we not find human remains in the diluvium? Their
absence is the more astonishing, as it is not uncommon
to find there the remains of elephants, rhinoceroses, and
other animals. If men, so civilized as to occupy themselves with commerce, lived on the banks of the Somme
at the commencement of the quaternary period, they
must have constructed habitations there, and these
would be seen now in the mass of diluvium which at a
later period filled up the valley; they would even be
perfectly preserved in it. Now this deposit has never
presented the least vestige of a habitation, nor even of
other products of human industry, excepting flint objects. Another consideration strengthens all these
grounds of doubt; worked flints, similar to those
which are claimed as diluvian, have been found in such
a position, that it has been necessary to attribute to

them a modern origin. M. Toillez, an archæologist and engineer of Mons, possesses a collection of four hundred axes, which for the most part are rough, and do not differ sensibly from those of St. Acheul; nevertheless, they have all been collected at the surface of the soil. Is it admissible to suppose that products so similar were manufactured, the one set at the commencement of the quaternary period, the other during the now existing period, seeing that an immense interval of time separates the two epochs?"

Here again we select the points of attack :—1. *The perfect preservation of the axes.*—"They look as if they had just come from the hands of the workmen." Say "*some* look," and then we shall reply, Quite right, M. Gras; some *do* look as if they had just come from the hands of the workmen. Assuredly they do—and very naturally too, seeing they have in reality just come from the hands of the workmen. We have seen abundance of forgeries, both from the valley of the Somme and from Yorkshire. There are indeed plenty of forgeries. Nevertheless there are some *real;* these however are comparatively few. No one ought to mistake the real geological flint-implements from the forgeries. No one who is used to break flints but ought to tell readily whether a flint was broken with an *iron* instrument or not. A modern hammer will not crack or flake a flint in the same way that a stone will. Try it, reader, and see for yourself.

Setting aside forgeries, there is even then no reason why the flint-implements should not be in good preservation. If first frozen into a mass of ice, then transported, enveloped in, and protected by that ice-casing, then dropped on the floor of the wide-spread river-flood by the melting of the ice, then covered over perchance by the soft materials of the summer stream, or left on the verdant marshy tract during the interval between the periodical floods, what was there to weather or otherwise injure so hard a substance as flint? Nothing that we know of. Moreover, the truth is, that as far as our experience goes—and we have seen more than a few of the fossil flint-implements—they are by no means *all* always so wonderfully perfect. Some are decidedly worn—even as much so as the gravel in which they are found.

2. *The astonishing multitude of these axes.*—Surely, no one thinks *one* man made the lot, or that they were all made at once. Geologists always cry out for "plenty of time." They ask for plenty of time—a whole geological age—for the formation of the gravel deposits. So therefore the primitive men had a *whole age* to chip flints in. The very quantity of elephant, and other bones, found in the gravel-beds shows nature did take an age to form them, unless we suppose a supernatural increase and growth of living beasts. followed by an equally supernatural and wholesale destruction. But in reality, *how* common are the true worked flints? We have seen *one* only from all the great gravel-beds round and under London, and miles of them have lately been cut through for the sewer-works. We have seen, may be, half a dozen from Suffolk, a like number from Bedford, two or three from Kent, and less than a dozen more from all parts of England. As to the Yorkshire specimens, we must know more about them, and *where* they came from, before we can say much about them. I suppose, however, whether ancient or modern, not more than a hundred exist from that, the largest county in England, and numbering as many acres as there are words in the Bible. M. Gras says, however, that in the rich collection of M. Boucher de Perthes. there are more than a thousand; that M. Toillez, of Mons, possesses four hundred; and that at St. Acheul the num

ber *found* in the compass of a hectare (two acres) has been estimated at more than 3.000! Now, does M. Gras mean that at St. Acheul two acres of gravel have been excavated for flint-implements? or does he mean that in proportion to the quantity of gravel actually excavated there, an estimate has been made of the probable number of 3,000 as existing in two acres of gravel? How many feet thick? There's a rub. Two acres, 30 feet thick, would contain some millions of tons of gravel, this proportion of flint-implements to the number and quantity of unworked flints and pebbles in which would be very small indeed. Take the total of 3,000 in another way, and suppose each man of a tribe numbering a hundred males to make or lose one new weapon every two years, from the age of twenty to the age of forty, after which period of lifetime we will suppose every man to be either useless, superannuated, or killed in battle or by wild beasts in the chase. Then it would only take three generations of this tribe to make or lose the quantity M. Gras thinks so enormous.

Really there is nothing wonderful in this total after all. When we come to look into it, we only wonder it is not more.

3. *That the worked flints were manufactured on the spot.*—Many might have been; certainly not *all*. We have already disposed of the assertion of the universal preservation of their perfect sharp edges. The sharp edge of a newly-broken flint will cut your fingers—try it; we have never seen the edges of a flint axe or even a fossil flint flake that would.

Some, we have said, were probably ice-borne down the annual floods. If Mr. Prestwich be right in his supposition of their being ice-chisels, in some localities where the primitive men had fishing-stations, many might be dropped through the holes they were used in breaking out. As to the commercial aspect which M. Gras suggests, it would neither make for, nor militate against, the antiquity of man. We are sorry to say, however, that we have not so high an opinion of the intellectual capacities of these our primitive ancestors —if *our* ancestors they really were, and perhaps they were not—as to believe them capable of commercial enterprises at all. Morever, the traffic in flint weapons pre-supposes the means of international communication; we doubt very much if the flint-implement men, who could do no more than *chip* stones—who did not know even how to grind them—had any means for this. The Veddahs of one tribe at this hour do not know the Veddahs of another tribe, their next neighbors; less than fifty miles of mere territory part them. For our own part, we think so poorly of the flint-implement men as to be scarcely inclined to feel any more pride in a pedigree from them, than from the much abused and hirsute gorilla.

4. *Why has this industrious population of the ancient world left no other trace of its existence? Why, above all, do we not find human remains?*—How many skeletons of all the known species of fossil monkeys all over the globe, have been exhumed from their stony tombs? Are there a hundred fragments in all the collections of all the museums and naturalists in every region and part of the earth? And have we found every kind of fossil monkey yet? No sane man will assert it. Human teeth have been found in Pleistocene strata as old as the gravel-beds; negative evidence we have seen too often to mean nothing, to trust it in a question like this. Human remains *have* been found with bones of the mammoth, and fossil deer and bear, although these are ignored. Those as yet found, we admit, *may* not be the remains of the flint-implement-making men.

"Wait patiently, they will yet be found." But will M. Gras declare that there are not in the gravel-beds of the Somme seams of brittle lignite; and will he venture to assert that these may not be the charred remains of huts?

Take another view. The beast, when he sickens to die, goes to some retired spot, and leaves his inanimate carcase on the soil. There it may become embedded, or the floods may lift and strand it on some shallow bank. Nature buries it or moulders it, and returns it dust to dust in her own way. When a man dies, the case is different. The cow weeps not for the death of the bull, the lion sheds no tears for the loss of the lioness, the hippopotamus scrapes no hole in the earth to bury its lifeless mate, the gorilla lights no fire to burn to ashes the mother of its progeny. The *lowest* of human beings must have had *human passions* and *human feelings*. The primitive wife, little sensible, as we can but conceive, of anything like fine sensations, would, degraded as ever we could possibly conceive her, naturally weep for the loss of her husband; and though no priest performed a marriage ceremony, in such relationship, notwithstanding, ever stood the union of *human* beings. The man would mourn for the loss of his helpmate. Death to *human* beings would always have had a different aspect to what death has to the beast. In the human heart there would be the innate desire to lay the lifeless corpse or its ashes *where* its resting-place could be visited. If the flint-implement men were *human*, such must have been, even in the first of this pristine race, the feelings which death would evoke; and if such the feelings, *burials* or *burnings* must have disposed of the mass of that primitive race. If burials, we must look elsewhere than to the *débris* of floods or the alluvia of river-beds for human bones.

We may search for a later but still early race near where the great monoliths and the gigantic stones of so-called Druids' temples exhibit their weather-beaten forms; but if cremation were practiced, then for all traces of the flint-implement makers, other than their works, we must trust to chance alone.

The massive bones of the great beasts could not escape the eye; the teeth and skulls of smaller animals would at once attract attention; but what notice would a few fragments of calcined bones among the *débris* and broken fragments obtain?

What explorer of caves, what digger in gravel-pits, has searched over the heaps of bone-bits always thrown aside as waste? In this respect we have followed the common way; but we are not without suspicion that more than once we have missed our chance.

5. *That worked flints, similar to those claimed as diluvial, have been found in such a position that it has been necessary to attribute to them a more modern origin.*—No instances are stated by M. Gras; we cannot, therefore, refute any cases to which he alludes by statements of the facts. Besides which, if such specimens exist under such circumstances, they may be forgeries; or they may be relics—and this is not at all unlikely—preserved by more modern tribes. We know that the savage races of the present day *do* sometimes treasure the weapons of their ancestors; and there are many other ways in which such occurences may be explained when the actual circumstances are given.

6. *That M. Toillez's axes have been collected at the surface of the soil.*—This is put as a "poser" by M. Gras; but strong as he thinks it, it goes down at once before a simple question. It is slaughtered by a breath. Do we not not find ordinary *gravel*-flints in myriads on the surface of the soil? Can you go

through any field, over any downs, across any chalk
country, and not pick up, if you please, tons upon tons,
or cart-load upon cart-load ? If one sort, why not the
other ? Is the proportion of flint-implements to unworked stones likely to be less in the disintegrated
gravel-bed, strewn over the soil, than in the solid untouched stratum lying intact in the earth ? And if not,
are we less likely to find flint-implements on the surface of the soil than in the gravel-beds beneath it ?
We are sure we need not reply to these questions—our
readers will have answered for themselves.

7. *Is it admissible to suppose that products so similar
were manufactured, the one set at the commencement of
the quaternary period, the other during the now existing
period, seeing that an immense interval of time separates
the two epochs ?*—Supposing the facts to be true—but
the facts are not stated by M. Gras, as already observed
—it might be so, if it be admissible to believe that
small tribes or scattered individuals of a nation or race
of mankind *could live on* after the *destruction* or *distribution* of the great bulk or mass of the nation or race.
Just as some modern uncivilized tribes are presumed to
be the descendants of once numerous and powerful peoples. Just as British and Celtic articles may be met
with in Saxon and Roman graves; just as medieval relics are still treasured in our houses, so may we always
expect to find some relics of more ancient races among
the relics of the more modern ones. The case put however by M. Gras is a presumption, and it is futile to fill
these pages with suppositions in reply to suppositions.
Let us go on therefore to consider M. Gras' final summary :—

" To all these difficulties, one single fact only can be
opposed, that, namely, of the absence of all apparent
disturbance in the diluvium ; but this fact is not a per-

emtory reason, for it may be explained in a plausible manner.

" Let us refer the manufacture of axes, which everything proves to have formerly been carried on in the valley of the Somme, to the origin of historic times. It is certain that the men occupied in this employment were not obliged to go very far to procure the first material that was necessary for them. By digging in the soil to a moderate depth, they found a great choice of flints ready to be cut. This was probably even the reason why this kind of industry sprang up in the country. The digging of flints might take place in two ways, by pits or by galleries. The first means was the most costly, since it was necessary to pass through the brown argillaceous-sandy diluvium before arriving at the flints, and because the removal of the rubbish must take place vertically. The digging by horizontal galleries opened on the side of the valley, taking advantage of the steep banks, was evidently preferable. The excavation of these ancient galleries is so far from being unlikely, that even at the present day such are still made for the extraction of gravel. I have seen one at St. Acheul, and I measured its dimensions approximately ; it was six mètres in length by one mètre ninety centimètres in height, and two mètres in breadth. This gallery supported itself well without props. It may be admitted that in former times the excavations were less in breadth and height, which would render them yet more solid.

" The flints freshly extracted, and not deprived of their quarry moisture, are much easier to work than those of which the drying has proceeded to some length. It is probable, consequently, that the ancient miners roughly formed in the interior of the galleries the axes destined to be polished. After this first labor, a selection was doubtless made ; the least shapely pieces, considered improper for sale, were rejected and left on the spot. When, after a length of time, the galleries, which had served at once as shops for mining and for rough hewing, had crumbled down, the chipped flints left on the floor were enveloped on all sides by the soil from whence they had been extracted. Supposing that the subsidence of the galleries was propagated up to the surface, the upper sand of argillaceous diluvium must have sunk a little, parallel to itself, without becoming mixed in any way with the grey flinty diluvium. If this was the real course of events, it is certain that at the end of some time all trace of disturbance must have been completely effaced. This explanation agrees well with the rude form of the flints disinterred—so rude, that it is difficult to understand how they can have been put to use in this state. It is confirmed by another peculiar circumstance, which had been held to be unimportant, but which, nevertheless, has much import. M. Albert Gaudry, who has been cited above, remarked that the nine worked flints discovered in his presence, lay nearly all palpably at the same level. Was not this level that of the floor of an ancient gallery ?"

This is how the learned Professor looks at the question from his own point of view, after, as he presumes, he has demolished his adversaries. After De Perthes, Prestwich, Lyell, Evans, we, of the oblique vision in M. Gras' opinion, have been out-argued and convicted of erroneous interpretations of the facts! Well! so, for the nonce, let us suppose the case. Is M. Gras, then, right in the views he promulgates in this summary? Assuredly not. If we are wrong, according to him, on one side of the barrier of facts, he is wrong on the other. If *our* geological interpretations do not agree with the evidence of facts, *his* historical speculations certainly do not.

Whatever eyes M. Boucher de Perthes has for looking at gravel beds—and being the first to pick out the flint implements would cause us to give him credit for sharp ones—we can for a certainty speak of the capabilities of Mr. Prestwich's organs. We have been over very many miles of gravel and drift deposits with him ; over country, every lane and turning in which is quite familiar ; and we do know, from experience, that if there be anything to be seen, he will see it. For more than twenty years of his life he has been incessantly studying over England and France, as a favorite speciality, these very quaternary beds ; and if any man's knowledge or judgment is to be relied upon for an opinion as to the age or nature of such deposits, assuredly it is his. Cautious in the extreme in adventuring conclusions, and fastidiously painstaking in collecting facts and testing the accuracy of his observations, no cooler intellect could discuss and put in intelligible order such intricate conditions as the gravel beds to the inexperienced present. Those who have read his masterly communications to the Royal Society of London will need no comments of ours to satisfy them of the accuracy of the views expressed, and of the ability of their author. But, to reply to M. Gras's suppositions. Referring the flint-implements to *historic* times for their origin, M. Gras states :—1. *That the makers were not obliged to go very far for their material.*—True, they were not obliged, *if*—and the whole summary involves a constant use of the little conjunction—*if* they *did make* the implements *on* the gravel-banks in which they have been imbedded. This is by no means certain : but one thing is quite sure, we have ourselves *seen*—and handled—a veritable flint implement from the valley of the Somme, which, although found in the gravel-bed, was undoubtedly and unmistakably made out of a flint-nodule taken *directly* out of the chalk rock.

In this case, therefore, the primitive manufacturer went at least to the side of the valley to get material which, according to M. Gras, he had, and quite as good, on the gravel-bank under his feet. If the manufacturer could be supposed to have worn breeches, he might be supposed to have pocketed a fine nodule which he chanced to fall in with on a pleasure-ramble ; but as he cannot be presumed to have so clothed his lower extremities, that presumption is untenable.

As a rule, we fancy that very many of the implements were made of flints directly taken from the chalk ; such flints would be preferable, generally, to gravel-flints, although suitable specimens could undoubtedly be collected from the gravel-beds, but not so abundantly as M. Gras infers. That some implements were made of large quaternary flint pebbles, the specimens from Herne Bay are indubitable evidence.

2. *The digging of the flints by means of pits or galleries.*—Setting aside the improbability of men digging for what they could find without labor on the surface, *what*, in the name of all mysteries, had those poor primitive savages to *dig with ?* Flint-implements ? It strikes us forcibly that, with one of those poor pointed tools, a man would soon be tired of the attempt to dig a hole in gravel, much less a gallery. Half a dozen strong men—and this supposes the ancient manufacturer to have kept a staff of workmen, unless he got voluntary help from his tribe—would make but sorry progress with those pointed flints. Even our stalwart miners would strike from such work with such tools. But *if*—we must use the little conjunction again—*if* the pits and tunnels *were* dug, were actually made, it is not true to suppose we should have no evidence of their former existence. The gravel would not sink into the excavations, and show no difference of structure at those spots which had been hollowed out of the beds ; for even such unsorted and heterogeneous deposits as gravel-beds are, they do distinctly show traces of former disturbances. We have clearly traced, by their appearances, disturbances made in gravel-beds by the

Romans and Saxons in forming their graves, or in digging for foundations of walls or pits; and what is likely to be distinctly apparent after the lapse of a thousand or more years, may be presumed to be at least detectable after the lapse of far longer ages. Moreover, *if* this explanation of M. Gras be acceded to, it involves the corresponding necessity of our finding the flint-implements in heaps or in narrow lines—where the pits and galleries have been—and *not* disseminated here and there, as they are, at least most usually, if not invariably. Supposing, as M. Gras does, that the subsidence into the galleries extended to the roof, there would be a furrow left at the surface, in which more recent deposits would accumulate, and if there were any sub-superficial coating of brick earth under the soil, that would bulge downwards in concentric, curved laminæ, such as we constantly see exposed in stone quarries when surface-clays have sunk down into fissures, and as we constantly observe in the sand and gravel pipes of the chalk districts, in which, too, we often find patches of older Tertiary clays, containing shells that have been imbedded in the overlying quaternary drifts.

7. *The rudeness of the implements suggestive of rough hewing for an after-finishing for sale.*—Rude as they are, and this is one of the points we dwell upon in proof of their antiquity, they were used in the state in which we find them, for otherwise we should find the *finished* examples elsewhere, which as yet, at any rate, we have done nowhere. We find stone and flint celts, polished and ground; but these, as we before observed, were used by the broad flat end. The large fossil flint-implements were all worked to a point, and which point, contrary to anything we know of the use of any other stone tool, ancient or modern, was the part used.

There is thus, besides the absence of chipping, one positive character at least which separates the fossil implements entirely from any other effort of savage industry. Will M. Gras assert he has ever seen a pointed weapon either ground or polished?

M. Gras further lays great stress on M. Gaudry having found nine worked flints on the same level. We might speak of levels in regularly stratified deposits, what *levels* are there in a gravel-bed?

Taking it for granted, however, nine were found on one level, is that number so large as to cause surprise? *If*—why may we not indulge in conjunctions?—if there were a fishing-station on the spot, would nine be a large number to be presumed to be lost during the sojourn of the fishermen there? Or is there not an infinity of incidents which might bring together so trifling a lot?

Finally, to close our comments, may we not justly ask M. Gras if the flint implements belong to historic times? *Who* were the men that used them?

———

Just now the gentlemanly Secretary of the Working Men's College, has handed me the London *Cornhill Magazine*, for August 1862, from the pages of which I take the following:—Is the human race making a new step on Darwinian principles toward the acquirement of some new organs, for which preparations are being made, and which may land us in the ten, or hundred thousandth generation in the possession of wings, or whatever other account of the fact is to be rendered? Certain it is that cases of late have occurred of the presence in the human subject, of SUPERNUMERARY MUSCLES OF THE CHEST! *Very* remarkable instances of three such supernumerary muscles, now for the first time observed and described, are given in the Transactions of

the Imperial Academy of St. Petersburg, recently pub
lished on the authority of Doctor Wenzel Gruber.
The most important and conspicuous of them rejoices
in the euphonious name of "Tensor Semi Vaginæ Ar-
ticulationes Humero Scapularis," and connects the
upper portion of the sternum (breast-bone) with the
upper end of the humerus, near the acromion. It is by
no means a feeble muscle, and must evidently impart
material additional strength to the inward contraction
of the shoulders. The other two are comparatively in-
significant.

Meismer and Auerbach have also recently discovered
a complete nervous apparatus lying under the mucous
layer of the intestines, and another and more important nervous plexus lying between the muscular walls of
the whole intestine from the pylorus downwards—a
plexus of nerves and ganglia of most extraordinary
formation, and doubtless function also.

———

The meaning of all these will be given in full in the
Second Volume of this Series, which volume is intended
to treat of The Human Body and the Human Soul—
their Origin, Nature, Constitution and Destiny, on the
Earth and off it. When it is ready (probably within
a few months,) it will be duly announced in the North,
as well as in the South, and will, it is believed, solve
several heretofore difficult problems.

———

CONCLUSION.

Mr. J. W. Jackson, of Scotland, a member of that
grand coterie of Thinkers now arising, and most assuredly destined, in the end, to totally revolutionize the
world of thought, both as to its methods and its results,
speaks eloquently in the *Future*, and of the future. He

maintains that History is not a mere chronicle of conflicting and isolated events, but a record of phenomena, developed in strict accordance with certain laws. Hence the possibility of attaining to the philosophy of it. Rousseau and some of his followers assert that the natural condition of man is savageism, but if so, he must, *many millenia* since, have emerged from his imperfect and primal state. On the verge of authentic history, and extending far away into the dim vista of tradition, we see the sublime shadows, vaguely looming in the distance, of great and already ancient nations, each with a language, religion, and political constitution, more or less peculiar to itself, and demonstrative of an origin even then long buried in a remote and forgotten antiquity. In addition to this, we have monumental evidence of a grandly-developed system of pre-historic civilization, not only from Britain to India, but also on the American Continent, from Canada to Peru. Of this Past, history is but a faint, and, in many instances deceptive echo. We are the heirs of long-buried generations, whose mighty labors and heroic deeds have left no trace upon the written page, and whose records, if they exist at all, are monumental, not literary. Judging by these, their minds must have been great, and their purposes grand ; for their public works, in proportion to the resources at their command, far transcend anything that later ages have accomplished. Such are the earth-works of America, the Cyclopean remains of Greece and Italy, and, lastly, the time-enduring pyramids of Egypt, which, however old, are probably among the latest tide-marks of this primeval period. Descending to the more recent age of tradition, we find society in India, Assyria, and Egypt, under hierarchical organization, with knowledge, and consequently power, especially concentrated in the hands of a few sacred and learned priesthoods, the holy ministers of religion, the revered administrators of the law, the skillful practitioners of medicine. and learned expositors of history and science. The clerisy of every order were then the clergy ; such were the Brahmins of Hindostan, the Magi of Babylon, and the priests of Mizraim. Such a system of civilization was, as we have said, concentrative and centripetal, wonderfully intensified as culture in a few favored minds, but leaving the masses wholly dependent upon the exoteric teaching and early tuition of these their divinely appointed and sacerdotal masters. This comparatively close and corporate system had undergone considerable modification among the classic nations of European antiquity ; philosophy, more especially among the Greeks, supplying the place of religion, and the philosophic sage superseding the saintly devotee. In such characters as Pythagoras, we see the process at the stage of transition; in Socrates and Plato it has attained to completion. The philosophy is, however, still moral rather than physical, and its principles are *a priori* rather than *a posteriori*, the master minds of that age descending from law to fact, rather than ascending from phenomena to the causes which have produced them. Intellectual culture. however, in its higher forms, was still the appanage of the favored few ; for only those peculiarly blessed by fortune or genius, could hope to obtain any considerable amount of knowledge, when every book was in manuscript, and a library of a hundred volumes would have purchased an estate of twenty farms. With Christianity in the West, and previously with Budhism in the East, a new era in civilization was inaugurated ; the old system of caste was ignored ; clergy and laity, prince and peasant, bond and free, were by these humanitarian faiths held equally amen-

able to the moral law, and regarded as equally heirs
of eternal beatitude.   Both synchronize with the
emergence of the human mind out of the sacerdotal
thraldom, the religious formalism and the caste prejudices of a previous era itself the product of an un-
lettered, traditional, and purely oral form of culture.
Budhism emerged out of Brahminism, the Judaism of
the farther East, as Christianity emerged out of Judaism, which, conversely, may be termed a modified form
of the Brahminism of the West.

A few words here upon the Genesis of Faith, which
is ever a result of the union between an old creed as
the male, and a new or strange philosophy as the female
element in human culture.   Thus this same Judaism
was the product of Patriarchal or Abrahamic theology,
the monotheism of the desert, combining with Egyptian
wisdom or philosophy in the exalted person of Moses,
the Menu or great law-giver of the Israelites.   While,
later again, Judaic monotheism as a male combined with
the Platonic philosophy of Greece as a female to produce Christianity, which, philosophically regarded, is
an adaptation of the Mosaic system to the wants and requirements of the European mind.   So we may feel assured that the Faith of the Future will be the result of
a union between the old Theology of (Judaic) Christianity, and that Science of Nature which constitutes our
existing philosophy, and which has never, during the
historic period at least, been embodied in any creed.
Of this faith Poets will be the Prophets, and sages the
Priests, and under it. Nature, as the Bride-Divine and
Universal Mother, will have due and honorable recognition among the Celestial Powers.

In the Middle ages we see the attempted reproduction
of a primeval time.   There is a highly organized hierarchy in the Papal Church which, fortunately, was cele-

bate, and so could not be made hereditary, like the corresponding priesthoods of India and Egypt in former
times, or like the contemporaneous feudal nobility, the
Cashatrya or Rajpoot caste of the West, where hereditary power and prestige are only now slowly on the
wane. The Dark Ages, as they are commonly termed,
were, of necessity, a compromise between the concentrative tendencies of a former past, and the diffusive
tendencies of an advancing future. Power and knowledge were still in a few hands, the privileges of birth,
everywhere except in the Church, and often even there,
predominated over the richest endowments of genius,
and for a long period it seemed that the world was once
more to be given up to the spiritual and temporal leadership of a favored few. Let us, however, do justice
to these Middle Ages, which were a grand period of re-
edification, during which the moral and physical temple
of humanity was rebuilt, and the foundation was laid
for that great start, which the human mind obtained at
the revival of learning. We under-estimate the civilization of the past, perhaps in part because it differs
from our own. Thus, for example, the men who reared
our Gothic cathedrals, and built our beautiful abbeys,
could not have been barbarians, but must have had
architectural taste and skill of the highest order, the
possession of which implies much else in correspondence
with it. The Papal faith and Aristotelian philosophy
of this time were in perfect harmony with each other
—that is, they were both *a priori*, and each taught with
an authority that dominated over independent reason.
The expansive tendency, however, was too strong, and
humanity burst its fetters, theologically, in the Reformation; philosophically, by the triumph of induction;
and geographically, by the discovery of America and
the way to the East round the Cape of Good Hope;

these liberalizing tendencies being confirmed and rein-
forced by the diffusive aptitudes for intellectual culture
placed at our command by the discovery of printing.
Luther and Bacon, Columbus and Guttenburg, co-oper-
ated in the one grand work of enfranchisement, which
is still proceeding, and of which Reformation and Revolutions are unavoidable results. The spirit of the
Middle Ages was synthetical, conservative, and *a priori*.
It built up and preserved all that it had inherited from
the past. It was an age of authority, not of reason ;
of religion, rather than of philosophy. Our Protestant
era is the very reverse of all this ; it is analytical, disintegrative, and even destructive. It pulls down the
strongholds of authority, and despises tradition. It is
ever appealing to reason against authority, and encour-
ages the independence of the many, in place of sanc-
tioning the power of the few. It discourages belief,
and is even prone to place philosophy above religion.
Strictly speaking, it is not a positive age at all, but
simply a revolutionary period of transition, between
two great eras of edification and conservation. Its result is natural philosophy, and its religion is the worship of nature, under the form of scientific culture.
The object of its higher idolatry is knowledge ; the god
of its more vulgar worship is money ; and both are
revered because each in its way is POWER. The
providential result of such an age. with its criticism
and its scepticism, its merchandise and its science, is
obviously to be—first, the sweeping away of old errors,
prior, doubtless, to the promulgation of new truths ;
and, secondly, the accumulation of material resources,
and the development of practical instrumentalities, to
be used under the higher spirit, and with the grander
aims of the future time. Priests and princes are alike
alarmed at the tendencies now becoming resistless and

all-pervasive of this disintegrative and destructive era.
And they may well be so, for should the flood continue
to rise, the ultimate submerging, both of the throne and
the altar, would be a question, not of circumstance, but
simply of time. The logical terminus of the movement
is a universal Pyrronism, under which faith and loy-
alty would utterly perish, and society be dissolved into
its elements, preparatory to its entire reconstruction.
France, at the latter end of the last century, approximated to this condition of things ; and, in her terror,
took refuge under the protection of a military despotism. No humanitarian movement, however, really
reaches this terminus, but is brought up by resistance
many stages short of so dire an ultimate. Thus it is
that we already see the symptoms of reconstruction,
restoration, of synthesis and re-edification already at
work. In religion we have our Mormonisms, Spiritu-
alisms, Revivalisms, and other convulsions of returning
life, which, under a certain aspect, are but the contortions of a galvanized corpse; and yet, under another,
are the pangs and rivings of birth taking place beneath
the ribs of death. In philosophy the leading minds are
becoming weary of the insignificance of mere facts,
and are beginning to demand the exercise of that reasoning power by which they may be harmoniously sys-
tematized, and thus converted from a weltering chaos
of phenomena into the order, beauty, and ONENESS of
a true creation. To accomplish this, more than mere
observers are required ; we must have thinkers—that
is, intellectual organizers, men of such grasp that they
can use the accumulated knowledge of the centuries as
mere subject-matter for their intellectual manipulation,
and who will, doubtless, succeed in eliminating from
this stupendous mass of experimental knowledge, those
profounder principles and grander views, which it

should legitimately produce, and of which, viewed from the causal sphere, it is the result.   Let us not, however, esteem too lightly the incalculable benefits which modern science confers, and is conferring, upon mankind. Its grander benefits must be universal, and can never, as of old, be confined to a class. or become the speciality of a few.   Already the printing-press places the grandest utterances of the profoundest wisdom at the service of the simplest peasant.   The Railway carries the artizan from town to town at a rate to which royalty, with all its couriers, could not even have approached in the last generation, while the Mail carries the letter of the humblest citizen with a rapidity and certainty to which the missive of monarchs never previously approached.

But let not the most timid Conservative take needless alarm ; the good already overbalances the evil. The forces of destruction are at work only upon error. The tide of revolution will sweep down nothing but injustice ; and criticism however searching, and scepticism, however hostile, will destroy nothing but untruth.   Already the roseate dawn of a second day is distinctly visible on the distant horizon; a great and sublime day of spirituality in religion. and of synthesis in philosophy, a day that doubtless will be as richly provided with its prophets and apostles, its poets and philosophers, as any that the world has yet seen, and in which not a favored few, but the countless millions of universal man will partake of the privileges, and share in the enlightenment of their instructions.

I began this book with a quotation from the *Tribune* —I end it with another from the same journal, December 16, 1863, which, beside being *apropos*, is also very suggestive, in more respects than its implied doubt of the correctness of the ordinarily accepted chronology :

" Music was the last of the arts to be perfected, and is the only romantic art left, for statues and temples were magnificently built four thousand or ten thousand years ago; and in the very heart of what is called the dark ages was the miracle of grandeur in architecture —the Cologne Cathedral : and now the statue means nothing—it has lost the hallowed signification which it enjoyed when it petrified virtue, and courage, and genius, and divinity —and architecture, too, has no longer any holy significance, it being a mere matter of more or less square feet, and more or fewer bricks, slabs, and tiles. Now, the idea of a church is a cosy library-sort of an affair, with pews and carpets—anti-asthmatic and anti-consumptive, and very comfortable and agreeable. The place carries no more sublime inspiration with it than a drawing-room. The age is simply one of anti-vastness, as applied to churches; and the sanctity of symbolism is, every day, more and more merged into secular actualities. But the ancient Egyptian walked through the enormous avenues to the temples, flanked with gods of stone—whose strength and size defy the ravages of years—and felt himself in a divine presence. The statue and the temple—to his simple idea was heaven on earth. And the Greek, so particular in selecting the site, the shape, the statues, and the various decorations of his temple, was wafted up to the Glorious Apollo or the Thundering Jove, as he sought the sacred shrine. So, too, the Christian of the Middle Ages, in entering sublime Cathedrals— whose marvelous grandeur cannot be fathomed by hearsay, but must be seen to be judged of—was exalted by their physical vastness and harmonious forms and colors, up to the seventh heaven of the apostle. But all that has passed away—the statue and the building no longer breathe a super-mundane language, because of their beauty, proportion and vastness. But music cannot be so cheapened, when on a pure, grand scale. With the advance of the epoch in mechanical means, it grows more and more into proportions, which are heroic, romantic—despite all the wonder-murdering tendencies of the age. So exalted has music become on a grand scale in England, above all other countries, that on a recent occasion five thousand performers—the body of singers being over four thousand, executed at the Sydenham Palace choral music, with an effect that all competent auditors and judges agree in saying, was preternatural for its largeness, its immensity—and bore comparison, musically, with other performances, as does Niagara with an ordinary little waterfall. It was, at turns, as vast as the undying chorus of nature on the sea-side, or lashed itself into a hell of declamatory vehemence and force, too great almost for the nerves of the auditors—and yet it was not noise, not dishevelled sounds, but tones in sequence and in combination as exactly measured and poised as the mathematics of the spheres, and as true evidences of the majesty of the Creator."

The same paper, in an abstract of a lecture on "The Lost Arts," by Wendell Phillips, reports him as saying that :

"We, as a people, were like the German, who always pulled off his hat when he spoke of himself. If we look back upon the past we may see the evidence that there is little that is new under the sun. He wished to show what the ancients had achieved. When England was a land of savages, art flourished in Asia. In one respect we have no conceit. We are willing to sit at the feet of the ancient poets. He heard the Italians say, that our artist, Powers, of Vermont, reminded them of Phidias. We are indebted to the past—even many of our newspaper jokes date back further than the days of Joe Miller. But he desired to call attention to the Useful Arts. Glass is a useful article, and the ancients knew more about it than we do, which fact is shown by the manner in which it was moulded and colored. He complimented Edward Everett's description of the telescope, but denied that Galileo was the first person to discover its use. He furnished facts to show that the ancients must have used telescopes, microscopes, and opera-glasses. The paintings of the past show that we cannot mix paints as well as the ancients could. In manufacturing metals, the ancients were our superiors. The orator spoke of a sword, so exquisitely made, that it could be put into a sheath, coiled up like a snake, without breaking. A Negro had tempered steel with an art which died with him, and it was not revived until a hundred years after. The ancients, it appears, had the steamboat and the canal, and they had the art of moving immense masses of rock—masses weighing three thousand tons each. Europe says, 'I made the canal.' China says, 'I made it a thousand years ago.' Egypt

growls from her granite lips, 'Keep quiet, children. I
made it five thousand years ago.' Stevens says he
found railroads (built thousands of years ago) whose
grooves were coated with iron. The use of guano is
not new. Animal magnetism may be traced to the
middle ages.* Cold water, as a remedial agent, is not
new. Revolving pistols and breech-loading cannon
are at least three hundred years old. Sherry coblers
are of ancient date, as is the fashion of drinking them
through straws. The balloon and the telegraph even
belonged to the past, Western wit, which consists of
exaggeration, such as Lowell delights in, is old. The
stereoscope is two hundred years older than Christianity, and the mowing-machine was used centuries
ago. Why did he speak thus of the wisdom of the
ancients? Because art was hidden in the bosom of
the aristocracy. In the printing-press, the only discovery of modern times, we see hope for the future.
Iron and fire cannot save civilization. Sublime and
noble principle, guided by wisdom and humanity. can
save it, if God intends to save it."

And now, reader, for a time, farewell. If I, by selection or otherwise, have added one ray of light to
your mind, I am well repaid for my labor—for labor,
indeed, it has been—necessitating an amount of travel,
reading, and research, and expense, that would scarcely
be credited. I leave the subject, then, by no means
exhausted, but at a point whence other men are called
to carry it on. Still, it is believed that the testimonies
herein adduced, especially in Part Third, are of such
an unimpeachable character, that no one rising from
their perusal and examination, but will concede that
we have clearly established the fact that this world
was once peopled by PRE-ADAMITE MEN!

----

* An error! for it was known in both Egypt and Nimroud, Syria.
and Nineveh, thousands, instead of hundreds of years ago, as is proved
by sculptures and paintings innumerable, some of which represent
the curative process, others those of inducing magnetic somnolence ;
others. still, the act of delivering dreamy oracles, a la the modern, so-
called, "clairvoyanta."

CPSIA information can be obtained at www.ICGtesting.com
Printed in the USA
BVOW03*1011270515

401571BV00010B/81/P